MW01253040

DISTRIBUTIVE AND PROCEDURAL JUSTICE

Distributive and Procedural Justice
Research and Social Applications

16100/

Edited by

KJELL TÖRNBLOM
University of Skövde, Sweden

and

RIËL VERMUNT
University of Leiden, The Netherlands and University of Skövde, Sweden

ASHGATE

Published by
Ashgate Publishing Limited
Gower House
Croft Road
Aldershot
Hampshire GU11 3HR
England

Ashgate Publishing Company
Suite 420
101 Cherry Street
Burlington, VT 05401-4405
USA

Ashgate website: http://www.ashgate.com

British Library Cataloguing in Publication Data
Distributive and procedural justice : research and social
  applications
  1. Distributive justice. 2. Judicial process 3. Distributive
  justice - Research 4. Judicial process - Research
  I. Törnblom, Kjell Yngve. II. Vermunt, Riël
  340.1'15

Library of Congress Cataloging-in-Publication Data
Distributive and procedural justice : research and social applications / edited by
Kjell Törnblom and Riël Vermunt.
      p. cm.
  Includes index.
  ISBN 978-0-7546-4766-9
  1. Distributive justice. 2. Fairness. 3. Justice, Administration of. I. Törnblom,
Kjell Yngve. II. Vermunt, Riël.

  HB523.D569 2007
  303.3'72--dc22

                                                                                2006036921

ISBN: 978-0-7546-4766-9

Printed and bound in Great Britain by MPG Books Ltd, Bodmin, Cornwall.

Contents

List of Figures

List of Tables

List of Contributors

Laurence Armand French has doctorates in sociology (PhD—University of New Hampshire) and psychology (PhD—University of Nebraska). He is Professor Emeritus of Psychology, Western New Mexico University; visiting professor of criminal justice, Grambling State University; and senior research associate of justice studies, the University of New Hampshire. He has over 250 publications including 12 books.

Celia M. Gonzalez is currently a doctoral student in Social Psychology at New York University. She received her Master of Arts degree in 2003, also from New York University, and her Bachelor of Science degree from the University of Illinois at Urbana-Champaign in 2001. Broadly, her research concerns social perception and group-directed behavior, with particular emphasis on the manner in which these processes are shaped by the quality of the individual's connection to relevant groups. Her recent research has examined the psychological motives underlying interest in procedural fairness and how these motives are stimulated or quelled in response to situationally induced feeling states.

Karen A. Hegtvedt is Professor of Sociology at Emory University (Atlanta, Georgia, USA). Her experimental and survey research focusses on issues of distributive justice. She and a collaborator are currently working on a series of experiments examining the impact of collective sources of legitimacy, group identity, and procedural justice on reactions to distributive injustice for oneself and for others. She is a former deputy editor of *Social Psychology Quarterly*.

Guillermina Jasso (PhD, Johns Hopkins) is Professor of Sociology at New York University and Research Fellow, Institute for the Study of Labor (IZA), Bonn, Germany. Her major research interests are sociobehavioral theory, distributive justice, status, international migration, mathematical methods for theory building, and factorial survey methods for empirical analysis. Recent work includes: "The Tripartite Structure of Social Science Analysis" (*Sociological Theory* 2004); "Culture and the Sense of Justice" (*Journal of Cross Cultural Psychology* 2005); "Immigration, Health, and New York City: Early Results Based on the U.S. New-Immigrant Cohort of 2003" (with D. S. Massey, M. R. Rosenzweig, and J. P. Smith, *Economic Policy Review 2005*); "Factorial Survey Methods for Studying Beliefs and Judgments." *Sociological Methods and Research* 2006; "Homans and the Study of Justice" (in A. J. Treviño (ed.), *George C. Homans: History, Theory, and Method* 2006); and "The Theory of Comparison Processes" (in P. J. Burke (ed.), *Contemporary Social Psychological Theories* 2006).

Elisabeth Kals is a Professor of Psychology (Social and Organizational Psychology) at the Catholic University of Eichstätt-Ingolstadt, Germany. Her research interests include applications of scientific psychology to various social, organizational, and individual problems. Currently, she focusses on the analysis and mediation of conflicts (environmental and political conflicts as well as conflicts in organizations and schools) and undertakes various consultancies in this field. Her books include *Mediation* (Leo Montada and Elisabeth Kals, 2001; 2nd edn 2007), *Arbeits- und Organisationspsychologie* (2006), *Verantwortliches Umweltverhalten* (1996).

Ali Kazemi received his PhD in Psychology from Göteborg University in Sweden and is currently a visiting lecturer and scholar in Social Psychology at the University of Skövde, where he also works at the Center of Social Justice Research. His current research interests include decision making in social dilemmas, fairness and conflict management in organizations, resource acquisition and conceptions of distributive justice, victim blaming and stereotyping, and social value orientation and procedural justice.

Holger Lengfeld earned his PhD in Sociology at Humboldt University of Berlin. He held research positions within the Interdisciplinary Social Justice Research Group at Humboldt University of Berlin (1998–2004) and within the Department of Sociology at Free University of Berlin (2004–2006). Currently, he is a Professor of Sociology at University of Hagen, Germany. His research fields are Social Stratification, European Integration, Sociology of Values and Sociology of Work. His publications include *Mitbestimmung und Gerechtigkeit* (Co-determination and Justice, 2003). He is a co-editor of *Verteilungsprobleme und Gerechtigkeit in modernen Gesellschaften* (Distributive Conflicts and Justice in Modern Societies, 2004) and of *Interdisziplinäre Gerechtigkeitsforschung* (Interdisciplinary Justice Research, 2002).

Steffen Mau is Professor of Political Sociology and Comparative Social Research at the Graduate School of Social Sciences (GSSS) at the University of Bremen. His research and writing focusses on welfare state attitudes, social justice, Europeanization and Transnationalization. His recent publications include *The Moral Economy of Welfare States. Britain and Germany Compared, Social Justice* (2003), *Social Justice, Legitimacy and the Welfare State* (edited with Benjamin Veghte, 2007), and *Welfare States: Construction, Deconstruction, Reconstruction* (edited with Stephan Leibfried, 2007).

Jacqueline Modde, PhD, was til recently an Assistant Professor of Social Psychology at the Radboud University of Nijmegen, the Netherlands. Dr Modde's research focused on the effects of procedural and distributive justice on norm-violating behavior in experimental settings. This research project resulted in a dissertation entitled *Procedural Fairness and Noncompliance*. She has also co-authored several articles regarding the topic of discrimination of psychiatric patients in the Netherlands. She currently lives in France.

Leo Montada is Professor of Psychology at the University of Trier, Germany, member of the European Academy of Sciences and founding President of the International Society of Justice Research (ISJR). He has chaired a research group "Justice, Responsibility, and Morality" publishing on issues as relative privilege, filial responsibility, moral emotions (guilt, resentment), justice problems in society (ecological justice and responsibility, unemployment, justice problems after the reunification of Germany), coping with losses and injuries by critical life events, etc. On the basis of these studies he criticized the economical theory of behavior. In the last few years, the psychology of conflict mediation is in the focus of his interest. A second revised edition of a book *Mediation*, coauthored by E. Kals, will appear 2007.

Elizabeth Mullen is an Assistant Professor at the Graduate School of Business at Stanford University. Her research interests include social justice and political psychology. Her current work focusses on how people's emotions and moral convictions influence their fairness reasoning and judgments, and on understanding the cognitive and motivational underpinnings of the left-right political divide.

Markus M. Müller is assistant professor in the Faculty of Philosophy and Education at the Catholic University Eichstätt-Ingolstadt in Germany. He received his PhD from Trier University with a dissertation on the role of justice in political conflicts (*Bedingungen der Konfliktlösung*, 2003). His research focusses on issues of social justice and trust in organizations, as well as conflict mediation, and he has undertaken a range of consultancies for public and private sector bodies on issues of sustainable development.

Nancy Picthall-French has three masters' degrees (two in education and one in psychology). She has taught at universities and currently is involved in the "no child left behind" initiative in the USA. Nancy and Laurence French have worked with Native Americans for over 30 years and have collaborated on numerous research projects.

Kjell Y. Törnblom is a Professor of Social Psychology, presently at the University of Skövde, Sweden, and previously (1990–2004) a Professor of Sociology at the University of Colorado at Denver. He has published in the area of justice in a variety of books (co-editor of *Resource theory: Explorations and applications*) and journals, (for example *Social Psychology Quarterly*, *Social Justice Research*, *European Journal of Social Psychology*, *Human Relations*, *Sex Roles*, *Journal of Cross-Cultural Psychology*, *International Journal of Intercultural Relations*, and *Acta Sociologica*) on topics like positive and negative resource allocations, intergroup relations, conflict and conflict resolution, integration between distributive and procedural justice and between justice and resource theories, and the impact of mode of resource production on justice conceptions.

Tom R. Tyler is a Professor at New York University. He teaches in the psychology department and the law school. His research explores the dynamics of authority in groups, organizations, and societies. In particular, he examines the role of judgments about the justice or injustice of group procedures in shaping legitimacy, compliance and cooperation. He is the author of several books, including *The Social Psychology of Procedural Justice* (1988); *Why People Obey the Law* (1990); *Trust in Organizations* (1996); *Social Justice in a Diverse Society* (1997); *Cooperation in Groups* (2000); and *Trust in the Law* (2002).

Riël Vermunt, PhD, is Associate Professor of Social and Organizational Psychology at Leiden University, the Netherlands. Dr Vermunt's research focusses on (integration of) procedural and distributive justice and its application in economic games and stress reduction. He has authored and co-authored more than 100 articles and chapters on these issues. Articles have appeared in *Journal of Applied Psychology*, *Journal of Applied Social Psychology*, *Social Justice Research*, and *European Journal of Social Psychology*. He is one of the founders of the International Society of Social Justice Research and he has co-founded the Dutch journal *Gedrag en Organisatie* (Behavior and Organization). In 1994, Dr Vermunt was visiting professor at the University of Colorado, Denver. Until 2006, Dr Vermunt was a visiting professor at the Department of Social Psychology at Skövde University, Sweden, where he cooperated with Kjell Törnblom, and Tomas Ståhl.

Sonja Wrobel is research assistant at the Collaborative Research Centre 597 'Transformations of the State', University of Bremen, Germany. In her PhD thesis, she analyzes the legitimization of recent pension reforms in Germany and France. She has published articles in the field of justice research with a special focus on the issue of intergenerational justice.

Preface

Justice is an increasingly salient issue within several contexts in today's unstable world. It is a fundamental problem in most groups, organizations, and societies and gains in importance with the increasing scarcity of our planet's resources. Discussions regarding which inequalities in the allocation of material as well as symbolic social resources are just and which are unjust have become more common within political and other institutional domains such as education, economy, family, and religion. Debated issues of justice and fairness concern taxes, the treatment of immigrants and ethnic groups, wages, pensions, employment, inequality between the sexes and across generations, access to and quality of health care, terrorism, war, etc.

This interdisciplinary and cross-national volume brings together theory and research by prominent scholars within the areas of distributive and procedural justice in the allocation of (scarce) social resources, not only featuring work within each area separately but also showing how combinations of the two justice orientations sometimes operate together to affect justice judgments and guide behavior. Most of the chapters are refined versions of presentations at the IXth International Social Justice Conference and held in June 2002 at the University of Skövde, Sweden. Rather than sorting the contents of the book along particular substantive themes, we have arranged the selected papers into three parts according to the type of justice they focus on—distributive, procedural, and both together as they operate interdependently. Each part is subdivided into two sections, basic research and applied research on current and important societal issues. A fourth and final part contains papers on issues pertaining to epistemology, method, and application.

As the reader will discover, the authors were not required to conform to a particular format for their chapters which cover various levels of analysis, from intra-personal to interpersonal to group and societal levels. Also, the organization and contents of this volume are primarily determined by the papers that were accepted for the conference. Collectively, they provide ample evidence of an exciting and lively international and multi-disciplinary field of inquiry that is diverse, insightful, theoretically well grounded, and useful at both individual and collective levels.

Several features of our approach are worth mentioning: *First*, we bring theory and research from each of the two parallel lines of inquiry (distributive and procedural justice) together, not only featuring work within each area separately, but also showing how they might operate simultaneously to form justice conceptions and guide behavior. *Second*, chapters cover various levels of analysis, from micro to macro (i.e., from intra-personal to inter-personal to group to societal and cultural levels). *Third*, most chapters contain an overview of theoretical and empirical research on a particular topic as well as an exemplary piece of relevant research. *Fourth*, we have selected contributions dealing with basic research as well as applied research on current and important societal issues. *Fifth*, the work contributed by our international group of researchers (10 Europeans—German, Dutch and Swedish—

and seven Americans) span several disciplines. *Sixth*, as already implied, this volume will complement the few existing social psychology monographs in the area. As organizational justice volumes focus on the meso level, our volume fills a gap by emphasizing the micro and macro levels.

Articles and chapters within this increasingly popular domain of social justice are spread over dozens of journals and books. In addition to bringing some of this work together under one roof, this volume complements similar efforts within the fields of industrial-organizational psychology, organizational behavior, and human resource management. The volume is particularly appropriate for courses in social psychology, psychology, sociology, political philosophy, and law, as well as for practitioners in various fields. It should also be of interest to anyone who cares about and is affected by issues pertaining to justice.

Most of the chapters are refined versions of some of the presentations at the IXth International Social Justice Conference and held in June 2002 at the University of Skövde, Sweden. The conference would not have been possible without the generous financial support that the University of Skövde provided with short notice. We would like to thank all contributors to this book for their outstanding work and their willingness to consider our suggestions for further improvements of their manuscripts. Thanks are also due to Louis E. Wolcher for his detailed and extensive comments on all chapters in the volume and to Louise Furåker who spent many hours formatting and proofreading the materials.

Kjell Törnblom
Riël Vermunt

Introduction

Distributive and Procedural Justice

Riël Vermunt
University of Leiden, The Netherlands

Kjell Y. Törnblom
University of Skövde, Sweden

Introduction

Distribution of scarce resources permeates almost all spheres and levels of social life. Scarce resources are not only distributed in the family, but also in the contexts of work, sports, friendship relations, the political arena, public organizations, legal settings, and more. Distribution of scarce resources is a problem affecting society at the micro, meso and macro levels. The micro level includes the family, friendship relationships, school, sport and work teams; the meso level includes work organization, the court, while the macro level includes political bodies, national economy, and others. In the family, for instance, problems with regard to the distribution of household tasks are common. In school, teachers have to decide how much attention to give to each student. On the meso level, public administrators are faced with the problem to determine whether or not to construct a new bus lane (see the chapter by Markus Müller and Elisabeth Kals in this volume) or how to tax different categories of citizens in the municipality for costs for water cleaning. The distribution and redistribution of income via taxation is an example of a distribution issue on the macro level.

People frequently evaluate the distribution of scarce resources in terms of justice or fairness. A child may evaluate the amount of his/her household chores as unfair, and citizens may evaluate their tax burden as fair. A well established finding is that fairness is of great importance and affect people's feelings and actions in social interaction. For instance, fairness has been linked to satisfaction with and acceptance of decisions, perceived legitimacy of authorities, task performance, organizational citizenship, anti-social behavior, employee theft, use of influence tactics, responses to layoffs, work satisfaction, commitment to groups and society, and more. It is not surprising that the social sciences spend considerable time, energy and financial resources to the study of scarce resource distribution and people's evaluation of it.

Traditionally, psychology focusses mainly on distribution processes at the micro level, while sociology leans toward the macro level approach. On the micro level, psychologists are concerned with the antecedents and consequences of justice evaluations. Chapters in the present volume are concerned with structural antecedents of people's justice evaluation of resource distribution (Kjell Törnblom and Ali Kazemi), motivational antecedents (Celia Gonzalez and Tom Tyler), cognitive and emotional antecedents (Elizabeth Mullen) as well as the attitudinal and behavioral consequences of people's justice evaluations (Markus Müller and Elisabeth Kals; Ali Kazemi; Karen Hegtvedt). The studies represented in those chapters are descriptive in nature in that they analyze how people form justice judgments and what the attitudinal and behavioral effects are of perceived fair or unfair resource distributions. Within the sociological tradition the normative approach to justice has received considerable attention. This approach is concerned with the question what a just distribution is or should be. The chapters by Steffen Mau and Sonja Wrobel, and Laurence French and Nancy Picthall-French are examples of the normative justice approach.

A resource distribution or allocation process frequently consists of an authority (a person or an institution possessing varying amounts of discretionary power to allocate resources) and one or more recipients of the allocated resource. The authority divides the resource between him/her and one ore more others or between others. In making the allocation decision authorities use distributive rules like equality (everyone receives the same amount), equity (the received amount of the resource matches contributions), or need (outcomes satisfy needs). A young child gets relatively more parental care than an older child because the young child needs it more; children doing more household chores will receive a higher allowance than those doing fewer chores; all children are taken to the movies by their parents irrespective of their age or gender. Thus, the received share of the resources may be evaluated in terms of various justice principles. Parents give a needy child more care then a less needy child because they find this distribution of care just.

In making allocation decisions authorities apply procedural rules—as distinct from distributive rules—to arrive at the decision. Three aspects of procedural rules maybe distinguished (see Vermunt, Van der Kloot and Van der Meer, 1993). The *structural* aspect refers to whether or not the procedural rule is part of the legal body of a country, family or organization. An example is the works council. In some countries works councils are formally arranged in the entrepreneur-bill, indicating that companies are obliged to install a works council. In other countries the entrepreneur-bill does not contain rules about the legal position of the works council. It might be assumed, therefore, that in countries with a legally regulated works council, workers have more say in some of the decisions of management than do workers in countries without a formally established works council. Another example is the presence or absence of a court or committee of appeal which citizens may attend in order to challenge an institutional decision. French and French (this volume) mention the installation of the Constitutional Act in 1982 in Canada to guarantee rights of Native Americans. Angola, for instance, has no separate juvenile justice system that offers protection against child labor.

However, it is generally agreed that legal arrangements are sometimes not applied in practice. We may label this aspect of procedural rules the *cultural* aspect. Management of companies with a works council may fully use the opportunities of the works council, try to reduce its influence, or even obstruct its ideas and advice. More concretely, management may or may not apply rules such as the accuracy rule, a rule that dictates that decisions are based on as much correct information as possible. Management in the works council may ask employees to voice their opinion, or they may refuse to do so (Leventhal, 1980). Most nations have laws that prohibit child labor, but world wide the percentage of child labor in 2004 was 15.8 per cent, which means that 218 million children from 5 to 17 years are forced to work and do not receive proper education. The third aspect of procedural rules is the *personal* aspect which includes the way decisions are communicated to the persons involved. Decisions may be communicated in a way that does or does not do justice to the persons involved (Bies and Moag, 1986).

Scarce resources are often partitioned into material resources, like money and goods and immaterial resources like respect and attention. Resources may have positive valence (e.g., a financial bonus or a winning lottery ticket) or negative valence like a punishment, financially or otherwise.

As an allocation event consists of an outcome and a procedure, the two aspects are inextricably connected to each other. Theoretical and empirical research has been and is still carried out within each of these domains, more or less independently of each other. During the last couple of decades researchers have increasingly focused their attention to how judgments of the distribution and the procedure combine to form (overall) justice conceptions. The assumption is that people take both aspects of the allocation event into account, when they determine whether or not a particular situation is just. The contributed chapters to this volume represent research in line with all three approaches, as is evident from their divisions into three corresponding parts of the book.

Distributive Justice

Distributive justice refers to the justice evaluation of the allocation outcome. What a recipient considers his/her just desert is dependent on several factors. One of the factors is the type of rule that is applied: the equity, equality or need rule. According to the equality rule an equal division of the shares will be seen as fair, while according to the equity rule the same division will be evaluated as unfair. Other factors are the valence of the outcome (an equal division of losses may be evaluated as unfair, while an equitable division may be seen as most fair for gains); the type of relationship between authority and recipient (the equity rule may be evaluated as more fair in a work relationship than in an intimate relationship); the way the resources are produced (see Törnblom and Kazemi, this volume—the equality distribution principle is likely to be endorsed for a good that is produced cooperatively by many, while the principle considered most just for the distribution of a good that is produced competitively by one person might be equity).

The equality rule seems to be the simplest rule to apply in practice. Everyone receives the same amount of a good irrespective of recipient characteristics or differences between recipients. Of course, as Messick (1993) noted, it may be difficult to divide a good equally when it is not divisible over the number of recipients. How may two chocolate bars be fairly divided among three children? Several strategies may be applied to solve this problem, but the cognitive processes to divide equally are as such not difficult. A more difficult task is to divide a good according to the need rule. The allocator has to estimate the need level of each recipient which is frequently a very complex task. However, the perceived need is often one-dimensional in nature rather than a combination of several need states. For instance, children may have a need for mother's attention during play. The child with the least competence is easy to detect and more attention will be directed to this child than to the others. The mother might explain the difference in attention by referring to the low competence of that child.

It is more difficult to allocate goods and evaluate the outcomes of the allocation decision when the equity rule is applied. The allocator and the recipients not only have to combine the delivered inputs (contributions, status, age), but they also have to compare the inputs of self and others. Several models have been proposed to describe how recipients combine information about inputs. Anderson (1976) proposed a cognitive algebra model to describe outcomes (salary or bonus) based on multiple input information, combining inputs additively could best predict the outcome. Harris (1983) was opposed to a monotonic relationship between input and output and made a strong case for a linear relationship between input and outcome. In a monotonic relationship the constraint of the relationship is that when the input increases so does the outcome as well. In a monotonic relationship an increment in the input will be related to an increment in the outcome, but the magnitudes of the increments are not the same: a small increase in the input, for instance, may go hand in hand with a large as well as a small increase in the outcome. In a linear relationship each increment in the input is related to an even larger increment in the outcome, although the increment in the input need not be of the same magnitude as the one in the outcome. When both increments are the same the product moment correlation will be one.

Another type of research in the distributive justice area has been carried out in which inputs and outcomes are given and the subject is asked to evaluate the fairness of the combination of inputs and outcomes is (Jasso, 1978, 1980, in this volume; Törnblom, Mühlhausen and Jonsson, 1991; Törnblom and Kazemi, this volume). Jasso states that an evaluation of the fairness of a reward can best be described as the difference between the natural logarithm of the actual reward and the just reward. Törnblom and associates showed that inputs are differently weighted for the formation of justice judgments dependent on the social relationship between the allocator and the recipient and the valence of the outcome.

This cognitive approach of distributive justice is challenged by Elizabeth Mullen in her contribution "The reciprocal relationship between affect and perceptions of fairness" (Chapter 1). Mullen states that affect is not only a by-product of cognitive processing, but asserts that affect influences fairness judgments as well. Specifically when people are confronted with negative events, negative affect prompt fairness reasoning. Negative outcomes such as under-reward and, to a lesser extent, over-reward, triggers affective responses that elicit cognitive reasoning about fairness of the events. Partly based on the cognitive appraisal approach, Mullen develops the Affective Model of Justice Reasoning (AMJR). The model claims a causal role for emotions of when and how people reason about fairness. Different emotions may elicit different types of information processing. Interestingly, the AMJR model predicts that outcomes and interpersonal treatment will elicit stronger affective reactions than procedural factors.

Kjell Törnblom and Ali Kazemi (Chapter 2, "Toward a resource production theory of distributive justice") elaborate on Törnblom's earlier work with regard to factors that influence distributive fairness judgments, such as type and valence of the allocated social resource, and the relationship between the allocator and recipients. In their contribution to the volume, the authors focus on mode of production as a factor affecting distributive justice judgments. Thus, the manner in which social resources are made is proposed to have an impact on distributive justice judgments and behavior. The content of this chapter is inspired by Marxist oriented critiques, and the goal is to lay a foundation for a new theoretical approach to distributive (as well as procedural) justice.

Distributive justice is concerned with the fair distribution of benefits and burdens, such as income, bonuses, and taxes. A particular kind of distribution of benefits and burdens takes place between different generations of citizens. In several countries in Europe the younger generation contributes to the benefits for the older generation and expects the same from the future generation. This arrangement can only continue if it is seen as fair and if sufficient solidarity exists between the generations. The issue how justice and solidarity are related is the subject of Chapter 3 by Steffen Mau and Sonja Wrobel ("Just solidarity: How justice conditions intergenerational solidarity"). The authors conceive of three ways in which justice and solidarity are related to each other: solidarity as a pre-condition of justice, solidarity and justice as mutually reinforcing processes and justice as a pre-condition of solidarity. A test of the relationships between justice and solidarity is conducted via an analysis of German parliamentary debates and survey data.

Procedural Justice

The history of procedural justice research is shorter than that of distributive justice research. In the beginning of the 1970s, Rawls (1971) and Thibaut and Walker (1975) were among the first to connect outcomes and procedures. Rawls discussed the issue of how to divide a pie between two persons as fair as possible. He suggested the use of a procedure in which the allocator, divides the pie and the other person chooses which piece s/he wants. With this procedure the allocator is likely to divide the pie as equally as possible, as an unequal division will motivate the choosing recipient to select the biggest part. Thibaut and Walker studied procedures in legal settings and compared people's satisfaction with two legal systems, the adversary system (as applied in the United States and England) and the continental system (as applied in Europe). Asking people about their satisfaction with their systems, the adversary system was considered more satisfying than the other system.

One of the factors that, according to Thibaut and Walker might have contributed to this difference in evaluation of the two systems is that in the adversary system the judge is a referee whose main task is to let both adversaries fight a fair match, while the jury decides about the verdict. In the continental system both tasks, the referee task as well as the final decision are performed by the judge and is seen as less impartial. In further research projects Thibaut and Walker also found that letting parties in a legal dispute have a say—to explain their motivation to handle the situation in this or that way—increased the fairness evaluation of the verdict. According to Thibaut and Walker, the reason for the difference in justice evaluations between voice and no-voice conditions is that parties involved in the dispute think that having voice increases their chances of getting a more positive outcome, e.g., a shorter incarceration. Thibaut and Walker concluded from these results that procedures are important because parties think that having a say may influence the final outcome, procedures offer parties real or imagined control over the outcome.

Research conducted by Tyler and his associates aimed at exploring the limits of the decision control hypothesis. Having voice was found to end in fair evaluation of the outcome and the process only if the authority gave due consideration to what the parties were saying. When they had the impression that what they brought forward was hardly listened to by the authority, outcome and process were evaluated less fair. Lind and Tyler (1988; Tyler and Lind, 1992) concluded that procedures are not only important with regard to outcomes, but have an important function of their own—a self-expressing function. Being granted the opportunity to voice ones opinion may be viewed as an indication of personal worth of being a full-fledged member of the group or society. The authors connected the function of procedures to group processes. The status of a group member is of vital importance to a member's behavior in the group. Status largely determines the type of activities a member is allowed to perform, the rewards s/he will receive, the type of members s/he is allowed to access and associate with, etc. One's status may be determined on the basis of several indicators. One is the interpersonal treatment by the group authority. A fair treatment is seen as an indication of high regard from the authority, while an unfair treatment is viewed as an indication of low regard. Procedural fairness, how fair the authority communicates with group members, is another status indicator. In an experiment conducted by Lind, Kanfer and Earley (1990), some participants got the opportunity to voice their opinion before the decision was taken (pre-decisional voice), others afterward (post-decisional voice), and still others were not allowed to voice their opinion at all (no-voice). Results suggested that the opportunity to voice one's opinion after the decision is made is considered more fair than no-voice, but less fair than a pre-decision voice. Although post-decisional voice had the same effect as no-voice (in both cases participants could not influence the decision) post-decision voice was evaluated as more fair than no-voice, presumably due to a self-expression function of voice. The group-value model and the more specific relational model of authority were thus developed to describe and explain the importance of procedures.

These models were followed by cognitive models of procedural fairness such as the fairness heuristic theory (Lind et al., 1993). Fairness heuristic theory (FHT) states that people often make fairness judgments quickly and without having full information about all aspects of the allocation decision process. Based on FHT, Van den Bos, Vermunt and Wilke (1997) assumed and confirmed that information about an aspect of the allocation process that is presented first has a larger impact on subsequent fairness judgments than information that is presented later. Moreover, Van den Bos et al. (1998) tested the FHT assumption that information about an aspect of the allocation process will serve as substitute for information that is lacking, although the substitute information is less relevant for fairness evaluation than the missing information.

Celia Gonzalez and Tom Tyler's contribution in Chapter 4 ("Why do people care about procedural fairness? The importance of membership monitoring") elaborates on the group-value model of procedural justice (Lind and Tyler, 1988) and the relational model of authority (Tyler and Lind, 1992). The chapter starts with the observation that procedural fairness judgments have a profound effect on people's social life, and that up til now no sufficient answer has been given to the question why procedural fairness has such a large impact people's emotions, opinions and behavior. Part of the answer should be sought in the importance of procedural fairness for group membership. According to Gonzalez and Tyler, group members frequently monitor the state of their group membership and their relationship with other members. The authors introduced the term membership monitoring for this activity, give examples of this activity and discuss several factors which increase the need for membership monitoring.

The relational model of authority is an important tool in explaining anti-normative behavior, as is suggested by Jacqueline Modde and Riël Vermunt in their contribution "The effects of procedural unfairness on norm-violating behavior" (Chapter 5). In earlier experiments Greenberg (1993) showed that fair procedures may attenuate the negative effects of unfair outcomes on theft. Participants were promised $5 for the performance of a task but received only $3. They then had the opportunity to take money for themselves. Participants who were treated unfairly took more money than fairly treated participants. The extent of this behavior diminished when interpersonal sensitivity and appropriate justification were provided. Modde and Vermunt wanted to demonstrate that procedural unfairness in itself may produce the same negative behavior as distributive unfairness. According to the relational model of authority, an unfair procedure is an indicator of low regard for the recipient (who then retaliates by stealing money if offered no other opportunities to gain respect). This is also predicted by Foa's (1971) resource theory of social exchange (see also Foa and Foa, 1974, 1976).

Markus Müller and Elisabeth Kals focus on the question how important procedural fairness is for conflict resolution (Chapter 6). In their contribution ("Interactions between procedural fairness and outcome favorability in conflict situations") the authors discuss the relationship between procedural fairness and cooperative behavior. In conflict situations people not only care about profit, but also about their relationship and future interaction with others. In that sense, behaving fairly is an important means to avoiding and resolving conflicts. In many social conflicts it is difficult or impossible to attain favorable outcomes, and the question is then how fair procedures might help reducing the hardiness of negotiating behaviors. The authors answer this question in a field study in which they collected data about people's reactions to local planning conflict.

Distributive and Procedural Justice

The introduction of the notion of procedural justice improves our understanding of people's justice evaluation of the entire allocation process. An allocation process consists of a distribution (an outcome) and a procedure, i.e., a set of rules that the allocator may apply when deciding the manner in which the outcome should be accomplished (Thibaut and Walker, 1975). The introduction of procedural fairness initiated a considerable amount of research in which the combined effects of distributive and procedural fairness were investigated. The main question was how distributive and procedural justice interacted to form justice judgments. It was assumed that people are motivated to attain fair outcomes, and some research was directed towards answering the question how procedural fairness might increase or decrease the perceived fairness of outcomes. Folger and associates (e.g., Folger, Rosenfield and Robinson, 1983) investigated the beneficial effects of justifications on resentment caused by relative deprivation. Greenberg (1993) showed that employee theft as a response to underpayment inequity decreased if employees were treated fairly. It was assumed that procedural fairness had a mitigating effect on perceived distributive unfairness.

Another line of research investigated the moderating role of procedural fairness on outcome favorability (Brockner and Wiesenfeld, 2005). Brockner and Wiesenfeld found that procedural fairness reduced the influence of outcome favorability when people evaluated others, while it increased its influence when people evaluated themselves. In other types of studies the attention shifted from the moderating role of procedural fairness toward the main role of procedural fairness. Van den Bos and associates (e.g., Van den Bos, Vermunt and Wilke, 1997) showed not only that procedural fairness had a beneficial effect on distributive unfairness, but that distributive fairness had a beneficial effect on procedural unfairness, as well, emphasizing the moderating role of distributive fairness.

Still another avenue of thinking was followed by Törnblom and Vermunt (1999). They emphasized that not only should the moderating role of distributive fairness and procedural fairness separately be taken into account but also the fairness of the entire allocation process. Törnblom and Vermunt started from the assumption that an allocation process can be conceived as a Gestalt consisting of several components, and that people form fairness evaluations of the whole process and not only on the basis of parts of it. The inclusion of all components of the allocation process (notably the outcome, the procedure, the type and valence of the allocated social resource, and the allocator-recipient relationship) will result in more precise predictions about the impact of justice evaluations on subsequent attitudes and behavior. In most social psychological research one or more of these aspects of the allocation process were neglected, resulting in less precise predictions of attitudes and behavior.

Whatever the exact nature of the relationship of distributive and procedural justice may be, several theoretical models have been developed in social psychology to account for the nature of fairness evaluations (see Greenberg and Colquitt, 2005, for a recent overview).

In his contribution "Distributive and procedural fairness promote cooperative conflict management" (Chapter 7) Ali Kazemi provides an extensive overview of the literature on how justice may contribute to fostering cooperation in interpersonal conflicts. Interpersonal conflicts are as much part and parcel of human life as is the drive to solve these conflicts. Kazemi assumes that fairness enhances cooperative conflict resolution via cooperative conflict management styles like integrating and obliging. Unfairness, on the other hand, increases the chances that aggressive management styles will be adopted. Data from a pilot study are presented in which distributive and procedural justice were varied. The interaction between the two kinds of justice was shown to affect cooperation in a conflict situation.

Karen Hegtvedt in her contribution "The talk of negotiators: Shaping the fairness of the process and outcome" (Chapter 8) focusses on how the content of negotiator communications affects distributive and procedural justice judgments. Although interpersonal justice (the perceived justice of the way allocation decisions are conveyed) was seen as an important component of justice judgments, little research attention has been devoted to this aspect. Hegtvedt states that not only do negotiator characteristics and characteristics of the negotiation situation affect the perceived justice of negotiations, but so does the content of the communication between negotiators as well. Participants in dyads performed a task in a laboratory setting after which individual performance, group performance, and group reward were assessed. Due to differences in instructions participants differed in their initial assessments of their individual rewards. Conflicts were created and the task was to solve this conflict by negotiation. Preset messages differing in aggression, conciliation and fairness were be used by participants, and the effects on distributive and procedural justice evaluations were analyzed.

In a detailed account of the position of Native Americans in the United States, Laurence French and Nancy Picthall-French state that the present position of the Native Americans is partly the result of former policies of the US Government. In their contribution "Social injustice in Indian country: Historical antecedents of current issues" (Chapter 9), they show that Native Americans face substantial distributive injustices in that their land and rights have been systematically taken from them. The authors describe the difference in culture between the dominant society and Native Americans with regard to their preferred ways of solving disputes. The dominant society's due process arrangements, with its emphasis on individual outcomes, differs greatly from the communal solutions sought by Native Americans. The importance of procedural justice or fairness in our western societies is based on cultural premises which emphasize a certain type of legal treatment. In other cultures these premises may not hold. For instance, in Japanese there is no word for fairness. In Native American culture conflict resolution is handled quite differently from main stream American culture. That is why this chapter is so interesting: it indicates the borderlines of effectiveness of justice, in this case procedural justice.

Distributive and Procedural Justice Research: Epistemology, Method and Application

How to measure people's justice judgments has been the subject of several debates. One of the issues is whether researchers are able to differentiate between justice judgments and satisfaction. Asking whether they are satisfied with their own pay, for instance, people will mainly take into consideration whether their pay satisfies their needs. But in answering that question people may also take into account (although to a lesser degree than satisfaction of their needs) whether or not their pay is seen as fair. Fairness will contribute to feelings of satisfaction as well. In addition, people may take into account whether or not their pay satisfies their needs also when evaluating its fairness. Evaluating ones pay as fair in a somewhat self-interested way may generate satisfaction as well. Thus, it is not surprising that researchers need to think twice about how measurements of justice judgments should be interpreted. This is the focus of Holger Lengfeld in his contribution to the volume ("Morality or self-interest: Do we really measure justice judgments in ordinary survey research?", Chapter 10). He notes that the main feature of justice judgments that differentiates the concept of justice from concepts like satisfaction is its moral component of. Referring to Rawls' concept of impartiality for making justice judgments in a moral sense, people often know their initial position and are therefore hardly able to make moral judgments. This position is of course untenable in empirical research, and Lengfeld's solution lies in the concept of partial impartiality: some positions more than others will make people "impartial". By identifying these positions Lengfeld is able to differentiate between justice judgments and satisfaction and reports the results from a survey among employees of German industries.

Another crucial issue with regard to measurement of justice judgments is the quantification of these judgments. With justice judgments reliably and validly quantified, it is possible to compare justice evaluations from different groups of people for different types of others in different situations. Guillermina Jasso in her contribution "Studying justice: Measurement, estimation, and analysis of the actual reward and the just reward" (Chapter 11), describes in detail how to measure and analyze justice judgments. Jasso gathered information via the factorial survey method about respondents' actual reward and just reward for fictitious others (rewardees). A comparison between the actual reward and the just reward in the justice evaluation function results in the justice evaluation. Including characteristics of the rewardees and of the situation in estimating the actual reward function and the just reward function results in micro and macro effects. Rewardee's characteristics may include, gender, occupation, and more. With examples from several surveys Jasso works out the direct as well as the indirect measures of the just reward.

How can our considerable social psychological knowledge about distributive and procedural justice processes be applied most efficiently for the purpose of reducing conflict? According to Leo Montada in his chapter entitled "Justice conflicts and the justice of conflict resolution" (Chapter 12), conflicts are the result of perceived injustice of outcomes and procedures. In his view, injustice is experienced when what people regard as their justified entitlements and claims are violated. Defining conflicts in this way opens up avenues to resolve conflicts. Montada emphasizes two major kinds of conflict resolution, trial and mediation, and makes a plea for mediation because it gives full consideration of the parties' normative views as well as their investments in the conflict. Both the normative views as well as personal investments in the conflict should be made clear to all parties involved in the conflict. Concrete steps to settle conflicts are discussed.

References

Anderson, N.H. (1976), "Equity Judgments as Information Integration", *Journal of Personality and Social Psychology*, **33**, 291–299. [DOI: 10.1037/0022-3514.33.3.291]

Bies, R.J. and Moag, J.S. (1986), "Interactional Justice: Communication Criteria of Fairness" in *Research in Organizational Behavior*. Lewicki, R.J., Sheppard, B.M. and Bazerman, M.H. (eds) (CT: JAI Press), 43–55.

Brockner, J. and Wiesenfeld, B. (2005), "How, When and Why does Outcome Favorability Interact with Procedural Fairness?" in *Handbook of Organizational Justice*. Greenberg, J. and Colquitt, J. (eds) (NJ: Lawrence Erlbaum), 525–553.

Foa, U.G. (1971), "Interpersonal and Economic Resources", *Science*, **71**, 345–351. [DOI: 10.1126/science.171.3969.345]

Foa, U.G. and Foa, E.B. (1974), *Societal Structures of the Mind* (IL: Charles C. Thomas Publisher).

Foa, U.G. and Foa, E.B. (1976), "Resource Theory of Social Exchange" in *Contemporary Topics in Social Psychology*. Thibaut, J.W., Spence, J.T. and Carson, R.C. (eds) (Morristown, N.J.: General Learning Press).

Folger, R., Rosenfield, D. and Robinson, T. (1983), "Relative Deprivation and Procedural Justification", *Journal of Personality and Social Psychology*, **45**, 268–273. [DOI: 10.1037/0022-3514.45.2.268]

Greenberg, J. (1993), "Stealing in the Name of Justice: Informational and Interpersonal Moderators of Theft Reactions to Underpayment Inequity", *Organizational Behavior and Human Decision Processes*, **54**, 81–103. [DOI: 10.1006/obhd.1993.1004]

Greenberg, J. and Colquitt, J., eds (2005), *Handbook of Organizational Justice* (NJ: Lawrence Erlbaum Associates).

Harris, R.J. (1983), "Pinning down the Equity Formula" in *Equity Theory: Psychological and Sociological Perspectives*. Messick, D.M. and Cook, K.S. (eds), 207–243 (NY: Praeger Publishing).

Jasso, G. (1978), "On the Justice of Earnings: A New Specification of the Justice Evaluation Function", *American Journal of Sociology*, **83**, 1398–1419. [DOI: 10.1086/226706]

Jasso, G. (1980), "A New Theory of Distributive Justice", *American Sociological Review*, **45**, 3–32. [DOI: 10.2307/2095239]

Leventhal, G. (1980), "What Should Be Done with Equity Theory?, New Approaches to the Study of Fairness in Social Relationships" in *Social Exchange: Advances in Theory and Research*. Gergen, K.G., Greenberg, M.S. and Willis, R.H. (eds), 27–55 (NY: Plenum Publishing).

Lind, E.A. and Tyler, T.R. (1988), *The Social Psychology of Procedural Justice* (NY: Plenum Publishing).

Lind, E.A., Kanfer, R. and Earley, C.P. (1990), "Voice, Control, and Procedural Justice: Instrumental and Non-Instrumental Concerns in Fairness Judgments", *Journal of Personality and Social Psychology*, **59**, 952–959. [DOI: 10.1037/0022-3514.59.5.952]

Lind, E.A., Kulik, C.T., Ambrose, M.L. and Park, M. (1993), "Individual and Corporate Dispute Resolution: Using Procedural Fairness as a Decision Heuristic", *Administrative Science Quarterly*, **38**, 224–251. [DOI: 10.2307/2393412]

Messick, D.M. (1993), "Equality as a Decision Heuristic" in *Psychological Perspectives on Justice*. Mellers, B.A. and Baron, J. (eds), 11–31 (NY: Cambridge University Press).

Rawls, J. (1971), *A Theory of Justice* (MA: Harvard University Press).

Thibaut, J.W. and Walker, L. (1975), *Procedural Justice: A Psychological Analysis* (NJ: Erlbaum).

Törnblom, K.Y. and Vermunt, R. (1999), "An Integrative Perspective on Social Justice: Distributive and Procedural Fairness Evaluations of Positive and Negative Outcome Allocations", *Social Justice Research*, **12**, 37–61.

Törnblom, K.Y., Mühlhausen, S.M. and Jonsson, D.R. (1991), "The Allocation of Positive and Negative Outcomes: When is the Equality Principle Fair for Both?" in *Social Justice in Human Relations*: *Vol.1. Societal and Psychological Origins of Justice*. Vermunt, R. and Steensma, H. (eds), (NY: Plenum Publishing).

Tyler, T. and Lind, E.A. (1992), "A Relational Model of Authority in Groups" in *Advances in Experimental Social Psychology*. Zanna, M.P. (ed.), 115–191 (CA: Academic Press).

Van den Bos, K., Vermunt, R. and Wilke, H. (1997), "Procedural and Distributive Justice: What is Fair Depends More on What Comes First than on What Comes Next", *Journal of Personality and Social Psychology*, **72**, 95–104. [DOI: 10.1037/0022-3514.72.1.95]

Van den Bos, K., Wilke, H., Lind, E. and Vermunt, R. (1998), "Evaluating Outcomes by Means of the Fair Process Effect: Evidence for Different Processes in Fairness and Satisfaction Judgments", *Journal of Personality and Social Psychology*, **74**, 1493–1503. [DOI: 10.1037/0022-3514.74.6.1493]

Vermunt, R., Van der Kloot, W.A. and Van der Meer, J. (1993), "The Effects of Procedural and Interactional Criteria on Procedural Fairness Judgments", *Social Justice Research*, **6**, 183–195. [DOI: 10.1007/BF01048476]

PART I
Distributive Justice

Chapter 1

The Reciprocal Relationship between Affect and Perceptions of Fairness

Elizabeth Mullen
Northwestern University, USA

The Reciprocal Relationship between Affect and Perceptions of Fairness

Current theories of justice focus on how variations in outcomes (i.e., distributive justice), procedures (i.e., procedural justice) and interpersonal treatment (i.e., interactional justice) influence people's perceptions of fairness (for reviews see Brockner and Wiesenfeld, 1996; Colquitt et al., 2001; Cropanzano et al., 2001). Although affect was a core component of early theories of distributive justice (e.g., equity theory), affect has largely been ignored in current justice theorizing (for an exception see Van den Bos, 2003). Moreover, when affect emerges as a theoretical construct, it is typically viewed as one of a number of possible consequences, rather than a potential cause, of people's perceptions of fairness (e.g., Brockner and Wiesenfeld, 1996; for reviews see Cropanzano and Greenberg, 1997; Cropanzano et al., 2001). The lack of attention given to affective influences on people's perceptions of fairness is surprising given that a) most philosophers (e.g., Solomon, 1990, 1994) and laypeople (e.g., Bies, 2001; Lupfer et al., 2000; Mikula, 1986, 1987; Mikula, Scherer and Athenstaedt, 1998) describe emotions such as anger and resentment as core components of their experiences of an injustice and b) considerable evidence exists that affective states can exert an influence on a wide range of dependent variables such as people's behavior, memory, information processing and attitudes (see Forgas, 1995, 2000, for reviews).

In this chapter, I outline how justice theorizing and research can be improved by incorporating affect. Consistent with other researchers, I will use the term *affect* to refer to a superordinate category that includes both moods and discrete emotions (Forgas, 2000). *Moods* refer to the more general, low intensity, diffuse affective states, such as feeling good or bad; whereas *emotions* are more specific feeling states (e.g., anger, sadness) that are tied to a specific eliciting target or event and are typically of higher intensity and shorter duration than moods (Forgas, 2000). Also, I will differentiate between incidental affect (affect that is unrelated to the focal event) and integral affect (affect that is elicited in response to the focal event; Bodenhausen, 1993), and I will discuss the influences of each type of affect on people's perceptions of fairness. I will argue that it is crucial to consider how people's integral affective reactions to events influence their perceptions of fairness.

This chapter is organized into four sections. In the first section, I review research that suggests that affect and perceptions of fairness are closely related. In the second section, I propose an Affective Model of Justice Reasoning (AMJR) that makes predictions about how integral affect influences people's perceptions of fairness. In particular, I argue that affect and perceptions of justice should be considered to have a reciprocal relationship. Moreover, I argue that people may only spontaneously reason about fairness when they experience negative affect in response to a negative event. In the third section, I review theoretical and empirical evidence supporting the notion that affect can be a causal factor in people's justice reasoning. In the final section, I outline the implications of the AMJR on how we study and theorize about people's perceptions of fairness and fairness reasoning, and suggest directions for future research.

Affect and Perceptions of Fairness

Beginning with equity theory in the 1960s, justice researchers traditionally have viewed affect as a consequence rather than a cause of people's justice judgments (Homans, 1961; Adams, 1965). For example, equity theory predicts that people evaluate the ratio of their inputs and outputs with the input/output ratio of a relevant comparison other when making their fairness judgments (Adams, 1965). Equal ratios lead to perceptions of fairness and satisfaction, whereas unequal ratios lead to perceptions of unfairness and emotional distress. Specifically, when people are under-benefited they are predicted to experience anger, whereas when people are over-benefited they are predicted to experience guilt. Moreover, the negative affect generated in response to an inequity is hypothesized to motivate people to take action to reduce the inequity.

Similarly, research on relative deprivation theory (Stouffer et al., 1949) has demonstrated that when people receive outcomes that are less than they desired, they experience negative affect (e.g., anger, resentment) that, in turn, motivates them to take corrective action (e.g., Crosby, 1976; for reviews see Olson, Hafer and Zanna, 1986; Olson and Hafer, 1996; Walker and Smith, 2002). In sum, some of the earliest work on distributive justice suggests that there is a strong link between perceptions of injustice and negative emotional reactions, and that negative emotional reactions are an important impetus for action.

Consistent with early work on equity and relative deprivation theories, qualitative research has demonstrated that people report experiencing an injustice to be an emotionally laden experience (Mikula, 1986, 1987; Bies, 1987, 2001; Mikula, Scherer and Athenstaedt, 1998; Bies and Tripp, 2001). For example, when participants were asked to report an event in which they had been unjustly treated by another person and then to describe their thoughts and feelings, they reported feeling (in order of decreasing frequency): a) anger, rage, and indignation, b) disappointment, c) surprise, d) physical symptoms of arousal and stress, and e) helplessness and depression (Mikula, 1986, 1987). Similarly, when asked to recall and describe situations that produced various discrete emotions (e.g., anger, sadness), people reported that perceptions of injustice were intimately involved in the experience of anger, disgust, sadness, fear, guilt and shame (Mikula, Scherer and Athenstaedt, 1998). Taken together, this research suggests that fairness and affect are intimately related, but does not firmly establish a causal direction between affect and fairness (i.e., affect and fairness may have a reciprocal influence on one another).

Finally, more recent laboratory research has revealed that variations in positive and negative features of outcomes and procedures are associated with people's discrete emotional reactions (Weiss, Suckow and Cropanzano, 1999; Cropanzano et al., 2000; Krehbiel and Cropanzano, 2000). In a series of studies, Cropanzano and his colleagues found that anger and frustration consistently were highest when people received an unfavorable outcome due to a procedure that was biased against them. In contrast, guilt and anxiety were highest when people received a favorable outcome due to a procedure that was biased in their favor (Weiss, Suckow and Cropanzano, 1999; Krehbiel and Cropanzano, 2000; see Stecher, 1995 for related work). Although Cropanzano and his colleagues suggest that variations in procedural and outcome fairness influence people's discrete emotional reactions, an alternative interpretation of this work is that variations in positive and negative features of outcomes and procedures influence people's discrete emotional reactions that, in turn, influence their perceptions of fairness. That is, positive and negative events could arouse different emotions that, in turn, shape people's assessments of whether something is fair or unfair.

In sum, research indicates that negative emotional reactions are associated with perceptions of unfairness (e.g., Adams, 1965; Mark, 1985; Weiss, Suckow and Cropanzano, 1999; Cropanzano et al., 2000), and people's negative affective reactions can at times motivate corrective action (e.g., Mark, 1985; Foster and Rusbult, 1999). Although these results normally are interpreted as evidence that perceptions of fairness or unfairness lead to positive or negative affect, respectively, existing research is unable to exclude the alternative explanation that initial affective reactions lead to perceptions of fairness or unfairness. Researchers typically argue that fairness judgments lead to affective reactions (rather than the converse) because they assume that fairness judgments are cognitively based. That is, a person reasons about the relevant information, forms a judgment that events were fair or unfair, and then feels anger or satisfaction (Adams, 1965; Kohlberg, 1969). However, I argue that people's affective reactions to outcomes or interpersonal treatment might be more primary than their fairness judgments (e.g., Zajonc, 1980; Haidt, 2001). Given that people's affective reactions can occur relatively quickly with little conscious cognitive processing (e.g., Lazarus, 1991), it seems unreasonable to assume that people's affective reactions only come into play *after* forming their fairness judgments. That is, there may be times when people's affective reactions to events occur before their more carefully reasoned fairness judgments, particularly in domains that are highly involving to participants. Thus, instead of regarding affect merely as a consequence of people's justice judgments, a more fruitful approach would entail incorporating the dynamic role of affect in people's perceptions of fairness. Specifically, justice theorizing could be greatly enhanced by considering how emotions elicited during the course of a justice-related encounter influence people's perceptions of fairness (cf. Scher and Heise, 1993). Therefore, in the next section, I outline an AMJR that posits a reciprocal relationship between affect and perceptions of fairness.

The Affective Model of Justice Reasoning

People often report justice-related events to be emotionally involving. Therefore, one could argue that emotions that arise during the course of a justice-related encounter have the power to influence people's perceptions of fairness and how they decide whether events were fair or unfair.

Figure 1.1 depicts the AMJR that posits an important role for integral affect in how people reason about fairness. In particular, the model predicts that people's initial appraisals of an event lead to their affective reactions and then their affective reactions influence whether and how they think about fairness. Moreover, the model predicts that people's fairness judgments then further refine their emotional reactions and appraisals of the event.

In particular, the AMJR predicts that people's concerns about fairness are shaped largely by their negative affective reactions to negative events (see Figure 1.1). Taylor (1991) defines a negative event as "one that has the potential or actual ability to create adverse outcomes for the individual" (p. 67). Negative events, such as seeing a valued employee fired (or being that employee), lead to negative affect that, in turn, prompts people's concern with fairness. The type of information processing that occurs in response to a negative event is hypothesized to vary as a function of the discrete emotion that is elicited. In particular, people who experience anger (a negative emotion associated with appraisals of certainty; Lazarus, 1991) are predicted to engage in motivated processing of information in search for evidence that events were unfair. That is, angry people should seek out information that is consistent with the conclusion that events were unfair and they should engage in biased processing of information (e.g., interpreting ambiguous procedural information as unfair). In contrast, people who experience sadness or disappointment (negative emotions associated with appraisals of uncertainty; Lazarus, 1991) are predicted to engage in more substantive information processing in an effort to understand the implications of the event and how it occurred. However, more careful processing does not imply that all information will be interpreted as being consistent with one's affective state. Thus, clear evidence of the fairness of the decision-making procedures after receiving an unfavorable outcome should mitigate the ill effects of the unfavorable outcome (e.g., see Lind and Tyler, 1988; Brockner and Wiesenfeld, 1996, 2005, for reviews). However, more ambiguous procedural information should be interpreted in affective consistent ways (Bower, 1981; Forgas, 1995). Thus, when people engage in more substantive processing in response to a negative or unfavorable outcome, they should conclude that an event was unfair when procedural information is ambiguous or negative, but not when procedural information is clearly positive. Moreover, the model predicts that people's judgments about the fairness of the event should also influence their original interpretations of the event and their affective reactions to the event. Thus, the model posits a reciprocal relationship between affect and perceptions of (un)fairness.

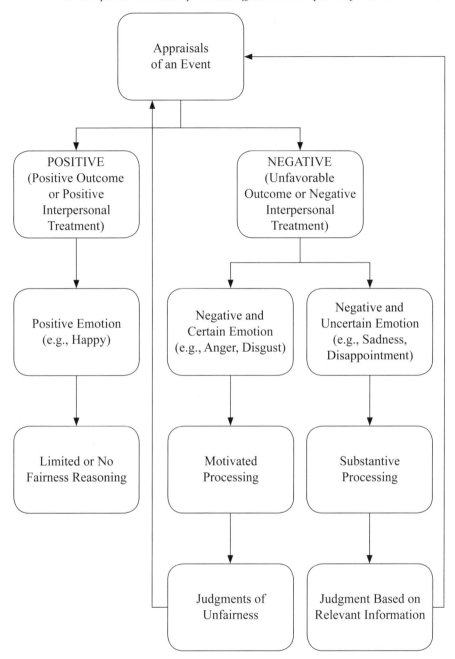

Figure 1.1   An Affective Model of Justice Reasoning

In contrast, when people appraise events to be positive and experience positive emotions, those positive emotions serve as a signal to people that all is right in their environment that, in turn, limits any motivation to engage in systematic fairness reasoning (e.g., Bless and Schwarz, 1999; Bless, 2000). Thus, events that lead to neutral or positive affect are not predicted to spontaneously prompt people's concerns with fairness (see also Scher and Heise, 1993; Rutte and Messick, 1995). If people are asked to provide a fairness judgment (e.g., in the context of a laboratory experiment), people will engage in heuristic or relatively shallow processing of information and be likely to conclude that events were fair. It is important to note, however, that positive emotions that are associated with appraisals of uncertainty (e.g., surprise) may be likely to lead to more information processing than positive emotions associated with appraisals of certainty (e.g., joy), yet the AMJR predicts that this additional processing will likely not include fairness reasoning.[1]

Some empirical evidence supports the notion that affect and perceptions of fairness are reciprocally related (Grote and Clark, 2001). For example, Grote and Clark (2001) conducted a longitudinal study of married couples' a) satisfaction with their marriage and b) perceptions of fairness in their marriage as they made the transition to first parenthood. Consistent with equity theory, the authors found that perceived unfairness in the division of household tasks predicted marital distress. However, the authors also found evidence that marital distress induced by the birth of a first child predicted later perceptions of unfairness. In other words, first parents demonstrated evidence of a cyclical process whereby perceived unfairness led to marital distress that, in turn, heightened the perceived unfairness. These results are consistent with the hypothesis that people's appraisal of events lead to affective reactions that, in turn, influence their perceptions of fairness and appraisals of the event.

Moreover, other research supports the notion that integral affect influences people's perceptions of fairness (e.g., Haidt, 2001; Mullen and Skitka, 2006). Consistent with the notion that people's affective reactions can guide their fairness judgments and reasoning, research has found that discrete emotions function either as a source of moral judgment (Haidt, Koller and Dias, 1993; Wheatley and Haidt, 2005) or as predictors of moral judgment (Rozin, Lowery, Imada, and Haidt, 1999). For example, Haidt's (2001) social intuitionist model argues that people often make moral judgments quickly and intuitively on the basis of their gut-level reactions, and that moral reasoning only comes into play when people are asked to justify their conclusions or when their intuitions conflict and thus prompt more careful

---

1   It is important to note, however, that people may sometimes engage in fairness reasoning in situations where they receive positive outcomes (e.g., in situations where they are over-rewarded and experience guilt). However, I posit that people's fairness reasoning in these situations is likely to be prompted by their feelings of guilt for being over-rewarded (i.e., a negative emotion) rather than by their positive outcome. People can justify positive outcomes as being deserved (Hegtvedt, 1990) and research has shown that it takes more of an over-reward than under-reward to generate a sense of injustice (Jasso, 1980). Therefore, the AMJR predicts that if people only experience positive affect in response to positive outcomes they will be unlikely to engage in fairness reasoning. However, when people are aware that their positive outcomes may be the cause of a negative outcome for another person (i.e., if one's over-reward causes another to be disadvantaged) then people will experience guilt (Hegtvedt and Killian, 1999), and their guilt should prompt them to think more carefully about fairness.

reasoning. Thus, people's intuitions and emotions are a significant driving force in their moral judgments. Similarly, neuropsychological research suggests that people generate affect in conjunction with moral judgment and that these affective states subsequently guide moral judgment and choice (Damasio, 1994; Greene and Haidt, 2002). For example, people's solutions to moral dilemmas vary as a function of the degree to which they are emotionally involved in the moral dilemma (Greene et al., 2001).

Finally, recent research on the role of people's moral convictions in fairness reasoning has found that outcomes that threaten people's core moral values lead people to experience anger and moral outrage that, in turn, leads them to devalue the fairness of the procedures and the outcome (Skitka, 2002; Mullen and Skitka, 2006). That is, when people are angered by outcomes that violate their moral standards they conclude that both the outcome and the procedures were unfair. In contrast, when outcomes support moral standards, people do not experience anger and consequently rate the outcome and procedures to be fair (Mullen and Skitka, 2006).

Taken together, a variety of evidence supports the hypothesis that people's integral emotional reactions to events might influence their perceptions of fairness and that their fairness judgments, in turn, might also influence their subsequent appraisals of the event and their affective reactions. Thus, the AMJR predicts that integral affect is not only an important consequence of perceptions of fairness or unfairness but is also an important causal factor in people's perceptions of fairness or unfairness. In the next section, I draw on research and theorizing on the role of incidental affect on people's judgments and information processing to provide additional support for the AMJR hypothesis that affect can be a causal factor in justice reasoning.

Incidental Affective Influences on Social Judgments

The majority of research investigating the influence of affect on social information processing has focused on judgments of people in good or bad moods rather than examining the effects of discrete emotions on people's judgments and information processing. Therefore, I first review theory and evidence that suggests that people's incidental moods can influence their fairness reasoning and judgments, and then I discuss the role of discrete emotions in people's perceptions of fairness.

Mood Effects on Information Processing and Judgments

Considerable research has supported the notion that people's incidental affective states influence their cognitions and judgments. For example, people's affective states influence their attributions (e.g., Forgas, Bower and Moylan, 1990), memory (e.g., Bower, 1981, 1991; Eich and Macaulay, 2000; Adolphs and Damasio, 2001; Bower and Forgas, 2001), information processing (e.g., Forgas, 1995, 2000; Clore, 2001; Fiedler, 2001), attitudes (Ito and Cacioppo, 2001; Petty, DeSteno and Rucker, 2001), solutions to moral dilemmas (Valdesolo and DeSteno, 2006), interpretations of behavior, impression formation, performance evaluations, and political judgments, among others (Forgas and Moylan, 1987; for reviews see Forgas, 1992, 1995, 2000;

Forgas and George, 2001). Taken together, this research is consistent with the notion that people's affective states have the potential to influence how fair or unfair they determine an event to be and the depth of information processing they engage in about the event.

People's moods can influence their judgments in a mood consistent direction either a) directly, when they use their current mood as information when making a judgment (e.g., Bless and Schwarz, 1999), or b) indirectly, through affective priming (Bower, 1981, 1991; Eich and Macaulay, 2000; Bower and Forgas, 2001). Research in the affect-as-information tradition has found that affect can directly influence people's judgments when they consult their current mood state to determine how they feel about an object. Affect is most likely to be used as information when people make judgments about highly typical or simple targets and when people do not experience motivational or situational demands for more detailed processing (Forgas, 1995). For example, when asked how fairly they are treated at work, people might consult their current mood state and use that information when forming their judgment (e.g., Van den Bos, 2003). Therefore, people in positive moods should conclude that they are more fairly treated than people in negative moods.

In contrast, affective priming influences the content of people's judgments indirectly by influencing the associated cognitions that are called to mind when making a judgment. In other words, research on affective priming suggests that people's emotional states make more accessible certain perceptual categories, themes, and ways of interpreting the world that are congruent with their emotional state. These mental sets then act as interpretive filters of reality and bias people's judgments (Bower, 1981, 1991; Bower and Forgas, 2001). Thus, people pay more attention to mood congruent information and process it more deeply relative to mood incongruent information. Affect is more likely to indirectly influence people's judgments through affective priming when they are engaged in more substantive, on-line information processing of novel or complex information about an event or target (Forgas, 1992, 1995).

Moreover, affect can also influence people's depth of information processing (e.g., heuristic or systematic, Forgas, 1992, 1995, 2000; Clore, 2001). Positive moods signal to people that all is right in their environment. People in positive moods therefore tend to engage in more spontaneous, heuristic, top-down processing of the situation, and rely more on their general knowledge structures. In contrast, negative affect signals to people that there is a problem in their environment, and therefore leads people to engage in more careful, systematic processing of the situation (e.g., Isen, 1984; Schwarz, 1990; Clore, Schwarz and Conway, 1994; Bless and Schwarz, 1999; Bless, 2000). Researchers investigating the effects of moods on information processing suggest that negative moods generally lead to more substantive processing. However, recent research suggests that not all negatively valenced emotions similarly influence information processing. For example, although anger and sadness both are negative emotions, they have been shown to have differing effects on people's information processing strategies. In particular, anger has been associated with more heuristic information processing whereas sadness has been associated with more substantive information processing (Bodenhausen, Sheppard and Kramer, 1994). In sum, considerable research supports the notion that people's affective states could influence the depth of information processing they engage in about fairness related events.

There is some evidence that people's incidental affective states can bias their fairness judgments. For example, people's incidental affective states exert an influence on their preferences for equality versus equity when distributing resources (e.g., Sinclair and Mark, 1991, 1992). Specifically, people in positive moods tend to allocate resources equally, whereas people in negative moods tend to allocate resources more equitably (O'Malley and Davies, 1984; Sinclair and Mark, 1991, 1992). Similarly, people in good moods show greater endorsement of macro-justice principles (e.g., guaranteeing a minimum income), whereas people in bad moods show greater endorsement of micro-justice principles (e.g., equity; Sinclair and Mark, 1991). These results are consistent with mood-induced differences in information processing and categorization (Sinclair and Mark, 1992). People in positive moods tend to rely on less careful processing and differentiate less between individuals, thus they allocate resources equally. In contrast, people in negative moods engage in more careful processing and tend to differentiate between individuals a great deal, thus they allocate according to equity principles. In sum, people's moods can influence their judgments of what is a fair allocation of resources.

Similarly, other research has found that people's incidental affective states can influence their perceptions of fairness (Van den Bos, 2003). In three studies, participants were induced to experience either a positive or negative affective state and then they received one of several outcomes (Study 1) or experienced one of several procedures that varied in their fairness (Studies 2 and 3; Van den Bos, 2003). When people had no relevant information for forming their fairness judgments (e.g., had no social comparison information to determine the fairness of the outcome they received) their perceptions of fairness were shaped by their incidental affective states. That is, participants in a negative mood rated the outcome they received to be less fair than participants in a positive mood. When participants had justice-relevant information, however, their affective states did not influence their perceptions of fairness. In sum, people's affective states can, at times, influence their perceptions of fairness in a mood consistent direction. However, the effects of incidental affective states on perceptions of fairness may be limited to situations that do not elicit strong integral affective reactions and in which people lack relevant information on which to base their decision.

Effects of Discrete Emotions on Information Processing and Judgments

Although most people would agree that valence is a very important, if not the most important aspect, of emotion (e.g., Smith and Lazarus, 1990), recent research suggests that considering other appraisal dimensions that usefully discriminate emotions can further advance our understanding of how people's emotions influence their judgments and information processing. Cognitive appraisal theories of emotion (e.g., Lazarus, 1991) suggest that different emotions are associated with different cognitive appraisals (e.g., congruence or incongruence with one's goals, accountability, certainty, coping potential; Smith and Lazarus, 1990). Recently, research on Appraisal Tendency Theory has found that discrete emotions can influence people's subsequent cognitive appraisals of new information in appraisal consistent directions (Lerner and Keltner, 2000, 2001; Tiedens and Linton, 2001; Lerner et al., 2003). Specifically, Appraisal Tendency Theory suggests that an emotion, once aroused, will influence people's subsequent interpretations of novel stimuli in an appraisal consistent manner. For example, anger (an emotion associated with appraisals of certainty) has been demonstrated to be associated with more optimistic appraisals of risk; whereas fear (an emotion associated with appraisals of uncertainty) has been demonstrated to be associated with more pessimistic appraisals of risk (Lerner and Keltner, 2000; Lerner et al., 2003). A considerable body of research supports the Appraisal Tendency Theory prediction that discrete emotions color people's subsequent judgment and behavior across a wide range of contexts (e.g., Keltner, Ellsworth and Edwards, 1993; Bodenhausen, Kramer and Susser, 1994; Raghunathan and Pham, 1999; DeSteno et al., 2000; Lerner and Keltner, 2000; Tiedens and Linton, 2001; Lerner et al., 2003).

Moreover, other research supports the notion that people's discrete emotions influence their information processing strategy (e.g., Bodenhausen, Sheppard and Kramer, 1994; Tiedens and Linton, 2001). For example, Tiedens and Linton (2001) found that emotions associated with appraisals of certainty (e.g., anger) were associated with heuristic processing whereas emotions associated with appraisals of uncertainty (e.g., fear) resulted in systematic processing. Thus, different discrete emotions (e.g., anger, sadness, fear) may have different effects on people's perceptions of fairness and fairness reasoning that would not be captured by simply considering the valence (positive or negative) of people's emotional state.

People have a wide range of emotional experience and researchers debate the best way to categorize emotions (see Ekman and Davidson, 1994 for a review). For the purposes of this chapter, it is enough to say that a range of discrete emotions exist (e.g., happiness, sadness, anger, disgust, surprise, fear) and that different discrete emotions might differentially influence people's fairness reasoning and judgments. Below, I consider three negative emotions that might be particularly useful for understanding the psychology of justice judgments. For a more detailed review of a broader range of emotions, including positive emotions, see Lazarus (1991).

Anger

Anger may be one emotion that is particularly likely to be associated with perceptions of injustice (e.g., Mikula, 1986, 1987; Lupfer et al., 2000; Bies, 2001). People frequently report anger towards others perceived to be personally responsible for causing harm (Weiner, 1995), and anger is associated with a desire to attack or punish people for their actions (Averill, 1982; Berkowitz, 1993; Shweder and Haidt, 2000; Skitka, Bauman and Mullen, 2004). Moreover, angry individuals may provide justification for their anger and desire to retaliate by deciding that events were unfair (Miller, 2001). Additionally, anger has been shown to lead to simpler, heuristic modes of information processing, and an increase in blame cognitions relative to other emotions (e.g., Berkowitz, 1993; Keltner, Ellsworth and Edwards, 1993; Tiedens and Linton, 2001). For example, Lerner, Goldberg and Tetlock (1998) found that participants who were primed to experience anger by witnessing a video of an injustice, made more punitive attributions toward a negligent tort defendant in a subsequent "unrelated" task than those not primed to experience anger. However, holding participants accountable for their decisions eliminated this difference, presumably because holding participants accountable forced them to engage in more substantive processing. Thus, angry people might be more likely to engage in heuristic or motivated processing of fairness-related information relative to people experiencing other emotions (e.g., happiness, sadness) and thus be more likely to arrive at a judgment that events were unfair.

Disgust

People experience disgust in response to extreme distaste for an object or in response to people who violate key cultural values (Lazarus, 1991; Rozin, Haidt and Cauley, 1999). People experiencing disgust frequently report experiencing nausea and typically want to distance themselves from the disgusting and offensive target (Rozin et al., 1999). Disgust has recently received increased attention in the moral reasoning literature due to work by Jon Haidt and his colleagues that suggests that people's feelings of disgust are intimately related to their moral judgments. People often report feeling disgust in response to moral transgressions and recent research has demonstrated that people's judgments about moral transgressions are more severe when accompanied by disgust (Wheatley and Haidt, 2005). If fairness judgments operate similarly to moral judgments, then people experiencing disgust may be more likely to judge events to be unfair relative to people who are not experiencing disgust.

Sadness

Sadness is another negatively valenced emotion, but unlike anger and disgust, sadness is associated with appraisals of uncertainty (Lazarus, 1991). Moreover, sadness tends to be associated with more systematic information processing (Bodenhausen, Kramer and Susser, 1994; Tiedens, 2001) relative to anger or positive emotions. Sadness is also associated with an increased tendency to make situational relative to personal attributions for a negative event (Keltner, Ellsworth and Edwards, 1993). Thus, given that sadness is associated with appraisals of uncertainty and a tendency to make situational attributions, sad people might be more willing to engage in more substantive information processing of fairness-related information before forming their fairness decisions relative to angry or disgusted people.

In sum, research suggests that people's affective states can color their subsequent judgments and influence their information processing strategies. Investigating how people's incidental affective states influence their judgments in subsequent unrelated contexts has advanced our understanding of the interplay between affect and cognition and has provided evidence that affect can be a causal factor in justice reasoning. The next necessary step to advance justice theorizing is to consider how people's integral emotions (i.e., emotions that are elicited during the course of a justice-related encounter) influence people's perceptions of fairness and fairness reasoning. The AMJR represents one attempt to take that next step.

Implications and Future Research

Positing a larger role for emotion in current theories of justice has several implications for how scholars theorize and test hypotheses about how people form their fairness decisions. First, the AMJR attempts to specify when justice considerations are a salient concern to people. In particular, the model predicts that people are not chronically concerned with fairness. Rather, people are more likely to think about fairness in response to a negative event. That is, people experience negative affect in response to a negative event and this negative affect prompts them to think about fairness. The type of information processing that occurs in response to a negative event is hypothesized to vary as a function of the discrete emotion that is elicited. In particular, anger is predicted to elicit motivated processing in support of the conclusion that events were unfair. In contrast, sadness or disappointment is predicted to lead people to engage in more substantive reasoning in an effort to understand how events could have turned out as they did. Finally, positive affect is not predicted to lead people to spontaneously engage in fairness reasoning at all. If people are asked to make a fairness judgment, however, they will rely on a heuristic strategy and conclude that events were fair. In sum, understanding how people's integral affective reactions to events influence their perceptions of fairness provides novel insight into *when* people are likely to be concerned with fairness and *how* they form their fairness decisions.

Second, the model implies that researchers need to pay more attention to people's integral affective reactions to fairness related events. Current theories of justice either treat affect as a consequence of fairness reasoning or, less frequently, consider incidental affective influences on perceptions of fairness. Although investigating the influence of incidental affect on people's perceptions of fairness has the advantages of allowing one to more conclusively demonstrate that affect influences people's perceptions of fairness and that justice judgments may be more subjective than heretofore believed (e.g., Van den Bos, 2003), it is limited because it fails to address the role of integral emotion in fairness reasoning. People's justice-related experiences are often highly emotionally involving. Thus, it seems reasonable to posit that the integral affect that is aroused in response to the focal event is likely to overwhelm people's incidental affective states. It is therefore crucial to gain a greater understanding of how integral affect and perceptions of fairness relate.

Third, the model implies that experiences of events judged to be fair and events judged to be unfair might be two qualitatively different experiences rather than mere opposites of one another. That is, judgments of fairness and unfairness may be arrived at through two very different processes. In particular, the AMJR predicts that people are much more likely to think about unfairness in response to negative events than fairness in response to positive events. The notion that people should think more about unfairness than fairness is consistent with other research that has found stronger effects for bad events than for good events on a) people's reactions to events, b) evaluations of close relationships, c) emotions, d) learning, e) neurological activation, f) social support, g) impression formation, and (h) information processing (see Baumeister et al., 2001, for a review). Similarly, Taylor's (1991) review of the literature revealed that negative events appear to elicit more "physiological, affective, cognitive, and behavioral activity and prompt more cognitive analysis than neutral or positive events" (p. 67). Moreover, other research has demonstrated that people take different approaches to allocating resources as a function of whether they are allocating benefits or burdens (e.g., Lamm and Kayser, 1978; Kayser and Lamm, 1980; Mannix, Neale and Northcraft, 1995; for a review see Törnblom, 1988). Thus, several lines of research are consistent with the notion that positive and negative events may inspire different types of fairness reasoning. Current theories of justice fail to adequately address the differences between perceptions of fairness and perceptions of unfairness, and future research should seek to remedy this shortcoming.

Fourth, the model predicts that people's affective reactions to events are more likely to be elicited by the outcomes and the interpersonal treatment they receive than by procedural factors (such as having an unbiased and impartial jury). Research has demonstrated that negative or unfavorable outcomes lead to anger (e.g., Adams, 1965) as does disrespect or negative interpersonal treatment (Bettencourt and Miller, 1996; Cohen et al., 1996). However, it is less clear whether procedural information (in the absence of outcomes) can elicit intense emotional reactions. Consistent with the notion that negative affective reactions should be more closely tied to outcomes or interpersonal treatment than procedures, research has found stronger effects for distributive than procedural justice on negative emotional reactions (Stecher, 1995; Mullen and Skitka, 2006). However, this is not to say that procedures are unimportant in justice reasoning, indeed they are posited to play an extremely important role in shaping people's reactions to negative outcomes or interpersonal treatment. In particular, people are predicted to evaluate procedural information if their negative affective reactions to outcomes or interpersonal treatment prompt them to engage in more substantive fairness reasoning. Clear evidence that procedures were fair should serve to mitigate the ill-effects of an unfavorable outcome (e.g., Cropanzano and Folger, 1991).

Finally, positing a greater role for emotions in justice reasoning highlights the interpersonal aspect of many justice situations and raises interesting questions about how the expression of emotion in interpersonal encounters influences people's perceptions of fairness. The expression of emotion helps to regulate social interactions (Keltner and Haidt, 1999). Thus, the expression of emotion by one individual may influence another person's perceptions of fairness or serve as a guide for regulating their behavior. Consider a boss who treats an employee rudely at work. If the employee expresses anger at the way his boss treated him, then perhaps fellow employees will come to perceive the boss's behavior as unfair. Moreover, if the employee expresses his anger to his boss, his anger can serve as a cue to his boss that perhaps she has offended her employee or behaved unfairly and thus she may choose to change her future behavior. That is, emotions expressed by one individual may provide other individuals with information about the fairness of the interaction.

In addition to exploring how people's emotional reactions to negative events caused by others (e.g., anger, disappointment) influence fairness reasoning, it would also be interesting to explore how shame or guilt expressed by the person responsible for the negative outcome or interpersonal treatment influence people's perceptions of fairness. Shame and guilt both involve negative affect, but guilt is experienced in response to a negative evaluation of one's own bad behavior; whereas shame is experienced in response to a negative evaluation of the entire self (Tangney, 1991). This distinction is consequential because guilt tends to be associated with reparative behavior for the bad act; whereas, shame is associated with the desire to hide or escape from the situation (Tangney, 1991). Thus, although both shame and guilt might accompany people's perceptions that they have behaved unfairly, these emotions might be associated with very different action tendencies and approaches to restore the injustice. Moreover, people's expression of shame or guilt for their behavior may influence how other people interpret whether their behavior was fair or unfair. Thus, in addition to exploring how emotions experienced by recipients of negative outcomes or interpersonal treatment influence their perceptions of fairness, it is also worth exploring how the expression of emotion by the person responsible for the wrong-doing influences perceptions of fairness.

Exploring how the expression of emotions influence perceptions of fairness in interpersonal encounters seems particularly relevant when one considers that many justice encounters occur in the context of on-going relationships (e.g., one repeatedly interacts with one's boss at work or one's partner at home). Therefore, it would also be interesting to explore how emotions that are elicited during one encounter (e.g., with one's boss) carryover to influence subsequent encounters with the same individual. Repeated negative interactions with the same individual over time have the potential to create a state of chronic negative affect that is called to mind anytime one interacts with that individual, potentially biasing one's perceptions of fairness. In sum, the influence of the expression of emotion in interpersonal encounters on people's perceptions of fairness has been relatively unexplored in the justice literature and deserves further research.

In addition to investigating how emotions influence perceptions of fairness in interpersonal encounters, future research should strive to sample a broad range of people's emotional reactions to events to provide insight into the complex manner that affect and justice interrelate. Moreover, the use of longitudinal designs to investigate how variations in interpersonal treatment and outcomes influence people's emotional reactions, and how those emotions once elicited, influence people's subsequent perceptions of fairness would help to tease apart the causal sequence between affect and perceptions of fairness (e.g., Grote and Clark, 2001). Similarly, examining when people spontaneously form fairness judgments by allowing people to provide more open-ended reactions to events (rather than explicitly asking people to form a judgment that something is fair or unfair) or using think aloud protocols might also provide insight into how affect and justice relate (e.g., Mikula, Scherer and Athenstaedt, 1998). Do people report experiencing emotions in response to events before they reason about whether the events were fair or unfair? Alternatively, do people first form their fairness judgments and then discuss their affective reactions? Similarly, do people spontaneously mention fairness when experiencing positive emotions generated by positive events? Using a broader array of methodologies has the potential to shed novel insight into these and other interesting questions about *when* people become concerned with fairness.

A model that posits a causal role for affect in how people reason about fairness also draws attention to the types of methodologies scholars currently use to answer questions related to *when* people are concerned with fairness. People can make fairness judgments in a variety of contexts. The prototypical fairness situation in the laboratory "involves the receipt or nonreceipt of some valued outcome by one person as a consequence of a decision made by another person, group, or institution" (Cropanzano et al., 2000, p. 49). However, more open-ended research demonstrates that there is often considerable divergence between the types of events people spontaneously report as an injustice and the one's that are typically studied in the laboratory (Mikula, 1986; Lupfer et al., 2000). Scholars should attempt to rectify this divergence by studying situations in the laboratory that have the potential to arouse people's emotions to some degree. If people only spontaneously initiate fairness reasoning when prompted to do so by their negative affective reactions (in the absence of being asked to provide a fairness judgment), then researchers interested in studying fairness judgments need to ensure that they create situations in the laboratory that are engaging and arousing for participants. Lerner (2003) has argued that it is unlikely that using the minimally involving laboratory techniques that most justice studies currently employ, that participants will experience strong emotions or express counter-normative responses. The lack of emotionally involving situations in the laboratory may limit our ability to understand how and when people reason about fairness.

The model proposed in this chapter is an initial attempt to incorporate affect as both a causal factor and a consequence of fairness reasoning. Future research will undoubtedly suggest boundary conditions and moderators to the proposed model. For example, individual difference variables such as people's levels of trait affect (Barsky and Kaplan, forthcoming), or the tendency for people to affectively react to events (e.g., affect intensity; Larsen and Diener, 1987) might be important moderators of people's emotional reactions to events and thus their fairness reasoning (e.g., Van den Bos et al., 2003). Moreover, one's relative status or power might influence whether emotions that are elicited during justice-related encounters are expressed. For example, status in a group is related to the expression of anger, embarrassment, contempt and fear (Keltner et al., 1998). Similarly, the degree of power one has might predict whether anger is expressed or repressed (Mackie, Devos and Smith, 2000). Finally, it is important to note that the AMJR was designed as a reactive rather than proactive model of justice. That is, the AMJR is most appropriate to situations in which people are reacting to events rather than proactively attempting to achieve justice. Future research is needed to model the role of affect in situations where people are proactively trying to achieve justice. One could predict that people's emotional reactions to imagined potential courses of action could help guide them to pursuing the most appropriate and just course of action (e.g., Damasio, 1994).

Conclusion

In conclusion, affect should be considered a relevant component of any theory of justice. Considerable research documents that affect is an integral part of people's experience of injustice (e.g., Adams, 1965; Mikula, 1986, 1987; Bies, 1987, 2001; Mikula, Scherer and Athenstaedt, 1998; Weiss, Suckow and Cropanzano, 1999).

Moreover, other research suggests that people's affective states can influence their perceptions of fairness (e.g., Grote and Clark, 2001; Van den Bos, 2003), and that emotions influence people's judgments in moral domains (e.g., Greene et al., 2001; Haidt, 2001). Most previous justice research has addressed the cognitive basis of justice judgments and has paid little attention to the role of affect in perceived justice and injustice (for an exception see Van den Bos, 2003). It is likely that both cognitive and affective factors influence people's perceptions of fairness and fairness reasoning, and thus current theories of justice would benefit from a greater understanding of how and when affect influences people's perceptions of fairness. The AMJR outlined in this chapter represents an initial attempt to incorporate integral affect into theories of justice. Even though the proposed model will inevitably be revised in light of new research findings, the ideas put forth in this chapter should nevertheless highlight that incorporating affect into theories of justice will advance our understanding of when people care about fairness and how they form their fairness decisions.

Author Note

I thank Christopher Bauman, Tracy Caldwell, Kjell Törnblom and Riël Vermunt for their helpful comments on an earlier version of this chapter.

References

Adams, J.S. (1965), "Inequity in Social Exchange" in *Advances in Experimental Social Psychology*, Vol. 2. Berkowitz, L. (ed.) (New York: Academic Press), 267–299.

Adolphs, R. and Damasio, A.R. (2001), "The Interaction of Affect and Cognition: A Neurobiological Perspective" in *Handbook of Affect and Social Cognition*. Forgas, J.P. (ed.) (Mahwah, NJ: Lawrence Erlbaum), 27–49.

Averill, J.R. (1982), *Anger and Aggression: An Essay on Emotion* (New York: Springer-Verlag).

Barsky, A. and Kaplan, S. (forthcoming), "If you Feel Bad, It's Unfair: A Quantitative Synthesis of Affect and Organizational Justice Perceptions", *Journal of Applied Psychology*. [PubMed 17227170]

Baumeister, R.F., Bratslavsky, E., Finkenauer, C. and Vohs, K.D. (2001), "Bad is Stronger than Good", *Review of General Psychology*, **5**, 323–370. [DOI: 10.1037/1089-2680.5.4.323]

Berkowitz, L. (1993), *Aggressions: Its Causes, Consequences, and Control* (Philadelphia: Temple University Press).

Bettencourt, B.A. and Miller, N. (1996), "Sex Differences in Aggression as a Function of Provocation: A Meta-Analysis", *Psychological Bulletin*, **119**, 422–447. [PubMed 8668747] [DOI: 10.1037/0033-2909.119.3.422]

Bies, R.J. (1987), "The Predicament of Injustice: The Management of Moral Outrage", *Research in Organizational Behavior*, **9**, 289–319.

Bies, R.J. (2001), "Interactional (In)Justice: The Sacred and the Profane" in *Advances in Organizational Justice*. Greenberg, J. and Cropanzano, R. (eds) (Stanford, CA: Stanford University Press), 89−118.

Bies, R.J. and Tripp, T.M. (2001), "A Passion for Justice: The Rationality and Morality of Revenge" in *Justice in the Workplace: From Theory to Practice (Vol. 2). Series in Applied Psychology*. Cropanzano, R. (ed.) (Mahwah, NJ: Lawrence Erlbaum), 197−208.

Bless, H. (2000), "The Interplay of Affect and Cognition: The Mediating Role of General Knowledge Structures" in *Feeling and Thinking: The Role of Affect in Social Cognition*. Forgas, J.P. (ed.) (Cambridge, UK: Cambridge University Press), 201−222.

Bless, H. and Schwarz, N. (1999), "Sufficient and Necessary Conditions in Dual-Process Models: The Case of Mood and Information Processing" in *Dual-process Theories in Social Psychology*. Chaiken, S. and Trope, Y. (eds) (New York: Guilford Publications), 423−440.

Bodenhausen, G., Sheppard, L.A. and Kramer, G.P. (1994), "Negative Affect and Social Judgment: The Differential Impact of Anger and Sadness", *European Journal of Social Psychology*, **24**, 45−62.

Bodenhausen, G.V. (1993), "Emotions, Arousal, and Stereotypic Judgments: A Heuristic Model of Affect and Stereotyping" in *Affect, Cognition, and Stereotyping*. Mackie, D.M. and Hamilton, D.L. (eds) (San Diego, CA: Academic Press), 13−37.

Bodenhausen, G.V., Kramer, G.P. and Susser, K. (1994), "Happiness and Stereotypic Thinking in Social Judgment", *Journal of Personality and Social Psychology*, **66**, 621−632. [DOI: 10.1037/0022-3514.66.4.621]

Bower, G.H. (1981), "Mood and Memory", *American Psychologist*, **36**, 129−148. [PubMed 7224324] [DOI: 10.1037/0003-066X.36.2.129]

Bower, G.H. (1991), "Mood Congruity of Social Judgments" in *Emotion and Social Judgments*. Forgas, J.P. (ed.) (Oxford: Pergamon), 31−53.

Bower, G.H. and Forgas, J.P. (2001), "Mood and Social Memory" in *Handbook of Affect and Social Cognition*. Forgas, J.P. (ed.) (Mahwah, NJ: Lawrence Erlbaum), 95−120.

Brockner, J. and Wiesenfeld, B.M. (1996), "An Integrative Framework for Explaining Reactions to Decisions: Interactive Effects of Outcomes and Procedures", *Psychological Bulletin*, **120**, 189−208. [PubMed 8831296] [DOI: 10.1037/0033-2909.120.2.189]

Brockner, J. and Wiesenfeld, B.M. (2005), "How, When, and Why Does Outcome Favorability Interact with Procedural Fairness?". in *Handbook of Organizational Justice*. Greenberg, J. and Colquitt, J.A. (eds) (Mahwah, NJ: Lawrence Erlbaum), 525−553.

Clore, G.L. (2001), "Affect as Information" in *Handbook of Affect and Social Cognition*. Forgas, J.P. (ed.) (NJ: Lawrence Erlbaum), 121−144.

Clore, G.L., Schwarz, N. and Conway, M. (1994), "Cognitive Causes and Consequences of Emotion" in *Handbook of Social Cognition*, Vol. 1. Wyer, R.S. and Srull, T.K. (eds) (Hillsdale, NJ: Erlbaum), 323–418.

Cohen, D., Nisbett, R.E., Bowdle, B.F. and Schwarz, N. (1996), "Insult, Aggression, and the Southern Culture of Honor: and 'Experimental Ethnography'", *Journal of Personality and Social Psychology*, **70**, 945–960. [PubMed 8656339] [DOI: 10.1037/0022-3514.70.5.945]

Colquitt, J.A., Conlon, D.E., Wesson, M.J., Porter, C.O.L.H. and Ng, K.Y. (2001), "Justice at the Millennium: A Meta-Analytic Review of 25 years of Organizational Justice Research", *Journal of Applied Psychology*, **86**, 425–445. [PubMed 11419803] [DOI: 10.1037/0021-9010.86.3.425]

Cropanzano, R. and Folger, R. (1991), "Procedural Justice and Worker Motivation" in *Motivation and Work Behavior*. Steers, R.M. and Porter, L.W. (eds) (NY: McGraw-Hill), 131–143.

Cropanzano, R. and Greenberg, J. (1997), "Progress in Organizational Justice: Tunneling through the Maze" in *International Review of Industrial and Organizational Psychology*, Vol. 12. Robertson, I.T. and Cooper, C.L. (eds) (NY: Wiley), 317–372.

Cropanzano, R., Rupp, D.E., Mohler, C.J. and Schminke, M. (2001), "Three Roads to Organizational Justice" in *Research in Personnel and Human Resources Management*, Vol. 20. Ferris, J. (ed.) (Greenwich, CT: JAI Press), 1–113.

Cropanzano, R., Weiss, H.M., Suckow, K. and Grandey, A.A. (2000), "Doing Justice to Workplace Emotions" in *Emotions at Work*. Ashkanasy, N., Hartel, C. and Zerbe, W. (eds) (Westport, CT: Quorum Books), 63–68.

Crosby, F. (1976), "A Model of Egoistical Relative Deprivation", *Psychological Review*, **83**, 85–113. [DOI: 10.1037/0033-295X.83.2.85]

Damasio, A. (1994), *Descartes' Error: Emotion, Reason, and the Human Brain* (Cambridge, MA: Bradford/MIT Press).

DeSteno, D., Petty, R.E., Wegener, D.T. and Rucker, D.D. (2000), "Beyond Valence in the Perception of Likelihood: The Role of Emotion Specificity", *Journal of Personality and Social Psychology*, **78**, 397–416. [DOI: 10.1037/0022-3514.78.3.397]

Eich, E. and Macaulay, D. (2000), "Fundamental Factors in Mood-Dependent Memory" in *Feeling and Thinking: The Role of Affect in Social Cognition*. Forgas, J.P. (ed.) (Cambridge, UK: Cambridge University Press), 109–130.

Ekman, P. and Davidson, R.J., eds (1994), *The Nature of Emotion: Fundamental Questions* (New York: Oxford University Press).

Fiedler, K. (2001), "Affective Influences on Social Information Processing" in *Handbook of Affect and Social Cognition*. Forgas, J.P. (ed.) (Mahwah, NJ: Lawrence Erlbaum), 163–185.

Forgas, J.P. (1992), "Affect in Social Judgments and Decisions: A Multiprocess Model" in *Advances in Experimental Social Psychology*, Vol. 25. Zanna, M. (ed.) (San Diego, CA: Academic Press), 227–275.

Forgas, J.P. (1995), "Mood and Judgment: The Affect Infusion Model (AIM)", *Psychological Bulletin*, **117**, 39–66. [DOI: 10.1037/0033-2909.117.1.39]

Forgas, J.P. (2000), "Affect and Information Processing Strategies: An Interactive Relationship" in *Feeling and Thinking: The Role of Affect in Social Cognition*. Forgas, J.P. (ed.) (Cambridge, UK: Cambridge University Press), 253–282.

Forgas, J.P. and George, J.M. (2001), "Affective Influences on Judgments and Behavior in Organizations: An Information Processing Perspective", *Organizational Behavior and Human Decision Processes*, **86**, 3–34. [DOI: 10.1006/obhd.2001.2971]

Forgas, J.P. and Moylan, S.J. (1987), "After the Movies: Transient Mood and Social Judgments", *Personality and Social Psychology Bulletin*, **13**, 467–477. [DOI: 10.1177/0146167287134004]

Forgas, J.P., Bower, G.H. and Moylan, S.J. (1990), "Praise or Blame? Affective Influences on Attributions for Achievement", *Journal of Personality and Social Psychology*, **59**, 809–819. [PubMed 2254856] [DOI: 10.1037/0022-3514.59.4.809]

Foster, C.A. and Rusbult, C.E. (1999), "Injustice and Powerseeking", *Personality and Social Psychology Bulletin*, **25**, 834–849.

Greene, J. and Haidt, J. (2002), "How (and where) Does Moral Judgment Work?" *Trends in Cognitive Sciences*, **6**, 517–523. [PubMed 12475712] [DOI: 10.1016/S1364-6613%2802%2902011-9]

Greene, J.D., Sommerville, R.B., Nystrom, L.E., Darley, J.M. and Cohen, J.D. (2001), "An fMRI Investigation of Emotional Engagement in Moral Judgment", *Science*, **293**, 2105–2108. [PubMed 11557895] [DOI: 10.1126/science.1062872]

Grote, N.K. and Clark, M.S. (2001), "Perceiving Unfairness in the Family: Cause or Consequence of Marital Distress?" *Journal of Personality and Social Psychology*, **80**, 281–293. [PubMed 11220446] [DOI: 10.1037/0022-3514.80.2.281]

Haidt, J. (2001), "The Emotional Dog and its Rational Tail: A Social Intuitionist Approach to Moral Judgment", *Psychological Review*, **108**, 814–834. [PubMed 11699120] [DOI: 10.1037/0033-295X.108.4.814]

Haidt, J., Koller, S.H. and Dias, M.G. (1993), "Affect, Culture, and Morality, or is it Wrong to Eat your Dog?" *Journal of Personality and Social Psychology*, **65**, 613–628. [PubMed 8229648] [DOI: 10.1037/0022-3514.65.4.613]

Hegtvedt, K.A. (1990), "The Effects of Relationship Structure on Emotional Responses to Inequality", *Social Psychology Quarterly*, **53**, 214–228. [DOI: 10.2307/2786960]

Hegtvedt, K.A. and Killian, C. (1999), "Fairness and Emotional Responses: Reactions to the Process and Outcomes of Negotiations", *Social Forces*, **78**, 269–303. [DOI: 10.2307/3005797]

Homans, G.C. (1961), *Social Behavior: Its Elementary Forms* (New York: Harcourt Brace Jovanovich).

Isen, A. (1984), "Towards Understanding the Role of Affect in Cognition" in *Handbook of Social Cognition*, Vol. 3. Wyer, R.S. and Srull, T.K. (eds) (Hillsdale, NJ: Erlbaum), 179–236.

Ito, T.A. and Cacioppo, J.T. (2001), "Affect and Attitudes: A Social Neuroscience Approach" in *Handbook of Affect and Social Cognition*. Forgas, J.P. (ed.) (Mahwah, NJ: Lawrence Erlbaum), 50–74.

Jasso, G. (1980), "A New Theory of Distributive Justice", *American Sociological Review*, **45**, 3–32. [DOI: 10.2307/2095239]

Kayser, E. and Lamm, H. (1980), "Input Integration and Input Weighting in Decisions on Allocations of Gains and Losses", *European Journal of Social Psychology*, **10**, 1–15.

Keltner, D. and Haidt, J. (1999), "Social Functions of Emotions at Four Levels of Analysis", *Cognition and Emotion*, **13**, 505–521. [DOI: 10.1080/026999399379168]

Keltner, D., Ellsworth, P.C. and Edwards, K. (1993), "Beyond Simple Pessimism: Effects of Sadness and Anger on Social Perception", *Journal of Personality and Social Psychology*, **64**, 740–752. [PubMed 8505705] [DOI: 10.1037/0022-3514.64.5.740]

Keltner, D., Young, R., Heerey, E.A., Oemig, C. and Monarch, N.D. (1998), "Teasing in Hierarchical and Intimate Relations", *Journal of Personality and Social Psychology*, **75**, 1231–1247. [PubMed 9866185] [DOI: 10.1037/0022-3514.75.5.1231]

Kohlberg, L. (1969), "Stage and Sequence: The Cognitive-Developmental Approach to Socialization" in *Handbook of Socialization Theory and Research*. Goslin, D.A. (ed.) (Chicago: Rand McNally), 347–480.

Krehbiel, P.J. and Cropanzano, R. (2000), "Procedural Justice, Outcome Favorability, and Emotion", *Social Justice Research*, **13**, 339–360. [DOI: 10.1023/A%3A1007670909889]

Lamm, H. and Kayser, E. (1978), "The Allocation of Monetary Gain and Loss Following Dyadic Performance: The Weight Given to Effort and Ability under Conditions of Low and High Intra-Dyadic Attraction", *European Journal of Social Psychology*, **8**, 275–278.

Larsen, R.J. and Diener, E. (1987), "Affect Intensity as an Individual Difference Characteristic: A Review", *Journal of Research in Personality*, **21**, 1–39. [DOI: 10.1016/0092-6566%2887%2990023-7]

Lazarus, R.S. (1991), *Emotion and Adaptation* (New York: Oxford University Press).

Lerner, J.S. and Keltner, D. (2000), "Beyond Valence: Toward a Model of Emotion-Specific Influences on Judgment and Choice", *Cognition and Emotion*, **14**, 473–493. [DOI: 10.1080/026999300402763]

Lerner, J.S. and Keltner, D. (2001), "Fear, Anger, and Risk", *Journal of Personality and Social Psychology*, **81**, 146–159. [PubMed 11474720] [DOI: 10.1037/0022-3514.81.1.146]

Lerner, J.S., Goldberg, J.H. and Tetlock, P.E. (1998), "Sober Second Thought: The Effects of Accountability, Anger, and Authoritarianism on Attributions of Responsibility", *Personality and Social Psychology Bulletin*, **24**, 563–574. [DOI: 10.1177/0146167298246001]

Lerner, J.S., Gonzalez, R.M., Small, D.A. and Fischhoff, B. (2003), "Effects of Fear and Anger on Perceived Risk of Terrorism: A National Field Experiment", *Psychological Science*, **14**, 144–150. [PubMed 12661676] [DOI: 10.1111/1467-9280.01433]

Lerner, M.J. (2003), "The Justice Motive: Where Social Psychologists Found it, How they Lost it, and Why they May not Find it Again", *Personality and Social Psychology Review*, **7**, 388–399. [DOI: 10.1207/S15327957PSPR0704_10]

Lind, E.A. and Tyler, T.R. (1988), *The Social Psychology of Procedural Justice* (NY: Plenum).

Lupfer, M.B., Weeks, K.P., Doan, K.A. and Houston, D.A. (2000), "Folk Conceptions of Fairness and Unfairness", *European Journal of Social Psychology*, **30**, 405–428. [DOI: 10.1002/%28SICI%291099-0992%28200005%2F06%2930%3A3%3C40 5%3A%3AAID-EJSP997%3E3.0.CO%3B2-U]

Mackie, D.M., Devos, T. and Smith, E.R. (2000), "Intergroup Emotions: Explaining Offensive Action Tendencies in an Intergroup Context", *Journal of Personality and Social Psychology*, **79**, 602–616. [PubMed 11045741] [DOI: 10.1037/0022-3514.79.4.602]

Mannix, E.A., Neale, M.A. and Northcraft, G.B. (1995), "Equity, Equality, or Need?" "The Effects of Organizational Culture on the Allocation of Benefits and Burdens", *Organizational Behavior and Human Decision Processes*, **63**, 276–286. [DOI: 10.1006/obhd.1995.1079]

Mark, M.M. (1985), "Expectations, Procedural Justice, and Alternative Reactions to Being Deprived of a Desired Outcome", *Journal of Experimental Social Psychology*, **21**, 114–137. [DOI: 10.1016/0022-1031%2885%2990010-1]

Mikula, G. (1986), "The Experience of Injustice: Toward a Better Understanding of its Phenomenology" in *Justice in Social Relations*. Bierhoff, H.W., Cohen, R.L. and Greenberg, J. (eds) (NY: Plenum), 103–123.

Mikula, G. (1987), "Exploring the Experience of Injustice" in *Issues in Contemporary German Social Psychology*. Semin, G.R. and Krahe, B. (eds) (London: Sage), 74–96.

Mikula, G., Scherer, K.R. and Athenstaedt, U. (1998), "The Role of Injustice in the Elicitation of Differential Emotional Reactions", *Personality and Social Psychology Bulletin*, **24**, 769–783. [DOI: 10.1177/0146167298247009]

Miller, D.T. (2001), "Disrespect and the Experience of Injustice", *Annual Review of Psychology*, **52**, 527–553. [PubMed 11148316] [DOI: 10.1146/annurev.psych.52.1.527]

Mullen, E. and Skitka, L.J. (2006), "Exploring the Psychological Underpinnings of the Moral Mandate Effect: Motivated Reasoning, Group Identification, or Anger?" *Journal of Personality and Social Psychology*, **90**, 629–643. [PubMed 16649859] [DOI: 10.1037/0022-3514.90.4.629]

O'Malley, M.N. and Davies, D.K. (1984), "Equity and Affect: The Effects of Relative Performance and Moods on Resource Allocation", *Basic and Applied Social Psychology*, **5**, 273–282. [DOI: 10.1207/s15324834basp0504_2]

Olson, J.M. and Hafer, C.L. (1996), "Affect, Motivation, and Cognition in Relative Deprivation Research" in *Handbook of Motivation and Cognition, The Interpersonal Context*, Vol. 3. Sorrentino, R.M. and Higgins, E.T. (eds) (New York: Guilford).

Olson, J.M., Hafer, C.L. and Zanna, M.P., eds (1986), *Relative Deprivation and Social Comparison* (Hillsdale, NJ: Lawrence Erlbaum).

Petty, R.E., DeSteno, D. and Rucker, D.D. (2001), "The Role of Affect in Attitude Change" in *Handbook of Affect and Social Cognition*. Forgas, J.P. (ed.) (Mahwah, NJ: Erlbaum), 212–236.

Raghunathan, R. and Pham, M.T. (1999), "All Negative Moods Are Not Equal: Motivational Influences of Anxiety and Sadness on Decision-Making", *Organizational Behavior and Human Decision Processes*, **79**, 56–77. [PubMed 10388609] [DOI: 10.1006/obhd.1999.2838]

Rozin, P., Haidt, J. and McCauley, C.R. (1999), "Disgust: The Body and Soul Emotion" in *Handbook of Cognition and Emotion*. Dalgleish, T. and Power, M. (eds), 429–445.

Rozin, P., Lowery, L., Imada, S. and Haidt, J. (1999), "The CAD Triad Hypothesis: A Mapping between the Other-Directed Moral Emotions, Disgust, Contempt, and Anger, and Shweder's Three Universal Moral Codes", *Journal of Personality and Social Psychology*, **76**, 574–586. [PubMed 10234846] [DOI: 10.1037/0022-3514.76.4.574]

Rutte, C.G. and Messick, D.M. (1995), "An Integrated Model of Perceived Unfairness in Organizations", *Social Justice Research*, **8**, 239–261. [DOI: 10.1007/BF02334810]

Scher, S.J. and Heise, D.R. (1993), "Affect and the Perception of Injustice", *Advances in Group Processes*, **10**, 223–252.

Schwarz, N. (1990), "Happy but Mindless?", "Mood Effects on Problem Solving and Persuasion" in *Handbook of Motivation and Cognition*, Vol. 3. Sorrentino, R.M. and Higgins, E.T. (eds) (New York: Guilford), 527–561.

Shweder, R.A. and Haidt, J. (2000), "The Cultural Psychology of the Emotions: Ancient and New" in *Handbook of Emotions*. Lewis, M. and Haviland-Jones, J.M. (eds) (New York: Guilford), 397–414.

Sinclair, R.C. and Mark, M.M. (1991), "Mood and the Endorsement of Egalitarian macrojustice Principles versus Equity-Based Microjustice Principles", *Personality and Social Psychology Bulletin*, **17**, 369–375. [DOI: 10.1177/0146167291174003]

Sinclair, R.C. and Mark, M.M. (1992), "The Influence of Mood State on Judgment and Action: Effects on Persuasion, Categorization, Social Justice, Person Perception, and Judgmental Accuracy" in *The Construction of Social Judgments*. Martin, L.L. and Tesser, A. (eds) (Hillsdale, NJ: Lawrence Erlbaum).

Skitka, L.J. (2002), "Do the Means Always Justify the Ends, or do the Ends Sometimes Justify the Means? A Value Protection Model of Justice", *Personality and Social Psychology Bulletin*, **28**, 588–597. [DOI: 10.1177/0146167202288003]

Skitka, L.J., Bauman, C.W. and Mullen, E. (2004), "Political Tolerance and Coming to Psychological Closure Following the September 11, 2001, Terrorist Attacks: An Integrative Approach", *Personality and Social Psychology Bulletin*, **30**, 743–756. [PubMed 15155038] [DOI: 10.1177/0146167204263968]

Smith, C.A. and Lazarus, R.S. (1990), "Adaptation" in *Handbook of Personality: Theory and Research*. Pervin, L. (ed.) (NY: Guilford Publications), 609–637.

Solomon, R.C. (1990), *A Passion for Justice* (Reading, MA: Addison-Wesley).

Solomon, R.C. (1994), "Sympathy and Vengeance: The Role of the Emotions in Justice" in *Emotions: Essays on Emotion Theory*. Van Goozen, S.H.M., Van de Poll, N.E. and Sergeant, J.E. (eds) (Hillsdale, NJ: Lawrence Erlbaum), 291–311.

Stecher, M.D. (1995), "The Distributive Side of Interactional Justice". Doctoral dissertation, University of Colorado.

Stouffer, S.A., Suchman, E.A., Devinney, L.C., Star, S.A. and Williams, R.M. (1949), *The American Soldier: Adjustment during Army Life Vol. 1* (Oxford, UK: Princeton University Press).

Tangney, J.P. (1991), "Moral Affect: The Good, the Bad, and the Ugly", *Journal of Personality and Social Psychology*, **61**, 598–607. [PubMed 1960652] [DOI: 10.1037/0022-3514.61.4.598]

Taylor, S.E. (1991), "Asymmetrical Effects of Positive and Negative Events: The Mobilization-Minimization Hypothesis", *Psychological Bulletin*, **110**, 67–85. [PubMed 1891519] [DOI: 10.1037/0033-2909.110.1.67]

Tiedens, L.Z. (2001), "The Effects of Anger on the Hostile Inferences of Aggressive and Non-Aggressive People", *Motivation and Emotion*, **25**, 233–251. [DOI: 10.1023/A%3A1012224507488]

Tiedens, L.Z. and Linton, S. (2001), "Judgment under Emotional Certainty and Uncertainty: The Effects of Specific Emotions on Information Processing", *Journal of Personality and Social Psychology*, **81**, 973–988. [PubMed 11761319] [DOI: 10.1037/0022-3514.81.6.973]

Törnblom, K.Y. (1988), "Positive and Negative Allocations: A Typology and a Model for Conflicting Justice Principles" in *Advances in Group Processes*. Lawler, E.J. and Markovsky, B. (eds) (Greenwich, CT: JAI Press), 141–168.

Valdesolo, P. and DeSteno, D. (2006), "Manipulations of Emotional Context Shape Moral Judgment", *Psychological Science*, **17**, 476–477.

Van den Bos, K. (2003), "On the Subjective Quality of Social Justice: The Role of Affect as Information in the Psychology of Justice Judgments", *Journal of Personality and Social Psychology*, **85**, 482–498. [PubMed 14498784] [DOI: 10.1037/0022-3514.85.3.482]

Van den Bos, K., Maas, M., Waldring, I.E. and Semin, G.R. (2003), "Toward Understanding the Psychology of Reactions to Perceived Fairness: The Role of Affect Intensity", *Social Justice Research*, **16**, 151–168. [DOI: 10.1023/A%3A1024252104717]

Walker, I. and Smith, H.J., eds (2002), *Relative Deprivation: Specification, Development, and Integration* (Cambridge, UK: Cambridge University Press).

Weiner, B. (1995), *Judgments of Responsibility: A Foundation for a Theory of Social Conduct* (New York: Guilford Publications).

Weiss, H.M., Suckow, K. and Cropanzano, R. (1999), "Effects of Justice Conditions on Discrete Emotions", *Journal of Applied Psychology*, **84**, 786–794. [DOI: 10.1037/0021-9010.84.5.786]

Wheatley, T. and Haidt, J. (2005), "Hypnotic Disgust Makes Moral Judgments More Severe", *Psychological Science*, **16**, 780–784. [PubMed 16181440] [DOI: 10.1111/j.1467-9280.2005.01614.x]

Zajonc, R.B. (1980), "Feeling and Thinking: Preferences Need no Inferences", *American Psychologist*, **35**, 151–175. [DOI: 10.1037/0003-066X.35.2.151]

Chapter 2

Toward a Resource Production Theory of Distributive Justice

Kjell Y. Törnblom
University of Skövde, Sweden

Ali Kazemi
University of Skövde and Göteborg University, Sweden

Introduction

> Any theory of distributive justice that fails to make provision for a principle of production of goods and merely insists upon the fairness and equity of distribution of such goods as lie at hand is gravely deficient. (Rescher, 1966, p. 89)

When benefits and burdens (e.g., salaries, employment, educational opportunities, taxes, layoffs) are considered unfairly allocated, people feel unjustly treated and are emotionally upset. Conflicts may emerge, and discussions about how justice should be established or restored are promptly initiated. Disagreements about what types of inequality are just and what types are unjust seem increasingly common in political and other contexts. Research on justice has increased considerably during the past three to four decades. Several studies have shown that justice is associated with satisfaction and decision acceptance (e.g., Greenberg, 1987; Lind et al., 1993), plays a fundamental role in conflict resolution (Lamm, 1986; Törnblom, 1988; Hegtvedt, 1992; Mikula and Wenzel, 2000; Kazemi in this book), contributes to psychological well-being (e.g., Prilleltensky, 2001), and to positive interpersonal (Lerner and Mikula, 1994) and inter-group relationships (Jost and Major, 2001). The experience of injustice, on the other hand, may have serious negative consequences on the individual, group, organizational, and societal levels (e.g., Miller and Vidmar, 1981; Mikula, 1986; Greenberg, 1990).

Social psychologists attempt to explain when, why and how individuals make justice judgments, how they react psychologically and behaviorally to the outcome of the judgment, and how reactions to (in)justice affect and are affected by the social context. There are two general types of justice judgments—*distributive* (i.e., the perceived fairness of final outcomes), and *procedural* (i.e., the perceived fairness of the decision making procedures referring either to the procedures in their instrumental capacity of generating the final outcomes, or to the procedures, per se, signalling one's social-relational standing). While procedural justice research concerns the formal procedures, a special form of procedural justice, *interactional justice*, focusses on the fairness of the interpersonal treatment received during the enactment of the procedures. There is, however, some controversy over whether or not interactional justice is simply an instance of the broader concept of procedural justice (see Lind and Tyler, 1988, and Tyler and Bies, 1990). Each one of the three types of justice subsumes a variety of rules or principles (i.e., criteria according to which justice is subjectively assessed by the individual).

We are here concerned with *distributive justice*, of which the most researched principles are equality, equity (contribution, merit), and need. However, a number of additional principles (e.g., winner takes all, justified self-interest, ownership rule, legality rule, status rule) have been distinguished by various theorists (e.g., Lerner, 1975; Leventhal, 1980; Reis, 1984). Some of these principles may be conceptualized in more than one way, resulting in more specific principles designated as "subrules" (Törnblom and Jonsson, 1985; see also Rescher, 1966, and Messick and Sentis, 1983). For example, the equality principle may be defined as equality-of-treatment, equality-of-results, and equality-of-opportunity; the contribution principle subrules include contribution-of-performance, contribution-of-effort, and contribution-of-ability.

A large number of studies have been conducted to understand why people frequently disagree about which principle should represent justice in a given context, and why a person may define justice in terms of a certain principle in one situation at one point in time, while at another point in time and/or in another situation a different principle is viewed as the appropriate representation of justice. Several of the factors that have been shown to affect people's justice conceptions were grouped into six general categories (Törnblom, 1992): factors that are relevant to 1) characteristics of the actor, 2) the contribution, 3) the social relationship, 4) the socio-cultural and historical context, 5) the outcome, and 6) the outcome allocation.[1]

This chapter focusses on (but it is not limited to) the fifth of the above mentioned categories, the outcome, and we will discuss the impact that different kinds of the allocated social resources may have on justice conceptions. More specifically, we will attempt a preliminary analysis of the possible impact the way different types of social resources are produced/acquired[2] may have on distributive justice conceptions.

---

1   1. The *actors* involved in situations of resource (outcome) allocation may be described as recipients, allocators, or both. Actors may be individuals, groups, or aggregates of people.

2. One or more actors may make *contributions* (i.e., make performances of various kinds and/or possess various ascribed and/or acquired characteristics) which may have a bearing on how resources are to be allocated on their own personal behalf or as representatives of a group.

3. Various types of *social relationship* may prevail among actors.

4. Contributions and outcome allocations occur within a *social, cultural, and historical context*.

5. Actors may receive *outcomes* (resources) of various sorts.

6. *Outcome allocations* and/or allocation procedures may be effectuated in a number of different ways, for different purposes, and according to various criteria (distribution and/or procedural principles).

2   We are unable at this stage to speculate whether or not the two processes of "production" and "acquisition" of a resource may differ in their impact on justice conceptions. The task of

As this is a first exploration into a new area of inquiry, we would like to point out at the outstart that we provide more questions than answers and hint at more issues than we are able to fully address in this chapter.

An analysis of the impact of mode of resource production on justice conceptions is likely to require a) a categorization of the multitude of resources people provide and receive. Instead of constructing our own typology we have adopted an already existing, useful, and well researched classification by Foa (1971). We also need b) a typology or inventory of factors related to the ways in which the various kinds of resources may be produced. To this end we present a first attempt at identifying some factors relevant to resource production/acquisition, starting out on the shoulders of Marx and his notion of "mode of production" which is one of the more central concepts within Marxist frameworks. We then propose a number of ways in which, and some reasons why, mode of resource production/acquisition (albeit conceived differently from Marx's notion) might affect distributive justice conceptions, thereby generating a number of empirically testable propositions.

People Care about the Ways Social Resources are Produced

There is a growing (global) concern about issues regarding the way goods (and other social resources) are produced and acquired. Groups of citizens frequently protest against the way tropical forests are depleted for the purpose of manufacturing furniture and paper to be sold for profit. Many worry about possible detrimental health effects of food products resulting from gene modification. People who are adequately enlightened to care about animals protest against exposing them to painful experiments for the production of cosmetics and new drugs, or against killing animals for fur, aphrodisiacs, ornaments, and accessories. Objections are expressed against how animals are stressed, tortured, mishandled, raised in too small cages, and robbed of their dignity in that they are treated as raw materials and valued merely on the basis of their use for the production of goods to satisfy human needs, luxurious desires and vanity. Children are still in this day and age exploited and used as cheap labor in various production and manufacturing processes. Money is laundered, counterfeited, and stolen. Information is acquired via (industrial) espionage, and status is sought via destruction of property, terrorism and other means. The list over dubious modes of production/acquisition that may elicit feelings of outrage can easily be made very extensive. On the other hand, some modes of production will have the opposite effect and awaken positive attitudes and emotions. To mention just one example, ecological production of dairy products may affect many consumers' attitudes and affective orientations toward these products in a positive direction.

Apparently, the mode of production may elicit intense feelings, moral emotions and evaluations (of which justice is one kind). We often react to transgressions of decent behavioral standards with moral indignation or outrage and other emotions and feelings. And the way we feel towards the way a resource was produced (towards

---

defining and analyzing the two processes will await future attention. In this chapter acquisition is subsumed under the notion of mode of production.

its mode of production) will likely, in turn, determine how we feel about the produced resource, per se. Even the identity of the resource producer (who is an integral part of the production aspect) and the allocator may affect the way the recipient feels about the resource (cf. Foa, 1971). Receiving praise from someone we consider a fool renders that resource (status) worthless, as compared to praise received from an admired person. Thus,

> *Assumption 1*: People's emotional reactions to the manner in which a resource is produced will influence their affective orientations toward the resource.

Apart from manners of production that may elicit positive or negative emotions, some modes of production are not likely to cause any emotional reactions at all. Why would, for instance, the manufacturing of bicycles arouse any particular emotions, especially if scarce resources are not squandered or at all used, wages for employees are fair and appropriate, and no children or other vulnerable categories of people are exploited as a work force? Thus, as the mode of production is not an issue (i.e., has no emotional relevance) in this case, there is no reason to assume that this factor would influence our affective reactions with regard to the resource, per se.

Although various modes of resource production are frequently criticized by citizens, it is surprising how little attention mode of production has attracted in the scientific literature on resource allocation and distributive/procedural justice. Considering the emotional and psychological impact the origin (production/ acquisition) of many of the resources we consume and use in our daily lives may have, it seems reasonable to be open to the possibility that our preferences with regard to their distribution and our views about the fairest way of allocating them might be affected as well.

Resource Characteristics and Conceptions of Distributive Justice

Social psychologists have primarily analyzed the impact of resources on perceived justice in terms of their a) nature, b) quantity, and c) valence. Scholars from various disciplines have discussed additional aspects as well, on the basis of which social resources may be described and distinguished, e.g., their scarcity (e.g., Greenberg, 1981; Hegtvedt, 2001), divisibility (e.g., Messick, 1995), status value (e.g., Berger et al., 1972), and fungibility[3] (Galvin and Lockhart, 1990). Blalock (1991) identified 10 dimensions along which resources can be distinguished and measured in his attempt at formulating a general theory of allocation processes.[4]

---

3   Fungibility refers to "the characteristic of an item having value regardless of who possesses it" (see Galvin and Lockhart, 1990, p. 1183). For example, "the value of currency derives from its ability to be exchanged for other goods, and its purchasing power does not vary according to its possessor." Other examples of fungible resources are air and water (cf. the notion of "particularism" within *Foa*'s resource theory framework).

4   Divisibility, once-and-for-all versus repeated allocations, retractibility, generalized value, depletion and replenishment, the degree to which they are subject to devaluation, the degree to which recipients share future power with allocators, valence, the degree of secrecy for allocation decisions, and monopoly control of goods and competition among allocators.

After brief discussions in this section of the impact of the nature, quantity, and valence of resources on justice evaluations, the chapter will narrow its focus to how the way in which the resource was produced might influence justice conceptions.

Resource Type

Initially, exchange and justice researchers paid little attention to the nature of the allocated resource, per se. However, *Foa* launched his resource theory of social exchange in 1971, defining "resource" as "any commodity—material or symbolic— which is transmitted through interpersonal behavior" (Foa and Foa, 1974, p. 36). Social resources were classified into six categories: love, services, goods, money, information and status[5] and arranged in a circular order along the two dimensions of particularism-universalism and concreteness-abstractness. Particularism is defined as the extent to which the value of a given resource is influenced by the identity of the provider or the relationship between provider and recipient. Thus, love is the most particularistic resource category, while money is the least particularistic (i.e., most universalistic) resource. The value of money is little, or not at all, dependent on the identity of the provider. Concreteness refers to the degree of tangibility (goods are concrete, while status is abstract).

Research testing *Foa*'s resource theory (e.g., Turner, Foa and Foa, 1971; Donnenwerth and Foa, 1974; Foa and Stein, 1980) indicates that the differential properties of resources may affect allocation and exchange processes in daily encounters. Thus, different resource classes may follow different rules of exchange. For instance, money can be separated from the immediate interpersonal situation and sent through a third person without loosing any of its inherent value, while love cannot be transmitted via a third party without a loss of its meaning and value. Further, all resources may not always be appropriate substitutes for each other, and increasing the amount of the improper reciprocated resource may not suffice to restore or sustain justice. Previous research (Donnenwerth, 1971; Teichman, 1971) indicates that, in the case of particularistic resources, people prefer reciprocation by similar resources, that is, proximal in the proposed circular order (money is usually preferred over love or status in return for goods), and that satisfaction diminishes as the similarity between the provided and received resource decreases.

Obviously, not all of these dimensions are *properties* of a resource, some (e.g., the last two) refer to "external" variables such as availability of information about allocation decisions and type of actor relationship.

5   "Love" is an expression of affectionate regard, warmth, or comfort. "Status" indicates an evaluative judgment that conveys prestige, regard or esteem. "Information" includes advice, opinions, instructions, or enlightenment but excludes those behaviors that could be classed as love or status. "Money" is any coin, currency, or token that has some standard unit of exchange value. "Goods" are tangible products, objects, or materials. "Services" involve activities that affect the body or belongings of a person and that often constitute labor for another' (Foa and Foa, 1976, p. 101).

The Impact of the Nature and Quantity of Resource on Justice Conceptions

Research suggests that people may define justice differently depending on the nature or property of the provided or received resource (Foa and Stein, 1980; Törnblom and Foa, 1983; Sabbagh, Yechezkel and Resh, 1994; McLean Parks et al., 1999). A distribution principle which is perceived as appropriate and fair for the allocation of a given resource may be viewed as less appropriate or even inappropriate and unfair for another, and more so the less proximal they are. Although findings vary between studies, people often prefer monetary rewards to be distributed equitably, while need and equality are frequently viewed as the most just allocation principles for the distribution of socio-emotional rewards like love and affection (e.g., Martin and Harder, 1994).

To explain these observations consider two possibilities. First, contrary to the more impersonal nature of some universalistic resources (e.g., money), the socio-emotional nature of particularistic resources (e.g., love and affection) is not very compatible with economically oriented exchanges and distributions. Thus, distributive principles like need and equality which reflect the "softer" aspects of people's existence (e.g., cooperation, caring, nurture, personal welfare) appear more suitable for the distribution of particularistic resources. Second, Foa (1971) and Foa and Foa (1974) suggested that it costs less to give a resource the more particularistic it is. For instance, giving away money or goods depletes your supplies while this is not true for love. Thus, affection and regard, for instance, are more "cost effective" than money and goods, unless cost is assessed in psychological/emotional terms. In the latter case, expressing and receiving negative valences of love and respect (i.e., hate and insult) may be extremely draining, thus costly, from an emotional standpoint. Thus, there is an interesting connection between the nature of a resource and whether or not the amount possessed is affected by its provision to others. To reiterate, the supply of universalistic resources (information excluded) decreases and may be depleted when provided which is not the case for all particularistic resources. Our supply of love does not decrease when provided to another. However, giving status in the shape of deference may lower one's own status position (e.g., Blau, 1964); subordination implies a loss of status.

Distribution principles may also vary with respect to their "cost-orientation". The contribution (equity) and need principles are more cost oriented than the equality principle (i.e., they emphasize rewards/resources according to some criterion of desert, such as performance, effort, ability, or need). Therefore, it seems reasonable to propose that universalistic social resources would be more likely than particularistic resources to be distributed according to the contribution principle, whereas particularistic resources are more likely than universalistic resources to be distributed according to the equality principle. Scarce resources are often allocated according to contribution or need principles of justice. Access to dialysis machines, for example, are often granted those in greatest need. Sometimes, however, equitable distributions may be considered more just than allocations according to needs. Younger patients, patients who are able to pay the most, high status patients, patients who occupy functionally important social positions, or patients who are likely to benefit the most from such treatment, etc., may be prioritized. Abundance or unlimited resource amount may allow for equal shares to all or may even make justice considerations unnecessary or irrelevant. Thus, it appears reasonable to suggest that scarce resources, in particular, are more likely to be allocated according to equity criteria rather than equally, while abundant social resources are more likely than scarce resources to be distributed according to the equality principle. In addition, the nature and quantity of resources may jointly affect the way a resource is fairly distributed. This is related to the observation that universalistic resources as compared to particularistic resources are limited, and thus are preferred to be distributed according to the contribution or need principles.

Resource Valence

There is a growing literature wrestling with the question whether or not the allocation of positive and negative resources (i.e., assets and liabilities) follow the same distributive justice principles. Research indicates that justice in the distribution of negatively valent resources (e.g., insults, hate, misinformation, and disservice) is often represented by different allocation rules than those endorsed for positively valent resources. For instance, people may have few objections to sharing others' profits and good fortunes equally, but they may strongly protest unless the distribution of losses is made according to merit (e.g., responsibility). Rather than going into detail in the present chapter about this research topic we refer the reader to existing reviews and research reports (see Törnblom, 1988 and 1992 for reviews; see also Törnblom and Jonsson, 1985; Meeker and Elliot, 1987; Jasso, 1998; Törnblom and Vermunt, 1999; Kazemi and Eek, forthcoming a).

Mode of Resource Production/Acquisition and Distributive Justice

As previously mentioned, a fourth characteristic of resources (in addition to their nature, quantity, and valence) which seems likely to influence people's justice conceptions is the way resources are produced. Their *mode of production* is said to determine how these resources (of consumption) are distributed. "The distribution of the means of consumption at any time is only a consequence of the distribution of the conditions of the production themselves. The latter distribution is a feature of the mode of production itself" (Marx, 1970, p. 10). Production—not consumption—is viewed as the most basic human need, and each mode of production is assumed to have its own mode of distribution and its own normative standards of justice. Therefore, a single focus on distributive justice is said to artificially and incorrectly separate the spheres of production and distribution.

However, the statement that the way resources are produced will determine their distribution is, however, more complex than what might appear at first. First, we need information about the extent to which, why, and precisely how justice evaluations of the distribution of various resources are affected by the way those resources are produced or acquired. Second, a thorough analysis related to the Marxist oriented critique would also require attention to the justice criteria according to which people prefer the means of production (rather than consumption) to be distributed. While these two issues are similar in that both deal with the impact of resource production, they are dissimilar in that the first concerns justice in the distribution of the produced resources intended for consumption, while the second issue refers to justice in the distribution of (access to, ownership of, and decision-making control over) the resources or means of production. Even though wages, for instance, may be fairly determined and distributed across positions, the access to these positions that entitle the incumbents to fair wages may be unfairly distributed.

These and related types of questions are seldom asked by researchers within the areas of distributive and procedural justice. Thus, attention appears warranted to the ways in which the organization of production is related to the distribution of the produced resources which, in turn, would require analyses of social structural aspects such as the ownership and control of the means of production, thus the hierarchy of power. This chapter will focus on how fairness in resource distribution may be affected by the way in which the resources, per se, are produced (while issues related to the social structural aspects will have to await analysis elsewhere). There is, for instance, surely a "difference between dividing a pie that [a person] has baked and dividing a pie that has drifted gently down from the sky" (Wolff, 1977, p. 207). Further, people probably prefer different distributive justice principles for resources that have been produced by the joint effort of all group members (cf. social dilemma research, e.g., Kazemi and Eek, forthcoming b) as opposed to resources produced by a single group member. These examples lend credibility to the contention that the mode of resource production may affect the way the produced resources are distributed. Our basic assumption, then, the raison d'être for the present essay, is:

> *Assumption 2*: Distributive[6] justice conceptions and behavior will be affected by the manner in which a resource is produced.

The Relevance of Mode of Production to Distributive Justice Conceptions Depend on the Nature of the Resource

Are there, contrary to the statement in Assumption 2, conditions under which a connection between resource production and justice in resource allocation might be very weak or even missing? Is the critique also relevant for other types of resources than goods (and services)? How may the production of social resources like love, services, and information be conceptualized (in comparison with the production of resources like material goods or money)? Is it even meaningful to speak of the "production" of love, for example? Would Marx really talk about mode of production when it comes to certain resources like affect and respect? If affirmative, would he argue that their mode of production determines their distribution? Surely, the way retirement funds are generated in a society (produced—via taxes or via private savings) will quite likely affect citizens' views about the fairest way to allocate pensions to entitled recipients. However, it does not seem reasonable, or even meaningful, to

---

6   We also expect procedural justice conceptions to be affected by mode of production, but space does not allow extensive elaborations regarding this aspect. For now, we have added a brief discussion in the last section of this chapter.

propose that the fairness of the amount of love a father gives to each of his children is affected by the way his love was produced or acquired! Similarly, to propose that the way a mother acquires time to help her two children with their home work determines the way she "calculates" how to fairly divide that time between them seems far fetched. Thus, it seems reasonable to maintain that mode of production may shape the distribution of some types of resources like goods, money, and information (i.e., universalistic resource classes). However, the way other resources like love, regard and, perhaps, services[7] (i.e., particularistic resource classes) are produced (if "production" is at all a meaningful notion to describe the generation of those resources) appear less or not at all relevant for their fair allocation. Thus,

> *Proposition 1:*[8] Mode of resource production/acquisition is more relevant for the distribution of universalistic than for particularistic resources.

A number of additional questions (i.e., the possible impact of a number of moderating variables) will be addressed later in order to understand the relevance of mode of resource production to how we think and act in terms of justice. For instance, as we have already indicated that not only the nature but also the valence of a resource appear to affect justice conceptions, we also ask whether valence might moderate the connection between mode of production and justice conceptions. First we turn to a brief discussion of Marx's usage of the notion of "mode of production" and how our own usage differs.

Extending the Notion of Mode of Production

We certainly do not claim to do justice to the meaning of mode of production within Marx's theoretical framework. However, as we are using the term mode of production differently than Marx did, a brief description of its meaning within his macro-theoretical framework seems appropriate and may hint at some possible connections between mode of resource production and distributive justice.

For Marx "mode of production" (the manner in which resources—mainly a variety of commodities—are produced) is "a distinct production structure in association with its superstructures" (Legros, 1977). It is based upon certain social arrangements and relationships, called "relations of production", and these may differ in different societies. Several modes of production may co-exist within a single society. The "relations of production" and the "forces of production" together define a specific mode of production. These two parts form the base that supports "a superstructure of government, laws, religion, culture and arts, education and

---

7   See the subsection "What type of resource was produced/acquired" under the "Concluding remarks" section for a discussion of the "production" of services.

8   An exception to this proposition would be a case where a recipient of a resource defines mode of production as the *procedure* by which the resource is distributed/acquired, e.g., 'my boss praised my services to the company with an insulting/disapproving frown on his face, thus "produced" the resource of status, esteem, or regard in a degrading way. We will discuss and attempt to specify a number of facets and elements of "mode of production" below.

ideas, in short, everything that isn't already included in the base" (Sweezy, 1981, p. 20). The "forces of production" is comprised of "technical procedures" (e.g., skills, knowledge, the patterning of behavior, the actual techniques and work effort necessary for production) and "technical means" (e.g., tools and other equipment needed for production). It is because the nature of the two components of mode of production (the relations and forces) vary geographically and historically that several types of mode of production may exist. The notions of forces, relations, and modes of production refer to a whole society (Olsen, 1978). Marx differentiated among five generic types of productive systems: primitive communism, ancient production, feudalism, capitalism, and socialism.

The distribution of the produced resources is determined by the "relations of production" component of mode of production. When surplus (above sustenance levels) is produced in a society, it is the way in which the expropriation of that surplus takes place that defines the specific mode of production. A capitalist mode of production, for instance, is characterized by class divisions where the privileged class is able to control the labor of subordinate classes and expropriate part of the product of their labor. Thus, the capitalist mode of production (which is based on private ownership of property and the means of production) and its mode of distribution may create inequalities and invite exploitation. Capitalism is unjust because the capitalist "is reaping the fruits of the worker's unpaid labor; he is exploiting him, taking from him what is justly his" (Wood, 1972, p. 263). On the other hand, the means of production within the socialist mode of production is based on social ownership. A study by Gorin (1980) found a greater degree of income equality in countries with the socialist mode of production, while capitalist modes were associated with inequality of income. Thus, a just mode of production is characterized by egalitarian societal arrangements as objectively assessed. Whether or not the individual's *subjective* justice perceptions correspond to objective assessments of justice as represented by equality (and/or need fulfillment) does not seem to have been an issue.

Our focus on production was originally inspired by Marxist critiques of the justice area, and the term mode of production was adopted from Marx's. However, due to the difficulties in operationalizing mode of production for the purpose of allowing the construction and empirical tests of social psychological hypotheses, our own usage of the term is so far more "general" but also more "narrow" than Marx's own usage. As we wanted to consider a number of different types of resources (in addition to economic resources as focused by Marx), we realized that the notion of mode of production, in its Marxist sense, is not appropriate for our purposes. In comparison with Marx's approach to production ours is a) social psychological, focusing on the individual's subjective experiences rather than objective conditions, thus b) micro-level rather than macro-level oriented, c) inclusive of different kinds of allocated social resources in addition to economic resources (Marx did not consider particularistic resources, for example), both of which may be d) positively as well negatively valent. Thus, for our purposes we allow the notion of mode of production to include a number of facets and elements which would probably fall outside of Marx's orientation and interests (perhaps mainly due to his analytic focus on the macro, societal rather than individual, level). On the other hand, Marx's notion certainly covers structural and dynamic aspects which are not included in our analysis.

In general, Marx's mode of production refers to[9] "the way in which the goods and services of the society are produced" (Olsen, 1978, p. 194). Of course, different types of social resources are produced in different ways and, as we shall see, a particular resource may be produced in more than one way. Thus, to answer the question "in what ways may the production of a particular social resource as well as qualitatively different types of resources be conceptualized and described", we are faced with the difficult task of constructing a categorization of different types of "modes of production". Toward this end we next present some initial ideas toward a categorization of various facets and elements relevant to our conceptualization of mode of production. As the purpose of our effort is to enable empirical tests of the general notion that the way social resources are produced affect preferences for their distribution, we escape some unnecessary restrictions imposed by the traditional usage of the term mode of production and can now start exploring a new direction of research within the justice area.

We now need to conceptualize, describe, and categorize the various ways in which the different types of resources may be produced/acquired. Again, some resources may be produced in more than one way, and some modes of production are likely to impact justice conceptions while others are not. We can at this stage only take some first and very preliminary steps toward the compilation of a list of ways in which some selected resource types may be produced (primarily ways that seem likely to impact justice conceptions). Apart from factors related to *how* resources are produced a number of moderator variables may come into play in, and affect, people's justice evaluations of a resource distribution (e.g., why and by whom resources are produced, type of resource and type of social relationship, all of which might shape the possible connection between mode of resource production and subsequent resource distribution). An extensive battery of new research questions is generated within the fields of distributive (and procedural) justice.

The next section is devoted to a presentation of a preliminary and incomplete "typology" of production relevant factors which we think might influence the distribution and justice evaluation of some (but not all) social resources.

Identifying the Components of Resource Production

To make the notion of mode of production manageable and amenable to empirical research, Marxist theorizing and concepts were only used as points of departure to generate new ideas of inquiry. We also indicated previously that the original meaning of mode of production is extended to include additional facets and elements. A useful conceptualization of mode of production for our purposes[10] may require the inclusion

---

9 "By mode of production we mean all those activities that human beings enter into in order to sustain themselves. These activities include skills and tools as well as the actions themselves, and they include the reciprocal impact of the actions on the natural environment and of the natural environment on human actions" (Olsen, 1978, p. 194).

10 For the purpose of understanding how it might affect the choice and justice evaluation of procedural and distributive principles in the allocation of positive and negative resources of consumption as well as production.

of at least the following *facets*: a) *how* it was produced, b) the *type of resource* that was produced, c) the *valence* of the produced resource, d) the *kind of investment* that was required, e) the *purpose* for which the resource was produced, f) *by whom* it was produced, g) *for whom* it was intended, h) *when* and i) *within what social context* it was produced (see Figure 2.1).

Each facet encompasses a number of *elements* that need to be identified. For example, the "how produced/acquired" facet may include the following (and several additional) elements: by purchase/sales, trade, gift, exploitation, theft, by chance, etc.; the *kind of resource type* facet covers goods, services, information, status, love, money (Foa, 1971); the *valence* of the produced resource may be specified by its identification as an asset or a liability; the *purpose* facet includes elements like for "own consumption" ("for use" in Marx's terminology), for "exchange" purposes[11] (again borrowing from Marx), for "survival",, etc.; and the *social context* facet includes social relational distinctions like cooperative, competitive, intimate, distant, and formal (see Figure 2.1).

It should be emphasized that the facets and elements included in this "typology" are tentative. In the absence of some kind of theory at this stage of development on the basis of which the choice of components would be less than arbitrary, some of the suggested facets and elements may very well be irrelevant or unimportant and others may need to be added. Thus, revisions will not doubt be needed.

Example Propositions about the Impact of Mode of Production on Distributive Justice Conceptions

The following propositions are merely a few samples out of the large number of testable statements that may be constructed on the basis of the various facets and elements associated with the notion of mode of production. Many of the listed propositions may be theoretically derived while others are more or less intuitively generated. Regrettably, space does not allow us to provide a rationale for each proposition. Further, the items on the provided list of propositions are more or less arbitrarily chosen, and the list can be considerably extended. Our modest intentions at this stage are merely to wet the appetite for future and more systematic theorizing with regard to the several issues we hint at in this chapter.

We now turn to some simple illustrative propositions about justice evaluations of three distribution rules as relevant for the facet a), how the resource may be produced. This section is then followed by a number of example propositions related to a few of the remaining facets (e, f, and i). These facets may be conceived of as moderator variables affecting the impact of mode of production on justice conceptions (see Figure 2.1).

---

11 It might be of interest to note that Marx lists eight types of "purpose for exchange", resulting in more specific distinctions than we need at this stage: Production 1) for exchange: 1.1) for exchange but not for exchange value, and 1.2) for exchange value, 1.2.1) for exchange value but not for maximum value, and 1.2.2) for maximum value, 1.2.2.1) for maximum value but not for capital accumulation, and 1.2.2.2) for capital accumulation (i.e., the capitalist mode of production).

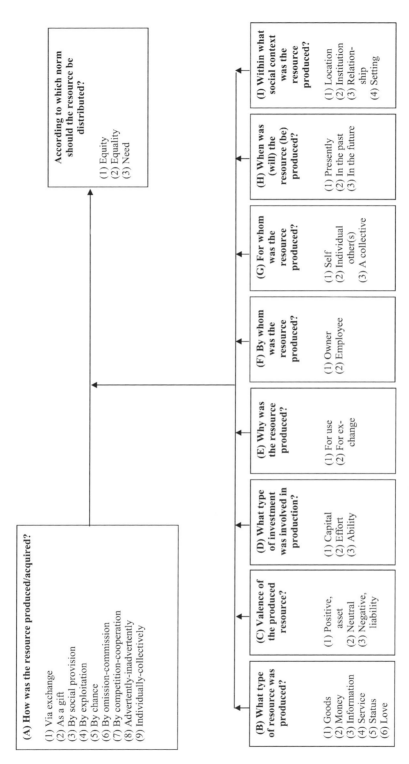

(A) How was the resource produced/acquired?

(1) Via exchange
(2) As a gift
(3) By social provision
(4) By exploitation
(5) By chance
(6) By omission-commission
(7) By competition-cooperation
(8) Advertently-inadvertently
(9) Individually-collectively

According to which norm should the resource be distributed?

(1) Equity
(2) Equality
(3) Need

(B) What type of resource was produced?

(1) Goods
(2) Money
(3) Information
(4) Service
(5) Status
(6) Love

(C) Valence of the produced resource?

(1) Positive, asset
(2) Neutral
(3) Negative, liability

(D) What type of investment was involved in production?

(1) Capital
(2) Effort
(3) Ability

(E) Why was the resource produced?

(1) For use
(2) For ex-change

(F) By whom was the resource produced?

(1) Owner
(2) Employee

(G) For whom was the resource produced?

(1) Self
(2) Individual other(s)
(3) A collective

(H) When was (will) the resource (be) produced?

(1) Presently
(2) In the past
(3) In the future

(I) Within what social context was the resource produced?

(1) Location
(2) Institution
(3) Relation-ship
(4) Setting

Figure 2.1   Modes of Resource Production/Acquisition and Associated Moderators

a) How was the Resource Produced/Acquired?

1) Exchange (e.g., Purchase, Buying-Selling, Trading, Bartering)

> *Proposition 2*: The contribution (equity) principle will be considered more just and appropriate than the equality principle for the allocation of social resources that are produced/acquired via bartering.

2) Gifts (e.g., Charity, Inheritance)

> *Proposition 3*: The contribution principle will be considered more just and appropriate than the equality and need principles for the allocation of social resources that are produced/acquired via inheritance.

> *Proposition 4*: The equality and need principles will be considered more just and appropriate for resources that are produced as gifts than for social resources that are produced/acquired by purchase.

3) Social Provisions (Welfare, Social Security, Charity)

> *Proposition 5*: The need principle will be considered more just and appropriate than the contribution principle for the allocation of social resources that are produced/acquired via social provisions (e.g., taxes).

4) Exploitation (e.g., Forcing, Depriving, Deceiving, Stealing)

> *Proposition 6*: For the distribution of resources that are produced/acquired via exploitation of the workers/producers, contributions are considered a more just criterion than equality by owners of the means of production (i.e., the exploiters) as well as by the exploited workers. They will, however, disagree about which contributions are relevant: the exploiters assess contributions in terms of ownership of means of production, while the exploited view contributions in terms of the work required for the production of the resources.

5) Chance (e.g., Lottery, Gambling)

> *Proposition 7*: The equality and need principles will be considered more just and appropriate than the contribution principle for the allocation of social resources that are produced/acquired by chance.

> *Proposition 8*: The equality and need principles will be considered more just and appropriate for the allocation of social resources that are produced/acquired by chance than for resources that are produced/acquired by purchase.

> *Proposition 9*: The contribution principle will be considered more just and appropriate for the allocation of resources that are produced/acquired by purchase than for resources that are produced/acquired by chance.

6) Omission vs. Commission

> *Proposition 10*: The contribution principle will be considered more just and appropriate than the equality and need principles for the allocation of social resources that are produced/acquired via commission.

Proposition 11: The contribution principle will be considered more just and appropriate for the allocation of social resources that are produced/acquired by commission than for resources that are produced/acquired by omission.

Proposition 12: The equality principle will be considered more just and appropriate for the allocation of social resources that are produced/acquired by omission than for resources that are produced/acquired by commission.

7) Competitively vs. Cooperatively

Proposition 13: The equality and need principles will be considered more just and appropriate than the contribution principle for the allocation of social resources that are produced/acquired cooperatively.

Proposition 14: The contribution principle will be considered more just and appropriate than the equality and need principles for the allocation of social resources that are produced/acquired competitively.

Proposition 15: The equality and need principles will be considered more just and appropriate for the allocation of social resources that are produced/acquired cooperatively than for resources that are produced/acquired competitively.

Proposition 16: The contribution principle will be considered more just and appropriate for the allocation of social resources that are produced/acquired competitively than for resources that are produced/acquired cooperatively.

8) Advertently vs. Inadvertently

Proposition 17: The greater the allocator's responsibility for (in particular unethical) resource production as perceived by the recipient or a third party, 1) the greater the magnitude of their emotional reactions to the mode of production, and 2) the more likely their distributive justice conceptions will be affected by the mode of production.

9) Individually vs. Collectively

Proposition 18: The equality principle will be considered more just and appropriate for the allocation of social resources that are produced/acquired collectively than for resources that are produced/acquired individually.

Examples of Predictions Involving Moderators of the Effects of Mode of Production on Justice Conceptions

Moderator E: Why, for What Purpose, was the Resource Produced/Acquired?
1) For Use (Consummatory Value)

Proposition 19: The need principle will be considered more just and appropriate than the contribution principle for the allocation of resources that are produced/acquired for the purpose of own use.

Proposition 20: The need principle will be considered more just and appropriate for the allocation of resources that are produced/acquired for the purpose of own use than for resources that are produced/acquired for the purpose of exchange.

2) For Exchange (Instrumental Value)

Proposition 21: The contribution principle will be considered more just and appropriate than the need principle for resources that are produced/acquired for the purpose of exchange.

Proposition 22: The contribution principle will be considered more just and appropriate for the allocation of resources that are produced/acquired for the purpose of exchange than for resources that are produced/acquired for the purpose of own use.

Moderator F: By Whom was the Resource Produced?
1) By Owner of Means of Production

Proposition 23: When the resource to be allocated is produced by the owner of the means of production, s/he is likely to consider equitable (self-maximized) distributions to be more just than equal distributions.

Proposition 24: Resource allocators are more likely to consider equitable (self-maximized) distributions to be more just than egalitarian distributions, when they are resource producing owners of the means of production as compared to when they are producing non-owners.

2) By Employee (Voluntary Exchange)

Proposition 25: Resource allocators are more likely to consider egalitarian distributions to be more just than equitable distributions, when they are resource producing non-owners of the means of production as compared to when they are producing owners of the means of production.

Moderator I: Within what Social Context Was the Resource Produced?
May mode of resource production have an impact on justice conceptions in all social contexts/spheres and within all kinds of social relationships (e.g., Deutsch, 1985; Fiske, 1991)? Different institutional and social relationships may be roughly characterized on the basis of their more or less unique resource profiles (i.e., resources that are particularly appropriate and transacted more frequently than others) (Foa and Foa, 1974). So, for example, may formal and economically oriented exchange relationships be described in terms of their typical transactions of universalistic resources (e.g., money and goods or services)? As we have suggested that mode of production is more salient when universalistic resources are distributed, it seems also reasonable to propose that the connection between mode of production and social relationship will be strongest within formal/impersonal/distant/economic contexts and weakest within informal/personal/close/non-economic contexts. Thus:

Proposition 26: The manner in which a resource is produced is more likely to have a bearing on distributive justice conceptions within impersonal, distant, formal, and economically oriented exchange relationships than within personal, close, intimate, informal, and communal relationships.

Proposition 27: The smaller the recipient's or third party's psychological distance to the act of production (and the producer), the greater the intensity of their emotional reactions to the mode of production, and the more likely these reactions will affect the recipient's or third party's distributive justice conceptions.

Emotional Mediators of the Impact of Mode of Production on Justice Conceptions

Our discussion so far has hinted at the possibility that mode of production may affect people's affective orientations towards the resource, per se. We may also recall Assumption 1 which suggested that people's emotional reactions to mode of production will impact their emotional reactions towards the resource. Further, it seems likely that a sentient person's emotional reactions towards a resource will mediate the effect of mode of production on conceptions of distributive justice. Certainly, mode of production may also have a direct impact on conceptions of distributive justice, as stated by Assumption 2. In order to systematically investigate the effect of mode of production on distributive justice conceptions, the following four models seem to be the most logical starting candidates: a) mode of production has a direct effect on distributive justice conceptions, b) emotional reactions to the mode of production mediate the effect of mode of production on distributive justice conceptions, c) emotional reactions to the produced resource moderate the effect of mode of production on distributive justice conceptions, d) emotional reactions to the produced resource mediate the emotional reactions to the mode of production which, in turn, mediate the effect of mode of production on distributive justice conceptions.

Mullen (in this book) observes that results from research on distributive justice is most frequently interpreted to indicate that 1) perceptions of *injustice* results in *negative affect*, *experiences* of injustice, and that 2) *negative affect* may lead to *action* (aimed at restoring justice). However, she also notes that 3) the causal connection between injustice and negative affect may be bi-directional. Thus, and consistent with the considerable amount of research that has shown that emotions are capable of influencing cognitions and evaluations (as well as behavior), it seems very plausible that *negative affect* may precede and result in perceptions of *injustice* (in addition to the other way around). This is the underlying assumption of models b, c and d above. Further, different types and magnitudes of negative affect may influence both the severity of perceived injustice as well as the manner in which the presence of injustice is assessed.

Mullen argues that affective reactions are probably more primary than justice judgments, because the latter activity is likely to require cognitive processing (a view shared by several other theorists, e.g., Scher and Heise, 1993). Thus, the formation of a justice judgment is assumed to take more time than the less conscious affective types of reactions which are more immediate, direct, and spontaneous. Negative affect would thus be experienced first and would then influence the definition of the situation in terms of justice. Mullen suggests that 4) negative affect may result from

unfavorable outcomes and *unfavorable allocation procedures*. The combination of
1) and 2) generates the following sequence: *perceptions of injustice* → negative
affect → action to restore justice (which is the most common way to conceive
of the relationship between the three variables). Together, 4) and 3) generate the
reverse order between justice perceptions and affect: unfavorable outcomes and
procedures → negative affect → *perceptions of injustice* (a less commonly assumed
relationship).

Previous research already suggests that unfavorable outcomes in terms of type
and amount of positive and negative resources may influence justice conceptions.
First, receiving an inappropriate type of resource in return for the one provided will
frequently cause frustration (i.e., negative affect—see Foa, 1971) which, in turn,
may result in a preference for the contribution principle to represent and guide the
restoration or establishment of distributive justice (O'Malley and Davies, 1984).
Second, being short-changed of a positively valent resource (e.g., receiving too low
a salary) or receiving a negatively valent resource (e.g., disrespect, misinformation,
etc.) may elicit negative affect as well and result in similar distributive justice
conceptions as in the previous example. Then, the nature, the amount and the
valence of resources may have a direct as well as an indirect (via affect) impact
on justice evaluations (and behavior). As Sprecher (1986, p. 319) noted, "Research
should consider how the relationship between inequity and emotions experienced
may depend on the specific types of resources measured".

It seems reasonable to propose that the same would hold true also for mode of
production, the way in which the resources have been produced. Thus, granted that
unfavorable outcomes and allocation procedures may generate (negative) affect (as
Mullen suggested), so might also the manner in which the allocated resources are
produced (as previously discussed). And these emotions may, in turn, affect justice
evaluations of both outcomes and procedures. Then, if events result in anger—events
that when later on are cognitively assessed and defined as unfavorable inequity or as
a violation of some other justice principle—is it also reasonable to assume that anger
resulting from disliked modes of production, in turn, will lead to preferences for
equity as the most just principle for subsequent resource allocation? If so, the impact
of mode of production on distributive justice conceptions is mediated by emotions.

Besides arguing that negative affect, in general, influences perceptions of injustice,
Mullen reminds us that 5) the negative affect associated with injustice subsumes a
variety of different emotions (e.g., anger, guilt, shame, sadness, disgust, resentment,
indignation, and fear). Thus, it seems reasonable to assume that different kinds of
emotions will elicit different perceptions of (the nature and severity of) injustice.
Further, different types of injustice might very well generate a) different conceptions
regarding the most just and appropriate distributive principle to adopt as a means to
restore justice and, perhaps in particular, b) the intensity with which justice restoring
behavior is expressed. *Anger* directed towards a harm-doer is often followed by
congruent behaviors aimed at restoring justice via *equitable* punishment. And, if
sadness is likely to predispose a person who is responsible for injustice to make
external causal attributions for this negative event (Keltner, Ellsworth and Edwards,
1993 cited in Mullen in this book), then equality would be the most reasonable choice
of a distribution principle to represent justice. If personal (internal) responsibility

attributions are not made, a basis for invidious distinctions is lacking. In such a case, it is meaningless to calculate proportionality between inputs and outcomes to assess personal entitlements or blame. Finally, as Mullen observes, 6) when it comes to reactions to one's own bad behavior, the emotion of *shame* seems to be associated with a desire to escape from the situation (Tangney, 1991), while *guilt* tends to result in behavior aiming at repairing the damage done. Thus, at least five propositions seem to emerge:

> *Proposition 28*: A victim of injustice who experiences anger (resulting from unfavorably unjust outcomes, procedures, or modes of resource production) is likely to consider the contribution principle for restoring justice to be more just than the equality and need principles.

> *Proposition 29*: A person responsible for injustice (in the form of unjust outcomes, procedures, or modes of resource production) who experiences sadness but makes external causal attributions for the unjust event is likely to consider the equality principle for restoring justice as more just than the contribution and need principles.

> *Proposition 30*: A person responsible for injustice (in the form of unjust outcomes, procedures, or modes of resource production) who experiences shame is less likely to attempt justice restoration (via any principle) than is a person experiencing anger, sadness, and guilt.

> *Proposition 31*: A person responsible for injustice (in the form of unjust outcomes, procedures, or modes of resource production) who experiences is more likely to attempt justice restoration (via any principle) than is a person experiencing sadness and shame.

> *Proposition 32*: A person who experiences anger (due to being the victim of unfavorably unjust outcomes, procedures, and modes of resource production) is more likely to attempt justice restoration (via any principle) than is a person experiencing sadness and shame.

Concluding Remarks and Some Directions for Future Research

We have scratched on the surface of a number of issues which must be more adequately addressed in order to fully develop a resource production theory of distributive (and procedural) justice. The present chapter is merely a modest beginning towards explorations of how and under what conditions mode of production may or may not affect justice judgments, and we will end this first expedition into uncharted territory by mentioning a few additional issues that appear to be important building blocks for further theorizing.

Do We Usually Know How Resources are Produced?

A prerequisite for mode of production to have an impact is availability and salience of information about the process of production. Availability and salience are, however, not to be taken for granted. As Olsen (1978) noted, production is usually hidden. The manner in which a fur coat is produced is unlikely to make a difference, if the prospective customer is unaware of the fact that it was produced by skinning four live dogs, or if the user of cosmetics does not know that the manufacture of her/his brand included painful and debilitating tests on the eyes of defenseless animals. For what products and under what conditions does what category of people have access to what type of information about resource production, and under what conditions do people care about how resources are produced? May possibly some kind of heuristics operate in the absence of knowledge about mode of production, just as in the case when the fairness and favorability of an anticipated distribution is inferred from knowledge about the procedure, or when the fairness of a procedure about which information is lacking is inferred from the fairness or favorability of the outcome (Lind et al., 1993; Törnblom and Vermunt, 1999). These and other questions need to be addressed to understand and predict the role of mode of production in justice judgments.

What Type of Resource was Produced/Acquired?

Resource type has for obvious reasons assumed an important role in our discussions sofar. Certainly, the kind of resource that is the end product of production activity needs to be specified, lest we are content with speaking about production in a vacuum. Analyzing resource production without specifying what is produced makes no more sense than analyzing resource allocation without specifying what is allocated. We know that resource type moderates justice judgments of distribution principles, and we have stated the proposition (see Proposition 1) that the type of resource produced is likely to conditionalize the impact of mode of production on justice judgments, in that mode of production presumably has a greater impact on justice conceptions when universalistic than when particularistic resources are involved.

Similarly, we also know that resource valence affect justice conceptions. As most of our propositions in this chapter contain statements that assume positive resource production and allocation, additional theoretical statements need to focus on the production and distribution of negatively valent resources as well (e.g., hate, misinformation, disservice, insult). Additional specific propositions regarding different types of positively and negatively valent resources will be derived in a different context.

Further, we have stated that 1) different types of social resources may be produced in different ways. For example, information may be produced/acquired via reading but not via purchase (of course, printed materials and lectures may be bought, but we need to assimilate this material by reading it or spending time listening to and learning about the contents). Goods, on the other hand, may be acquired via purchase but not via reading. We have also stated that 2) a particular resource can be produced in more than one way. Money may be produced via counterfeit methods, theft, inheritance, or earned through work, and status may be produced through verbal praise or by presentation of status symbols like medals, diplomas and other awards.

A systematic and extensive analysis of the major ways in which selected resources may be produced/acquired is, of course, beyond the scope of this chapter. It would not only be a topic for a separate chapter of its own, but also a cumbersome but seemingly important task towards the construction of a solid foundation for future research on the effects of mode of production. A reasonable beginning might be based on our present list of elements belonging to the "how produced" a) facet of production. For example, can all (positively as well as negatively valent) resources that are classifiable under Foa's (1971) six resource categories be produced/acquired in all of the 10 ways listed? It may be possible for some but not for others. It is certainly possible to acquire (as well as create deficits, the negative valence, of) money in all 10 ways, but it does not make much sense to conceive of love as produced via lottery, gambling or inheritance. Further, it appears impossible to produce positively valent resources for the recipient by exploiting her, and people may certainly be deprived of all six types of resources by force and deceit.

We would also like to call attention to some interesting observations regarding certain "resource transformations" that might occur due to certain linkages among the *production* (origin), *possession*, and *distribution* of social resources. These certainly seem relevant in this context, although their role and significance as moderators will have to await future exploration.

"Resource-of-Origin" and "Resource-of-Possession" Linkage

A resource possessed by a person may have its origin in a different kind of resource. In other words, a resource of possession may have been produced/acquired via an identical or via a dissimilar type of resource. For example, the code for a safety box (i.e., information) may be (illegitimately) purchased (via monetary bribes), it may be acquired by inflicting pain on the owner until s/he reveals the correct code (negative service in *Foa*'s resource classification scheme), or it may be obtained via written instructions in the manual (i.e., information) published by the manufacturer. Whether or not the impact of mode of production on justice conceptions is moderated by whether or not the resource-of-possession and the resource from which the resource-of-possession originated is identical or dissimilar is an interesting question for future investigation. As far as we know, the literature provides no theoretical or empirical clues at this point in time.

"Resource-of-Possession" and "Resource-of-Distribution" Linkage

A resource of possession may be distributed in the form of an identical or in the form of a different kind of resource. In other words, a resource possessed by P may be transformed into another when provided to O. For example, a person's car repairing know-how (i.e., information) may be written down and provided to someone as instructions (i.e., information), or it be transformed into the act of repairing her car (i.e., service). Whether or not the impact of mode of production on justice conceptions is moderated by the form in which the produced resource is allocated (i.e., identical or dissimilar form) is another interesting question for future investigation. Again, we have found no theoretical or empirical clues in the literature.

Resource Production and its Distribution may Coincide

The two stages or processes of production and distribution/provision of a resource may coincide in that its production and distribution are identical, i.e., one and the same process. Certainly, material goods, for example, have to be produced (and possessed) before they can be provided to somebody. This is not so, however, in the case of services: the moment a service is rendered or distributed (e.g., repairing someone's car or mowing a lawn) it is simultaneously produced/materialized (via energy, effort, know-how and time expenditure) on the basis of information or knowledge concerning how to perform the service. Thus, a service does not exist, has not been produced (and can not be possessed) before it is provided. Only a "pre-potent" resource, e.g., information, which allows the performance of a service exists. In other words, a service is produced/materialized the moment it is allocated—as opposed to other resources like goods and money! The massage I give does not exist before I give it, my service of mowing your lawn is not "produced" until I've provided the service. Apparently, *production is sometimes identical with distribution.* Whether or not the impact of mode of production on justice conceptions is moderated by instances in which production and distribution constitute one process, rather than two separate processes, is still another interesting question for future investigation that seems to lack previous theoretical and empirical attention.

Mode of Production and Procedural Justice

As we have so far focused our attention on the effect of mode of production on distributive justice, one of the next logical steps to be taken toward further development is an extension to *procedural justice*. The process by which resources are allocated seems perhaps even more likely than the outcome distribution to be affected by several of the factors that are associated with resource production. For example, if resources are produced/acquired via exploitation of the workers/ producers, it seems unlikely that the exploiters (i.e., the owners of the means of production who in that capacity occupy positions of power) would give the workers any say (voice) with regard to how resources should be allocated. It seems reasonable to assume that this mode of production would affect several additional procedural justice rules too, in this case resulting in the violation of a number of rules (e.g., the correctibility, ethicality, representativeness, standing, respect, and consistency rules). And resources produced collectively may result in endorsement and application of of the representativeness rule as the most just procedural principle.

Further, if unethical and unjust procedures were used in the production of resources, restoration of justice may very well take place via just allocation procedures that meet the criteria of ethicality, consistency, representativeness, etc. Similar strategies have been used to restore distributive justice, e.g., "transrelational equity" and "equity with the world"; inequity within one relationship may be compensated via equity restoring behavior within another relationship (Austin and Walster, 1975).

Finally, as previously stated, production and distribution may coincide, as when a service is provided (the service does not exist, is not produced, before it is provided to the recipient), or in the case of physical love-making (which does not exist before it takes place). And as the distribution of a service or love-making is accomplished via a process or procedure, we realize that it is equally true that production and procedure may coincide as well. Thus, it appears reasonable to assume that mode of production will affect procedural justice conceptions and behavior as well—maybe even to a greater extent than it affects distributive justice conceptions and behavior.

The Origin of Resources: Production Versus Acquisition

The resource P possesses may have been *produced* (manufactured, crafted, built, written, etc.) by P him/herself. Resources may be produced in a multitude of ways, 10 of which were listed previously. Also, once produced by P somebody else may acquire the already existing resource. Like in the case of production, some resources can be *acquired* in several ways, while the acquisition of others is much more restricted. Money, for example, can be acquired by earning it through work, stealing, counterfeiting, receiving it as a gift or award, inheriting, finding, winning by lottery, through investment pay-offs, etc., while the ways in which love and affection can be acquired is relatively restricted to a very limited number of ways.

Some resources can be acquired in ways in which other resources can not be acquired. Information containing industrial secrets may be acquired through espionage, while affection or services can not. Is the distinction between production and acquisition significant in the sense that the nature or dynamics of the two processes might carry different implications for distributive and procedural justice conceptions? If so, would the nature and amount of power accruing the owner of resources differ due to whether resources were produced by the owner or acquired by the owner from somebody else (e.g., inherited) and thus (at least partly) explain the different impact production and acquisition might have on justice conceptions? Answers to questions like these will tell us whether we need one or two (or more) theories to account for the impact of resource origin on justice conceptions.

The Role of Power and Perspective Taking

The relationship between mode of production and power constitutes a crucial focus for future theory and research about the role of production among other determinants of cognitive, affective, and behavioral justice phenomena. Related to this issue is the perspective from which events are perceived. Whose justice conceptions are we referring to: the power holder/owner of the means of production, the producer/ non-owner of the means of production, the resource recipient, other persons who are affected one way or the other, or the outside observer? These distinctions are necessary and will help make theorizing more systematic and meaningful.

Mode of Production and Social Dilemma Research

The distinction between production and acquisition brings our thoughts to an area of inquiry which appears closely related to the subject of this chapter. Research on public good social dilemmas concerns how members of a collective through individual contributions realize or maintain a common resource (i.e., social resource production) from which all can benefit. Certainly, collectively owned resources (called public goods within this research tradition) may be produced and acquired in a variety of ways. Once public goods are produced, the question of their distribution arises. The ways in which they were produced certainly has a bearing on the manner in which they are shared among eligible recipients.

In their research, Kazemi, Eek and Gärling (2005a, 2005b, 2006) investigated the effects of group goal or group orientation (i.e., performance-oriented versus socio-emotional goals) on public good distribution. Group goal concept can be subsumed under facet (E, the purpose of production), a moderator, which is a category in our mode of production typology. In several studies Kazemi, Eek and Gärling showed that group goals affect the allocation of public goods. Thus, group goal provided a reason for why the resource was produced and what the purpose of its distribution was, and thereby influenced the way people allocated the good to those who collectively had provided it.

We began this chapter with a reference to criticisms (mainly by philosophers and Marxist oriented sociologists) that theory and research in the field of distributive justice has neglected to take the issue of resource production into account and thereby focused on resource distribution in an unbalanced way. What at the outset seemed to be a rather simple question—"Do the ways in which social resources are produced affect our allocation preferences and conceptions of distributive justice?"—has turned out to be a very complex theoretical problem with a large number of implications. Due to the absence of social psychological theory and research on this topic, our present venture has mainly resulted in some guiding ideas that might assist in breaking new grounds. These ideas now need to be thoroughly analyzed, systematized, and combined into a more coherent theoretical framework, exposing them to empirical tests and exploring their implications for existing and future research on distributive and procedural justice.

Acknowledgments

We would like to express our appreciation to Barry Markovsky, Jonathan Turner and Louis E. Wolcher for their encouraging comments on this chapter.

References

Austin, W. and Walster, E. (1975), "Equity with the World: The Transrelational Effects of Equity and Inequity", *Sociometry*, **38**, 474–496. [DOI: 10.2307/2786362]

Berger, J., Zelditch, M., Jr, Anderson, B. and Cohen, B.P. (1972), "Structural Aspects of Distributive Justice: A Status Value Formulation" in *Sociological Theories in Progress*. Berger, J., Zelditch, M., Jr and Anderson, B. (eds) (Boston: Houghton Mifflin Company), 119–146.

Blalock, H.M., Jr (1991), *Understanding Social Inequality. Modeling Allocation Processes* (Newbury Park, CA: SAGE Publications, Inc.).

Blau, P.M. (1964), *Exchange and Power in Social Life* (New York: John Wiley & Sons, Inc.).

Deutsch, M. (1985), *Distributive Justice: A Social Psychological Perspective* (New Haven: Yale University Press).

Donnenwerth, G.V. (1971), "Effect of Resources on Retaliation to Loss". Doctoral dissertation, University of Missouri, Columbia.

Donnenwerth, G.V. and Foa, U.G. (1974), "Effect of Resource Class on Retaliation to Injustice in Interpersonal Exchange", *Journal of Personality and Social Psychology*, **29**, 785–793. [DOI: 10.1037/h0036201]

Fiske, A.P. (1991), *Structures of Social Life: The Four Elementary Forms of Human Relations* (New York: Free Press).

Foa, E.B. and Foa, U.G. (1976), "Resource Theory of Social Exchange" in *Contemporary Topics in Social Psychology*. Thibaut, J.W., Spence, J.T. and Carson, R.C. (eds) (Morristown, NJ: General Learning Press), 99–131.

Foa, U.G. (1971), "Interpersonal and Economic Resources", *Science*, **71**, 345–351. [DOI: 10.1126/science.171.3969.345]

Foa, U.G. and Foa, E.B. (1974), *Societal Structures of the Mind* (Springfield, IL: Charles C. Thomas Publisher).

Foa, U.G. and Stein, G. (1980), "Rules of Distributive Justice: Institution and Resource Influences", *Academic Psychology Bulletin*, **2**, 89–94.

Galvin, R.F. and Lockhart, C. (1990), "Discrete Idiosyncratic Goods and Structural Principles of Distributive Justice", *Journal of Politics*, **52**, 1182–1204. [DOI: 10.2307/2131687]

Gorin, Z. (1980), "Income Inequality in the Marxist Theory of Development: A Cross-National Test", *Comparative Social Research*, **3**, 147–174.

Greenberg, J. (1981), "The Justice of Distributing Scarce and Abundant Resources" in *The Justice Motive in Social Behavior: Adapting to Times of Scarcity and Change*. Lerner, M.J. and Lerner, S.C. (eds) (New York: Plenum Publishing), 289–316.

Greenberg, J. (1987), "Reactions to Procedural Injustice in Payment Distributions: Do the Ends Justify the Means?" *Journal of Applied Psychology*, **72**, 55–61. [DOI: 10.1037/0021-9010.72.1.55]

Greenberg, J. (1990), "Organizational Justice: Yesterday, Today, and Tomorrow", *Journal of Management*, **16**, 399–432. [DOI: 10.1177/014920639001600208]

Hegtvedt, K.A. (1992), "Bargaining for Justice: A Means to Resolve Competing Justice Claims", *Social Justice Research*, **5**, 155–172. [DOI: 10.1007/BF01048705]

Hegtvedt, K.A. (2001), "When Rewards Are Scarce: Equal or Equitable Distributions?" *Social Forces*, **66**, 183–207. [DOI: 10.2307/2578907]

Jasso, G. (1998), "Exploring the Justice of Punishments: Framing, Expressiveness, and the Just Prison Sentence", *Social Justice Research*, **11**, 397–422. [DOI: 10.1023/A%3A1022171207173]

Jost, J.T. and Major, B., eds (2001), *The Psychology of Legitimacy: Emerging Perspectives on Ideology, Justice, and Intergroup Relations* (Cambridge, UK: Cambridge University Press).

Kazemi, A. and Eek, D. (forthcoming a), "Effects of Group Goal and Resource Valence on Allocation Preferences in Public Good Dilemmas", *Social Behavior and Personality*.

Kazemi, A. and Eek, D. (forthcoming b), "Promoting Cooperation in Social Dilemmas Via Fairness Norms and Social Goals" in *New Issues and Paradigms in Research on Social Dilemmas*. Biel, A., Eek, D., Gärling, T. and Gustafsson, M. (eds) (New York: Springer).

Kazemi, A., Eek, D. and Gärling, T. (2005a), "Effects of Fairness and Distributive Goal on Preferred Allocations in Public Good Dilemmas", Göteborg Psychological Reports, 35, No. 4 (Göteborg, Sweden: Göteborg University, Department of Psychology).

Kazemi, A., Eek, D. and Gärling, T. (2005b), "Effects of Fairness, Group Goal, and Cooperation on Allocation Preferences in Step-Level Public Good Dilemmas", Göteborg Psychological Reports, 35, No. 5 (Göteborg, Sweden: Göteborg University, Department of Psychology).

Kazemi, A., Eek, D. and Gärling, T. (2006), "The Interplay between Greed, Fairness and Group Goal in Asymmetric Public Good Dilemmas". Manuscript submitted for Publication.

Lamm, H. (1986), "Justice Considerations in Interpersonal Conflict" in *Justice in Social Relations*. Bierhoff, H.W., Cohen, R.L. and Greenberg, J. (eds) (New York: Plenum Publishing), 43–63.

Legros, D. (1977), "Chance, Necessity, and Mode of Production: A Marxist Critique of Cultural Evolutionism", *American Anthropologist*, **79**, 26–41. [DOI: 10.1525/aa.1977.79.1.02a00030]

Lerner, M.J. (1975), "The Justice Motive in Social Behavior: Introduction", *Journal of Social Issues*, **31**, 1–20.

Lerner, M.J. and Mikula, G., eds (1994), *Entitlement and the Affectional Bond: Justice in Close Relationships* (New York: Plenum Publishing).

Leventhal, G.S. (1980), "What Should Be Done with Equity Theory?". in *Social Exchange: Advances in Theory and Research*. Gergen, K.J., Greenberg, M.S. and Willis, R.H. (eds) (New York: Plenum Publishing), 27–55.

Lind, E.A. and Tyler, T.R. (1988), *The Social Psychology of Procedural Justice* (New York: Plenum Publishing).

Lind, E.A., Kulik, C.T., Ambrose, M. and de Vera Park, M.V. (1993), "Individual and Corporate Dispute Resolution: Using Procedural Fairness as a Decision Heuristic", *Administrative Science Quarterly*, **38**, 224–251. [DOI: 10.2307/2393412]

Martin, J. and Harder, J.W. (1994), "Bread and Roses: Justice and the Distribution of Financial and Socioemotional Rewards in Organizations", *Social Justice Research*, **7**, 241–264. [DOI: 10.1007/BF02334833]

Marx, K. (1970), *Critique of the Gotha Programme* (New York: International Publishers).

McLean Parks, J., Conlon, D.E., Ang, S. and Bontempo, R. (1999), "The Manager Giveth, the Manager Taketh Away: Variation in Distribution/Recovery Rules Due to Resource Type and Cultural Orientation", *Journal of Management*, **25**, 723–757. [DOI: 10.1016/S0149-2063%2899%2900023-9]

Meeker, B.F. and Elliot, G.C. (1987), "Counting the Costs: Equality and the Allocation of Negative Group Products", *Social Psychology Quarterly*, **50**, 7–15. [DOI: 10.2307/2786885]

Messick, D.M. (1995), "Equality, Fairness, and Social Conflict", *Social Justice Research*, **8**, 153–173. [DOI: 10.1007/BF02334689]

Messick, D.M. and Sentis, K. (1983), "Fairness, Preference, and Fairness Biases" in *Equity Theory: Psychological and Sociological Perspectives*. Messick, D.M. and Cook, K.S. (eds) (New York: Praeger Publishing), 61–94.

Mikula, G. (1986), "The Experience of Injustice: Toward a Better Understanding of its Phenomenology" in *Justice in Social Relations*. Bierhoff, H.W., Cohen, R.L. and Greenberg, J. (eds) (New York: Plenum Publishing), 103–124.

Mikula, G. and Wenzel, M. (2000), "Justice and Social Conflict", *International Journal of Psychology*, **35**, 126–135. [DOI: 10.1080/002075900399420]

Miller, D.T. and Vidmar, N. (1981), "The Social Psychology of Punishment Reactions" in *The Justice Motive in Social Behavior*. Lerner, M.J. and Lerner, S.C. (eds) (New York: Plenum Publishing), 145–172.

O'Malley, M.N. and Davies, D.K. (1984), "Equity and Affect: The Effects of Relative Performance and Moods on Resource Allocation", *Basic and Applied Social Psychology*, **5**, 273–282. [DOI: 10.1207/s15324834basp0504_2]

Olsen, M.E. (1978), *The Process of Social Organization: Power in Social Systems*, 2nd edn (New York: Holt, Rinehart & Winston).

Prilleltensky, I. (2001), "Cultural Assumptions, Social Justice, and Mental Health" in *Cultural Cognition and Psychopathology*. Schumaker, J. and Ward, T. (eds) (Westport, CO.: Praeger), 251–265.

Reis, H.T. (1984), "The Multidimensionality of Justice" in *The Sense of Injustice: Social Psychological Perspectives*. Folger, R. (ed.) (New York: Plenum Publishing), 25–61.

Rescher, N. (1966), *Distributive Justice: A Constructive Critique of the Utilitarian Theory of Distribution* (New York: The Bobbs-Merrill Co., Inc.).

Sabbagh, C., Yechezkel, D. and Resh, N. (1994), "The Structure of Social Justice Judgements: A Facet Approach", *Social Psychology Quarterly*, **57**, 244–261. [DOI: 10.2307/2786879]

Scher, S.J. and Heise, D.R. (1993), "Affect and the Perception of Injustice", *Advances in Group Processes*, **10**, 223–252.

Sprecher, S. (1986), "The Relation between Inequity and Emotions in Close Relationships", *Social Psychology Quarterly*, **49**, 309–321. [DOI: 10.2307/2786770]

Sweezy, P.M. (1981), *Four Lectures on Marxism* (New York: Monthly Review Press).

Tangney, J.P. (1991), "Moral Affect: The Good, the Bad, and the Ugly", *Journal of Personality and Social Psychology*, **61**, 598–607. [PubMed 1960652] [DOI: 10.1037/0022-3514.61.4.598]

Teichman, M. (1971), "Satisfaction from Interpersonal Relations Following Resource Exchange". Doctoral dissertation, University of Missouri, Columbia, Missouri.

Törnblom, K.Y. (1988), "Positive and Negative Allocations: A Typology and a Model for Conflicting Justice Principles" in *Advances in Group Processes,* Vol 5. Lawler, E. and Markovsky, B. (eds) (Greenwich, CT: JAI Press), 141–168.

Törnblom, K.Y. (1992), "The Social Psychology of Distributive Justice" in *Distributive Justice from an Interdisciplinary Perspective*. Scherer, K.R. (ed.) (Cambridge, UK: Cambridge University Press), 177–284.

Törnblom, K.Y. and Foa, U.G. (1983), "Choice of a Distribution Principle: Crosscultural Evidence on the Effects of Resources", *Acta Sociologica*, **26**, 161–173.

Törnblom, K.Y. and Jonsson, D.R. (1985), "Subrules of the Equality and Contribution Principles: Their Perceived Fairness in Distribution and Retribution", *Social Psychology Quarterly*, **48**, 249–261. [DOI: 10.2307/3033685]

Törnblom, K.Y. and Jonsson, D.R. (1987), "*Distribution v Retribution*: The Perceived Justice of the Contribution and Equality Principles for Cooperative and Competitive Relationships", *Acta Sociologica*, **30**, 25–52. [DOI: 10.1177/00016 9938703000102]

Törnblom, K.Y. and Vermunt, R. (1999), "An Integrative Perspective on Social Justice: Distributive and Procedural Fairness Evaluations of Positive and Negative Outcome Allocations", *Social Justice Research*, **12**, 39–64. [DOI: 10.1023/A%3A1023226307252]

Turner, J.L., Foa, E.B. and Foa, U.G. (1971), "Interpersonal Reinforcers: Classification, Interrelationship and some Differential Properties", *Journal of Personality and Social Psychology*, **19**, 168–180. [DOI: 10.1037/h0031278]

Tyler, T.R. and Bies, R.J. (1990), "Interpersonal Aspects of Procedural Justice" in *Applied Social Psychology in Business Settings*. Carroll, J.S. (ed.) (Hillsdale, NJ: Lawrence Erlbaum).

Wolff, R.P. (1977), *Understanding Rawls* (Princeton, NJ: Princeton University Press).

Wood, A.W. (1972), "The Marxian Critique of Justice", *Philosophy and Public Affairs*, **1**, 244–185.

Chapter 3

Just Solidarity: How Justice Conditions Intergenerational Solidarity

Steffen Mau
University of Bremen, Germany

Sonja Wrobel
University of Bremen, Germany

1. The Disciplinary Divide

Justice and Solidarity: Conceptual Foundations

In order to define the concept of justice, Plato coined the term "suum cuique", to each his own. Subsequently, Aristotle distinguished between distribution and rectification as constituent parts of justice. Rectificatory justice relates to the economic exchange among individuals, which is based on the principle of equivalence between performance and counter-performance. Distributive justice, however, alludes to the relation between society as a whole and the individual and is concerned with the fair distribution of honors, public office, material goods, or anything else that can be divided between members of a community (Aristotle, 1980). In this context, the principle of proportional equality claims that individuals should be treated unequally (in proportion to their merits) but according to the same standards. As a consequence of the Aristotelian division, justice can be regarded as either being an individual virtue or as a characteristic of the political and societal sphere. Normative theory since the Enlightenment has concentrated on the latter aspect. In reaction to the development of sovereign states during the sixteenth century, justice theories were concerned with the individual's rights vis-à-vis the state. In this context, the idea of normative individualism claimed that binding decisions must be based on the agreement of every person who is affected by the decision. Hobbes (1998 [1651]) and Locke (1976 [1690]), the founders of social contract theory, transferred this idea to the state by conceptualizing it as a voluntary union among the people. In exchange for guaranteeing the citizens' security, the just state is equipped with the monopoly of legal power.

Normative individualism represents the logical precondition for liberal universalist claims with regard to rules of justice. In accordance with this principle, the Kantian categorical imperative claims that philosophical rules must be formulated in a way that rational deliberation will result in everyone's agreement. As a precondition for universal agreement, however, it will be necessary to abstract from one's own personal preferences and contextual restrictions. Once these conditions are fulfilled, rationality drives the agreement to a rule. Therefore, theories of justice and liberal ethics in general are to apply in exactly the same manner to every person, regardless of the context. They are thus based on the premise that "moral rules must not contain spatial or temporal restrictions, and—as a consequence—must not be directed towards particular communities; there is no special moral status for those who belong to us" (Bayertz, 1998, p. 13; translation by the authors).

In contrast to this formal concept of justice, solidarity refers to the qualitative dimension of social relations. The term describes social relations that are based on mutual closeness and reciprocity and focuses on the individual's collective orientations and cooperative behavior resulting eventually in stable social structures. On the individual level, solidarity includes the notions of support and assistance which have to be based on the acceptance of particular duties. As a consequence, the concept of solidarity cannot be objectively applied to a given social situation but must be actively valued by the individuals involved. On a more abstract level, solidarity represents an ideal social structure which is closely linked to the aspects of social integration and social cohesion. In this context, the concept of solidarity has been interpreted in different ways. It may be conceptualized as a particular form of social cooperation that originates from the interdependence of interests. From this point of view, the cooperative aspect of solidarity refers to an actor's assumptions about the intentions of other actors. This argument shows a considerable overlap between solidarity and the perception of personal advantage. However, it is important not to reduce solidarity to the aspect of cooperation alone. Instead, the affective dimension occurring in a number of factual forms of solidarity has to be taken into account as well. Concepts based on this aspect therefore emphasize the role of feelings of togetherness among the members of social groups as inherent to solidarity. Social and emotional closeness as well as sympathy represent the essential source of solidarity with other group members (Thome, 1998, p. 238). By the same token, the link between the concepts of solidarity and the common good has frequently been emphasized, because existing solidarity is viewed as prerequisite to the solution of many common good problems.

Two Perspectives on the Problem of Social Integration

While normative theory advocates the concept of social justice, sociology generally refers to social solidarity (cf. Bayertz, 1998, p. 12ff). There seems to be something of a "natural" division of labor between these two disciplines. So why do we not simply leave it at that and accept that each of them is driven by a specific research interest? Taking a closer look, it becomes obvious that normative theories of justice as well as sociological conceptions of solidarity share a common interest: both disciplines seek to explore the foundations of social integration and a stable social order, but their conclusions are based on different concepts. When sociologists speak of solidarity, they refer to the aspect of social integration. A short look at Durkheim's seminal work is enough to realize that the core element of his sociological analysis aims at combining the concepts of solidarity and social integration. In his early work on *The Division of Labour in Society* (1999 [1893]), he concentrates on the problem of how social integration might be guaranteed in modern societies that are characterized by an increasing degree of labor differentiation and individualization. In contrast to his contemporary Tönnies (1935 [1887]), who observes a loss of solidarity and the weakening of social bonds, Durkheim detects a transformation from mechanic to organic solidarity. Social similarity represents a precondition of mechanic solidarity, which is derived from the collective consciousness. In the transformation process, social similarity is replaced by social differentiation and the resulting new dependency relations. Organic solidarity is then characterized by solidarity among different but interdependent individuals. Moreover, Durkheim regards the division of labor as valuable because the manifold relations resulting from social exchange create emotional bonds and therefore solidarity between individuals. Moral bonds develop via interdependence and complementarities creating positive emotions of closeness as well as duties, which both stabilize the relations among the members of a group (Baurmann, 1999).

The late (collectivistic) Durkheim (1912) revised the architecture of the argument he had developed in the *Division of Labour*. He then argued that solidarity does not result from inter-individual relations of social exchange, but that it follows from the relations between the individual and the collective as a whole. Actions based on solidarity are a consequence of the loyalty towards the collective as well as a result of an over-individual morality. The importance of shared beliefs and general normative orientations for the development of solidarity relations is rarely contested. When duties and solidarity relations are discussed in the context of social integration, the embeddedness of solidarity in culture, traditions and in value communities usually plays an important role. This embeddedness might be conceptualized as "deep-rooted convictions of a general backwards-oriented nature that have an immediate, authoritative and quasi-religious effect or as closeness like it exists between relatives" (Hondrich and Koch-Arzberger, 1992, p. 18; translation by the authors). In these cases, a shared background can be expected with regard to the concepts of what is good and right. Social integration is therefore deduced from the fact that individual identity is linked to the community. When individuals find "their position, their identity, their purpose, their satisfaction and their aims in the lap of such a community" (Engelhardt, 1998, p. 438; translation by the authors), solidarity becomes ubiquitous.

In this context, the questions of how much social solidarity is necessary among the members of a society in order to guarantee social cohesion and which are the conditions of stability for this kind of solidarity remain ever-present. Since individualization poses challenges to dense community networks and since a collective consciousness cannot be taken for granted in the context of modern societies, the possible sources and functions of solidarity are a subject of lively discussion. Also in modern societies, the functional and self-interested interplay among the members of a society alone cannot guarantee social integration; solidarity relations need to complement and back the instrumental cooperation (Kaufmann, 1984). However, one also can identify forms of solidarity that are inherent to modern societies. The variety of factual solidarity-based relations that human beings develop, no matter if they are private support-networks, welfare arrangements or new associative networks, point to the fact that the potential of solidarity does not simply vanish in societies which are increasingly differentiated and individualized.

The aforementioned perspective on social integration has to be distinguished from approaches within normative theory that analyze the integration of society from a *top-down* perspective. From this point of view, social integration is derived from the assumption that societies are based on normative principles. As a consequence, societal institutions are able to develop authority and to successfully deal with the conflicting interests of their members. Rawls' *A Theory of Justice* (1971) represents an example of normative theories that claim to establish a theoretical foundation of social cohesion. As an allusion to social contract theory, the Rawlsian society is conceptualized as a group of individuals who are confronted with the problem of how to distribute social resources in a manner that is satisfactory and legitimate to all of them. On the grounds of equal rights and freedoms, social and economic inequalities have to be designed in a way that all parties to the treaty regard as adequate. According to Rawls, social inequalities are justified as long as they increase the position of the least well-off, and as long as public positions are accessible for everyone. The legitimacy of social inequalities is based on the idea that they create incentives for productive behavior that will result in a general increase of welfare. The resulting gains will then have to be used for an improvement of the situation of those who are worst off. The development of these distributive rules is based on the fictitious concept of the "veil of ignorance". This term constitutes a metaphor for the idea that people will decide impartially when they do not know their own social position and personal preferences: if I do not know how big my share of the scarce societal resources will be, I had better insist on a fair distribution of goods. Rawls' concept of justice as fairness is therefore based on the idea of combining a deliberative procedure with the idea of impartiality.

Moreover, Rawls emphasizes the moral and social advantages of his justice concept. He claims that respecting his justice rules will lead societies to a balanced and fair social equilibrium that is grounded on the acceptance of institutionalized norms. Justice as the most important institutional virtue will result in reciprocal acknowledgment of the members of a society as well as in acceptance of the institutionalized norms. Justice as fairness is based on the idea that people will acknowledge and behave according to these normative principles, which will positively influence the quality of social relations. In Rawls' concept, fairness works as a precondition for the development of solidarity relations (Zoll, 2000, p. 189).

It is obvious that normative theory and sociology approach the subject of social integration from different directions. Nonetheless, both disciplines cannot avoid reflecting upon the link between solidarity and justice. Normative theorists regard the establishment of just rules as logically prior to the development of social relations, while sociologists conceptualize social solidarity as context-bound and point to those instances when people take responsibility for each other. In their view, social integration is based on feelings of togetherness and responsibility for the community. However, neither perspective elaborates on the mutual effects and relations between solidarity relations and norms of justice.

2 Bridging the Disciplinary Divide

The Normative Content of Solidarity Relations

For a better understanding of the relationship between justice and solidarity, it appears useful to emphasize the norm-generating potential of solidarity relations. Honneth (2000, p. 7) argues that the moral content of affective solidarity relations cannot be understood by only referring to the formal aspect of impartiality. In other words, the moral aspect of a social order is insufficiently captured if one neglects the social meaning attached to social relations. Justice research shows that although distributive justice attitudes indeed relate to formal criteria such as impartiality or rational reasoning, the attitudes are strongly influenced by the individual's social positioning. In this context, we have to distinguish between two classes of justice judgments: on one hand we find norm-based judgments which are independent from contextual influences and which result from deliberative reasoning; on the other hand there are judgments that can be regarded as individual preferences (Liebig, 2001). The latter type of justice attitude implies that distributive preferences might be heavily influenced by social bonds or social positions.

The controversy between communitarians and liberals reflects some of the central aspects of this distinction. Communitarianism has provided strong arguments for the importance of social communities in generating normative orientations. It is argued that social participation is the only way through which moral commitments may emerge (Honneth, 1995). However, since moral commitments based on solidarity are closely associated with social bonds, their generalization and extension beyond the community remains unlikely. Consequently, this kind of solidarity is reserved to the members of a group, be it a nation, a neighborhood or a family. State institutions based on law and bureaucracy may help to extend the scope of solidarity, but attempts to encompass more and more people may also endanger the socio-moral underpinnings of solidarity (Taylor, 1995, p. 106).

Many sources of solidarity within the society are closely linked to emotional and affective relationships between people. Social psychology has pointed out that personal relations and networks are indispensable for the production of moral orientations. Accordingly, the ability to make moral judgments and to behave morally largely depends on people's interactions with others, which result in feelings of empathy and mutual understanding (Hoffman, 1990). Melden (1977, p. 18) underlines: "It is this moral concern for other persons, rather than principles and priority rules, which provides us with a rationale for resolving many or most of the moral conflicts that arise, easily and without hesitation." For the development of moral judgments, it is essential that people learn to take each other's perspective and that they are able to mitigate conflicting interests. Friendship relations, for example, are regarded as central for any moral understanding because they support the development of interpersonal norms such as trust, reliability and reciprocity. Those norms in turn represent important components of the moral consciousness. It has been argued that these norms are not confined to specific friendships but that they have a tendency to become generalized instead (Keller, 1986). In other words, social relations can be conceived of as the locus of moral socialization and moral competence. The fact that universal moral attitudes are developed within the context of social relations does not mean that all types of moral obligations might be dissociated from "their" social origins. Empirical evidence suggests that the morality of social care, for example, is difficult to disconnect from the specificity of social bonds (see Bertram, 1992). Because it is inherently related to the embeddedness of individuals, it appears difficult to "harmonize" solidarity with a contractual approach to social justice.

By looking at the role that normative elements of affective solidarity relations play for solidarity with strangers, one can identify a more direct link with concepts of social justice. In such cases, justice might represent the cognitive-motivational basis of solidarity acts. Solidarity with the unemployed, with suppressed people or with the victims of a natural catastrophe, for example, represents a type of solidarity that is not based on social closeness or pre-existing social relations (Hondrich and Koch-Arzberger, 1992, p. 13). Such solidarity in fact transcends the boundaries of the community, although it still refers to a specific group in a situation of misfortune. It has been demonstrated that the pro-social commitment in favor of under-privileged groups is indeed a moral undertaking which rests on feelings of moral outrage or shame (Montada and Schneider, 1989). In cases like this, people often perceive a justice gap between their own and the others' less fortunate social situation (Montada, Schmitt and Dalbert, 1986). Alternatively, moral outrage might be caused by ascribing responsibility for social misery to a third party. In this context, social engagement is to be understood as a form of social protest against those considered responsible (Bierhoff and Küpper, 1998, p. 272f).

Solidarity as a Norm that Converges with Justice Norms

Besides the aforementioned perspective, we can distinguish those approaches that regard solidarity itself as a normative principle and thus establish a close relationship to justice norms. Montada (1999) favors a concept of solidarity that is less focused on social relations and serves to explain social action instead. He suggests to conceptualize solidarity sociologically as a social norm and psychologically as a normative belief. Consequently, the concept of solidarity is not the object of explanation but the explanatory factor guiding the analysis and providing information about social action. By conceptualizing justice as solidarity, Krettenauer (1998) even goes one step further. His idea is based on Durkheim's concept of moral individualism, which describes a specific modern orientation implying the willingness to consider the needs and interests of others and to moderate one's personal interests based on the moral principle that all members of society are equal. Based on this, he asks how solidarity-based action is possible under conditions of an increasing individualization and the decline of traditional community bonds. He explicitly alludes to solidarity sentiments that go beyond a collective-solidarity tradition, namely those which correspond to concepts of distributive justice (see Folger, 1984). This approach does not relate individual inputs (expenses, efforts, achievements) to outcomes (rewards), as claimed by equity theory. Conceptions of distributive justice rather refer to a perception of justice that concentrates on the distribution of outcomes only. This type of judgment refers to considerations of resource allocation as they are expressed in claims for social equality or minimum standards. It does not articulate itself through a liability towards specifically bonded persons or groups but through the moral claim that everyone should be provided equally with the necessary minimum of social resources.

> As a subjectively binding justice orientation, such a moral claim can motivate the willingness to redistribute resources in favor of the structurally disadvantaged. Justice as solidarity therefore turns out to be not only thinkable but indeed feasible. A distributive concept of justice may cause the solidarity-based acceptance of responsibilities towards the structurally disadvantaged. If this type of responsibility is not rejected but actually accepted, the cognitive-motivational ground for just action based on solidarity remains within the scope of Durkheim's concept of moral individualism. (Krettenauer, 1998, p. 83, translation by the authors)

In the context of a distributive conception of justice, solidarity comes into play to the extent that pro-social action goes beyond particular social relations. Here, solidarity refers to the acknowledgment of irrefutable individual claims for necessary material and social goods. This idea draws on normative standards that endure regardless of the specific connection between aid giver and aid receiver and that refer exclusively to considerations of neediness. Krettenauer stresses that empathy and compassion cannot constitute the dominant motives for such solidarity-based action because such motives do not apply universally. They rather result in the (undue) preference of those persons with whom we have an emotionally closer connection. As an extension of Kohlberg's theory (Colby and Kohlberg, 1986), the development of moral autonomy is conceived as a key factor to understanding this kind of universal solidarity-based responsibility. It appears that the genesis of a generalized empathy is linked to the development of moral autonomy. Furthermore, it seems that individualism does not necessarily go along with increased egoism. The aforementioned universal solidarity-based commitment is therefore no longer related to specific community bonds but rather to cognitive-moral standards containing a high level of independence from such particular bonds. One should note, however, that the convergence of solidarity and justice is based on a narrow concept of solidarity. This concept might be helpful with regard to the idea of universality but, in fact, it only encompasses parts of the socially significant solidarity relations.

Norms of Justice as Stabilizers of Solidarity

A third way of linking solidarity with justice might be developed by studying the stability conditions of solidarity arrangements. Sociological theory generally regards justice as a stabilizer of different forms of solidarity-based exchange, given that this exchange is not solely achieved through a congruence of material interests. It is assumed that the perception of justice contributes to people's willingness to participate in the production of public goods (Rothstein, 1998). This argument is based on the idea that only when the exchanges and distributions are perceived as just, are individuals willing to put aside their self-interests and to commit themselves to solidarity arrangements. The less affective solidarity relations are, the more they must be stabilized by the attainment of prevailing norms of justice.

The welfare state can be considered as an ideal-typical example of the inability of redistributive arrangements to produce and consolidate solidarity without a corresponding normative infrastructure. The acceptance of resource redistribution in the context of welfare state transfers neither depends on the tax burden nor on the social policy aims alone. Acceptance is also connected to the perception of a fair distribution of burdens. This perception refers to the contributions made by all the other participants within a solidarity arrangement and therefore includes other tax-payers' contributions as well as the activities of those who receive benefits. The discovery of "free-riding" has an especially negative impact on the willingness of those persons who have complied with solidarity-based duties. People who try to avoid individual contributions to the public good and who instead try to secure unjustified advantages for themselves represent this dilemma. Consequently, with regard to supporting the unemployed, it is quite important whether the benefit receiver is accused of abusing these benefits or not. Empirical evidence suggests that the way welfare state clienteles are perceived (for instance with regard to the reasons for unemployment or efforts made to find a new job) strongly influences the social acceptance of unemployment insurance (Hamann, Karl and Ulrich, 2001). Besides one's own contribution to the production of public goods, the contributions made by other participants also represent an important aspect of people's willingness to show solidarity. A person is more likely to do so if the other persons concerned with the production of public goods also fulfill their solidarity-based duties and thus socially cooperate.

Levi's theory of "contingent consent" (1991, 1993; Rothstein, 1998) points out that people are willing to participate in solidarity arrangements and to overcome their narrow self-interests under three conditions. Firstly, if the institutional regulations converge with acknowledged norms of social justice and fairness; secondly, if they can trust others to participate in collective arrangements as well; and thirdly, if the implementation of social measures is perceived as non-discriminatory and fair. In this context, Offe (1999) speaks of a "moral plausibility" of institutions, which encourages individuals to support institutions also for the reason that the incorporated justice principles possess social validity. When this can be taken for granted, individuals may act on the assumption that the other social actors also acknowledge and support the institutions. The moral plausibility of distributive systems suggests that the social counterpart also acknowledges the system's normative foundations and that he or she is therefore willing to cooperate. According to this idea of the system's normative foundation, solidarity systems that are based on the assumption that people put aside their utility maximizing interests can only function when the idea is reflected in the mainstream attitudes towards justice. When institutions and their distributive rules correspond with individual ideas of justice, the conditions for social cooperation improve, and it becomes likely that solidarity orientations are strengthened. With regard to the welfare state, it has been argued that the solidarity arrangements of the welfare state themselves can be norm-generating (Rothstein, 1998; Mau, 2003). Thus, regarding the institutional architecture of welfare state arrangements, it can be assumed that the normative rules and their distributive implications promote a habitual loyalty of those who participate (Hinrichs, 1994, p. 140).

By now we have discussed three perspectives that aim at bridging the disciplinary divide between normative theoretical and sociological approaches towards solidarity and justice. The first perspective is built on the idea that affective social relations contribute to the general normative orientations of the individual. It is claimed that individual conceptions of justice are formed and influenced by contextual factors such as the personal experience of solidarity. The second view states that solidarity partly converges with justice. From this perspective, solidarity does not relate to specific social contexts but can be regarded as a universal norm that is directed towards the "generalized other". The third point of view argues that justice norms function as stabilizers of solidarity relations. Solidarity can only be developed in environments that are perceived as just in the sense that nobody is seeking individual advantages at the others' expense.

In the following section, we will confront these theoretical considerations with some empirical illustrations related to the topic of intergenerational justice—a fair division of benefits and burdens between generations. In the context of welfare state adjustments to the challenges of globalization and the slowing-down of economic growth, intergenerational relations have become a central issue. Intergenerational justice and solidarity have been debated in the context of pension reforms, family policy and fiscal policy in more general terms. In our analysis, we concentrate on the field of pension policy in Germany, which has been at the centre of reform debates for nearly a decade now. We will first look at parliamentary debates about pension reforms before we turn to the analysis of attitudes about intergenerational justice. In both parts, we will provide pointers for the question of how the relation between solidarity and justice is empirically being referred to.

3 Justice and Solidarity in the Context of Intergenerational Relations

Intergenerational Justice and Solidarity in Parliamentary Debates about Pension Reform

Our analysis includes three parliamentary debates that were held in the Bundestag, Germany's main legislative chamber, in the course of three consecutive periods of legislation. Each of the three debates represents the second and final lecture of a pension reform bill. The first bill, the "Pension Reform Act 1999", introduced the so-called *demographic factor*, which includes the integration of the average life expectancy into the pension calculations. The 2001 "Pension Modernization Act" established a *new pension pillar* in the form of a state-subsidized private pension scheme that was added to the public one. In the third debate, the members of parliament discussed the "Pension Sustainability Act 2004". It introduced the so-called *sustainability factor*, indexing the level of pensions to labor-market development.

During the period under review, five parties were represented in the German Bundestag: the conservative *CDU/CSU*, the liberal *FDP*, the Green Party *Bündnis 90/Die Grünen*, the social-democratic *SPD* and the socialist *PDS*. The German party

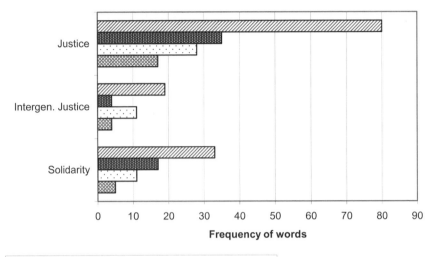

Frequency of words

Figure 3.1   Intergenerational Justice and Solidarity in Parliamentary Debates

system is characterized by a competition between the two major parties, the CDU/ CSU and the SPD (Schmidt, 2003). With two exceptions, when these two parties have been governing together,[1] government has alternated between them. Since WWII, social policy bills have traditionally been adopted by both major parties' votes. This inter-party consensus was kept up until the governing CDU/CSU introduced the Pension Reform Act 1999. For the first time since the 1957 pension reform, a major pension reform bill was not supported by both CDU/CSU and SPD. This break up was due to changes in the political environment such as the slowing-down of economic growth, mass unemployment, demographic changes and the resulting increase in pension policy expenditures. Since then, parliamentary debates about pension reforms have become much more controversial, especially with regard to normative justifications (Schmidt, 2000, p. 274ff).

Our content analysis of the three debates primarily aims at the links made between the terms "solidarity" and "intergenerational justice".[2] In a first step, we carried out a computer-supported text search in order to identify the text passages referring to these concepts.[3] In a second step, we analyzed the references between intergenerational justice and solidarity with regard to the question of whether and to what extent they reflect the above theoretical distinctions. The results of the text search are displayed in Figure 3.1. At first glance, it is obvious that politicians

---

1   Governments including both the CDU/CSU and the SPD are labeled "grand coalitions". In the Federal Republic's history, this has been the case twice (from 1966 to 1969 and from 2005 to the present).

2   The 1997 and 2001 debates contain about 30,000 words each, while the 2004 debate consists of 15,000 words.

3   The computer search was not directed towards the exact phrases but to the respective word families instead.

used the term justice more than twice as often as the term solidarity. This might be explained by reference to the "nature" of the German public pension system, which is generally regarded as typically "Bismarckian" (Bonoli, 1997). This means 1) that the pension system is financed on a contributory basis and 2) that it is focused on status-preservation. Contributions are paid by both employers and employees on the basis of wages. Compared to this contributory component, the system's solidarity-related elements are rather weakly developed. They mainly refer to the acknowledgment of child care and education periods in the calculation of pensions. Because only very limited time periods are acknowledged as equivalent to regular pension contributions, the system is said to allow for distribution over a lifetime rather than among contributors (Rürup, 2002). Accordingly, contributory justice plays an important role in debates about pension policy, whereas solidarity is addressed less frequently.

Politicians referred least frequently to intergenerational justice. This is probably due to the fact that the terminology was only recently "invented" and introduced into the German political debate. An analysis of German quality newspapers has shown that the term first occurred during the second half of the 1990s (Nullmeier, 2004). In the context of pension policy debates, it soon became a key reference, and it is generally used to point to a lack of justice in the public pension system. The discussion relates to labor market transformations and demographic changes, which have been taking place in Germany in the course of the last decades. As a consequence of improved life expectancy, payments to pensioners are increasing. In addition, low birth rates worsen the ratio between the pensioners and the active working population. Therefore, in pay-as-you-go systems like the German one, a decreasing proportion of the working population has to pay pension contributions for an increasing number of pensioners (Schmähl, 2000). It is exactly this problem that is addressed by the term intergenerational justice. In our text sample, all references to intergenerational justice are related to this problem. Nonetheless, the relatively small number of hits indicates that intergenerational justice seems to be a less well-entrenched concept than solidarity and justice. Moreover, it can be observed that the frequency of references to all three norms decreases from the first to the last debate. We assume that this decrease in normative statements is due to a growing consent about the necessity of reform. In the first debate, the government and the opposition engaged in a dispute about the consequences that the government had to draw from the demographic development with regard to the public pension system. In contrast, the need to make adjustments in the pension system was widely acknowledged in 2001 and even more so in 2004.

In a qualitative analysis, we addressed the question of how the politicians made connections between solidarity and justice in the parliamentary debates. First of all, it can be observed that solidarity and justice were only rarely connected by the speakers. Connections were counted when both terms occurred in the same paragraph *and* when there was a logical link between them. Overall, there were nine instances in which the speakers mentioned solidarity and justice together, each of them referring to the sphere of intergenerational relations.

In our theoretical discussion, it was first claimed that affective social relations contribute to the individual's general normative orientations. In our text sample, only one passage referred to this idea. The speaker argued that solidarity between the young and the elderly is a characteristic of family relations. However, by means of the pay-as-you-go system, the pension system structure includes an institutionalized form of solidarity between the generations. The integration of solidarity norms into the pension system represents one of the reasons why many people consider the system as just (Norbert Blüm, 10 October, 1997).[4] This argument is based on the assumption that solidarity as a family value shapes and influences peoples' perception of justice.

The second argument holds that solidarity and justice norms partly overlap. Five of our nine passages match this perspective, which is based on the idea that solidarity and justice converge because both can be classified as universal norms. With regard to the parliamentary debates, this viewpoint works as a "catch-all" category including all instances in which solidarity and justice were referred to in equal terms. Typically, text passages of this type claimed that the pension system must be based on intergenerational justice as well as on intergenerational solidarity. The parliamentary speakers thus refer to solidarity and justice as normative foundations of the pension system, thereby classifying them as universally applicable norms. However, the relation between them remains rather unspecified.

Finally, the third position argues that justice works as a stabilizer of solidarity relations. We have found four text passages supporting this view, all of them describing intergenerational justice as a precondition for intergenerational solidarity.[5] A typical argument of this type stated that the young generation's trust in the public pension system had to be re-established in order to avoid the system's collapse. For this purpose, the pension reform bill under discussion should be designed in accordance with the norm of intergenerational justice (Kerstin Müller, 26 January, 2001).[6] All text passages that were counted as belonging to this type emphasized in a similar way the need for intergenerational justice as a precondition for the young generation's willingness to show solidarity with the pensioners' generation. These references obviously relate to the idea of contingent consent as discussed above: politicians believe that the young generation is only willing to be solidaristic towards the pensioners when the pension system as a whole is considered just. By contrast, the young are assumed to withdraw their solidarity once they get the impression that the system provides advantages for the elder generations at the young generation's expense. Overall, references of this type seem to represent the most stable and well-entrenched linkage between the concepts of solidarity and justice within the parliamentary debates.

It can be concluded that evidence regarding all theoretical arguments can be found in the debates. However, the small size of our sample indicates that politicians do not

---

4 At that time, Norbert Blüm was Secretary of State for employment in the German federal government. He is a member of the conservative CDU, which is rooted in the Christian tradition. Conservative politicians therefore often refer to Catholic social theory, which generally regards the family as society's core element.

5 One passage was counted twice, as it fits the first as well as the third perspective.

6 In 2001, Kerstin Müller was co-chair of the Green Party.

usually regard solidarity and justice as conceptual siblings. By contrast, there seems to be a party-political divide with regard to the use of these concepts.[7] While speakers of the Conservative Party, the Liberal Party and the Green Party more often refer to the concept of intergenerational justice, the social democrats as well as members of the Socialist Party rather emphasize the importance of solidarity. Nevertheless, the idea of justice as a precondition for solidarity-based behavior seems to have been most deeply internalized by the parliamentary speakers.

Generational Justice from the Perspective of Attitude Research

A second area of research that gives us some evidence for the links between justice and solidarity is empirical attitude research. Within the academic debates, it is often pointed out that the pension system produces winner and loser cohorts. This "intergenerational accounting" argument is based on the ideal of equity within a lifetime's contributions and benefits. It is argued that the pensions of the generations who have retired during the last two decades show a very favorable proportion of contributions and benefits on average. In contrast, this proportion will deteriorate considerably for the generations who will retire in the decades to come. As a consequence, many researchers contend that the younger generations—when faced with the perspective of retrenchment—will no longer be willing to finance the older generation's pensions. The pension system, it is said, sets the old against the young. Intergenerational accounting approaches therefore predict that the younger generations will withdraw from the generational contract, since it works to their disadvantage (Moody, 1988; Johnson, Conrad and Thompson, 1989).

However, although the issue of intergenerational justice ranks high on the public agenda, the results of attitude research do not confirm the impression of the pension system's legitimacy crisis. Surveys report that the German pension system still enjoys a high degree of support across all generations (Rinne and Wagner, 1995; Mau, 2003). Similar results are to be found for most European Union countries (Kohl, 2003; see Figure 3.2). Data from the Eurobarometer 56.2 (2001) show that 55 per cent of all respondents in the EU-15 countries strongly agree with the statement that "everyone should have the right to a state minimum pension". On the whole, positive responses amount to 90 per cent. Moreover, 52 per cent state that the protection of elderly people against the risk of poverty is a major task of good old age provision (strong and weak agreement together form 92 per cent of the responses).

On the basis of such findings it can be pointed out that distributional balance sheets seem not to be decisive for the issue of support and neither that relations of solidarity and reciprocity weaken generational conflicts. Experimental studies in economics have shown that the younger generation is willing to support pay-as-you-go systems, even though they promise lower returns than other investments (Veall, 1986). There is strong evidence for the role of solidarity considerations when people evaluate different pension schemes. Individual utility that aims at optimizing the relation between current working income and future pension transfers is by no

---

7   This finding does not relate to the links between solidarity and justice, but to those passages that refer to either solidarity or justice.

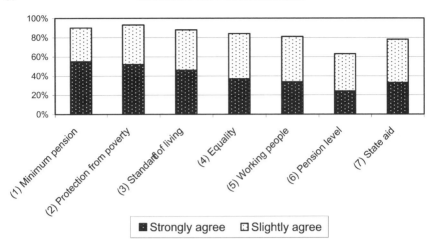

Figure 3.2   Attitudes on Aims and Principles of Pension Schemes in the EU-15
*Data basis: Eurobarometer 56.2 (2001); 1) A guaranteed minimum pension should be a
basic social right of every citizen. 2) The primary goal of a good pension scheme should
be to protect elderly people against the risk of poverty. 3) A good pension scheme should
allow everybody to maintain an adequate standard of living relative to their income before
retirement. 4) A good pension scheme should contribute to greater equality in income and
living conditions among the elderly. 5) Those who are now working have a duty to ensure,
through their taxes and contributions, that elderly people have a decent standard of living.
6) The amount of one's pension should be strictly based on the amount of contributions one
has paid into the pension scheme. 7) People who cannot pay sufficient contributions into a
pension scheme (e.g. the unemployed, those on low earnings) should receive some extra help
from the state for old age.*

means the only parameter determining pension scheme preferences. Considerations
in this context obviously also comprise the social situation of the pensioner
generation and ideas of intergenerational justice. In other words, it is crucial for the
younger generation that the elderly can enjoy a decent living standard. Some studies,
therefore, refer to an existing "intergenerational altruism" which motivationally
underpins the existing pension schemes (Van der Heijden, Nelissen and Verbon,
1995). Furthermore, it has been argued that public transfers from the young to the
old represent just one side of the intergenerational exchange. On the other side, there
are large transfers from the elderly to the younger generation, which countervail the
redistributive bias and, hence, diminish potential and actual conflicts (Kohli, 1999;
Attias-Donfut and Arber, 2000).

Dallinger and Liebig (2004) have criticized the body of literature that deals with
the acceptance of the pension system, because most of the studies do not explicitly
ask for justice evaluations. In their own study, based on data from the International
Social Justice Project, they could show that the younger cohorts judge the pension
system as being much more unjust than the cohort beyond or shortly before retirement
age. However, across all age groups there is a tendency to criticize the pension
system as unjust towards the younger generation. Even in the cohort born between
1900 and 1940, nearly half of the respondents agree with the statement that the

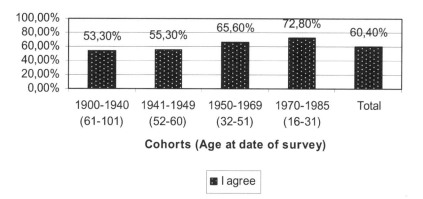

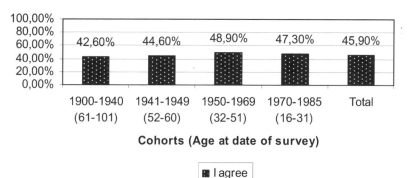

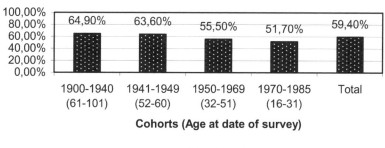

Figure 3.3   Attitudes to the Pension System in Germany
Source: Dallinger and Liebig, 2004.

current pension system works to the disadvantage of the younger generation. For the youngest group of respondents, agreement with this statement ranks slightly higher than 70 per cent. Interesting results also emerge with regard to the insurance principle resulting in earnings-related pension levels. Elderly respondents favor pensions based on the insurance principle more than the younger ones. At the same time, a large proportion of respondents is in favor of a basic pension that is independent from former earnings or employment status. Forty-four per cent of the elderly and 47 per cent of the younger cohort support this idea of a basic pension. The authors assume a close nexus between perceptions of justice and preference formation, in the sense that a weakening of the insurance principle increases the support for a basic pension model. The results indicate that underneath the overwhelming support for the state pension system "justice problems" could indeed occur. Therefore, it is not unlikely that perceptions of injustice may turn into legitimacy problems if the younger cohorts feel that the distribution of burdens and benefits within the state pension system works more and more to their disadvantage.

Linked to our discussion of the relationship between solidarity and justice, the survey data suggest that the governmental responsibility to provide a decent standard of living for the elderly, as well as the generational duty to support the preceding generation, are well-established social norms. It could be that the very existence of the welfare state institutions also influenced people's normative orientations and the approval of state responsibility. As in the context of family relations, experiences of solidarity made within the context of the welfare state may have a positive impact on people's views. Furthermore, given the wide acceptance of state responsibility for the elderly, and given the fact that pension schemes are large-scale institutions encompassing millions of citizens, it might well be that people's solidarity converges with justice norms. In this case, generalized solidarity attitudes instead of the personal relations between the young and the old foster the willingness to support redistribution from the young to the old. Intergenerational altruism, for example, is likely to be a social norm that cannot be explained by special ties but rather by reference to universal norms, such as the support for a provision of a decent living standard for the elderly. In this context, the third nexus between solidarity and justice with justice conditioning solidarity arrangements can be emphasized as well. The pension system's legitimacy and solidarity ambitions depend on perceptions of intergenerational justice (Mau, 2003). Systems working at the expense of the younger generations risk losing support in the long run. Although one still finds a good deal of support for the basic principles of state pension systems, it has been shown that especially the younger generations have a propensity to view the pension system more critically. This in turn may have a negative impact on their motivation to show solidarity with the older generation. Hence, for the survival of solidarity motivation within the context of the welfare state, it is essential that the system is perceived as just, i.e. that benefits and burdens are distributed justly across generations and cohorts.

Conclusion: How Justice Conditions Intergenerational Solidarity

The disciplinary divide between sociology and normative theory was the starting point of this chapter. "Divide" refers to how solidarity and justice are used as concepts in both disciplines to understand social integration. While sociology emphasizes that solidarity develops in specific social contexts, normative theory— by contrast—aims to show the anonymous character and universal applicability of justice rules. Curious to see whether this common interest in the problem of social integration allows bridging the disciplinary divide, we first discussed three potential connections between solidarity and justice from a theoretical perspective. The first argument claims that individual conceptions of justice are formed and influenced by contextual factors such as the personal experience of solidarity. The second view states that solidarity may partly converge with justice if it becomes a universalist norm. The third point of view argues that solidarity can only be developed in environments that are perceived as just in the sense that nobody is seeking individual advantages at the others' expense.

In a second step, our theoretical considerations were confronted with empirical observations from parliamentary debates and survey data in the context of welfare state arrangements. This empirical "test" has shown that people actually make links between solidarity and justice. With regard to attitudes, the idea that individual concepts of justice are formed and influenced by contextual factors such as the personal experience of solidarity within families remains rather abstract. Therefore, this link is difficult to validate by reference to our survey data alone. In the parliamentary debates, however, this idea was applied with regard to the transfer of family values to the pension system. The claim that justice and solidarity converge because both represent universal norms finds more support in both the surveys and the debates. There is a high level of agreement for the aims and principles of pension systems across the European countries. This agreement cannot exclusively be explained by reference to individual social ties but has to be regarded as a form of generalized solidarity towards others. Politicians have referred to this idea by mentioning solidarity and justice as equally universal principles within the pension system. Nevertheless, they generally remained vague with regard to the content of these norms. Last but not least, the argument that justice works as a stabilizer of solidarity relations seems to be very prominent. Although the survey results do not support the public impression of a legitimacy crisis, they show that especially the younger generations consider the pension system to be unfair. It was suggested that for the long-term viability of the generational solidarity established by the pension system, it is crucial that the system is viewed as just. Turning to the parliamentary debates, it becomes obvious that politicians are especially sensitive with regard to this idea. They particularly emphasize the need for a just system in order to avoid a withdrawal of solidarity on the part of the younger generations.

Although presently, there is no sound evidence for such a withdrawal, the political sensitivity with regard to this issue points to the need for an intensified exchange about the normative foundations of welfare arrangements and their role in the context of social integration. While solidarity and justice often refer to different dimensions, the analysis indicates that there are areas in which they overlap. In order to fully grasp the problems of injustice within the pension system and the erosion of solidarity between the generations, it seems adequate to consult both the justice and the solidarity perspective. Despite the general perception of a disciplinary divide, both perspectives should rather be regarded as complementary, and they might be able to integrate some of the others' insights into their own disciplinary horizon. Normative theory, for instance, could question the rigidity of their assumptions about the rationality and self-sufficiency of human nature. In contrast, sociology might be criticized for often leaving aside those normative considerations that go beyond personal experience. Social integration needs to be regarded from both perspectives, as our analysis of the link between intergenerational solidarity and justice has shown with regard to the pension system.

References

Aristotle (1980), *The Nicomachean Ethics* (Oxford: Oxford University Press).

Attias-Donfut, C. and Arber, S. (2000), "Equity and Solidarity across the Generations" in *The Myth of Generational Conflict. The Family and State in Ageing Societies.* Arber, S. and Attias-Donfut, C. (eds) (London, New York: Routledge), 1–21.

Baurmann, M. (1999), "Durkheims individualistische Theorie der Arbeitsteilung" in *Soziale Integration.* Friedrichs, J. and Jagodzinski, W. (eds) (KZfSS-Sonderheft. Opladen: Westdeutscher Verlag), 85–114.

Bayertz, K. (1998), "Begriff und Problem der Solidarität" in *Solidarität. Begriff und Problem.* Bayertz, K. (ed.) (Frankfurt/M.: Suhrkamp), 11–35.

Bertram, H. (1992), "Moralische Sozialisation" in *Handbuch der Sozialisationsforschung 2.* Hurrelmann, K. (ed.) (Frankfurt/M.: Suhrkamp), 717–744.

Bierhoff, H.W. and Küpper, B. (1998), "Sozialpsychologie der Solidarität" in *Solidarität. Begriff und Problem.* Bayertz, K. (ed.) (Frankfurt/M.: Suhrkamp), 263–196.

Bonoli, G. (1997), "Classifying Welfare States: A Two-Dimension Approach", *Journal of Social Policy*, **26**, 351–327. [DOI: 10.1017/S0047279497005059]

Colby, A. and Kohlberg, L. (1986), "Das moralische Urteil: Der kognitionszentrierte entwicklungspsychologische Ansatz" in *Gesellschaftlicher Zwang und moralische Autonomie.* Bertram, H. (ed.) (Frankfurt/M.: Suhrkamp), 130–162.

Dallinger, U. and Liebig, S. (2004), "Gerechtigkeit zwischen den Generationen in der wohlfahrtsstaatlichen Alterssicherung" in *Verteilungsprobleme und Gerechtigkeit in modernen Gesellschaften.* Liebig, S., Lengfeld, H. and Mau, S. (eds) (Frankfurt, New York: Campus), 97–132.

Durkheim, E. (1912), *Les formes elémentaires de la vie religieuse* (Paris: Librairie Félix Alcan).

Durkheim, E. (1999 [1893]), *Über soziale Arbeitsteilung* (Frankfurt/M.: Suhrkamp).

Engelhardt, H.T., Jr (1998), "Solidarität: Postmoderne Perspektiven" in *Solidarität. Begriff und Problem.* Bayertz, K. (ed.) (Frankfurt/M.: Suhrkamp), 430–452.

Eurobarometer 56 (2001), "Public Opinion in the European Union" (Brussels: European Commission).

Folger, R. (1984), "Emerging Issues in the Social Psychology of Justice" in *The Sense of Injustice*. Folger, R. (ed.) (New York: Plenum Publishing), 3−24.

Hamann, S., Karl, A. and Ulrich, C.G. (2001), *Entsolidarisierung? Leistungen für Arbeitslose im Urteil von Erwerbstätigen* (Frankfurt/M.: Campus).

Hinrichs, K. (1994), "Restrukturierung der Sozialpolitik?", "Das Beispiel der Gesundheitspolitik" in *Grenzen des Sozialversicherungsstaates. Leviathan Sonderheft 14*. Riedmüller, B. and Olk, T. (eds) (Opladen: Westdeutscher Verlag), 119−145.

Hobbes, T. (1998 [1651]), *Leviathan* (Oxford: Oxford University Press).

Hoffman, M.L. (1990), "Empathy and Justice Motivation", *Motivation and Emotion*, **4**, 151−172. [DOI: 10.1007/BF00991641]

Hondrich, K.-O. and Koch-Arzberger, C. (1992), *Solidarität in der modernen Gesellschaft* (Frankfurt/M.: Fischer).

Honneth, A. (2000), *Das Andere der Gerechtigkeit. Aufsätze zur praktischen Philosophie* (Frankfurt/M.: Suhrkamp).

Honneth, A., ed. (1995), *Kommunitarismus. Eine Debatte über die moralischen Grundlagen moderner Gesellschaften* (Frankfurt/M.: Campus).

Johnson, P., Conrad, C. and Thompson, D. (1989), "Introduction" in *Workers Versus Pensioners: Intergenerational Justice in an Ageing World*. Johnson, P., Conrad, C. and Thompson, D. (eds) (Manchester, New York: Manchester University Press), 1−16.

Kaufmann, F.-X. (1984), "Solidarität als Steuerungsform—Erklärungsansätze bei Adam Smith" in *Markt, Staat und Solidarität bei Adam Smith*. Kaufmann, F.-X. and Krüsselberg, H.-G. (eds) (Frankfurt/M.: Campus), 158−184.

Keller, M. (1986), "Freundschaft und Moral: Zur Entwicklung der moralischen Sensibilität in Beziehungen" in *Gesellschaftlicher Zwang und moralische Autonomie*. Bertram, H. (ed.) (Frankfurt/M.: Suhrkamp), 195−223.

Kohl, J. (2003), "Breite Zustimmung für Beibehaltung des Renteniveaus auch bei *steigenden Beiträgen*". *Einstellungen zur Altersicherung im europäischen Vergleich*. Informationsdienst Soziale Indikatoren (ISI) *29*, 1-5.

Kohli, M. (1999), "Private and Public Transfers between Generations: Linking the Family and the State", *European Societies*, **1**, 81−104.

Krettenauer, T. (1998), *Gerechtigkeit als Solidarität. Entwicklungsbedingungen sozialen Engagements im Jugendalter* (Weinheim: Deutscher Studien Verlag).

Levi, M. (1991), "Are there Limits to Rationality?" *Archives Europeénnes de Sociologie*, **31**, 130−141.

Levi, M. (1993), "The Construction of Consent: Administration, Compliance and Governability *Programm*", Working Paper No. 10, Research School of Social Science, Australian National University, Canberra.

Liebig, S. (2001), "Lessons from Philosophy? Interdisciplinary Justice Research and Two Classes of Justice Judgments", *Social Justice Research*, **14**, 265−287. [DOI: 10.1023/A%3A1014367907348]

Locke, J. (1976 [1690]), *The Second Treatise of Government (An Essay concerning the True Original, Extent and End of Civil Government) and a Letter Concerning Toleration* (Oxford: Blackwell).

Mau, S. (2003), *The Moral Economy of Welfare States, Britain and Germany Compared* (London, New York: Routledge).

Melden, A.S. (1977), *Rights and Persons* (Berkeley: University of California Press).

Montada, L. (1999), "Solidarität als Norm für Soziales Handeln", *Ethik und Sozialwissenschaften*, **10**, 221–223.

Montada, L. and Schneider, A. (1989), "Justice and Emotional Reactions to the Disadvantages", *Social Justice Research*, **3**, 313–344. [DOI: 10.1007/BF01048081]

Montada, L., Schmitt, M. and Dalbert, C. (1986), "Thinking about Justice and Dealing with One's Own Privileges: A Study of Existential Guilt" in *Justice in Social Relations*. Bierhoff, H.W., Cohen, R. and Greenberg, J. (eds) (New York: Plenum Publishing), 125–143.

Moody, H.R. (1988), "Generational Equity and Social Insurance", *Journal of Medicine and Philosophy*, **13**, 31–56. [PubMed 3283283]

Nullmeier, F. (2004), "Die politische Karriere des Begriffs "Generationengerechtigkeit" und seine wissenschaftliche Bedeutung", *Generationengerechtigkeit*, **4**, 3–9.

Offe, C. (1999), "How Can we Trust our Fellow Citizen?". in *Democracy and Trust*. Warren, M. (ed.) (Cambridge, UK: Cambridge University Press), 42–87.

Rawls, J. (1971), *A Theory of Justice* (Cambridge, MA: Harvard University Press).

Rinne, K. and Wagner, G. (1995), "Zufriedenheit mit dem sozialen Sicherungssystem und seiner *Finanzierung* in *Westdeutschland*", *Diskussionspapier 95-20* (Bochum: Ruhr Universität, Fakultät für Sozialwissenschaften).

Rothstein, B. (1998), *Just Institutions Matter* (Cambridge, UK: Cambridge University Press).

Rürup, B. (2002), "The German Pension System: Status Quo and Reform Options" in *Social Security Pension Reform in Europe*. Feldstein, M. and Siebert, H. (eds) (Chicago: University of Chicago Press), 137–163.

Schmähl, W. (2000), "Increasing Life Expectancy, Retirement Age and Pension Reform in the German Context", *Journal of Ageing and Social Policy*, **11**, 61–70. [DOI: 10.1300/J031v11n02_07]

Schmidt, M.G. (2003), *Political Institutions in the Federal Republic of Germany* (Oxford, New York: Oxford University Press).

Schmidt, V.A. (2000), "Values and Discourses in the Politics of Adjustment" in *Welfare and Work in the Open Economy. From Vulnerability to Competitiveness*. Scharpf, F.W. and Schmidt, V.A. (eds) (Oxford, New York: Oxford University Press), 229–309.

Taylor, C. (1995), *Philosophy and the Human Sciences* (Cambridge, UK: Cambridge University Press).

Thome, H. (1998), "Soziologie und Solidarität: Perspektiven für die empirische Forschung" in *Solidarität. Begriff und Problem*. Bayertz, K. (ed.) (Frankfurt/M.: Suhrkamp), 217–262.

Tönnies, F. (1935 [1887]), *Gemeinschaft und Gesellschaft: Grundbegriffe der reinen Soziologie* (Leipzig: Buske)

Van der Heijden, E.C.M., Nelissen, J.H.M. and Verbon, H.A.A. (1995), *Altruism and Fairness in a Public Pension System*, Center for Economic Research Discussion Paper No. 9537, Tillburg University.

Veall, R. (1986), "Public Pensions as Optimal Social Contracts", *Journal of Public Economics*, **31**, 237−251. [DOI: 10.1016/0047-2727%2886%2990020-4]

Zoll, R. (2000). *Was ist Solidarität heute?* (Frankfurt/M.: Suhrkamp).

PART II
Procedural Justice

Why Do People Care about Procedural Fairness? The Importance of Membership Monitoring

Celia M. Gonzalez
New York University, USA

Tom R. Tyler
New York University, USA

Procedural fairness has long been recognized as a key determinant of people's thoughts, feelings, and behaviors. In social spheres as diverse as the family, the work organization, and the legal arena, people react to how fairly they are treated. The effects of procedural fairness have been repeatedly demonstrated on a variety of meaningful outcomes (see Folger and Cropanzano, 1998; Tyler and Blader, 2000; Cohen-Charash and Spector, 2001; Colquitt et al., 2001), suggesting that group members' interest in matters of procedural fairness is both considerable and widespread. Our concern is not with the existence of procedural justice effects, but with understanding why such effects occur. In other words, our focus is on the psychological motives underlying this interest in procedural justice.

In this chapter we will highlight the role that people's motivation to clarify the state of their connection to an in-group has in driving their interest in knowing more about procedural fairness. The value of procedural fairness for providing insight into the quality of one's social relationships will be discussed. Examining the interface of these two factors, a framework for understanding the psychology of procedural fairness in the light of such motivations will be set forth. Further, the situational conditions that may elicit such concern as well as the individual differences that may predispose a greater interest in such information will be discussed.

Procedural Fairness in Social Life

Effects of Procedural Fairness

One common social experience is that of being affected by a decision made by another person. What factors shape people's responses in these situations? While there are surely many contextual parameters that influence the way an individual thinks about, feels about, and acts in response to, such exchanges, procedural fairness has consistently been shown to determine responses in a variety of domains. Procedural fairness has been shown to impact reactions to situations as diverse as those experienced in legal settings (e.g. Lind et al., 1980), in educational institutions (e.g. Tyler and Caine, 1981), in interactions with co-workers (e.g. Folger and Konovsky, 1989), and in dealing with the law enforcement authorities (e.g. Tyler, 1990). A good deal of research had demonstrated that procedural fairness influences the intra-psychic and interpersonal responses of those on the receiving end of the decision-making processes. What is the nature and the scope of these effects?

The receipt of fair or unfair procedures exerts a strong impact on the recipient. So much so, that the experience of unfairness has been proclaimed to be one of the most affectively evocative experiences in social life (e.g. Miller, 2002). In general, negative affective states are elicited as a consequence of, or in reaction to, unfair procedures, and positive affective states are brought on by fair procedures (e.g. Scherer, 1997; Mikula, Scherer and Athenstaedt, 1998; Hafer and Correy, 1999; Weiss, Suckow and Cropanzano, 1999; Cropanzano et al., 2000). Both global mood states and specific constellations of positive and negative emotions are aroused by issues of procedural fairness.

Procedural fairness also affects people's attitudes about the arenas in which the procedures were enacted. Evaluations of decision-makers, such as those involving their perceived legitimacy (e.g. Tyler, 1990), are affected by procedural fairness. But also attitudes toward the group in which procedures are enacted are affected by the quality of these procedures. For instance, job satisfaction (e.g. Tyler and Blader, 2000), and the intention to stay within or to leave the group (e.g. Donovan, Drasgow and Munson, 1998) are all influenced by procedural fairness.

The effects of procedural fairness are not limited to feeling-based and attitudinal responses. That is, they are not confined within the mind of the recipient of the procedures. Rather, they also translate into the way that people behave. Issues of procedural fairness shape actions as multiply determined as those contributing to job performance (Konovsky and Cropanzano, 1990) and extra role behavior (Moorman, 1991). Even the inclination to engage in destructive behaviors, such as workplace theft, is well predicted by the receipt of fair or unfair procedures in the workplace (Skarlicki and Folger, 1997).

As proposed by Brockner and colleagues (Brockner, Ackerman and Fairchild, 2001), we can approach identifying the factors underlying an interest in procedural fairness by focusing our attention on the conditions under which procedural fairness effects are strong versus the conditions under which such effects are minimal or nonexistent. To account for the various circumstances in which the influence of procedural fairness is strong in nature or more limited, there are several theoretical frameworks that speak to the factors motivating an interest in procedural fairness. Though there are a number of interesting perspectives regarding the psychological foundations of procedural fairness concerns, we will center our discussion on those that have focused empirically on the examination of such differences in effects.

When are Procedural Fairness Effects Most Pronounced, and Why

A number of models have been put forth which speak to the motives underlying an interest in procedural fairness. At the inception of research in this area, procedural fairness was conceived of as a means of securing fair (i.e. equitable) outcomes (Walster, Bercheid and Walster, 1973; Thibaut and Walker, 1975). These theorists argued that procedural fairness was meaningful to individuals in conflict situations because of their underlying interest minimizing the likelihood of being taken advantage of and maximizing the likelihood of attaining desirable or fair outcomes. A primary focus of this work was on the fairness of opportunities for voice provision, as through this type of channel one could provide input into the decision-making process.

When Leventhal (1980) considered processes such as bias suppression and correctability, the decision-making procedures that were thought to fall under the rubric of procedural fairness were extended beyond voice procedures. Still though, concerns for resource preservation and acquisition were thought to be the key factors inspiring interest in procedural fairness. These resource-focused orientations asserted the importance of procedural fairness and built a solid foundation for considering procedural fairness as a unique dimension of people's justice concerns. Several other frameworks for understanding interest in procedural fairness have been introduced to the literature in more recent years.

One common finding in justice research is that affect associated with experiencing or not experiencing procedural fairness is stronger when the procedure leads to an undesirable outcome. When the end result of the procedures used is desirable, the fairness of the procedures used to reach that outcome exerts less of an influence on what are typically quite positive reactions to those making the decision (Brockner and Wiesenfeld, 1996). However, when an undesirable outcome is reached, procedural fairness information is relied upon to a greater degree when reacting to the decision-maker, the group in which the decision was made, and various other facets of the social situation.

Why might this be? To account for these findings, Brockner and Wiesenfeld (1996) postulated the existence of a sense-making mechanism. For most people receiving an undesirable outcome, especially in the context of a valued social group, is an unwelcome surprise. Because of the unexpected and unwanted nature of such an event, confusion ensues, and greater information processing is evoked in response. This desire to further delve into the available information leads to a more thorough consideration of the otherwise underutilized information regarding procedural fairness.

With a focus on the information processing and cognitive mechanisms at work when making use of fairness related information, uncertainty management models present a broader but related framework for understanding the reasons when and why people are affected by issues of fairness. Based on the idea that the possibility of exploitation is inherent in group membership (e.g. Lind, 1995), the uncertainty management perspective (and its predecessor fairness heuristic theory), focuses on understanding procedural fairness as it functions to resolve uncertainty in social situations (Lind and Van den Bos, 2002; Van den Bos, 2001; Van den Bos and Lind, 2002). From this perspective, people are more inclined to rely upon fairness information in general, and procedural fairness in particular, when they are lacking information about, or are uncertain about, the parameters of a given situation. The heuristic function of fairness information has been emphasized, as it can be used to 'fill in the gaps,' and can serve as the basis for other inferences, when alternative sources of information are inadequate or altogether lacking.

As evidence for this perspective, and for the functional utility of fairness for resolving uncertainty, variations in fairness more strongly affect other judgments when operating with limited information directly relating to these other judgments, or when needing to make a snap judgment. For instance, procedural fairness can substitute for knowing whether or not someone is trustworthy (Van den Bos, Wilke and Lind, 1998), for knowing whether or not an outcome is fair or desirable (Van den Bos et al., 1998), or for knowing what other people received in similar circumstances (Van den Bos et al., 1997). In addition, after focusing on even general issues of uncertainty, the effects of fairness are stronger than they are otherwise (Van den Bos and Miedema, 2000; Van den Bos, 2001; Van den Bos et al., 2005).

While it has been demonstrated that issues of procedural fairness exert a stronger influence on judgments under conditions of uncertainty than when all necessary information is readily available, uncertainty management frameworks do not speak to the issue of *why* procedural fairness information, over other types of information, would be sought to resolve these uncertainties. Without referring to other theoretical frameworks, what precisely it is about procedural fairness that makes it useful under conditions of uncertainty remains unclear. For an understanding of why people care about issues of procedural fairness, and an explication of the characteristics of procedural fairness that lend it distinct significance in the mind of recipients, we can look to a different set of models.

Relational models of procedural justice (Lind and Tyler, 1988; Tyler and Lind, 1992; Tyler and Blader, 2003) argue that people can discern the state of their connection to an organization through the fairness of the decision-making procedures used by a representative of that organization in the course of an interaction. From this perspective, the decision-making procedures enacted by a group representative provide the group member with information about his or her relationship to the group at large. The receipt of fair procedures indicates that the group values the group member, whereas the receipt of unfair procedures indicates that the group does not.

What evidence is there supporting this framework? Indeed, procedural fairness effects are particularly pronounced for those who are more invested in group membership and diminished for those who place little importance on the group in which the procedures are enacted. Reactions are stronger when fair or unfair decision-making procedures are used by an in-group authority rather than an out-group authority (e.g. Smith et al., 1998; Tyler et al., 1998; Duck and Fielding, 2003). In addition to differences which hinge on the presence or absence of group membership, the *strength* of a group member's sense of connection to the group influences the magnitude of reactions to the procedures. For instance, greater in-group identification leads to more extreme reactions to incidents of procedural fairness or unfairness (e.g. Brockner, Tyler and Cooper-Schneider, 1992; Tyler and Degoey, 1995; Huo et al., 1996). Based on this work, it seems clear that there is at least some relationship between an interest in group membership and sensitivity to procedural fairness.

So far we have discussed three factors that affect the importance placed on procedural information. People are more affected by issues of procedural fairness when these procedures lead to negative or undesirable outcomes, when uncertainty about the social situation (or about other issues) is made salient, and when the recipient is more strongly invested in the group in which the procedures are enacted. In this chapter we will discuss a membership monitoring orientation to understanding procedural fairness. This approach incorporates insights derived from relational models of procedural fairness and an appreciation of the situational contingencies and epistemic motives put forward by uncertainty management models to understanding when and why people care about procedural fairness.

The Interface of Procedural Fairness Effects and Membership Monitoring

What do we mean by membership monitoring? When we talk about membership monitoring we are referring to a person's interest in the presence, duration, stability, or quality of their connection to an in-group, and/or to other in-group members. The groups that we belong to shape and define our identity (e.g. Tajfel and Turner, 1986; Hogg and Abrams, 1988), serve as the basis for self-esteem (e.g. Abrams and Hogg, 1988; Rubin and Hewstone, 1998), and aid in the procurement of valuable opportunities and resources (e.g. Caporael and Brewer, 1991; Brewer, 1997). Rooted in the notion that successfully constructing, maintaining, and regulating social connections is one of the most fundamental considerations of human existence (e.g. Baumeister and Leary, 1995; Deci and Ryan, 2000; Andersen and Chen, 2002), we argue that people are deeply driven to be aware of the state of their membership in groups.

There are many factors that may affect the desire to scrutinize the state of one's membership in a given group. The nature of one's membership in meaningful social groups, such as the family, peer groups, and the community, is highly dynamic and subject to change over time. These changes promote social uncertainty as positions, roles, and relationships to others, transform to accommodate these shifts in the arrangement of the social network. As such, people are motivated to scrutinize, clarify, and reassess the nature of their place within the group, and this is especially necessary when it seems as though the quality of the connection to the group is on the verge of changing dramatically.

It is fairly easy to think of detrimental events that would lead one to experience concern about the state of their membership. Threat of restructuring or downsizing may lead employees to wonder whether they are in danger of being pushed out of the organization, and cast doubt upon what had been perceived to be a stable employee-organization relationship. Receiving a negative performance evaluation or being passed over for a promotion may lead one to question the extent to which he or she is valued by the organization. When one is being excluded, losing recognition, or has other indications that social bonds are deteriorating, they should be more inclined to assess the state of their connections to others. This is consistent with other work (e.g. Gardner, Pickett and Brewer, 2000; Pickett, Gardner and Knowles, 2004) including that which serves as the foundation of, and articulates the specifications of, uncertainty management models (Lind, 2001).

However, with respect to any given group, the creation or maintenance of high levels of enmeshment and dependence may be undesirable for the individual (Snyder and Fromkin, 1980; Breakwell, 1986; Tajfel and Turner, 1986; Turner, 1987; Brewer, 1991). Furthermore, interest in assessing the state of one's connection to a social group may even be more prominent when this connection seems to be becoming stronger rather than weaker (e.g. Ruble, 1994; Ruble and Seidman, 1996). Some events, which are arguably beneficial in nature, may also evoke the impulse to examine the nature of one's connection to the organization more closely. Status assessment motives need not only be engaged when it seems as though one's social bonds are breaking. While the experience of beneficial events may not carry with it the immediate threat of expulsion from the group, it may still lead to enhanced membership scrutiny. We argue that the same motive to clarify one's connection to a given group can be catalyzed by the possibility of gaining entrance, advancing within the group, or otherwise receiving indications that the connection to the group is becoming stronger. When it seems as though one's connection to a group is dynamic and subject to change, either becoming stronger or weaker, the desire to assess one's place within that group should be heightened.

Changes in one's formal position within a group, or structural changes of the group itself, are likely sufficient to promote examination of one's relationship with other group members or one's connection to the group as a whole. But less formal events can also bring about similar reactions. For instance, being the last person picked to be involved in a particular project, or being invited to a party by a group of previously aloof co-workers, can evoke the same sort of membership related considerations.

Though certain experiences and social situations can contribute to this membership monitoring mechanism being more or less engaged, this does not mean that membership monitoring is entirely determined by the situation. There is also room for individual variation in this regard. Without much difficulty we can call to mind examples of individuals who seem to be membership monitors in overdrive. Even seemingly trivial interactions are remembered in detail. In the search for underlying motives and the meaning behind other group member's behaviors, memories of these interactions are examined for evidence of the nature of one's place within the group. Theories regarding the membership relevant implications of people's behaviors are examined, discarded, and reassessed. A given exchange can be the topic of analysis, rumination, and discussion with others for days. In stark contrast, others approach interactions with group members with relative indifference. Some people rarely appreciate the status implications of exchanges with fellow group members. If they do, the first available understanding of the event is sufficient and they do not engage in much beyond superficial processing of the status implications of the event. Some people are certainly less vigilant about monitoring their membership in a group than are other group members.

We have devoted a good deal of discussion to the situational influences on membership monitoring and to individual variations in the proclivity to monitor group membership. This should not be taken so as to suggest that these are wholly independent influences. Rather, we also acknowledge that some types of individuals may also be more readily susceptible to the influence of situations that would catalyze membership concerns, whereas others may be impervious to such matters. We argue that the drive to monitor the state of membership in a given group, whether evoked by situational cues, determined by individual differences, or shaped by the interaction between the two, will direct interest in procedural fairness due to the status relevance of this information.

Evidence for a Membership Monitoring Model of Procedural Fairness

Social life abounds with circumstances that can lead one to evaluate, or reevaluate, their connection to a social group. It seems reasonable to suggest that when in membership monitoring mode, people would exhibit greater sensitivity to information that can communicate the state of his or her connection to the group in question, relative to when curiosity about group membership has been satisfied. When monitoring one's membership in a given social group, status relevant information should be disproportionately extracted from interactions with other group members. Though each interpersonal and intragroup interaction is saturated with many complex pieces of social information, procedural fairness is one element of such experiences that is particularly rich with status relevant connotations.

The fairness of procedures enacted by a representative of an in-group can provide the recipient with a unique opportunity to gain insight into the state of his or her connection to the group as a whole. As such, we argue that when the motivation to clarify, scrutinize, or otherwise monitor the state of one's membership in a group is evoked, procedural fairness will be called upon in the service of resolving any ambiguities regarding the quality of one's connection to the group.

If we look to the existing literature on procedural fairness there are several lines of evidence that lend support to the assertion that people make use of procedural fairness information to monitor their membership in in-groups. Interactions with authorities can affirm or disaffirm one's status in that group (Tyler, Degoey and Smith, 1996; Tyler and Blader, 2000). When procedures are not informative of the state of one's membership in a group they exert less influence on judgments. For instance, when the individual enacting the procedures is an out-group member procedural fairness effects are minimized (Smith et al., 1998; Tyler et al., 1998; Duck and Fielding, 2003). When the decision maker is an in-group member, but is required to make use of fair or unfair procedures for reasons beyond his or her control, the influence of procedural fairness on the recipients' subsequent judgments is attenuated (Okimoto and Tyler, 2006).

In addition, people who chronically are not invested in group membership, or are low in identification with a given group, are typically less interested in the fairness of procedures used within that group (e.g. Brockner, Tyler and Cooper-Schneider, 1992; Tyler and Degoey, 1995; Huo et al., 1996).

There is also evidence for a membership monitoring approach to understanding procedural fairness when examining reactions to contextual or situational factors that alter the perceived state of one's connection to an in-group, however momentarily. In one example, people reported their thoughts about a group that was of great consequence. In this case it was their work organization. Compared to those employees who viewed membership in their work organization as stable and unchanging, employees in danger of being laid off from their workplace were more sensitive to the fairness of the decision-making procedures of workplace authorities (Brockner et al., 1990).

There may be a variety of explanations for the results of correlational studies such as the study discussed above. But a very similar pattern of response can be seen in experimental studies as well. For instance, in one such study (De Cremer, 2002) participants were assigned to groups and informed that this was on the basis of meaningful criteria, providing a basis of shared similarity amongst participants. They then were told that they were either peripheral group members (presumably experienced as a demotion in intragroup standing) or core group members (presumably confirming existing bases for membership). A representative of the group then treated participants either fairly or unfairly. Those for whom the connection to the group had challenged were more sensitive to the way they were treated by the representative than were those whose status was confirmed.

In a different set of experimental studies (Gonzalez and Tyler, 2006a), participants were made to feel like membership in a valued social group, their university, was threatened or assured. Under membership threat conditions they not only expressed more curiosity about their place within this valued group, and drew more membership related inferences based from the receipt of fair or unfair procedures from an in-group representative, but also used procedural fairness more when formulating social judgments. The extent to which status relevant information was extracted from the fairness of procedures at least partially determined the extent to which variations in procedural fairness affected social responses.

In contrast, other findings indicate that enhanced feelings of connection to, belonging in, or inclusion in, a group magnifies the influence of procedural fairness (Van Prooijen, van den Bos and Wilke, 2004). These conclusions are largely drawn from responses of participants assigned to novel or non-interacting arbitrarily-defined groups, in which there is likely little esprit de corps. While these findings may seem entirely at odds with those of De Cremer (2002) and Gonzalez and Tyler (2006a), they are fairly consistent when viewed from a membership monitoring orientation.

The present perspective provides one means of reconciling these seemingly conflicting findings by accounting for the influence of current feelings about group membership *in the context of* one's existing connection to the group. Contrary to the position that either the experience of social bonds strengthening or weakening unilaterally facilitates interest in procedural fairness, we argue that a *disruption* in regards to the state of one's existing relationship to a group, be it in a positive or negative direction, prompts enhanced reliance on procedural fairness information, as this information can be used to clarify such matters.

Evidence for a membership monitoring approach is more directly gained by recent research by Gonzalez and Tyler (2006b). In this series of studies participants' pre-existing connection to an in-group were either measured or manipulated. Participants were then induced to feel as though their connection to the group was weak or strong. For those who were initially deeply invested in group membership, experiencing the sense that membership in the group was threatened led to greater interest in issues of procedural fairness. However, it did not for those who were disinvested in group membership, or made to adopt more of an independent orientation to group membership. The effects of procedural fairness, instead of becoming weaker, were sometimes even more pronounced when made to feel as though they were becoming closer to the group. This interest in procedural fairness was indicated by the amount of time spent attending to procedural fairness information as well as the extent to which this information was reflected in judgments about, and evaluations of, their experience. When participants' current feelings about their connection to the group were in direct conflict with the nature of their history with the group, this heightened the desire to clarify their intragroup status, and procedural fairness information was recruited to this end. Complimenting this work nicely, research by Van Prooijen and colleagues (Van Prooijen, Van den Bos and Wilke, 2002) demonstrates that the effects of procedural fairness are particularly strong when issues of social status have been made salient.

There is some evidence in the literature supporting a membership monitoring approach to understanding procedural fairness. Adopting such an orientation opens up a variety of opportunities for exploring the conditions under which procedural fairness is the most meaningful to individuals.

Situational Factors Shaping Membership Monitoring

As discussed, there are innumerable situational factors that can increase interest in assessing, or reassessing, one's place within the group. The influence of procedural fairness can be curtailed or can flourish depending on the conditions at hand. Existing literature indicates that whether or not the procedures lead to a valuable outcome, whether the decision maker is or is not trusted, and whether these processes take place in an in-group or out-group, all change the nature of procedural fairness effects. A membership monitoring approach suggests a variety of other situational contexts that could shape the importance placed on issues of procedural fairness.

Changes in intragroup dynamics, such as those brought on by transitions in leadership, shifting patterns of social alliances, and incorporation of new members or departure of previous members, can cause ripples in the social fabric of the group that reach beyond those whose actions initiated the change. For instance, in a work organization, events such as mergers, promotions, transfers, and changes in the composition of work groups, all contribute to the almost constant need to reassess one's standing in their work organization. In social situations in which the quality of group membership is subject to change rather than fixed, and intragroup standing is fluid rather than static, occurrences that may catalyze a reexamination of one's relation to fellow group members are more frequently encountered. An interest in procedural fairness should be encouraged by conditions such as these, in that they necessitate the assessment and the negotiation of group membership.

Other theoretical models also predict that when social changes imply that one's connection to an in-group is becoming weaker, procedural fairness will be more impactful than when one's connection to a group is stable. A membership monitoring approach further posits that interest in procedural fairness will also be heightened under circumstances in which it seems that one's connection to a group may be becoming stronger. We will discuss two examples of situationally located events which, from this perspective but not others, would be expected to affect the extent to which membership monitoring mechanisms are engaged, and shape procedural fairness effects.

Potential Entrance

When might one be more inclined to assess the quality and nature of their connection to a given group? Arguably, one of the most critical times to do so would be when deciding whether or not to join a group. Clearly people belong to at least some groups in which there is little or no choice about accepting or declining the opportunity to enter. Membership in groups such as females, adolescents, or Caucasians, are all examples of ascribed group memberships. However a great number of our group memberships are (or at least were at the inception) volitional in nature. These groups vary in importance, and are relevant to many disparate domains of social life.

Becoming a member of some types of group may require little consideration, such as when deciding which gym or which knitting circle to join. However, when people think about joining other types of groups, such as choosing which college to attend or which job to take, the decision making process is likely to be more complicated and seriously undertaken. When contemplating entrance to important social groups such as universities and work organizations, people are highly motivated to consider what they think their place within that group would be. When it comes time to make such a choice, particularly when selecting between multiple options, people often agonize about which group will best meet their needs. Determining which group one will fit in best with, will be treated well in, and will be able to excel within, is no easy task. By virtue of not yet being a member, one has limited experience with these groups, and membership related judgments are speculative in nature.

Even though in this case membership is anticipatory or prospective, one's connecting to the group is potentially changing and becoming stronger. As such, procedural fairness should exert a strong effect on what feels like a momentous decision. We argue that elements of procedural fairness embedded within interactions with group members or representatives of such a group would be deeply considered as the basis for membership-related forecasts.

Promotion and Advancement

Another circumstance in which a membership monitoring approach might lead to counterintuitive predictions is when considering advancement within a group. As discussed previously, several other perspectives advise that procedural fairness is most important when negative outcomes are received or when one's connection to a group seems to be waning. By allowing for the possibility that even upwards movement within a group can direct status assessment motives, it seems likely that promotions within an organization would also increase sensitivity to issues of procedural fairness.

Promotions in the workplace, and the responsibility and social adjustments associated with them, lead to the experience of anxiety (e.g. Campion, Lord and Pursell, 1981). Moving up the organization ladder can prompt questions such as "Why did they promote me—do they really respect me or were they required to place a woman in this position?" "How will the coworkers I left behind feel about me now that I am a supervisor?" "Will those in my new peer group ever really view me as an equal?" It is easy to imagine that those who have been recently promoted would be more interested in, and attentive to, the receipt of procedural fairness, than if their position within an organization had been stable.

A longitudinal study of the effects of promotion decisions on management professors who were being considered for tenure (Ambrose and Cropanzano, 2003) provides some indirect evidence to this effect. Under such circumstances we would expect the possibility or the experience of being promoted to strongly evoke the need to assess one's status and scrutinize one's relationship with others at the university. Shortly before the tenure decision was made, and shortly after tenure was granted, perceived fairness of procedures strongly shaped recipients' reactions such as commitment to the university and, conversely, turnover intentions. At these two time points, procedural fairness exerted greater influence on the criterion variables than did other forms of social information (such as distributive fairness).

Importantly, reactions of those promoted were also measured two years after the promotion decision was made. At this point, presumably recipients' place within the organization had stabilized, they had likely become acclimated to this promoted position, and as such the need to monitor membership should have subsided. The impact of procedural fairness was significantly weaker at this point in time than it had been when status assessment was an imperative. This minimized effect of procedural fairness is consistent with expectations based on a membership monitoring model.

Individual Differences Shaping Membership Monitoring

Understanding the reasons why situational parameters affect interest in procedural fairness is important. In situations promoting membership monitoring, procedural fairness effects are greater. Based on an appreciation of the motivations underlying these situational influences, it is likely that certain individual difference characteristics also shape the extent to which membership monitoring mechanisms are engaged, and result in interest in procedural fairness.

Existing Evidence

Several lines of existing research which make use of an individual difference approach are relevant to the relationship between membership monitoring and procedural fairness. For instance, some work indicates that people with interdependent self-construal are more strongly affected by issues of procedural fairness (e.g. Brockner et al., 2005). This may be because people who conceive of themselves as interdependent are chronically more motivated to assess the state of their connections to others, and this leads to greater interest in procedural fairness. Derived from the same logic, those with a stronger need to belong may be more habitually interested in their place within a given in-group. It is indeed the case that the need to belong is positively related to responsiveness to the receipt of fair or unfair procedures (De Cremer and Blader, 2006).

There is some evidence suggesting that certain individual difference characteristics, which may be related to a proclivity toward membership monitoring, are also related to interest in procedural fairness. There are a number of other dimensions upon which individuals vary, which we expect to relate to membership monitoring, and thus an interest in procedural fairness. For illustrative purposes we will mention and discuss two such factors.

Contingencies of Self Worth

There are many potential sources from which people can base a sense of their personal value, their self-esteem, or their self-worth. And people can differ widely in the domains that are most relevant to their feelings about themselves. Research in this area has demonstrated that individuals reliably differ in their proclivity to derive a sense of self-worth from factors such as their appearance, their relationship with their family, or being a 'good person' (Crocker et al., 2003). One such basis of self-worth, contingency upon others' approval, is conceptualized as the extent to which self-esteem is determined by whether others hold the individual in high or low regard (Crocker et al., 2003; Park, Crocker and Mickelson, 2005).

Individuals vary in the degree to which they are affected by what others think of them. How might this individual difference characteristic play out in the intragroup context? It seems likely that group members for whom self-worth is highly contingent on approval from others (relative to those whose self-worth is less contingent on this factor) would be more concerned about their place within the in-group and more motivated to keep track of their intragroup status. This would also suggest that group members for whom self-esteem is highly contingent on approval from others would exhibit greater interest in procedural fairness. Lending some evidence to this idea, the tendency for self esteem to be unstable amplifies reactions to procedural fairness (e.g. De Cremer and Sedikides, 2005). However, from a membership monitoring perspective, we would argue that staking one's feelings of self-worth on approval from others *in particular* (over and above other contingencies of self-worth or self-esteem instability in general) should lead to interest in issues of procedural fairness.

Attachment to Groups

Individual differences regarding tendencies to monitor membership in specific groups, not just general personality characteristics, should also affect interest in procedural fairness. Consider the following example. People have mental models of the self as a member of a given group, and of that group as it relates to him or her. Research on attachment to groups has focused on two independent dimensions of patterns of attachment between one's self and a group (Smith, Murphy and Coats, 1999). Attachment anxiety is characterized by the perception of the self as unworthy of group membership and the group as potentially rejecting. An avoidant orientation toward a group would be reflected in perceptions of the self as independent of the group, and the group as undeserving of investment. If one is low on both dimensions, the self is viewed as secure in membership, and membership is valued.

These patterns of attachment may direct interest in group relevant information in different ways. To the extent that attachment anxiety fosters perceptions that group membership is valued but unstable, this should lead to greater desire to monitor group membership. We would argue that this then would be associated with more attention to the procedures enacted by in-group representatives. In contrast, avoidance seems to be associated with reduced interest in group membership. Thus, the impact of procedural fairness should be lesser with an avoidant orientation to group membership.

Insights Gained by Considering the Importance of Membership Monitoring

Features of the Membership Monitoring Model

Situational factors, one's orientation toward groups in general, and one's orientation to the particular group in question, can all contribute to the extent to which one is motivated to assess or monitor the state of his or her place within a group. This curiosity should evoke heightened sensitivity to status relevant information. Furthermore, from a membership monitoring perspective, this should be reflected in the desire to acquire, attention paid to, and processing of such information. Procedural fairness information is called upon in service of this clarification motive due to the status-implicative power of the receipt of fair or unfair procedures. When one is motivated to monitor their place within a group, procedures take on special importance.

Of course, issues of procedural fairness do not incessantly dominate group members' thoughts about intragroup situations. Relative indifference to procedural fairness may be demonstrated for a variety of reasons. Perhaps the state of one's group membership has been confirmed through some other source of information. Or perhaps concern about one's place in a given group is largely lacking. That is, interest in issues of procedural fairness should be lessened, or negligible, when membership monitoring drives are either mitigated or altogether absent. In addition, we would not expect membership monitoring motives to manifest themselves in attention paid to procedures if the status relevant inferences that could be drawn from procedural fairness have been constrained by other parameters of the situation. This understanding of the conditions that foster or curtail the impact of procedural fairness allows us to look at established findings in a new way.

Reconsidering Established Findings

Through the lens of a membership monitoring approach, we can think differently about the motivations underlying established procedural fairness effects. In one example of how an appreciation of membership monitoring motives can help extend our understanding of procedural fairness, let us consider the procedure by outcome interaction. Procedural fairness effects are often stronger when the procedures result in negative rather than positive outcomes. For instance, when one does not receive a raise while other co-workers do, or when one receives a speeding ticket while another commuter driving equally fast does not, people are especially concerned with the fairness of decision-making procedures used to reach this kind of outcome (for reviews see Brockner and Wiesenfeld, 1996; Tyler and Blader, 2000).

This may be due to the status relevant messages carried by the receipt of undesirable outcomes (Berger, Cohen and Zelditch, 1972; Homans, 1976). The receipt of an undesirable outcome can prompt one to question the state of their connection to the social group (e.g. the work organization or the local community), and may engage a status assessment mechanism. That is, it may be this motivation to monitor one's membership to the group that stimulates an interest in procedural fairness following the receipt of such an outcome. There are two interesting implications of adopting a membership monitoring understanding of this effect.

First, if indeed this procedure by outcome interaction is brought about by the sense that the quality of membership is changing, assuaging these concerns would lead to the attenuation of this effect. That is, if one was assured that the quality of group membership was stable, even following the receipt of a negative outcome, procedural fairness effects may not be larger than following the receipt of a favorable outcome, as the need to monitor one's membership would be satisfied.

Second, the receipt of other types of outcomes that suggest that one's connection to the in-group is in a state of flux may also kindle increased interest in issues of procedural fairness. Perhaps being granted an outcome that surpasses expectations and precedents would also signal that one's connection to the group was becoming stronger. If so, this could engage the membership monitoring mechanism, and lead to greater interest in the fairness of the procedures producing that outcome.

In addition to contributing to our understanding of existing phenomena, adopting a membership monitoring approach may also allow us to ask new questions that warrant empirical investigation.

Conclusions

It is our hope that a consideration of the features and parameters of this membership monitoring approach opens up new and fruitful directions of research on procedural fairness. We have discussed several novel situations under which procedural fairness effect may be more pronounced (entrance to a group and promotion within a group). To compliment our understanding of the conditions under which procedural fairness effect may be more pronounced, adopting a membership monitoring approach also allows us to consider a host of new personality and individual difference factors that could shape interest in procedural fairness. We suggested that between-person variation in qualities related to membership monitoring motives (including approval-based contingencies of self-worth and styles of attachment to a group) should be related to interest in, or reactivity to, procedural fairness. This aspect of our approach has the potential to add to a growing body of literature that demonstrates that interest in procedural fairness can be influenced by recipients' individual difference characteristics.

The extent to which membership monitoring motives shape sensitivity to the receipt of fair or unfair procedures has been the primary focus of this chapter. While we cannot highlight the benefits of such an approach enough, this is not to say that perceptions of fairness or unfairness are unaffected by components of the membership monitoring process. Recent research has indicated that the extent to which a given procedure is viewed as more or less fair can be influenced by both fluctuations in feeling states (Van den Bos, 2003) and social concerns (Van Prooijen, Van den Bos and Wilke, 2005). Further, one's expectations and concern about his or her connections to others can affect perceptions of the way they are treated (e.g. Downey and Feldman, 1996). As such, it is likely that perceptions of procedures are also shaped by the factors that both engage, and contribute to, the membership monitoring process. With this in mind, how do these processes interact? When will group members be motivated to perceive procedures as accurately as possible, so as to gain an accurate understanding of their connection to an in-group, and when will their perceptions be biased in ego-serving or group-serving directions? Though a full discussion of these issues is beyond the scope of this chapter, certainly our understanding of the utility and operation of issues of fairness in the intragroup context would benefit greatly from a nuanced understanding of these complex processes.

In this chapter we have sought to build on previous conceptions of the factors underlying an interest in procedural fairness by advancing a membership monitoring model. In doing so, we can more precisely anticipate which individuals will care about procedural fairness, and can better understand the conditions under which interest in issues of procedural fairness will predominate. More importantly, however, a more complete appreciation of the reasons why people care about procedural fairness can be gained.

References

Abrams, D. and Hogg, M.A. (1988), "Comments on the Motivational Status of Self-Esteem in Social Identity and Intergroup Discrimination", *European Journal of Social Psychology*, **18**, 317–334.

Ambrose, M.L. and Cropanzano, R. (2003), "A Longitudinal Analysis of Organization Fairness: Examination of Reactions to Tenure and Promotion Decisions", *Journal of Applied Psychology*, **88**, 266–275. [DOI: 10.1037/0021-9010.88.2.266]

Andersen, S. and Chen, S. (2002), "The Relational Self: An Interpersonal Social-Cognitive Theory", *Psychological Review*, **109**, 619–645. [PubMed 12374322] [DOI: 10.1037/0033-295X.109.4.619]

Baumeister, R.F. and Leary, M.R. (1995), "The Need to Belong: Desire for Interpersonal Attachments as a Fundamental Human Motivation", *Psychological Bulletin*, **117**, 497–529. [PubMed 7777651] [DOI: 10.1037/0033-2909.117.3.497]

Berger, J., Cohen, B.P. and Zelditch, M., Jr (1972), "Status Characteristics and Social Interaction", *American Sociological Review*, **37**, 241–255. [DOI: 10.2307/2093465]

Breakwell, G.M. (1986), *Coping with Threatened Identities* (London: Methuen).

Brewer, M.B. (1991), "The Social Self: On Being the Same and Different at the Same Time", *Personality and Social Psychological Bulletin*, **17**, 4750–4782.

Brewer, M.B. (1997), "On the Social Origins of Human Nature" in *The Message of Social Psychology: Perspectives on Mind in Society*. McGarty, C. and Haslam, S.A. (eds) (Malden, MA: Blackwell Publishers), 54–62.

Brockner, J. and Wiesenfeld, B.M. (1996), "An Integrative Framework for Explaining Reactions to Decisions: Interactive Effects of Outcomes and Procedures", *Psychological Bulletin*, **120**, 189. [PubMed 8831296] [DOI: 10.1037/0033-2909.120.2.189]

Brockner, J., Ackerman, G. and Fairchild, G. (2001), "When do Elements of Procedural Fairness Make a Difference? A Classification of Moderating Differences" in *Advances in Organizational Justice*. Greenberg, J. and Cropanzano, R. (eds) (Stanford, CA: Stanford University Press), 179–212.

Brockner, J., De Cremer, D., Van den Bos, K. and Chen, Y.-R. (2005), "The Influence of Interdependent Self-Construal on Procedural Fairness", *Organizational Behavior and Human Decision Processes*, **96**, 155–167. [DOI: 10.1016/j.obhdp.2004.11.001]

Brockner, J., DeWitt, R.L., Grover, S. and Reed, T. (1990), "When it is Especially Important to Explain Why: Factors Affecting the Relationship between Managers' Explanations of a Layoff and Survivors' Reactions to the Layoff", *Journal of Experimental Social Psychology*, **26**, 389–407. [DOI: 10.1016/0022-1031%2890%2990065-T]

Brockner, J., Tyler, T.R. and Cooper-Schneider, R. (1992), "The Influence of Prior Commitment to an Institution on Reactions to Perceived Unfairness: The Higher They Are, the Harder They Fall", *Administrative Science Quarterly*, **37**, 241–261. [DOI: 10.2307/2393223]

Campion, M.A., Lord, R.G. and Pursell, E.D. (1981), "Individual and Organizational Correlates of Promotion Refusal", *Journal of Voacational Behavior*, **19**, 42–49. [DOI: 10.1016/0001-8791%2881%2990048-8]

Caporael, L.R. and Brewer, M.B. (1991), "Reviving Evolutionary Psychology: Biology Meets Society", *Journal of Social Issues*, **47**, 187–195.

Cohen-Charash, Y. and Spector, P.E. (2001), "The Role of Justice in Organizations: A Meta-Analysis", *Organizational Behavior and Human Decision Processes*, **86**, 278–321. [DOI: 10.1006/obhd.2001.2958]

Colquitt, J.A., Conlon, D.E., Wesson, M.J., Porter, C.O.L.H. and Ng, K.Y. (2001), "Justice at the Millennium: A Meta-Analytic Review of 25 years of Organizational Justice Research", *Journal of Applied Psychology*, **86**, 386–400. [DOI: 10.1037/0021-9010.86.3.386]

Crocker, J., Luhtanen, R.K., Cooper, M.L. and Bouvrette, A. (2003), "Contingencies of Self-Worth in College Students: Theory and Measurement", *Journal of Personality and Social Psychology*, **85**, 894–908. [PubMed 14599252] [DOI: 10.1037/0022-3514.85.5.894]

Cropanzano, R., Weiss, H.M., Suckow, K.J. and Grandey, A.A. (2000), "Doing Justice to Workplace Emotion" in *Emotions in the Workplace: Research, Theory, and Practice*. Ashkanasy, N.M. and Haertel, C.E. (eds) (Westport, CT: Greenwood Publishing Group, Inc.), 49–62.

De Cremer, D. (2002), "Respect and Cooperation in Social Dilemmas: The Importance of Feeling Included", *Personality and Social Psychology Bulletin*, **28**, 1335–1341. [DOI: 10.1177/014616702236830]

De Cremer, D. and Blader, S.L. (2006), "Why do People Care about Procedural Fairness? The Importance of Belongingness in Responding and Attending to Procedures", *European Journal of Social Psychology*, **36**, 211–228. [DOI: 10.1002/ejsp.290]

De Cremer, D. and Sedikides, C. (2005), "Self-uncertainty and Responsiveness to Procedural Justice", *Journal of Experimental Social Psychology*, **41**, 157–173. [DOI: 10.1016/j.jesp.2004.06.010]

Deci, E.L. and Ryan, R.M. (2000), "The 'What' and 'Why' of Goal Pursuits: Human Needs and the Self-Determination of Behavior", *Psychological Inquiry*, **11**, 227–268. [DOI: 10.1207/S15327965PLI1104_01]

Donovan, M.A., Drasgow, F. and Munson, L.J. (1998), "Perceptions of Fair Interpersonal Treatment Scale: Development and Validation of a Measure of Interpersonal Treatment in the Workplace", *Journal of Applied Psychology*, **83**, 683–692. [PubMed 9806012] [DOI: 10.1037/0021-9010.83.5.683]

Downey, G. and Feldman, S.I. (1996), "Implications of Rejection Sensitivity for Intimate Relationships", *Journal of Personality and Social Psychology*, **70**, 1327–1343. [PubMed 8667172] [DOI: 10.1037/0022-3514.70.6.1327]

Duck, J.M. and Fielding, K.S. (2003), "Leaders and their Treatment of Subgroups: Implicatiosn for Evaluations of the Leader and Superordinate Group", *European Journal of Social Psychology*, **33**, 387–401. [DOI: 10.1002/ejsp.153]

Folger, R. and Cropanzano, R. (1998), *Organizational Justice and Human Resource Management* (Thousand Oaks, CA: Sage).

Folger, R. and Konovsky, M.A. (1989), "Effects of Procedural and Distributive Justice on Reactions to Pay Raise Decisions", *Academy of Management Journal*, **32**, 115–130. [DOI: 10.2307/256422]

Gardner, W.L., Pickett, C.L. and Brewer, M.B. (2000), "Social Exclusion and Selective Memory: How the Need to Belong Influences Memory for Social Events", *Personality and Social Psychology Bulletin*, **26**, 486–496.

Gonzalez, C.M. and Tyler, T.R. (2006a). "Responses when Group Membership is Threatened: Greater Influence of Procedural Fairness with Greater Need for Status Assessment". Unpublished manuscript.

Gonzalez, C.M. and Tyler, T.R. (2006b). "The Interplay of Inclusionary Status Cues and Group Identification Shapes Sensitivity to Procedural Fairness". Unpublished manuscript.

Hafer, C.L. and Correy, B.L. (1999), "Mediators of the Relation between Beliefs in a Just World and Emotional Responses to Negative Outcomes", *Social Justice Research*, **12**, 189–204. [DOI: 10.1023/A%3A1022144317302]

Hogg, M.A. and Abrams, D. (1988), *Social Identifications: A Social Psychology of Intergroup Relations and Group Processes* (London, New York: Routledge).

Homans, G.C. (1976), "Commentary", *Advances in Experimental Social Psychology*, **9**, 231–244.

Huo, Y.J., Smith, H.J., Tyler, T.R. and Lind, E.A. (1996), "Superordinate Identification, Subgroup Identification and Justice Concerns: Is Separatism the Problem, is Assimilation the Answer", *Psychological Science*, **7**, 40–45. [DOI: 10.1111/j.1467-9280.1996.tb00664.x]

Konovsky, M.A. and Cropanzano, R. (1990), "Perceived Fairness of Employee Drug Testing as a Predictor of Employee Attitudes and Job Performance", *Journal of Applied Psychology*, **76**, 698–707. [DOI: 10.1037/0021-9010.76.5.698]

Leventhal, G.S. (1980), "What Should Be Done with Equity Theory? New Approaches to the Study of Fairness in Social Relationships" in *Social Exchange*. Gergen, K., Greenberg, M. and Wilis, R. (eds) (New York: Plenum Publishing), 27–55.

Lind, E.A. (1995), "Justice and Authority in Organizations" in *Politics, Justice, and Support: Managing the Social Climate of the Work Organization*. Cropanzano, R. and Kacmar, K.M. (eds) (Westport, CT: Quorum), 83–96.

Lind, E.A. (2001), "Fairness Heuristic Theory: Justice Judgments as Pivotal Cognitions in Organizational Relations" in *Advances in Organizational Behavior*.

Greenberg, J. and Cropanzano, R. (eds) (San Francisco, CA: New Lexington Press), 56–88.

Lind, E.A. and Tyler, T.R. (1988), *The Social Psychology of Procedural Justice* (New York: Plenum Publishing).

Lind, E.A. and Van den Bos, K. (2001), "When Fairness Works: Toward a General Theory of Uncertainty Management", in *Research in Organizational Behavior.* Staw, B.M. and Kramer, R.M. (eds) (Greenwich, CT: JAI Press), 181–223.

Lind, E.A., Kurtz, C.A., Musante, L., Walker, L. and Thibault, J. (1980), "Procedure and Outcome Effects on Reactions to Adjudicated Resolutions of Conflicts of Interest", *Journal of Personality and Social Psychology*, **39**, 643–653. [DOI: 10.1037/0022-3514.39.4.643]

Mikula, G., Scherer, K.R. and Athenstaedt, U. (1998), "The Role of Injustice in the Elicitation of Differential Emotional Reactions", *Personality and Social Psychology Bulletin*, **24**, 769–783. [DOI: 10.1177/0146167298247009]

Miller, D.T. (2002), "Disrespect and the Experience of Injustice", *Annual Review of Psychology*, **52**, 527–553. [DOI: 10.1146/annurev.psych.52.1.527]

Moorman, D.H. (1991), "Relationship between Organizational Justice and Organizational Citizenship Behaviors: Do Fairness Perceptions Influence Employee Citizenship?" *Journal of Applied Psychology*, **76**, 845–855. [DOI: 10.1037/0021-9010.76.6.845]

Okimoto, T.G. and Tyler, T.R. (2006). Is compensation enough?: Relational concerns in responding to unintended harm. Unpublished manuscript.

Park, L.E., Crocker, J. and Mickelson, K.D. (2005), "Attachment Styles and Contingencies of Self-Worth", *Personality and Social Psychology Bulletin*, **30**, 1243–1254. [DOI: 10.1177/0146167204264000]

Pickett, C.L., Gardner, W.L. and Knowles, M. (2004), "Getting a Cue: The Need to Belong and Enhanced Sensitivity to Social Cues", *Personality and Social Psychology Bulletin*, **30**, 1095–1107. [PubMed 15359014] [DOI: 10.1177/0146 167203262085]

Rubin, M. and Hewstone, M. (1998), "Social Identity Theory's Self-Esteem Hypothesis: A Review and some Suggestions for Clarification", *Personality and Social Psychology Review*, **2**, 40–62. [PubMed 15647150] [DOI: 10.1207/ s15327957pspr0201_3]

Ruble, D.N. (1994), "A Phase Model of Transitions: Cognitive and Motivational Consequences", *Advances in Experimental Social Psychology*, **26**, 163–214.

Ruble, D.N. and Seidman, E. (1996), "Social Transitions: Windows into Psychological Processes" in *Social Psychology: Handbook of Basic Principles*. Higgins, E.T. and Kruglanski, A.W. (eds) (New York: Guilford Publications), 830–856.

Scherer, K.R. (1997), "The Role of Culture in Emotion-Antecedent Appraisal", *Journal of Personality and Social Psychology*, **73**, 902–922. [DOI: 10.1037/0022-3514.73.5.902]

Skarlicki, D.P. and Folger, R. (1997), "Retaliation in the Workplace: The Roles of Distributive, Procedural, and Interactional Justice", *Journal of Applied Psychology*, **82**, 434–443. [DOI: 10.1037/0021-9010.82.3.434]

Smith, E.R., Murphy, J. and Coats, S. (1999), "Attachment to Groups: Theory and Management", *Journal of Personality and Social Psychology*, **77**, 94−110. [PubMed 10434410] [DOI: 10.1037/0022-3514.77.1.94]

Smith, H.J., Tyler, T.R., Huo, Y.J., Ortiz, D.J. and Lind, E.A. (1998), "The Self-Relevant Implications of the Group-Value Model: Group Membership, Self-Worth, and Treatment Quality", *Journal of Experimental Social Psychology*, **34**, 470−493. [DOI: 10.1006/jesp.1998.1360]

Snyder, C.R. and Fromkin, H.L. (1980), *Uniqueness: The Human Pursuit of Difference* (New York: Plenum Publishing).

Tajfel, H. and Turner, J.C. (1986), "The Social Identity Theory of Intergroup Behaviour" in *Psychology of Intergroup Relations*. Worchel, S. and Austin, W.G. (eds) (Chicago: Nelson-Hall), 7−24.

Thibaut, J. and Walker, L. (1975), *Procedural Justice: A Psychological Analysis* (Hillsdale, NJ: Erlbaum).

Turner, J.C. (1987), "A Self-Categorization Theory" in *Rediscovering the Social Group: A Self-Categorization Theory*. Turner, J.C., Hogg, M.A., Oakes, P.J., Reicher, S.D. and Wetherell, M.S. (eds) (Oxford: Basil Blackwell), 42−67.

Tyler, T.R. (1990), *Why People Obey the Law: Procedural Justice, Legitimacy, and Compliance* (New Haven: Yale University Press).

Tyler, T.R. and Blader, S.L. (2000), *Cooperation in Groups: Procedural Justice, Social Identity, and Behavioral Engagement* (Philadelphia: Taylor & Francis).

Tyler, T.R. and Blader, S.L. (2003), "The Group Engagement Model: Procedural Justice, Social Identity, and Cooperative Behavior", *Personality and Social Psychology Review*, **7**, 349−361. [PubMed 14633471] [DOI: 10.1207/S15327957PSPR0704_07]

Tyler, T.R. and Caine, A. (1981), "The Role of Distributional and Procedural Fairness in the Endorsement of Formal Leaders", *Journal of Personality and Social Psychology*, **41**, 642−655. [DOI: 10.1037/0022-3514.41.4.642]

Tyler, T.R. and Degoey, P. (1995), "Collective Restraint in Social Dilemmas: Procedural Justice and Social Identification Effects on Support for Authorities", *Journal of Personality and Social Psychology*, **69**, 482−497. [DOI: 10.1037/0022-3514.69.3.482]

Tyler, T.R. and Lind, E.A. (1992), "A Relational Model of Authority in Groups", *Advances in Experimental Social Psychology*, **25**, 115−191.

Tyler, T.R., Degoey, P. and Smith, H.J. (1996), "Understanding why the Justice of Group Procedures Matters", *Journal of Personality and Social Psychology*, **70**, 913−930. [DOI: 10.1037/0022-3514.70.5.913]

Tyler, T.R., Lind, E.A., Ohbuchi, K., Sugawara, I. and Huo, Y.J. (1998), "Conflict with Outsiders: Disputing within and across Cultural Boundaries", *Personality and Social Psychology Bulletin*, **25**, 115−191.

Van den Bos, K. (2001), "Uncertainty Management: The Influence of Human Uncertainty on Reactions to Perceived Fairness", *Journal of Personality and Social Psychology*, **80**, 931−941. [PubMed 11414375] [DOI: 10.1037/0022-3514.80.6.931]

Van den Bos, K. (2003), "On the Subjective Quality of Social Justice: The Role of Affect as Information in the Psychology of Justice Judgments", *Journal of*

Personality and Social Psychology, **85**, 482–498. [PubMed 14498784] [DOI: 10.1037/0022-3514.85.3.482]

Van den Bos, K. and Lind, E.A. (2002), "Uncertainty Management by Means of Fairness Judgments", *Advances in Experimental Social Psychology*, **34**, 1–60. [DOI: 10.1016/S0065-2601%2802%2980003-X]

Van den Bos, K. and Miedema, J. (2000), "Toward Understanding why Fairness Matters: The Influence of Mortality Salience on Reactions to Procedural Fairness", *Journal of Personality and Social Psychology*, **79**, 355–366. [PubMed 10981839] [DOI: 10.1037/0022-3514.79.3.355]

Van den Bos, K., Lind, E.A., Vermunt, R. and Wilke, H.A.M. (1997), "How do I Judge my Outcome when I do not Know the Outcome of Others? The Psychology of the Fair Process Effect", *Journal of Personality and Social Psychology*, **72**, 1034–1046. [PubMed 9150583] [DOI: 10.1037/0022-3514.72.5.1034]

Van den Bos, K., Poortvliet, P.M., Maas, M., Miedema, J. and van den Ham, E.-J. (2005), "An Inquiry Concerning the Principles of Cultural Norms and Values: The Impact of Uncertainty and Mortality Salience on Reactions to Violations and Bolstering World-Views", *Personality Journal of Experimental Social Psychology*, **41**, 91–113.

Van den Bos, K., Wilke, H.A.M. and Lind, E.A. (1998), "When do we Need Procedural Fairness? The Role of Trust in Authority", *Journal of Personality and Social Psychology*, **75**, 1449–1458. [DOI: 10.1037/0022-3514.75.6.1449]

Van den Bos, K., Wilke, H.A.M., Lind, E.A. and Vermunt, R. (1998), "Evaluating Outcomes by Means of the Fair Process Effect: Evidence for Different Processes in Fairness and Satisfaction Judgments", *Journal of Personality and Social Psychology*, **74**, 1493–1503. [DOI: 10.1037/0022-3514.74.6.1493]

Van Prooijen, J.-W., Van den Bos, K. and Wilke, H.A.M. (2002), "Procedural Justice and Status: Status Salience as Antecedent of Procedural Fairness Effects", *Journal of Personality and Social Psychology*, **83**, 1353–1361. [PubMed 12500817] [DOI: 10.1037/0022-3514.83.6.1353]

Van Prooijen, J.W., Van den Bos, K. and Wilke, H.A.M. (2004), "Group Belongingness and Procedural Justice: Social Inclusion and Exclusion by Peers Affects the Psychology of Voice", *Journal of Personality and Social Psychology*, **87**, 66–79. [PubMed 15250793] [DOI: 10.1037/0022-3514.87.1.66]

Van Prooijen, J.-W., Van den Bos, K. and Wilke, H.A.M. (2005), "Procedural Justice and intragroup Status: Knowing where we Stand in a Group Enhances Reactions to Procedures", *Journal of Experimental Social Psychology*, **41**, 664–676. [DOI: 10.1016/j.jesp.2004.12.003]

Walster, E., Bercheid, E. and Walster, G.W. (1973), "New Directions in Equity Research", *Journal of Personality and Social Psychology*, **25**, 151–176. [DOI: 10.1037/h0033967]

Weiss, H.M., Suckow, K. and Cropanzano, R. (1999), "Effects of Justice Conditions on Discrete Emotions", *Journal of Applied Psychology*, **84**, 786–794. [DOI: 10.1037/0021-9010.84.5.786]

Chapter 5

The Effects of Procedural Unfairness on Norm-Violating Behavior

Jacqueline Modde
Radboud University Nijmegen, The Netherlands

Riël Vermunt
University of Leiden, The Netherlands

Many studies have been conducted in various settings to examine effects of procedural fairness on peoples' cognitive, affective and behavioral reactions to decisions. A substantial amount of studies have paid attention to noncompliance with decisions made by authorities and norm-violating behavior as a reaction to unfavorable and/or unfair outcomes. In most of these studies, the moderating effect of procedural fairness was investigated in settings like the legal area (see also Fuller, 1969) and organizations. Most of these studies were surveys, whereas very few studies were conducted in the laboratory. In the legal area, Tyler (1984, 1990, 1994) has conducted several surveys in which he studied reactions of respondents who reported having some experience with legal authorities and found that procedural justice judgments influenced evaluations of authorities. Authorities who implemented unfair procedures were perceived as not measuring up to criteria of trustworthiness, respectfulness and/or neutrality. As a result they were perceived as less legitimate than authorities who implemented fair procedures. Perceived legitimacy influenced respondents' acceptance of decisions and their compliance with laws: the more an authority was seen as legitimate, the more people were willing to obey and comply. Lind et al. (1993) studied decisions made in federal court and found that procedural justice judgments correlated strongly with acceptance of the courts' decision. MacCoun et al. (1988) investigated litigants in cases involving automobile claims and found that judgments of procedural fairness correlated with intentions to accept or reject the arbitrator's decision. In Dutch research, van Schie and Wiegman (1995) investigated reactions of crime victims after experiences with police and court. Results of this study indicate that victims who perceived procedures implemented by police and court as unfair had higher intentions to break the law and had a more negative view of the judicial system than victims who felt that procedures had been fair. An indirect effect was found on self reports of actual offenses committed by respondents: perceived procedural unfairness correlated with a more negative view of the judicial system and this in turn influenced actual transgressions of the law. Similar results were obtained by Wemmers (1996) in a longitudinal study among victims of crime in the Netherlands. Although procedural fairness did not correlate directly with compliance with the law, it did influence satisfaction with performance of the judicial system, which in turn influences support for the system and sense of duty to obey the law. Actual transgressing behavior was correlated strongly with sense of duty and support (Wemmers, 1996). It can be concluded that procedural fairness fosters positive attitudes towards authorities and leads to more compliance with laws, while procedural unfairness diminishes satisfaction with the system and leads in the end to more breaches of the law.

The influence of procedural fairness was also examined in studies that were conducted in organizational settings. Greenberg (1994) found that clerical employees were more likely to accept a smoking ban when the ban was introduced in a procedural fair manner. He also found that turnover-intention and organizational commitment was influenced by procedural fairness, which was operationalized as information-thoroughness and social sensitivity from the management. Parks (1995) found that reactions of workers of various organizations that recently underwent significant changes were influenced by procedural fairness: procedural unfairness caused workers to make negative statements, shirk work and engage in behaviors like theft, accepting kickbacks and hostile behavior. Greenberg (1997) found in a study on the reactions of employees to a pay-cut that norm-violating, disruptive behavior (theft, sabotage) is more likely to occur when procedural justice is low, while more constructive ways of behavior in organizations can be promoted by implementing fair procedures. Thus, in several studies, procedural injustice increased behavior in organizations that can be described as noncompliance as well as anti-social, like employee theft, sabotage and active and passive forms of aggression (cf. Ciacalone and Greenberg, 1997). Skarlicki and Folger (1997) investigated the relationship between distributive justice, procedural justice, interactional justice and organizational retaliation behavior, which was defined as adverse reactions to perceived unfairness by disgruntled employees toward their employer, and includes several acts of sabotage and petty theft. They found that inequitable outcomes did not generate retaliation when either procedural or interactional fairness was high, i.e., a fair procedure or fair interpersonal treatment from authorities refrained employees from reacting with disruptive behavior towards the organization, even when obtained outcomes were judged to be unfair. Thus, procedural and/or interactional justice seem to compensate for distributive unfairness in some cases. Innes, Barling and Turner (2005) studied workplace aggression of employees with two jobs and different supervisors. In this within-person, between jobs design it was shown that situational factors like interactional justice and abusive supervision explained more variance than individual difference factors like self-esteem and history of aggression. However, in a study conducted by Dietz et al. (2003) negative effects of procedural unfairness on aggression in the workplace could not been shown. Aggression in the workplace was predicted by violent crime rates in the community in which the plant resided.

Some studies about effects of procedural fairness have been conducted in the laboratory. These studies focus on the occurrence of *resentment* (Folger et al., 1983; Taylor et al., 1987, Cropanzano and Folger, 1989), *satisfaction/discontent* (LaTour, 1978; Lind and Lissak, 1985, Folger and Martin, 1986) *intention to protest* (Greenberg, 1989; Vermunt et al., 1993), *intention to engage in action against a denying agent* (Greenberg, 1987, 1995) and *commitment to the decision made by the authority*

(Korsgaard, Schweiger and Sapienza, 1995; Sapienza and Korsgaard, 1996). In general, these studies show that procedural fairness diminishes negative reactions to inequitable outcomes and that negative reactions of the non-complying kind are utmost present when outcomes are unfair or unfavorable and procedural fairness is low.

Conclusions from Empirical Evidence

All studies conducted in the field or in the laboratory examine reactions to negative outcomes and the moderating effect of procedural justice on reactions to negative or inequitable outcomes. Greenberg (1990) and Greenberg and Scott (1996) for example argue that employee theft occurs as a reaction to inequity, either as a way to get restitution (and gain material benefits) or as a way to retaliate (harm the offender in some way). Greenberg and Scott claim that procedural aspects, in particular justification of inequitable or negative outcomes, and interpersonal sensitivity from the decision-maker towards those involved, prevent antisocial behavior as a reaction to *inequitable outcomes*. In other words, it seems that resentment, norm-violations and retaliation as a result of frustration about an outcome can be reduced substantially if procedural fairness is high. However, it is not yet demonstrated that procedural unfairness in itself will produce the same negative behavior as distributive unfairness. If the assumptions of the relational model of authority are correct, people should feel resentment when they are denied a fair procedure, and thresholds to engage in reprehensible conduct is likely to be lowered, even in the absence of an inequitable or unfavorable outcome. However, there are hardly any laboratory studies that focus on norm-violating behavior as a reaction to *procedural unfairness without the presence of an inequitable or unfavorable outcome*. Thus, a direct causal influence of procedural unfairness on norm-violating behavior remains yet to be demonstrated. Furthermore, the studies that link experiences of an unfair or unfavorable outcome in combination with procedural unfairness to norm-violating behavior (cf. Tyler, 1990) are correlational, with data gathered through self reports.

In summary, we may conclude that there is considerable evidence that the experience of procedural unfairness is linked with the occurrence of norm-violating behavior, but that a causal relationship between the experience of procedural unfairness and norm-violating behavior remains to be demonstrated. Accurate conclusions regarding a causal relationship between procedural unfairness, perceived legitimacy and norm-violating behavior, requires a study of this relationship in a controlled setting, preferably studying the noncompliant behavior itself rather than a self report of past or intended behavior. This is hardly ever done, because of obvious problems in operationalizations of norm-violating behavior: to elicit socially undesirable behavior in the laboratory is not easy and perhaps morally dubious. It is not surprising that most laboratory studies focus on resentment or protest behavior instead of norm-violating behavior. An exception can be made for the study by Greenberg (1993) who conducted a controlled laboratory setting with theft as a reaction to underpayment. This study falls in the category of studies that examine the moderating effect of procedural fairness on reactions to inequity. Participants in this study were promised 5 dollar to perform a clerical task. After performing the task, half of the participants were told that they would be paid only $3 (i.e. they were underpaid). The remaining participants were paid $5, which was considered an equitable payment. The experimenter systematically manipulated the quality of the justification used as the basis for establishing this rate of pay. The decision was either justified by referring to directly acquired information from an identified expert source, which was independently double checked, or based upon information from hearsay, from an unidentified person of unknown expertise. Furthermore, the interpersonal sensitivity shown to participants with respect to their pay-rate was systematically varied. High levels of interpersonal sensitivity were characterized by expressing concern for participants, while low levels expressed disinterest with participants' outcomes. After manipulation, participants were invited to take the amount of money they were supposed to take from a hand-full of bills and coins left on a desk, and leave the rest. Participants were thus given the opportunity to steal money from the experimenter. Greenberg investigated the moderating effects of validity of information and interpersonal sensitivity on participants' inclination to steal money (amounts in excess of $3 were considered theft). Interpersonal sensitivity and proper justification (validity of information) were considered operationalizations of procedural fairness. Greenberg found indeed that theft was greatest in the low valid information/low sensitivity condition. In other words, when underpayment was not justified properly and the experimenter's decision to underpay was communicated in an insensitive way, theft was greater than when underpayment was justified properly and interpersonal sensitivity in communicating the decision was high. Greenberg thus studied norm-violating behavior *as a reaction to distributive injustice*, while proper justification of the inequitable payment diminished the stealing behavior. In other words, elements of procedural justice (adequate explanation and interpersonal sensitivity) moderated the reaction to *distributive* injustice.

As stated before, the central assumption of the relational model of procedural fairness, however, is that fair procedures have intrinsic value to people, regardless of outcomes. The question remains whether being subjected to an unfair procedure elicits norm-violating behavior, regardless of the outcome, i.e. whether violations of the more formal criteria for fair procedures will cause people to retaliate against the authority in a norm-violating manner. Such an effect should be demonstrated in a setting in which the outcome is not influenced by the nature of the implemented procedure. We argue that procedural injustice per se should have an effect on the attitude of participants towards the experimenter, their willingness to comply to a decision made by the experimenter and their propensity to engage in norm-violating behavior when given the opportunity to do so. To demonstrate this, it is necessary to separate procedure and outcome, i.e. the choice for a particular procedure should not influence the outcome-expectation of participants.

The Experiment

In this study we examine the effects of procedural injustice per se by disengaging the procedure from the outcome, so participants experienced either a fair or an unfair procedure, but the choice for either procedure made no difference in relation to the outcome participants expected and received. Regardless of procedure, all participants received the same outcome. The influence of procedural unfairness on norm-violating behavior, in this study operationalized as committing fraud (stealing), was studied in the controlled setting of a laboratory in order to establish a causal relationship between experience of procedural unfairness and norm-violating behavior.

To state hypotheses about the effects of unfair procedure on norm violation we refer to the group-value model (Lind and Tyler, 1988) as well as to the refined version of this model, the relational model of authority (Tyler and Lind, 1992). Implementation of an unfair procedure by an authority will lead to decreased legitimacy of that authority and this will undermine the motivation to comply and obey. In this experiment, the experimenter is, in the eyes of the participants participating in this experiment, in charge of the procedure and makes the decisions. Thus, we assume that an unfair procedure will diminish legitimacy of the experimenter. Furthermore, we assume that decreased legitimacy of the experimenter's authority will reduce the motivation to comply with decisions and feelings of moral obligation (Tyler, 1990). Moreover, based on General Strain theory (Agnew and Raskin White, 1992) we expect that participants who are deprived of a fair procedure will experience negative emotions (Frijda, Kuipers and Ter Schure, 1989) and will engage in norm-violating behavior as a form of corrective action more often than participants who have been granted a fair procedure.

By also varying outcome-importance we were able to examine limits of the procedural justice effect. Tyler (1990) states, that procedural unfairness is only effective in situations where outcome importance is high. Acceptance of a negative outcome is no longer determined largely by fairness of the procedure in such cases. One could argue that when the outcome is important, for example, when large amounts of money are at stake, a fair procedure will not be effective anymore to refrain people from undertaking corrective action, i.e. stealing. Thus, even when the procedure is fair, being withheld from a desirable outcome may elicit stealing behavior in participants, despite the fair procedure.

Summarizing, we predict that participants in the unfair procedure condition will steal more money (Hypothesis 1a) and more frequently (Hypothesis 1b) than participants in the fair procedure condition and that high outcome importance will elicit more stealing behavior than low outcome importance (Hypothesis 2).

Method

Participants
Participants were 145 freshman students at Leiden University, who volunteered to participate in this study. The students were recruited at the History department and the department of Medicine. As part of the recruitment procedure they were promised two euro for their participation in the experiment, which would take them approximately 15 minutes.

Design
A 2 × 2 factorial design was used in which the independent variables were Procedure (Unfair, Fair) and Outcome Importance (a bonus of 2 or 10 euro which participants

could earn on top of the 2 euro they were promised at the recruitment). Procedural fairness was operationalized as consistency over time (cf. Leventhal, 1980). Research (Greenberg, 1986, van den Bos, Vermunt and Wilke, 1996) has indicated that once people expect a procedure, deviation from the expected procedure will lead to a reduction in perceived procedural fairness. People will evaluate procedural inconsistency as unfair, because the authority takes the liberty to break an agreement, which is an indication of lack of respect for those involved. Violation of the consistency rule is expected to elicit negative procedural fairness judgments.

We subjected half of the participants to a consistent procedure and the other half to an inconsistent procedure. The dependent variables were perceived legitimacy of the experimenter (operationalized as trustworthiness, politeness and suitability for his task), mood (experience of negative emotions by participants) and norm violating behavior, operationalized as the amount of money participants took in excess of the amount they were allowed to take.

Procedure
Participants were scheduled six at a time and were placed in separate cubicles behind a computer screen and a keyboard. They were requested to perform a task which was described as a recently developed estimation test. It was communicated to the participants that the experimenter's goal was to validate the test and to investigate the reactions this test would elicit in people. The test was presented on the computer screen; participants were told that their computers were connected to the main computer in the adjacent room and that the experimenter communicated with them by means of the computer network. Actually, all communication was preprogrammed. The estimation test consisted of a series of a rectangular figure containing black and white squares which was shown on the screen for five seconds. The participants' task was to estimate the amount of black squares (cf. De Gilder and Wilke, 1990). There were four subtests, each consisting of five rectangular figures. Participants were told that after completion of these four subtests a second task would be administered which would only take about five minutes. They learned that for participating in this second part of the experiment, they would receive a bonus of 2 euro in the condition of low outcome importance or 10 euro in the condition of high outcome importance. The rationale was given that this second part of the experiment was the most important part and that a relatively large amount of extra money would be paid to motivate participants to make a good effort on the test in the first part of the experiment, because only participants with a sufficient grade on subtest four in the first part would be allowed to participate in the second part.

Participants in the Unfair Procedure condition were told that *everyone with a sufficient grade on subtest four* would be allowed to participate in the second part of the experiment and earn the bonus, whereas participants in the Fair Procedure condition were told that participation in the second part would be determined by *a lottery among those with a sufficient grade on subtest four*. Participants were informed that their grades would be determined by comparing their estimations to the actual amount of black squares per trial, and averaging the deviations per subtest (five trials). All participants received bogus feedback about their grades on the subtests; they all learned that the criterion for a sufficient grade was a maximum difference of 10 between the actual amount of black squares and the participant's estimate of the amount of black squares. Participants learned that their first and second grade were considerably above the criterion (16 and 14, respectively) their third just met the criterion (10) and the fourth one point below the criterion (9). The purpose of this feedback was to give participants the impression that their performance was not entirely a matter of chance, because they were improving, but to keep them ignorant about their chances to participate in the second part. Due to the ambiguity of the task participants had to form their expectations completely on the feedback they received from the experimenter. After each subtest participants answered a few questions and, after some time during which the experimenter was "correcting" the test, they received their grades on the computer screen. After the completion of four subtests participants in the Fair Procedure condition received a message, telling them that they would be entering the lottery which would determine whether or not they would participate in Part 2. Participants in the Unfair Procedure condition received a message from the experimenter, telling them that the experimenter had decided to change the procedure; instead of basing his decision on their grade on subtest four, the experimenter decided by drawing lots who would participate in the second test. This change in procedure was a violation of the consistency criterion as formulated by Leventhal (1980). Participants received no information regarding the reasons for this change in procedure, or any excuse or justification. At this point all participants answered questions about their mood (are you angry, irritated, insulted), questions about the experimenters' performance (did the experimenter treat you fairly, did he prove to be trustworthy, did he behave politely and was he a capable person for the job) and questions about their outcome expectations and the importance they attached to obtaining a favorable outcome.

After participants had answered the questions the experimenter went to the participants in their cubicles and asked them to wait for the results of the lottery to appear on their screen. The experimenter asked participants to take money if the lottery was negative and they were not allowed to participate in test 2. For all participants the lottery was negative. The experimenter put a money box containing an amount of 20 euro in coins of several different values on the desks in each cubicle, telling the participants that they could take their own pay when they left. The rationale given for this procedure was that the experimenter was not able to correct tests on the main computer, draw the lots on the computer and pay the participants the amount they earned at the same time for all six participants. The experimenter told the participants that the lots would be drawn by the computer and that he did not know who was drawn in and who was not, so he did not know who was to receive 2 or 10 euro. He furthermore made the impression that he was unaware of the exact amount of money he left by saying: "it looks like there's enough money for you here, whether you will participate in the second part or not, but if it is not sufficient, let me know". After the experimenter had left the cubicle, the participants received the results of the drawing on the screen and were all informed they had been drawn out, and that they had subsequently earned 2 euro for their participation. All participants were thus informed about the amount of money that they were entitled to, which was consistent with the amount of money that was promised them for their invested time (about 15 minutes). Participants were then informed that they could take the money they had earned and leave; the impression was made that there would be no more contact between the experimenter, who was in the adjacent room, and the participants. The participants could thus take more money than they were allowed to and were given the impression that the experimenter would be not able to tell how much was actually taken by whom. Upon leaving the cubicles, participants were intercepted in the corridor, and debriefed about the true purpose of the experiment. It was stressed that the experimenters were interested in differences between groups of participants and not in individual norm violations. All participants were paid €1 extra as a compensation for the deception and they all agreed to this procedure. The amount of money that participants had left in the cubicles was numbered and counted by two persons after the participants had left; thus, the experimenters did not know which specific participants had stolen money.

Results

Manipulation Checks

In order to prevent participants from getting suspicious about the true purpose of the experiment, we did not ask participants directly to give their opinion on the fairness of the procedure. Instead, a number of dependent measures were obtained, which were considered to be an indication of participants' feelings of injustice. These dependent measures were (bad) mood and judgment of the experimenter.

We asked participants after the (change in) procedure, but before the results of the lottery were communicated to them to indicate to what extent they were in a bad mood, that is, to what extent they felt angry, irritated and insulted (scale from $1 =$ not at all, $7 =$ very much). Analysis of variance of these combined three variables (Cronbachs'Alpha $= 0.82$) as dependent variable and consistency and outcome importance as independent variables showed that inconsistently treated participants on the average were in a more negative mood than consistently treated participants ($M = 2.7$ vs. $M = 1.9$, $F_{(1/140)} = 15.04$, $p < 0.000,1$, scale $1 =$ not at all, $7 =$ very much). Outcome importance did not affect mood.

Participants were also asked to judge the person and the actions of the experimenter.

They indicated on a response scale ranging from 1 to 7 to what extent they felt the experimenter had treated them fairly, had proved to be trustworthy, had behaved politely and was perceived as a capable person for the job. ANOVA with consistency and outcome importance as independent variables indicated that in the inconsistent procedure condition, participants judged the experimenter as less trustworthy (scale from $1 =$ not at all trustworthy to $7 =$ very trustworthy, $M = 4.9$ vs. $M = 5.4$, $F_{1,143} = 5.49$, $p < 0.05$) and felt that they were treated less fair (scale from $1 =$ not at all fair to $7 =$ very fair, $M = 5.4$ vs) $M = 6.0$, $F_{1,143} = 7.19$, $p < 0.01$) than participants in the consistent procedure condition. Participants did not differ in the extent to which they felt the experimenter had been polite (consistent procedure: $M = 5.2$, inconsistent procedure: $M = 5.0$, $F_{1,140} = 0.5$, N.S.) and capable for the job (consistent procedure: $M = 5.5$, inconsistent procedure: $M = 5.2$, $F_{1,140} = 1.5$, N.S., both on a 1–7 scale). No other significant main or interaction effects were found. We conclude from these indirect measures that participants in the inconsistent procedure conditions experienced more negative emotions and perceived more injustice than participants in the consistent procedure conditions and that our manipulation of procedural fairness was successful.

To check the manipulation of outcome importance, participants were asked how important it was for them to participate in the second part. The difference between participants in the low outcome importance condition ($M = 3.4$) and participants in the high outcome importance condition ($M = 3.9$, $F_{1,142} = 2.8$, $p = 0.10$, measured on a scale from 1 = not at all important to 7 = very important) was nearly significant. We have to conclude therefore that our manipulation of outcome importance was not completely as intended.

In order to check for a difference in outcome expectation between participants in the consistent procedure condition and participants in the inconsistent procedure condition, we asked participants to indicate what they thought their chances would be to participate in Part 2. On a scale with three response categories (1 = "probably not", 2 = "have no idea", 3 = "probably so"), there was no significant difference between consistently treated participants ($M = 2.1$) and inconsistently treated participants ($M = 2.0$, $F_{1,142} = 1.60$, N.S.). On the average, participants had no notion of their chances to continue. There was thus no perceived connection between the choice of procedure and the likelihood of obtaining a desired outcome.

Norm-Violating Behavior

Out of 145 participants, 39 participants took more money than the €2 that was agreed upon. In total, an amount of €51.70 was stolen. The smallest amount that was stolen by a participant was a quarter (25 cents); the largest amount 6 euro. In the consistent procedure condition, 12 participants stole money and in the inconsistent procedure condition 27 participants ($\chi^2 = 7.77$, *d.f.* = 1, $p < 0.01$), so consistency of the procedure had a significant effect on the number of participants engaging in norm violating behavior.

We also determined whether stealing participants in the inconsistent procedure condition stole more money than stealing participants in the consistent procedure condition; A 2 × 2 analysis of variance was performed with consistency and outcome importance as independent variables and the amounts of stolen money per participants as dependent variable. A logarithmic transformation was performed on the amounts of money stolen to correct for a skewed distribution. The results of this analysis show that participants in the inconsistent procedure condition stole more money than participants in the consistent procedure condition (inconsistent procedure: $M = 1.0$ vs. consistent procedure: $M = 0.32$, $F_{1,37} = 7.41$, $p < 0.01$). The amount of money stolen in the inconsistent procedure condition by 27 participants was €41.4; mean amount stolen was €1.53; in the consistent procedure condition 12 participants stole €10.30; mean amount €0.85. Outcome importance had no significant effect on the number of participants that stole, nor on the amount of money that was stolen, and no interaction effect was found. Hypotheses 1a and 1b (Participants will steal more often and more money in the inconsistent procedure condition than in the consistent procedure condition) were thus confirmed, but we could not confirm Hypothesis 2, concerning the effect of outcome importance (in the high outcome importance condition more participants will steal than in the low outcome importance condition). Gender, a variable which was not included a priori in the design, proved to have a significant effect on norm violating behavior; men appeared to steal more often than women (43 per cent vs. 18 per cent, $\chi^2 = 10.55$, p = 0.001) and stole more money ($M = 1.3$) than women ($M = 0.5$, $F_{1,142} = 8.65$, p < 0.005).

Discussion

The induction of an unfair procedure was considered successful; we consider the more negative mood and the more negative judgment of the experimenter in the inconsistent procedure condition strong indicators of perceived procedural injustice. The fact that the answers to the questions "has the experimenter behaved politely" and "is the experimenter capable for his job" did not show a difference for the consistently and inconsistently treated participants can be explained by two reasons: the term "politely" was often not connected to the implemented procedure, but more to the way the experimenter was dressed, the way he talked, etc. Secondly, our freshmen-participants never participated in an experiment before and felt they had no standards to evaluate whether the experimenter was capable for his job, as several participants stated on their questionnaire. Capability thus seemed not the correct expression for measuring legitimacy of the experimenter for this group of participants.

Participants in the consistent and inconsistent procedure conditions did not differ from each other in their estimation of their chance to pass on to the next test in which they could earn extra money. Nearly all participants indicated that they had no idea about their chances to pass on, and so the procedure of deciding by lottery was not a more unfavorable one than the referent procedure that was announced beforehand. Participants were then informed that they were eliminated by lottery: a negative outcome which was not unfair or inequitable to the participants because it was dependent on chance: all participants, thus, received the same outcome. Therefore, we assume that the increase in norm violating behavior in the inconsistent procedure condition may be attributed to the unfairness of the procedure and not to a reduction in outcome expectation.

Outcome importance was not successfully induced and thus had no effect on norm violation. A plausible explanation may be that good test performance and the chance of earning a bonus were much more salient to participants than the exact amount of money they could earn, or that the difference in amount of money that could be earned was just not large enough to be salient.

In the experiment described here, we have examined a type of noncompliant reaction to procedural injustice that is not often studied in the laboratory. In the study conducted by Greenberg (1993) participants reacted to distributive injustice by compensating themselves; they stole money, as did the participants in our study, but they only took what was promised to them beforehand. The question can be raised if this can be considered stealing, since participants did not take money in excess of what was promised to them for their cooperation. Our participants, however, were paid the amount that was promised to them for their participation, the norm-violating stealing behavior thus cannot be considered a reaction to inequity. The choice for an unfair procedure did not influence participants' outcome expectancies, so the increase in stealing behavior cannot be attributed to frustration as a reaction to lowered outcome expectancies, but must be attributed to the experience of procedural injustice.

The results of this study can be explained in terms of the relational model of authority (Tyler and Lind, 1992). Because we eliminated possible outcome effects on the judgments of the procedure, participants in this experiment did not relate the procedural decisions to the chance of getting favorable outcomes, so it is impossible that a self-serving bias caused by anticipation of enhancement of the chance to get a favorable outcome colored the procedural justice judgments or influenced mood and behavior. We must conclude, therefore, that in our study the reactions to procedural injustice were brought about by other than instrumental concerns, as is the central assumption of the relational model. According to the model the explanation for the increase in norm-violating behavior can be found in decreased legitimacy of the authority (in this study operationalized as trustworthiness) which leads to a decrease in motivation to comply with the decision made by the authority. We were unable, however, to demonstrate a direct relationship between judgments of the legitimacy of the experimenter and norm-violating behavior, probably due to our choice of items which seemed not completely appropriate to measure legitimacy. As has been found in other studies, the links between attitudes, self reports and actual behavior are sometimes weak.

The fact that procedural unfairness may elicit stealing behavior in people is remarkable. It must be noted, that much effort was placed in designing the experiment so that perceived risk of being caught in the act was minimized. Several pilot studies were conducted to create circumstances in the laboratory in which participants fully believed that the experimenter was absolutely unable to trace any theft. In other words, opportunity and temptation were made as salient as possible. In this respect, opportunity (cf. Rational Choice theory) is also an important predictor of deviant behavior as illustrated by the 12 participants in the fair procedure conditions who took the opportunity to enrich themselves by stealing. Furthermore, participants were given no opportunities to make a protest or communicate with the experimenter during the experiment,[1] so they really had no other possibility to react to the unfair treatment than by stealing. When given the opportunity, participants will probably prefer protest as a reaction to unfairness over a norm-violating reaction as stealing. It must also be noticed that about two-third of the participants resisted temptation and abstained from stealing.

A last remark must be made regarding the relationship between the authority and the participants in this study. Participants did not know the experimenter and were students of another faculty located in a different building. Former interactions or

---

1   The announcement about the lottery was made by computer, and the deposition of the moneybox by the experimenter in the cubicles was a very brief encounter, since the experimenter pretended to be in a hurry and did not wait for a reaction from the participants, but left immediately after his short speech.

expectations for future interactions were thus absent. It can be argued that when a more enduring relationship with an authority is present, chances of norm-violating responses after one negative experience are much smaller.

Revenge or retaliation, respectively, are viewed as employees' responses to organizational injustice, and as such may potentially be "prosocial, productive, and beneficial" (Bies and Tripp, 2004, p. 68). Folger and Skarlicki (2004) have long argued that retaliation may serve the interests of organization members and the organization itself, in that employee mistreatment may be prevented by moral watchdogs, whose actual or potential retaliation serves to keep abusive managers in check.

References

Agnew, R. and Raskin White, H. (1992), "An Empirical Test of General Strain Theory", *Criminology*, **30**, 475–499. [DOI: 10.1111/j.1745-9125.1992.tb01113.x]

Bies, R.J. and Tripp, T.M. (2004), "The Study of Revenge in the Workplace: Conceptual, Ideological, and Empirical Issues" in *Counterproductive Work Behavior: Investigations of Actors and Targets*. Fox, S. and Spector, P.E. (eds) (Washington, DC: APA Press).

Ciacalone, R.A. and Greenberg, J. (1997), *Antisocial Behavior in Organizations* (Thousand Oaks, CA: SAGE Publications).

Cropanzano, R. and Folger, R. (1989), "Referent Cognitions and Task Decision Autonomy: Beyond Equity Theory", *Journal of Applied Psychology*, **74**, 293–299. [DOI: 10.1037/0021-9010.74.2.293]

De Gilder, D. and Wilke, H. (1990), "Processing Sequential Status Information", *Social Psychology Quaterly*, **53**, 340–351. [DOI: 10.2307/2786739]

Dietz, J., Robinson, S.L., Folger, R., Baron, R.A. and Schulz, M. (2003), "The Impact of Community Violence and an Organization's Procedural Justice Climate on Workplace Aggression", *Academy of Management Journal*, **46**, 317–326.

Folger, R. and Martin, C. (1986), "Relative Deprivation and Referent Cognitions: Distributive and Procedural Justice Effects", *Journal of Experimental Social Psychology*, **22**, 531–546. [DOI: 10.1016/0022-1031%2886%2990049-1]

Folger, R. and Skarlicki, D.P. (2004), "Beyond Counterproductive Work Behavior: Moral Emotions and Deontic Retaliation v Reconciliation" in *Counterproductive Work Behavior: Investigations of Actors and Targets*. Fox, S. and Spector, P.E. (eds) (Washington, DC: APA Press).

Frijda, N., Kuipers, P. and Ter Schure, E. (1989), "Relations among Emotions, Appraisals, and Emotional Readiness", *Journal of Personality and Social Psychology*, **57**, 212–228. [DOI: 10.1037/0022-3514.57.2.212]

Fuller, L. (1969), *The Morality of Law* (New Haven: Yale University Press).

Greenberg, J. (1986), "Determinants of Perceived Fairness of Performance Evaluations", *Journal of Appled Psychology*, **71**, 340–342. [DOI: 10.1037/0021-9010.71.2.340]

Greenberg, J. (1987), "Reactions to Procedural Injustice in Payment Distributions: Do the Ends Justify the Means", *Journal of Applied Psychology*, **72**, 55–61. [DOI: 10.1037/0021-9010.72.1.55]

Greenberg, J. (1989), "Cognitive Re-Evaluation of Outcomes in Response to Underpayment Inequity", *Academy of Management Journal*, **32**, 174–184. [DOI: 10.2307/256425]

Greenberg, J. (1990), "Employee Theft as a Reaction to Underpayment Inequity: The Hidden Costs of Pay-Cuts", *Journal of Applied Psychology*, **75**, 561–568. [DOI: 10.1037/0021-9010.75.5.561]

Greenberg, J. (1993), "Stealing in the Name of Justice: Informational and Interpersonal Moderators of Theft Reactions to Underpayment Inequity", *Organizational Behavior and Human Decision Processes*, **54**, 81–103. [DOI: 10.1006/obhd.1993.1004]

Greenberg, J. (1994), "Using Socially Fair Procedures to Promote Acceptance of a Work Site Smoking Ban", *Journal of Applied Psychology*, **79**, 288–297. [PubMed 8206818] [DOI: 10.1037/0021-9010.79.2.288]

Greenberg, J. (1995), "Employee Theft" in *The Blackwell Dictionary of Organizational Behavior*. Nicholson, N. (ed.) (Oxford, England: Blackwell), 160–161.

Greenberg, J. (1997), "The Quest for Justice on the Job: Essays and Experiments", *Contemporary Psychology: A Journal of Reviews*, **42**, 738–763.

Greenberg, J. and Scott, K.S. (1996), "Why do Workers Bite the Hand that Feeds Them?" *Research in Organizational Behavior*, **18**, 111–156.

Innes, M., Barling, J. and Turner, N. (2005), "Understanding Supervised-Targeted Aggression: A Within-Person, between Jobs Design", *Journal of Applied Psychology*, **9**, 731–739. [DOI: 10.1037/0021-9010.90.4.731]

Korsgaard, M.A., Schweiger, D. and Sapienza, H. (1995), "Building Commitment, Attachment and Trust in Decision Making Teams: The Role of Procedural Justice", *Academy of Management Journal*, **38**, 60–84. [DOI: 10.2307/256728]

LaTour, S. (1978), "Determinants of Participant and Observer Satisfaction with Adversary and Inquisitorial Modes of Adjudication", *Journal of Personality and Social Psychology*, **36**, 1531–1545. [DOI: 10.1037/0022-3514.36.12.1531]

Leventhal, G.S. (1980), "What Should Be Done with Equity Theory?, New Approaches to the Study of Fairness in Social Relationships" in *Social Exchange: Advances in Theory and Research*. Gerge, K.J., Greenberg, M.S. and Willis, R.H. (eds) (New York: Plenum Publishing), 27–54.

Lind, E.A. and Lissak, R.I. (1985), "Apparent Impropriety and Procedural Fairness Judgments", *Journal of Experimental Social Psychology*, **21**, 19–29. [DOI: 10.1016/0022-1031%2885%2990003-4]

Lind, E.A. and Tyler, T.R. (1988), *The Social Psychology of Procedural Justice* (New York: Plenum Publishing).

Lind, E.A., Kulik, C.T., Ambrose, M. and De Vera Park, M.V. (1993), "Individual and Corporate Dispute Resolution: Using Procedural Fairness as a Decision Heuristic", *Administrative Science Quarterly*, **38**, 224–251. [DOI: 10.2307/2393412]

MacCoun, R.J., Lind, E.A., Hensler, D.R., Bryant, D.L. and Ebener, P.A. (1988), *Alternative Adjudication: An Evaluation of the New Jersey Automobile Arbitration Program* (Santa Monica, CA: Rand).

Parks, J.M. (1995), *Unpublished Manuscript* (Minneapolis: University of Minnesota).

Sapienza, H.J. and Korsgaard, M.A. (1996), "Procedural Justice in Entrepreneur-Investor Relations", *Acadamy of Management Journal*, **39**, 544–574. [DOI: 10.2307/256655]

Skarlicki, D.P. and Folger, R. (1997), "Retaliation in the Workplace: The Roles of Distributive, Procedural, and Interactional Justice", *Journal of Applied Psychology*, **82**, 434–443. [DOI: 10.1037/0021-9010.82.3.434]

Spector, P.E. and Fox, S. (2002), "An Emotion-Centered Model of Voluntary Work Behavior: Some Parallels between Counterproductive Work Behavior (CWB) and Organizational Citizenship Behavior (OCB)", *Human Resource Management Review*, **12**, 269–292. [DOI: 10.1016/S1053-4822%2802%2900049-9]

Taylor, D.M., Moghaddam, F.M., Gamble, I. and Zellerer, E. (1987), "Disadvantaged Group Responses to Perceived Inequality: From Passive Acceptance to Collective Action", *Journal of Social Psychology*, **127**, 259–272.

Tyler, T.R. (1984), "The Role of Perceived Injustice in Defendants' Evaluations of their Courtroom Experience", *Law and Society Review*, **18**, 51. [DOI: 10.2307/3053480]

Tyler, T.R. (1990), *Why People Obey the Law* (New York: Plenum Publishing).

Tyler, T.R. (1994), "Psychological Models of the Justice Motive: Antecedents of Distributive and Procedural Justice", *Journal of Personality and Social Psychology*, **67**, 850–863. [DOI: 10.1037/0022-3514.67.5.850]

Tyler, T.R. and Lind, E.A. (1992), "A Relational Model of Authority in Groups", *Advances in Experimental Social Psychology*, **25**, 115–191.

Van den Bos, K., Vermunt, R. and Wilke, H. (1996), "The Consistency Rule and the Voice Effect: The Influence of Expectations on Procedural Fairness Judgments", *European Journal of Social Psychology*, **26**, 411–428. [DOI: 10.1002/%28SICI%291099-0992%28199605%2926%3A3%3C411%3A%3AAI D-EJSP766%3E3.0.CO%3B2-2]

Van Schie, E.G. and Wiegman, O. (1995), 'De Effecten van Slachtofferschap en van Misdrijven en de Reacties van het Strafrechterlijk Systeem op Normovertredend Gedrag'. Universiteit Twente: Interimrapport, deel 2.

Vermunt, R., Wit, A., Van den Bos, K. and Lind, E.A. (1993), "The Effects of Unfair Procedure on Negative Affect and Protest", *Social Justice Research*, **9**, 109–121. [DOI: 10.1007/BF02198075]

Wemmers, J.M. (1996), *Victims in the Criminal System: A Study into the Treatment of Victims and its Effect on their Attitudes and Behavior*, Dissertation (Leiden: Leiden University).

Chapter 6

Interactions between Procedural Fairness and Outcome Favorability in Conflict Situations

Markus M. Müller
Catholic University of Eichstätt-Ingolstadt, Germany

Elisabeth Kals
Catholic University of Eichstätt-Ingolstadt, Germany

Procedural Fairness and Conflict Behavior

Since the seminal psychological theories of justice in the 1960s and 1970s (Adams, 1965; Thibaut and Walker, 1975; Walster, Walster and Berscheid, 1978), justice research and theorizing has developed greatly and new, more specified theories have been proposed. Initially, the focus of researchers and theorists had been on justice evaluations of distributions within or between groups or populations. In recent years, issues like the allocation or distribution of material resources or symbolic goods, rights, duties, positions, power, opportunities, taxes, etc., the fairness of procedures of decision making (i.e. whether the procedure is based on fair rules) and interpersonal treatment (i.e. whether the persons involved feel that they are treated in a fair and respectful way) have become equally important (Skitka and Crosby, 2003). According to Leventhal (1980) a procedure is considered as fair if it is consistently applied across persons and situations (consistency principle), if the authorities are not biased by self-interest or ideologies (bias-suppression principle), if the information used is accurate (accuracy principle), if decisions can be corrected once there is new relevant information (correctability principle), if all parties involved in the issue have an opportunity to participate in the procedure (representativeness principle), and if the procedure is compatible with general moral and ethical standards (ethicality principle) (see also Fuller, 1969). Although there are close connections between both types of fairness (Folger, 1996; Törnblom and Vermunt, 1999), there are differences in the psychological processes underlying procedural and distributive fairness evaluations. One of the differences is demonstrated in the fair process effect: if parties involved in a conflict perceive the process of conflict settlement as fair, they may accept outcomes that are less favorable than they had initially expected.

Studies on the fair process effect (see Lind and Tyler, 1988; van den Bos et al., 1997) showed that satisfaction with outcomes depends not only on favorability and distributive fairness, but also on the procedures that are applied in the distribution process. For instance, if the procedure is perceived as fair people may be satisfied with an outcome even though it is not fair and/or to their benefit. A large number of studies have shown that this effect is rather stable across situations and settings. For example, Tyler and Folger (1980) studied the satisfaction of citizens with police encounters. They found that citizens were most satisfied with the police if procedural fairness criteria had been met. Satisfaction was independent of the actual outcome of the encounter, e.g., receiving a ticket for violating a traffic rule. Similarly, Thibaut and Walker, in their classic studies on procedural justice, showed that satisfaction with outcomes in criminal trials is influenced to a large extent by the fairness of the court procedure and less by the (un)favorability of the penalty imposed by the judge (Thibaut and Walker, 1975). Later research has shown that the fair process effect also applies to organizational and other settings. For example, in a recent meta-analysis of 190 organizational justice studies, Cohen-Charash and Spector (2001) showed that procedural justice is closely related to pay satisfaction, suggesting that a lower payment can be accepted if the procedure that has led to the payment is perceived to be fair. There is ample evidence, as these examples illustrate, that procedural justice can have impacts on the satisfaction with outcomes in a variety of contexts. Moreover, Cohen-Charash and Spector (2001) show that not only evaluations such as pay satisfaction are related to perceived procedural justice. Both in field studies and laboratory settings, procedural fairness also predicted behavior, such as work performance (a positive relationship of $r = 0.45$) and counterproductive work behavior (a negative relationship of $r = -0.22$). We will look at the relationship between fairness and behavior more closely later, but we will first focus on the role of justice in conflict situations.

The concern of this chapter is on interpersonal conflict situations (as distinguished from intrapersonal conflicts) characterized by an incompatibility of actions, goals, values, beliefs, etc. between two or more persons and not only within a person (Montada and Kals, 2001). Cooperation or non-cooperation are often considered to be the result of strategic choices serving to maximize outcomes for the individual. As mutual cooperation frequently results in the best possible outcome for the individual (depending on the pay off structure of the conflict), it would be a wise strategy for people who want to maximize their outcomes to cooperate, provided the conflict partners cooperate as well. In the case of non-co-operating conflict partners, self-interested individuals would likely choose a non-cooperation strategy as well in order to avoid potential losses. This tendency has been described as "tit-for-tat" strategy (Axelrod, 1984).

Self-interest is not the only motive or goal that guides behavior in conflict situations (Biel, 2000). Justice related studies have shown that procedural fairness can be an important factor for behavior in social conflicts. Hegtvedt and Cook (1987) reviewed existing research on the role of distributive and procedural justice in bargaining situations. With regard to procedural justice, they identified three important questions: First, what are the ground rules in bargaining situations, how do they emerge, and which role do they play in guiding individual behavior? Second, how does reciprocal concession-making guide decisions in bargaining? And third, what is the role of appeals to justice in the process? In all, the review shows that procedural justice can guide behavior in bargaining and lead to fairer behavior of the participants. For example, the work of Bartos and colleagues has shown (Bartos, 1977; Bartos et al., 1983, cited in Hegtvedt and Cook, 1987) that concession making can be an effective strategy to enhance cooperation if the concessions are considered as reciprocal, which means that none of the parties makes smaller concessions than another in order to take advantage of the process. Mikula and Wenzel (2000) described four functions of justice in social conflicts: First, (in)justice can evoke conflicts, second, it can be used as a rhetoric to support one's one position, third, justice principles can help to find ways of conflict resolution, and fourth, the labeling of a solution as just can help generate acceptance of the solution. The third function is especially important in the context of our study: procedural fairness can enhance cooperative behavior in groups, and thus facilitate conflict resolutions for the benefit of all. For example, De Cremer (2003) studied the consequences of perceived respect on behavior in an experimental social dilemma situation. The results show that respect can enhance contributions in dilemmas compared to non-respect (De Cremer, 2003). Outside the laboratory, Tyler and Blader (2000) report a study showing that in a work organization, cooperative behavior in favor of the organization is best predicted by perceived procedural justice. The results from the meta-analysis from Cohen-Charash and Spector (2001) mentioned above also link procedural fairness perceptions to behavior.

In addition, research results point to the fact that a lack of procedural fairness can lead to protest behavior and deviant behavior. Greenberg (1987) studied fairness reactions to payment distributions in different conditions of outcome favorability and fairness of procedure. In the fair condition, subjects were told that their payment depended on their task performance. Payment in the unfair condition, on the contrary, was claimed to be dependent on their choice of room for the experiment, which was arbitrary and unrelated to the actual task. Greenberg found a significant interaction between outcome and procedure: the fairer the procedure, the more the unfavorable outcome was perceived as fair. This interaction of outcome favorability and procedural fairness closely reflects findings on the fair process effect: A fair procedure can reduce dissatisfaction with unfavorable outcomes, and it can lead to the evaluation of an unfavorable outcome as fair. Moreover, the most dissatisfactory constellation was that of unfair procedure and unfavorable outcome. In that condition, 43.75 per cent of the subjects chose to take a paper strip with a telephone number of an "Ethical Responsibility Board to Report any Unfair Treatment in Human Experimentation". None of the subjects in the other conditions picked up the phone number, including those unfairly, but favorably treated. Greenberg's interpretation was that protest behavior may be a result of unfair treatment associated with negative distributions.

Effects of procedural fairness and favorability of outcomes on emotional reactions were found by Krehbiel and Cropanzano (2000). In a laboratory experiment, the authors varied procedural justice (high/low) and outcome favorability (favorable/ unfavorable) and investigated their influence on emotional states (measured by a questionnaire). Outcome favorability had main effects on emotions of happiness (favorable outcomes) and disappointment (unfavorable outcomes). Anger and frustration were highest in the unfair/unfavorable condition, meaning that there was an interaction of fairness and outcome favorability quite similar to Greenberg's results. While Greenberg had observed protest behavior when unfair procedures lead to unfavorable outcomes, Krehbiel and Cropanzano found emotions of anger and frustration associated with this kind of pattern. Moreover, it should be noted that in the unfair process/favorable outcome condition, not only positive emotions like satisfaction were found. In this condition, significant amounts of guilt and anxiety were also recorded. Although the authors themselves do not elaborate on this point, the findings suggest that the combination of unfair procedures and favorable results may generate feelings of satisfaction as well as guilt. The latter are moral reactions indicating that a moral principle has been violated (see also the research on existential guilt, Montada and Schneider, 1989). The emotional reactions reflect equity theory's (Walster, Walster and Berscheid, 1978) early assumption that unfair overreward leads to less satisfaction than outcomes that are both fair and favorable.

These findings show that favorability of outcomes and procedural fairness can interact in a way that low procedural fairness leads to anger-related emotions and protest behavior when outcomes are unfavorable to the individual. This implies that these interactions are not only relevant for cognitive appraisals of the outcome (cf. the fair process effect), but also for emotional and behavioral processes. Based on the findings of these studies, the present study was designed to examine how procedural fairness and outcome favorability can influence behavioral tendencies in conflict resolution, namely hardness of negotiation and cooperation.

Hard negotiating was defined as taking one's own position uncompromisingly without considering the outcomes of others (Fisher and Ury, 1981). It is very similar to the concept of toughness (Bartos, Teitz and McLean, 1983, cited in Hegtvedt and Cook, 1987), which the authors define as the "bargainer's insistence on having his or her own way" (Hegtvedt and Cook, 1987, p. 124). Diverging positions are often at the basis of interpersonal conflicts, because they seem incompatible to the conflict partners, as for example in a bargain between a seller and a buyer, when both insist on two different prices for the product without reaching an agreement. In manuals of negotiation and conflict resolution (e.g., Fisher and Ury, 1981; Montada and Kals, 2001), this strategy of hard negotiation is often considered to be unproductive even for self-interested negotiators, since it only promotes short-term self-interest and neglects the advantages of mutual win-win solutions that can be reached through cooperation. Cooperation, then, was defined as the support of solutions to the benefit of as many people as possible (see Montada and Kals, 2001).

As Deutsch (2000) has pointed out, the hard negotiation and cooperative strategies are often not exclusive, but compatible. This means that both strategies can be an option for a negotiator depending on the situation: A person who cooperates unconditionally, which is cooperation without considering the fact that the others might not cooperate, might be easily exploited by non-cooperators. On the other hand, a hard negotiating behavior without considering the possibility of cooperation might result in win-lose solutions even when an agreement for the benefit of all conflict partners (win-win) would have been possible. Therefore, using both strategies as possible options in the course of conflict resolution may lead to constructive solutions without running the risk of being taken advantage of. We therefore expect that cooperation and hardness will be positively related, but not completely interchangeable.

How do procedural fairness and outcome favorability relate to cooperation and hardness? If the findings on the procedural fairness effect are extrapolated to social conflicts, it can be hypothesized that high degrees of perceived procedural fairness can reduce hard negotiating in the face of an expected unfavorable outcome. In this case, hardness (especially the type of hardness that is unconditional, that rules out cooperation) can be considered as similar to protest. Protest behavior signifies that the individual considers the existing order unsatisfying and therefore assumes responsibility for action (Tyler and Smith, 1997). Hard negotiation can also imply that the existing conflict between the parties is seen as unsatisfying. A hard negotiator will focus on his or her own position in order to reach an outcome that s/he considers most compatible with his or her self-interest, thus focusing solely on their own outcomes (Fisher and Ury, 1981). When a person expects disadvantages, a fair process could lead to milder negotiation, thus less hardness. As a second line of relationship, we expect that a process perceived as unfair should lead to greatest degrees of hardness in negotiation if subjects expect unfavorable outcomes for themselves. This hypothesis is based on Greenberg's (1987) findings that the highest levels of protest occurred when an unfair process was followed by an unfavorable outcome. Social protest is often caused by perceived injustice (Tyler and Smith, 1997), and we expect that unfair process in the face of expected disadvantages will lead the negotiator to focus on their self-interest in an uncompromising way, thus negotiate harder. To extend existing research, we are also interested in exploring the effects of procedural fairness when the expected outcomes are favorable. When a fair process is accompanied by favorable outcomes, then happiness and other positive emotions have been reported (Krehbiel and Cropanzano, 2000). So, if the persons are motivated solely by the maximization of self-interest, then the process that leads to these aims should be irrelevant if they expect advantages. Therefore, we would expect a zero-correlation of procedural fairness with either hardness or cooperation in the case of positive outcome favorability. But if people are motivated by fairness as well, then procedural fairness should be positively related with cooperation and unfavorably with hardness even in the case of expected advantages. However, existing theories do not allow for a clear derivation of hypotheses in this case.

The Study

The conflict chosen for the study was a local planning conflict in the community of Trier in Germany. In the beginning of the year 2000, the city administration planned to build a new bus lane to connect the town center in the Mosel river valley with the outskirts situated on the hills around the town. According to the statistics, existing roads would not be able to support the growing traffic in the near future, and new roads could not be built. So the idea was proposed to support public transport and to build a tunnel route from the center to the hills that could only be used by buses to guarantee this connection.

But the issue did not stay within the city administration. Several groups in the community had begun to participate in the discussion about the project, arguing either in favor of or against the new bus lane. One group was formed by inhabitants of a neighborhood situated east of the train station. This part of the town had so far been a very quiet, low-traffic area with family homes and some of the richer, influential citizens living there. Their concern was primarily that the bus lane would change the area by causing more traffic noise and constructing activities. They argued that the new constructions would affect the city surroundings in an unfavorable way, because the tunnel and especially its entering points would be built into a former vineyard and this would deteriorate the aspect of the city. Another group, positive towards the project, was an activist group for the enhancement of an environmentally sound traffic. Its members argued that the project would represent a clear statement in favor of public transport, thus enabling the city to reduce car traffic. It should be noted that the air quality in Trier, due to a high volume of traffic and the geographical location of the city, is relatively low compared to other cities in Germany. According to this group, a reduction of car traffic would contribute to the improvement of air quality. A third group composed by students of the university (which is located on the hills) represented a less organized but nevertheless large and important group of people who were in favor of the project. They considered the existing bus connections between the city and the university unsatisfying. A fourth group had been formed by inhabitants of a city block located in an area highly affected by the existing traffic routes. These people argued that a project as expensive as the new bus lane would not be efficient in reducing traffic, because the people in the city would not be willing to use buses instead of their own car. Therefore, they were in favor of the promotion of car traffic by building new roads or investing money in existing roads. Still other groups were involved in the discussions as well. The constructions and the new bus connections would have an impact on nearly the entire population of Trier, resulting in high levels of interest and participation in discussions about the project.

In sum, the arguments brought up were diverse: the effectiveness of public transport in reducing car traffic was questioned. Some people were afraid that the tunnel would imply new buildings that might affect the appearance of the city and its surroundings; people living on the upper hills were in part hoping for better bus connections to the city; others preferred solutions in favor of car traffic; and those living near the location at which the tunnel would be built feared unfavorable consequences by the growing bus traffic and the construction activities. Finally, the issue was raised whether the city would be able to finance the project, and there was concern whether this would affect the realization of other important projects in the community. These are only some of the topics discussed, and articles in the local newspaper as well as discussions at assemblies of interest groups or panel discussions organized by the city administration showed considerable interest in the issue not only by interest groups, but also by the general population.

The study was planned during spring 2000. In June 2000 the city council decided to demand a formal evaluation of the project and explore possibilities for financial support by the regional and national administration. The results of this evaluation were due in spring 2001. This created a time slot within which no further decisions or developments were to be expected. It was, then, a timely occasion for the administration of the questionnaire.

Method

Procedure

The research was conducted as a questionnaire study. The questionnaire was distributed from October 2000 through January 2001 among the population of Trier. As the general population as well as specific interest groups were to be represented in the questionnaire, several strategies for its distribution were used. First, articles addressing the general population were placed in the local newspaper. Additionally, special interest groups were directly contacted by phone calls or during regular group meetings. On these occasions, the questionnaires were directly handed out to the respondents, or selected individuals were given a number of questionnaires to distribute among their peers.

Respondents

Out of about 600, a total of 309 people answered the questionnaire. The sample used for the following analyses was further reduced to n = 110 by considering only those respondents who were highly affected by the issue. The conditions for inclusion were responses to more than two items that respondents expected positive or unfavorable consequences by the bus lane (see measures paragraph for details on this scale) and that they had no missing values on the other variables used for the analysis. In the subsample were 45 women and 64 men (one person did not report their sex). Their age varied between 15 and 75 years, with a large number of respondents (44.5 per cent) between 20 and 29 of age. Persons with higher education were overrepresented, 78.1 per cent having a bachelor degree or higher. The higher education of the sample is also due to the fact that the people living in the areas which were most affected are either students who would use the new bus line or upper middle class or upper class people with academic education.

Instrument

The questionnaire started with a general introduction and some information about the issue. It then included all the scales described below. As the study was part of a larger study about conflict, the questionnaire also contained scales that are not included in the present report. The questionnaire ended with some items tapping demographical information (gender, age, school, living area, etc.).

Measures

The scales included in the study were constructed especially for the questionnaire. The scale construction will be described in detail in the following sections, and an English translation of all items is provided in Appendix A.

Hardness and Cooperation

The focus of the study were the variables hardness and cooperation in conflict resolution. We chose to operationalize hardness and cooperation as *readiness* for behavior, because actual behavior was not observed. The concept of readiness refers to commitments for classes of behaviors rather than intentions that are directed towards very specific behaviors. Readiness for behavior had proven do be a valid proxy for actual behavior in previous studies (Montada, Kals and Becker, forthcoming). The degree of cooperation was assessed on the basis of agreements to seven items along six-point scales (1 = strongly disagree, 6 = strongly agree). Example: "I am willing to recognize the concerns of all people involved in the conflict as legitimate" (Reliability $\alpha = 0.82$). The hardness scale consisted of four items with the same six-point scale. Example: "I am willing to take up my own position on the conflict issues uncompromisingly." (Reliability $\alpha = 0.72$.) A high score on the scales means that respondents are more inclined to use a strategy of hardness or cooperation in the conflict.

Procedural Fairness

The procedural fairness rules were based on Leventhal's (1980) criteria: consistency, bias-suppression, accuracy, correctability, representativeness, and ethicality. Thus, six items, each representing one of the six criteria, were used to measure procedural fairness. Two sentences were used to construct each item. The first sentence informed about the fairness principle and the second the extent to which this principle was perceived to be realized in the conflict (example: "For a just decision-making concerning the new bus lane it is essential that everyone has equal opportunities getting his/her opinion heard. In the decision-making process concerning the new bus lane this is granted."; Reliability $\alpha = 0.88$). A six-point scale was used (1 = strongly disagree, 6 = strongly agree), where a high score means that the respondents consider the criteria of procedural fairness to be fulfilled.

Outcome Favorability

In order to measure the valence attached to the proposed bus lane by the subjects, a subjective measure of perceived personal (dis)advantages was used. Subjects rated their concern about five different issues (quality of life in their neighborhood; mobility; ecological quality of their neighborhood; worth of real estate; realization of other personally important issues (like, for example, the construction of roads or the reparation of damaged paving, etc.) on 7-point scales ranging from -3 ("very negative consequences") to +3 ("very positive consequences"). These five issues were used as they had proven to be objects of concern in panel discussions and local gatherings as well as in the media. In order to avoid a tendency towards the middle point, we added an option "I am not concerned" to each single item. In order to ensure that the respondents felt concerned by the issue, we used information only from individuals who reported to be affected by at least three issues (n = 110). Example: "The proposed tunnel has the following consequences for my mobility (by bus, car, etc…)" (reliability $\alpha = 0.96$). A high positive score represent expected personally favorable outcomes from the bus lane and, a high negative score indicates unfavorable outcomes.

Results

First, bivariate (Pearson) correlations between all variables were analyzed. All correlations, along with information on the variables, are shown in Table 6.1. As

Table 6.1   Means, Standard Deviations, N, and Intercorrelations of the Variables

				r		
Variable	M	S	N	2 Procedural Justice	3 Hardness	4 Cooperation
1 Outcome favorability[1]	0.56	1.57	110	0.33**	0.05	0.18
2 Procedural justice[2]	3.38	1.17	110		0.06	0.10
3 Hardness[3]	3.58	1.14	110			0.49**
4 Cooperation[4]	4.43	0.82	110			

[1]*Scale ranging from -3 (only disadvantages) to +3 (only advantages)*
[2]*Scale ranging from 1 (strongly disagree) to 6 (strongly agree)*
**$p < 0.01$

predicted, a significant correlation was found between hardness and cooperation ($r = 0.49$; $p < 0.01$). This means that both strategies are complementary (and can be used by the same individuals) rather than independent (zero-correlation) or exclusive (negative correlation). This correlation has to be considered in further analyses. Neither hardness or cooperation correlated significantly with procedural fairness and outcome favorability. Procedural fairness and outcome favorability were positively correlated ($r = 0.33$, $p < 0.01$).

Moderator Hypotheses

We tested for the hypotheses that procedural fairness and outcome favorability interact in their relationship with strategies in conflict resolution. The tests were performed using multiple regression analysis. In order to reduce the risks of multicollinearity, all variables were z-standardized before the analyses are carried out (Aiken and West, 1991).

Cooperation
The regression analysis in which cooperation is regressed on outcome favorability, procedural fairness and the interaction term of procedural fairness and outcome favorability revealed a small interaction effect: $R^2 = 0.06$. This effect was significant ($p < 0.05$, see Table 6.2).

As already mentioned, a significant correlation was obtained between hardness and cooperation. Therefore, in a second step, hardness was also included in the analyses as a predictor of cooperation, allowing control for potential partial correlations being responsible for the effect. In the regression equation with hardness as additional predictor, the product favorability x fairness did not have significant effect on cooperation ($\beta = 0.03$; $F = 0.12$). The significant interaction effect of outcome favorability and procedural fairness on cooperation could only be explained by the variance that cooperation had in common with hardness, and not by the unique variance of cooperation as such. Thus, it can be concluded that outcome favorability does not moderate the effect of procedural fairness on cooperation.

Table 6.2   Moderated Regression, Criterion: Cooperation, Predictors: Procedural Fairness, Outcome Favorability and the Product Term Fairness × Favorability (All Variables are Z-standardized)

Criterion	Predictor variables	R^2	B	SE B	r	beta	F
Cooperation	Outcome favorability		0.13	0.10	0.13	0.13	1.67
	Procedural fairness.	0.02	0.01	0.10	0.01	0.01	0.01
	Favorability × fairness	0.06	0.14	0.06	0.22	0.22	5.15*
	(constant)		-0.05				
F_{ges} = 2.44	d.f. = 3/106						

*0.01 < p< 0.05 **p < 0.01*

Note: The interaction is not significant when hardness is used as additional predictor in the equation (see text for details).

Hardness

Multiple regression analyses were also computed for hardness as dependent variable. As shown by Table 6.3, a significant effect (p < 0.01) of the product favorability x fairness was found (R^2 = 0.13).

Again, this effect was controlled for, in a second step, using cooperation as an additional predictor. Unlike the analyses to explain cooperation, this time the effect of the product favorability x justice remained significant even with cooperation as predictor ($\beta = 0.26, F = 9.94, p < 0.01$). There was therefore an interaction effect between outcome favorability and procedural fairness on hardness in conflict resolution. As illustrated in Figure 6.1, the pattern can be described as follows. The relationship between procedural fairness and hardness was negative when outcome favorability was negative. In other words, when people expected disadvantages, they were willing to negotiate harder if they also perceived the process as unfair. A fair process would on the other hand reduce hardness when people expect disadvantages. However, the relationship between procedural fairness and hardness turned out to be positive when outcome favorability was positive. When people expected advantages, a fair process yielded even greater hardness, whereas an unfair process reduced hardness. When both outcome favorability and procedural fairness were moderate, hardness was also moderate.

Table 6.3   Moderated Regression, Criterion: Hardness, Predictors: Procedural Fairness, Outcome Favorability and the Product Term Fairness × Favorability (All Variables are Z-standardized)

Criterion	Predictor variables	R^2	B	SE B	r	beta	F
Hardness	Outcome favorability		0.00	0.07	0.04	0.00	0.00
	Procedural fairness	0.00	0.13	0.11	0.06	0.13	1.7
	Favorability × fairness	0.13	0.23	0.04	0.34	0.36	15.54**
	(constant)		-0.09				
F_{ges} = 5.35*	d.f. = 3/106						

*0.01 < p< 0.05 **p < 0.01*

Note: The interaction remains significant when cooperation is used as additional predictor in the equation (see text for details).

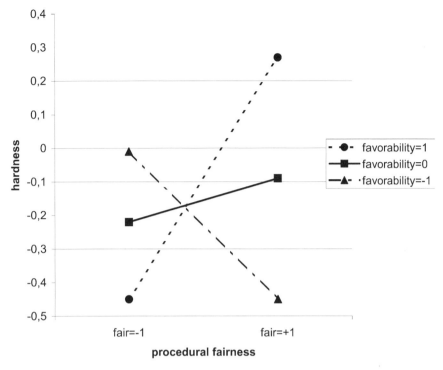

Figure 6.1   Relationships between Procedural Fairness and Hardness for Three Levels of Outcome Valence

Discussion

In this study we examined the effects of procedural fairness and outcome favorability on cooperation and hardness in conflict resolution. The study involved a real-life conflict between different opinions about how the construction of a new bus lane/tunnel should be planned in the German city of Trier. Data were gathered by means of questionnaires (n = 309), and the present data were based on a sub-sample of 110 persons who reported to be directly affected by the new bus lane in at least three areas of life. The results showed that there were no significant main effects of outcome favorability and procedural fairness on cooperation and hardness. Moreover, there was a significant correlation between hardness and cooperation, which supported the hypothesis that strategies in conflict resolution may in part be adopted simultaneously and are therefore positively related. There was a small interaction effect on cooperation, but this effect was not stable when the intercorrelation of hardness and cooperation was controlled for.

Results from correlational and multivariate analyses supported the hypothesis concerning hardness. As predicted, high levels of hardness were found when unfavorable outcomes were associated with low procedural fairness. This finding reflects results of earlier studies on procedural fairness which show that protest behavior may be a result of unfair procedures when the outcomes are unfavorable to the subjects (Greenberg,

1987). This supports the idea that the interactive effects of outcome favorability and procedural fairness on protest behavior can be applied to conflict resolution strategies. Hardness (like protest behavior) can result from unfair procedures when the people involved also expect to be disadvantaged. In addition, the hypothesis derived from research on the fair process effect was also supported in that hardness was low when the process was perceived to be fair, even though disadvantages were expected. The significant interaction effect of outcome favorability and procedural fairness on hardness was stable when the correlation between hardness and cooperation was controlled for. Thus, the findings are especially relevant for hard strategies independent of cooperation. Although there was a close relationship between both strategies, an important part of the variance of both was independent of one another. What does this mean in the context of conflict resolution? Our interpretation is that hardness and cooperation can be compatible if the individuals pursue a tit-for-tat-like strategy. They will employ either hardness or cooperation depending on the behavior of the other conflict partners and their own expectation about the other's future behavior. Research as well as manuals of conflict resolution often describe this kind of "conditional cooperation" (Axelrod, 1984) as a very successful means to reach mutually agreeable results.

However, the most interesting interactions were found for hardness independent of cooperation. This part of the variance in the hardness variable, when cooperation was partialed out, may be described as "unconditional hardness", a strategy of hard negotiation which will not switch to cooperation even if conflict partners actually do cooperate. Such a strategy of uncompromising toughness and realization of own positions has been described as unproductive for one's own as well as the conflict partners' benefits (Fischer and Ury, 1981). This kind of hard negotiating may lead to destructive results of the process of conflict resolution, since it is often accompanied by a win-lose orientation (Thompson and Nadler, 2000) which, in turn, may be an obstacle to constructive win-win solutions. Thus, the results suggest that expectations for disadvantages from an unfair process might lead to problematic situations in the course of conflict resolution which might finally cause the negotiation to fail.

The effect of expected advantages (positive outcome favorability) is less well documented in its relationship to procedural fairness on strategies in conflict resolution. Existing research suggests that a fair process with favorable outcomes will lead to happiness and positive emotions (Krehbiel and Cropanzano, 2000), but the translation to behavior in conflicts has not yet been made. The findings not only suggest that positive outcome favorability may result in low hardness when procedural fairness is low, but also that advantages may lead to harder negotiating when people feel that the process is fair. This finding is surprising as it seems to imply that even when people expect that their self-interests will be met, they are still sensitive to procedural fairness information. In this case, rather than enhancing cooperation, fairness will lead to more hardness. Thus, a high degree of procedural fairness may have both constructive and destructive consequences for conflict resolution behavior.

One possible interpretation of this effect is that while expected losses may result in fear, expected advantages might result in greed, i.e. a desire to maximize personal gains without considering the outcomes of others. Thus, hardness in conflict resolution might be an expression of both emotions: An individual who fears potential losses will negotiate hardly to prevent these losses, when s/he perceives that the interests or needs of the conflicting partners will not be considered properly (which might happen when procedural fairness is perceived as low). This fear can be reduced when a party in the conflict experiences the procedure as fair. It seems that greed is enhanced when one expects advantages and the procedure is perceived as fair. However, these interpretations of a mediating effect of the emotions of greed and fear should be tested directly in further studies.

There are further limitations to the interpretations. First, the data stemmed from a questionnaire study. Therefore, causal interpretations should be made with caution. One should keep in mind that the cross-sectional nature of the data only allows for causal speculations based on correlations. Experimental studies should further investigate the validity of the causal interpretations. Second, the number of variables used in the study is limited. For example, the effects of fear and greed as emotions should be investigated in future research, as well as the effect of fairness criteria that are relevant to interpersonal treatment (Bies and Moag, 1986; Blader and Tyler, 2003).

In conclusion, we found that procedural fairness may have differential effects on conflict resolution strategies. Fairness did not affect cooperation or hardness directly, but only via moderation of outcome favorability. Thus, establishment of procedural fairness may reduce hardness when people expect disadvantages, and may therefore be beneficial to a constructive process of conflict resolution. On the other hand, there seems to be reason to be cautious when people expect advantages. In this case fairness might lead to more uncompromising hardness. This could become an obstacle to cooperative solutions, because the people involved in the conflict might focus their own position. They will insist on a resolution that will provide them with the best outcome, without taking the possibility of win-win solutions for the benefit of all conflict partners into account. Further studies should validate and extend the findings in experimental laboratory settings as well as in the field.

Appendix A

Items (translated from the German questionnaire)

Cooperation

(1 = "strongly disagree" ... 6 = "strongly agree")

1. I am willing to demand a decision on the issue that benefits as many people as possible.
2. I am willing to recognize the concerns of all people involved in the issue as legitimate.
3. I am willing to invest that all citizens are thoroughly and comprehensively informed about the project planning of the issue.
4. I am willing to understand even strongly uttered annoyance of stakeholders in the issue.
5. I am willing to set back my personal interests if this helps finding a decision that satisfies as many people as possible.

6. I am willing to mediate between stakeholders during excited discussions around the issue.
7. I am willing to take up my own position on the issue uncompromisingly.

Hardness

1. I am willing to insist on a quick end of the laborious discussions about the issue.
2. I am willing to accept the disadvantages of others in order to carry my own points in the issue.
3. I am willing to convince other people that too much deference is not helpful if one wants to obtain one's goals in the process of the issue.
4. I am willing to take all fears of people involved in the issue seriously.

Outcome Favorability

(-3 = "only disadvantages" … +3 = "only advantages")

The option A (completely tunneled route) would have effects on…

A. …my living quality in my residential quarter (structural modifications, changes in traffic, etc.).
B. …my possibilities to be mobile (by bus, car, etc.).
C. …the environmental quality in my direct living space (air quality, state of the landscape).
D. …the value of my own immovables (estates, houses, apartments).
E. …the realization of other public measures that are of equal importance for me.

Procedural Justice

(1 = "strongly disagree" … 6 = "strongly agree")

For a just decision-making concerning the issue it is essential…

1. …that everyone has the same possibility to get a hearing of his opinion
   In the decision-making process concerning the issue this is granted.
2. …that those who take part in the decision-making do not pursue any personal interests.
   In the decision-making process concerning the issue this is granted.
3. …that prior to the decision there is a comprehensive and precise search for information.
   In the decision-making process concerning the issue this is granted.
4. …that decisions, once made, can be rectified in the case of legitimate objections.
   In the decision-making process concerning the issue this is granted.

5. ...that the criteria for evaluating the options are elaborated clearly from the very beginning.
   In the decision-making process concerning the issue this is granted.
6. ...that political decisions must be justified in public.
   In the decision-making process concerning the issue this is granted.

References

Adams, J.S. (1965), "Inequity in Social Exchange", *Advances in Experimental Social Psychology*, **2**, 267–299.

Aiken, L.S. and West, S.G. (1991), *Multiple Regression: Testing and Interpreting Interactions* (Newbury Park, CA: Sage).

Axelrod, R. (1984), *The Evolution of Cooperation* (New York: Basic Books).

Biel, A. (2000), "Factors Promoting Cooperation in the Laboratory, in Common Pool Resource Dilemmas, and in Large-Scale Dilemmas: Similarities and Differences" in *Cooperation in Modern Society: Promoting the Welfare of Communities, States, and Organizations*. Vugt, M..V., Snyder, M., Tyler, T.R. and Biel, A. (eds) (London: Routledge), 25–41.

Bies, R.J. and Moag, J.S. (1986) "Interactional Justice: Communication Criteria of Fairness" in *Research on negotiation in organizations*, Vol. 1. Lewicki, R. J., Sheppard, B. H. and Bazerman, M. H. (eds). (Greenwich, CT: JAI Press), 43–55.

Blader, S.L. and Tyler, T.R. (2003), "A Four-Component Model of Procedural Justice: Defining the Meaning of a "Fair" Process", *Personality and Social Psychology Bulletin*, **29**, 747–758. [PubMed 15189630] [DOI: 10.1177/0146167203029006 007]

Cohen-Charash, Y. and Spector, P.E. (2001), "The Role of Justice in Organizations: A Meta-Analysis", *Organizational Behavior and Human Decision Processes*, **86**, 278–321. [DOI: 10.1006/obhd.2001.2958]

De Cremer, D. (2003), "Noneconomic Motives Predicting Cooperation in Public Good Dilemmas: The Effect of Received Respect on Contributions", *Social Justice Research*, **16**, 367–377. [DOI: 10.1023/A%3A1026361632114]

Deutsch, M. (2000), "Cooperation and Competition" in *The Handbook of Conflict Resolution: Theory and Practice*. Deutsch, M. and Coleman, P.T. (eds) (San Francisco, CA: Jossey-Bass), 21–39.

Fisher, R. and Ury, W. (1981), *Getting to Yes: Negotiating Agreement without Giving In* (Boston, MA: Houghton Muffin).

Folger, R. (1996), "Distributive and Procedural Justice: Multifaceted Meanings and Interrelations", *Social Justice Research*, **9**, 395–416. [DOI: 10.1007/ BF02196992]

Fuller, L. (1969), *The Morality of Law* (New Haven: Yale University Press).

Greenberg, J. (1987), "Reactions to Procedural Injustice in Payment Distributions: Do the Means Justify the Ends?" *Journal of Applied Psychology*, **72**, 55–61. [DOI: 10.1037/0021-9010.72.1.55]

Hegtvedt, K.A. and Cook, K.S. (1987), "The Role of Justice in Conflict Situations", *Advances in Group Processes*, **4**, 109–136.

Krehbiel, P.J. and Cropanzano, R. (2000), "Procedural Justice, Outcome Favorability and Emotion", *Social Justice Research*, **13**, 339–360. [DOI: 10.1023/A%3A1007670909889]

Leventhal, G.S. (1980), "What Should Be Done with Equity Theory? New Approaches to the Study of Fairness in Social Relationships" in *Social Exchange: Advances in Theory and Research*. Gergen, K.J., Greenberg, M.S. and Willis, R.H. (eds) (New York: Plenum Press), 27–55.

Lind, E.A. and Tyler, T.R. (1988), *The Social Psychology of Procedural Justice* (New York: Plenum Publishing).

Mikula, G. and Wenzel, M. (2000), "Justice and Social Conflict", *International Journal of Psychology*, **35**, 136–135. [DOI: 10.1080/002075900399439]

Montada, L. and Kals, E. (2001), *Mediation* (Weinheim: Beltz).

Montada, L. and Schneider, A. (1989), "Justice and Emotional Reactions to the Disadvantaged", *Social Justice Research*, **3**, 313–344. [DOI: 10.1007/BF01048081]

Montada, L., Kals, E. and Becker, R. (2007), "Willingness for Continued Social Commitment: A New Concept in Environmental Research", *Environment and Behavior*, **39**(3), 287–316.

Skitka, L.J. and Crosby, F.J. (2003), "Trends in the Social Psychological Study of Justice", *Personality and Social Psychology Review*, **7**, 282–285. [PubMed 14633467] [DOI: 10.1207/S15327957PSPR0704_01]

Thibaut, J. and Walker, L. (1975), *Procedural Justice: A Psychological Analysis* (Hillsdale, NJ: Erlbaum).

Thompson, L. and Nadler, J. (2000), "Judgmental Biases in Conflict Resolution and how to Overcome Them" in *The Handbook of Conflict Resolution: Theory and Practice*. Deutsch, M. and Coleman, P.T. (eds) (San Francisco, CA: Jossey-Bass Inc.), 213–135.

Törnblom, K.Y. and Vermunt, R. (1999), "An Integrative Perspective on Social Justice: Distributive and Procedural Fairness Evaluations of Positive and Negative Outcome Allocations", *Social Justice Research*, **12**, 39–64. [DOI: 10.1023/A%3A1023226307252]

Tyler, T.R. and Blader, S.L. (2000)*Cooperation in Groups: Procedural Justice, Social Identity, and Behavioral Engagement*. (Philadelphia, PA: Taylor & Francis).

Tyler, T.R. and Folger, R. (1980), "Distributional and Procedural Aspects of Satisfaction with Citizen-Police Encounters", *Basic and Applied Social Psychology*, **1**, 281–292. [DOI: 10.1207/s15324834basp0104_1]

Tyler, T.R. and Smith, H.J. (1997), "Social Justice and Social Movements" in *Handbook of Social Psychology*, Vol. 2. Gilbert, D., Fiske, S. and Lindzey, G. (eds) (New York, NY: McGraw-Hill), 595–629.

Van den Bos, K., Lind, E.A., Vermunt, R. and Wilke, H.A.M. (1997), "How do I Judge my Outcome when I do not Know the Outcome of Others? The Psychology of the Fair Process Effect", *Journal of Personality and Social Psychology*, **72**, 1034–1046. [PubMed 9150583] [DOI: 10.1037/0022-3514.72.5.1034]

Walster, E., Walster, G.W. and Berscheid, E. (1978), *Equity: Theory and Research* (Boston, MA: Allyn & Bacon).

PART III
Distributive and Procedural Justice

Chapter 7

Distributive and Procedural Fairness Promote Cooperative Conflict Management

Ali Kazemi

University of Skövde and Göteborg University, Sweden

Distributive and Procedural Fairness Promote Cooperative Conflict Management

> I think of justice as akin to the oil within an engine. It allows the many parts within the engine to interact without the friction that generates heat and leads to breakdown. Similarly, justice allows people and groups to interact without conflict and societal breakdown. (Tyler, 2000, p. 117)

Conflicts are a ubiquitous aspect of human social life. They can be handled cooperatively as well as competitively (e.g., Deutsch, 1990). As cooperative conflict management breed positive outcomes, it should be encouraged (De Dreu, 1997). One way of promoting cooperation in managing interpersonal conflicts is to make distributive and procedural fairness[1] concerns salient. Decades of research have demonstrated the significance of social justice for people's cognitions, emotions, and behavior (e.g., Törnblom, 1992; Tyler and Lind, 1992).

The primary goal of this chapter is to highlight the role of fairness for managing interpersonal conflicts in the workplace. The basic idea is that fairness promotes cooperative conflict management. Fairness concerns involve distributive and procedural aspects, independent of and in interaction with each other. Cooperation in interpersonal conflicts means taking your own as well your opponent's point of view into consideration or to downplay your own preferences. Competition, in contrast, means focusing and promoting your own preferences. Cooperative (integrating, compromising, and obliging) and competitive (dominating and avoiding) conflict management strategies are discussed and examined in this chapter. Specifically, results from a scenario study are presented in which the independent and combined effects of distributive and procedural justice on willingness to endorse each one of these strategies to manage a workplace conflict with a superior, from an employee's point of view, are investigated.

---

1   The following terms are used interchangeably throughout this chapter: a) justice and fairness, and b) distributive/distribution and outcome.

Fairness and Interpersonal Conflicts

Social psychologists study people's subjective experiences and perceptions of justice in the context of resource allocation (Törnblom, 1992). This is important as social psychological analyses of justice do not consider justice as an objectively definable quality, making it distinct from normative conceptions of justice common in political sciences and philosophy. In the context of conflict resolution, social psychologists investigate the way that perceptions and representations of justice affect how conflicts arise, develop, and are resolved. Pruitt and Kim (2004) defined interpersonal conflict as *"perceived divergence of interest*, a belief that parties' current aspirations are incompatible. In other words, conflict is a belief that if one party gets what it wants, the other (or others) will not be able to do so" (italics in the original, p. 8).

A thorough understanding of conflicts is important as conflicts may be destructive to the welfare of individuals and societies (e.g., Deutsch, 1985; Levine and Thompson, 1996). Rahim and Magner (1995) differentiated and validated five interpersonal conflict management strategies along two basic dimensions: concern for self and concern for others. The first refers to the extent a person aims at fulfilling her own goals and needs. The second dimension refers to the extent she is concerned with the goals and needs of other parties. The *integrating* conflict management strategy consists of a high concern for both self and the other party. This is a win-win style in that parties aim at a thorough understanding of both positions and a solution of the conflict that maximizes the chances of fulfilling both parties' needs. The *obliging* strategy involves self-sacrifice and thus means low concern for self and high concern for the other party. The *dominating* strategy involves high concern for self and low concern for the other party. Dominating can be viewed as a zero-sum strategy in that everything the dominating person gains, the other party looses. The *avoiding* strategy involves low concern for self as well as for the other party. To postpone an issue to an undecided point in time or pretend that a conflict does not exist are concrete examples of the avoiding strategy. The *compromising* strategy involves moderate concern for self as well as for the other party. To meet the other party half way is to compromise and involves giving up some resource to reach a solution.

Henceforth, I will refer to the strategies of integrating, obliging, and compromising as *cooperative* strategies as they all share a concern for the other party in a conflict. However, as integrating is a strategy that also involves a high concern for self it is, in a sense, a strategy that aims at maximizing the individual's own benefits. On the concern-for-self dimension, the compromising style follows integrating. An individual employing the compromising strategy is willing to give up something important to self in return for something else. The obliging strategy, in contrast, is the one strategy that only considers the interests of the other party (i.e., self-sacrifice). Viewed in light of this characteristic, the obliging can be perceived as the most cooperative strategy. The dominating strategy is diametrical to the obliging strategy in that an individual adopting the former strategy only cares about own outcomes and totally neglects those accrued to others. The avoiding strategy has also been proposed to be competitive in that an individual using it believes that even though it brings harm to herself, it will drag the opposing party down to the misery as well. The dominating strategy is the most *competitive* strategy as it only focusses on promoting own interests at the cost of the other party's interests.

According to Deutsch (2000, p. 63), "The relationship between conflict and justice is bidirectional. Injustice breeds conflict, and destructive conflict gives rise to injustice" (p. 63). He discusses different types of connections between justice and conflict. First, he notes that perceived injustice starts and maintains conflicts. Thus, when people feel that their interests or voice are not taken into account, or when they perceive decision making procedures to be inconsistent or against basic rules of ethics (Leventhal, 1980), their confidence in the system will be damaged. Conflicts may also concern which distributive fairness norm that should prevail or how a particular distributive fairness norm should be applied. For instance, how should opportunities to higher education be allocated? According to merit, equality, or need? If merit is chosen as the basis for the allocation decision, how should it be measured in a fair manner? Should one use tests, grades, or work experience? Finally, justice can be viewed as a negotiation technique in the sense that one party self-righteously claims to be morally superior to the other party and, accordingly, blames the other to be the cause of the conflict and demands compensation to restore justice.

In a similar vein, Mikula and Wenzel (2000) discuss the following four functions of justice for social conflicts. The *trigger* function refers to the observation that a social conflict may be initiated i) when entitlements are violated by an agent who after being identified can be held responsible for it, and no social accounts are provided; ii) when an individual being exposed to injustice demands compensation or restoration; and iii) when the causal agent is punished in some way for an act of injustice. The *argument* and the *acceptance* functions pertain to the fact that references to justice assign greater legitimacy to decisions made and provide acceptable arguments for a certain course of action. The *resolution* function refers to justice enhancing the sense of trust between the conflicting parties, defining the range of acceptable solutions, and restraining self-interested claims. Thus, fairness or justice not only initiates, maintains, legitimizes, and escalates social conflicts, but also facilitates their resolution. The focus in this chapter is on investigating the role of distributive and procedural justice for willingness to resolve or manage conflicts cooperatively and competitively.

In the social justice literature, two major types of justice judgments are discussed. Distributive justice refers to the perceived fairness of the final shape or the outcome of a resource allocation event, while procedural justice pertains to the way in which the final allocation is accomplished. Justice scholars suggest that the effects of fairness cannot be meaningfully examined unless both aspects are taken into account (e.g., Brockner and Wiesenfeld, 1996; Törnblom and Vermunt, 1999). Brockner and Wiesenfeld (1996) maintained that distributive and procedural aspects often interact to affect individual reactions, or as they put it: "The effects of what you do depend on how you do it" (p. 206). An analysis of 45 independent samples revealed that procedural fairness was more positively associated with individuals' reactions when distributive (outcome) fairness was low, and that distributive fairness was more positively associated with individuals' reactions when procedural fairness was low. Brockner and Wiesenfeld discussed the following four explanations of this outcome by procedure interaction. *Referent cognitions theory* (Folger, 1986,

1993) posits that when outcomes are conceived as unfair, people tend to imagine if better outcomes would be obtained if a different procedure had been used. *Self-interest* or *instrumental hypothesis* (Thibaut and Walker, 1975) argues that the perceived favorability of future outcomes is assumed to be greater when procedures are perceived as fair. Thus, people conclude from unfair procedures that decisions were made arbitrarily which in turn implies a lower degree of favorability of future outcomes. By contrast, *group-value theory* (Lind and Tyler, 1988) postulates that when procedures are unfair, the two important needs of identity and self-esteem are not fulfilled, and that may lead people to attend more to the favorability of the outcomes. According to *attributional explanations* (e.g., Bem, 1972; Lind and Lissak, 1985), the relationship between procedural fairness and outcome favorability is mediated by the causal attributions people make for the outcomes they receive or the activities they perform. For instance, when organizational decision procedures are unfair, people may infer that their pro-organizational activities are externally motivated. Conceiving their behavior as externally caused may thus explain why people predominantly focus on the expected receipt of favorable outcomes when procedural fairness is low.

Törnblom and Vermunt (1999) presented a theoretical framework of social justice in the context of positive and negative outcome allocations, the Total Fairness Model (TFM). TFM views the resource allocation event as a structured unity or a configuration consisting of three interdependent components. More specifically, they suggested that distribution, procedure, and outcome valence are three inherent aspects of every allocation event. Törnblom and Vermunt proposed that favorable and unfavorable outcome distributions can be accomplished in different ways. Thus, it is necessary to make a distinction between the valence of a resource and the valence of the outcome distribution. Resource valence refers to "the evaluation of the transacted resource, per se and, in fact, the *type* or nature of the allocated resource", whereas outcome valence refers to "the perceived result of the transaction of a particular positively or negatively valent resource, e.g., delivering love and withdrawing disaffection are likely to be perceived as positive outcome valence, while withdrawing love and delivering disaffection would be viewed as negative outcome valence" (p. 42; see also Törnblom, 1988, for a detailed discussion). They argued that previous social justice research i) has erroneously used the terms "outcome favorability" and "outcome fairness" interchangeably (e.g., Brockner and Wiesenfeld, 1996); ii) has failed to recognize that positive and negative outcome allocations can be accomplished in different ways (i.e., the distinctions between outcome favorability, resource valence, and outcome valence); and iii) has neglected to address the effects of various fairness configurations on fairness judgments and other (e.g., organizational) outcomes. The fairness configurations were derived by dichotomizing and combining distribution, procedure, and outcome valence.

Empirical Study

There is substantial empirical evidence supporting the contention that fairness affects employees' attitudes and behaviors toward organizations (for meta-analytic reviews see Cohen-Charash and Spector, 2001; Colquitt et al., 2001; for narrative reviews see Greenberg, 1990b; Cropanzano et al., 2001). To name a few examples, Hollinger and Clark (1983) surveyed employees from three different industry segments. Approximately one-third of those employees admitted to have stolen some form of company property during their tenure. Theft was shown to be positively related to employees' feelings of exploitation. In a related vein, Greenberg (1990a) measured employee theft rates when wages were reduced by 15 per cent during a short period of time in a sample of non-union employees working in manufacturing plants. Employees who reported feeling underpaid stole approximately twice as much as those feeling equitably paid. Moreover, the magnitude of the perceived inequity and the rate of employee theft were lower when adequate explanations were offered for reductions in payment, than when the reductions were inadequately explained. Konovsky and Folger (1991) made the observation that the perceived fairness of layoff procedures was negatively correlated with layoff victims' willingness to press charges against their former employer. Skarlicki and Folger (1997) reported that retaliation (e.g., theft or sabotage) was related to outcome fairness only when interactional[2] and procedural justice was low. Predicting positive organizational outcomes, Moorman (1991) found that employees who perceived interactional justice to be high in their organizations to a greater extent engaged in organizational citizenship behavior, i.e., spontaneous organizational behavior, behaviors that are not formally required but that help the organization, than those employees who perceived it to be low.

Reviews of the organizational justice literature have revealed a paucity of research examining the impact of fairness concerns on organizational conflict management (e.g., Greenberg, 1990b; Cohen-Charash and Spector, 2001). To the best of my knowledge, only one published empirical study has specifically investigated this issue. Rahim, Magner and Shapiro (2000) found that employees' perceptions of organizational justice were positively related to their use of more cooperative styles (i.e., integrating, obliging, and compromising) when managing conflicts with their superiors. Employees' perceptions of organizational justice did not significantly predict use of competitive styles (i.e., dominating and avoiding). The Rahim et al. study had two methodological limitations. First, questionnaire (i.e., correlational) data were reported making causal effect conclusions impossible. Second, in studies using self-reports, the possibility of common method variance may be an issue (Podsakoff and Organ, 1986). Common method variance arises when measures on the criterion and predictor variables come from the same source and any defect in the source may contaminate both measures. As a result, correlations between measures may be spurious. To overcome these limitations, an experimental scenario study was

---

2 Studies have shown that people also react to their perceptions of the interpersonal treatment they receive from authorities, called interactional justice (e.g., Bies and Moag, 1986). When authorities are interactionally just, that is, polite, kind, show respect, they convey a message that the people affected by the decisions are significant and worthy. Tyler and Bies (1990), however, subsequently included interactional justice as the informal aspect of the general concept of procedural justice. See also Cropanzano et al. (2001) for a discussion of this controversy.

designed in which the fairness of an outcome and how the outcome was accomplished (i.e., procedure) was manipulated to examine how various fairness configurations influence willingness to use cooperative and competitive conflict management strategies in the context of a workplace conflict between a subordinate and her superior.

As already mentioned, previous research on the relationship between fairness and organizational behavior indicates that "positive" employee behaviors are associated with higher levels of organizational justice and "negative" employee behaviors are associated with low levels of organizational justice as manifested by the management (e.g., Hollinger and Clark, 1983; Greenberg, 1990a; Moorman, 1991; Skarlicki and Folger, 1997). I argue here that cooperative strategies of interpersonal conflict management may be viewed as "positive" organizational behaviors and competitive strategies, primarily aimed at maximizing own interests, as "negative" organizational behaviors. Thus, it is hypothesized that people are willing to employ cooperative conflict management strategies to a *greater* extent when distributions and procedures enacted by organizational management are fair rather than unfair. Conversely, it is hypothesized that people are *less* willing to use competitive strategies when distributions and procedures are fair rather than unfair. Moreover, it is hypothesized that perceived fairness of conflict management strategies mediates the effects of distributive and procedural justice on willingness to use different conflict management strategies.

Method

Participants and Design
A total of 160 undergraduates participated in the study (28 males with a mean age of 29.9, SD = 7.5; 132 females with a mean age of 31.5, SD = 8.7). The mean work experience for males and females were 9.5 (SD = 7.9) and 10.8 (SD = 8.6) years, respectively. Participants were randomly assigned and responded to one of four scenarios in a 2 (Distribution: fair vs. unfair) × 2 (Procedure: fair vs. unfair) between-subjects factorial design.

Procedure
Participation was voluntary and responses to questionnaire items were solicited during regular class meetings. The participants read scenarios describing a conflict of interest between an employee and a supervisor at work (translated from Swedish):

> Last week you went to the company's cafeteria to close a deal with a client. When you were about to leave the cafeteria, you realized that your coat was missing in the wardrobe and that the company keys were in its pocket.
>
> The next day you told your supervisor what had happened. Later on your supervisor came to your office and said that the company is going to charge you SEK 20.000 (approximately equivalent of USD 2600) for changing the locks. You cannot afford this. It is now a fact that there is a conflict between what your supervisor demands and what you want to accept.

In the *unfair distribution condition*, participants were asked to imagine that "You had seen the sign 'The wardrobe is attended' at the cafeteria entrance." In the *fair distribution condition*, the participants were asked to imagine that "You had seen the sign 'The wardrobe is unattended' at the cafeteria entrance." Thus, outcome fairness was operationalized with regard to whether or to what extent the employee was responsible for loosing the company keys.

Furthermore, half of the participants learned that "Your supervisor provided you with a opportunity to voice your opinion about the decision" (*fair procedure condition*), whereas the other half learned that "Your supervisor did not provide you with a opportunity to voice your opinion about the decision" (*unfair procedure condition*).

The participants were asked to imagine themselves involved in the depicted scene and make their responses with this in mind. Following each scenario, participants rated their willingness to employ five interpersonal conflict management strategies. Items tapping interpersonal conflict management strategies were adapted from Rahim and Magner (1995). The statements read: "I would try to keep my disagreement with my supervisor to myself in order to prevent hard feelings (Avoiding)"; "I would try to bring all our concerns out in the open so that our disagreement can be resolved in the best possible way (Integrating)"; "I would propose a middle ground to resolve the disagreement (Compromising)"; "I would accommodate the wishes of my supervisor (Obliging)"; "I would firmly pursue my side of the issue (Dominating)". Subsequently, each strategy was rated for perceived fairness. Finally, participants made outcome and procedural fairness judgments. All questions were answered on 7-point rating scales ranging from "to a very small extent" or "not fair" (1) to "to a very large extent" or "very fair" (7). Participation in the study required approximately 10 minutes.

Results

Outcome judgments
A 2 (Distribution) × 2 (Procedure) analysis of variance (ANOVA) on the item tapping fairness judgment of the outcome yielded significant main effects of distribution, $F_{1,156} = 102.32, p < 0.001, \eta^2 = 0.396$; procedure, $F_{1,156} = 11.37, p = 0.001, \eta^2 = 0.068$; and a distribution by procedure interaction, $F_{1,156} = 5.93, p = 0.016, \eta^2 = 0.037$.

The outcome was perceived as fairer when the distribution was fair ($M = 4.5, SD = 2.0$) rather than unfair ($M = 1.8, SD = 1.4$). Similarly, the outcome was perceived as fairer when the procedure was fair ($M = 3.6, SD = 2.3$) rather than unfair ($M = 2.7, SD = 2.0$).

The main effects of distribution and procedure were qualified by an interaction indicating that a fair distribution was perceived as fairer when the procedure was fair rather than unfair, $t(156) = 4.11, p < 0.001$. However, an unfair distribution was not perceived as less unfair when accomplished by a fair rather than an unfair procedure, $t < 1$, indicating that procedural fairness had no enhancement effect on the perceived fairness of outcome when the distribution was unfair. Means are depicted in Table 7.1.

Table 7.1   Means and Standard Deviations of Fairness Judgments of Outcome and Procedure

| | Distribution | | | |
| | Fair Procedure | | Unfair Procedure | |
Fairness Judgments	Fair	Unfair	Fair	Unfair
Outcome	5.3 (1.8)	3.7 (2.0)	1.9 (1.5)	1.7 (1.4)
Procedure	5.2 (1.8)	1.4 (0.78)	3.4 (1.8)	1.3 (0.66)

Note: Higher values indicate more positive ratings of the dependent variable. Entries within parentheses are standard deviations.

Procedure judgments

A 2 × 2 ANOVA on the item tapping fairness judgments of the procedure yielded significant main effects of distribution, $F_{1,156} = 20.25$, $p < 0.001$, $\eta^2 = 0.115$; procedure, $F_{1,156} = 182.27$, $p < 0.001$, $\eta^2 = 0.539$; and a distribution by procedure interaction, $F_{1,156} = 16.31$, $p < 0.001$, $\eta^2 = 0.095$.

The procedure was perceived as fairer when the distribution was fair ($M = 3.3$, $SD = 2.4$) rather than unfair ($M = 2.4$, $SD = 1.7$). Similarly, the procedure was perceived as fairer when the procedure was fair ($M = 4.3$, $SD = 2.0$) rather than unfair ($M = 1.4$, $SD = 0.72$).

As to the interaction, a fair procedure was perceived as fairer when the distribution was fair rather than unfair, $t(156) = 6.04$, $p < 0.001$. An unfair procedure was perceived as equally unfair regardless of the fairness of the distribution, $t < 1$. Means are depicted in Table 7.1.

Willingness to employ

A 2 × 2 multivariate analysis of variance (MANOVA) was performed on willingness to employ five conflict management strategies. Means are depicted in Table 7.2. The analysis revealed two multivariate main effects of distribution, $F_{5,152} = 4.33$, $p < 0.001$, $\eta^2 = 0.125$, and procedure, $F_{5,152} = 4.23$, $p < 0.001$, $\eta^2 = 0.122$. Subsequent ANOVA's revealed no significant effects of distribution or procedure on willingness to endorse the avoiding, integrating, or compromising strategies, all F's < 1; significant main effects of distribution, $F_{1,156} = 3.91$, $p = 0.05$, $\eta^2 = 0.024$; procedure, $F_{1,156} = 15.29$, $p < 0.001$, $\eta^2 = 0.089$; and a distribution by procedure interaction, $F_{1,156} = 4.60$, $p = 0.034$, $\eta^2 = 0.029$, on obliging; and a main effect of distribution, $F_{1,156} = 18.03$, $p < 0.001$, $\eta^2 = 0.104$, on dominating.

The main effect of distribution on obliging showed that the willingness to endorse the obliging strategy was greater when the distribution was fair ($M = 3.2$, $SD = 2.1$) rather than unfair ($M = 2.6$, $SD = 1.9$). The main effect of procedure on obliging showed that the willingness to endorse the obliging strategy was greater when the procedure was fair ($M = 3.5$, $SD = 2.2$) rather than unfair ($M = 2.3$, $SD = 1.6$). The distribution by procedure interaction on obliging suggested that a fair procedure enhances the effect of a fair distribution on willingness to use the obliging strategy, $t(156) = 4.28$, $p < 0.001$.

The main effect of distribution on dominating indicated that the willingness to use the dominating strategy was greater when the distribution was unfair ($M = 3.1$, $SD = 1.9$) rather than fair ($M = 2.0$, $SD = 1.3$).

Table 7.2 **Means and Standard Deviations of Willingness to Employ and Perceived Fairness of Conflict Management Strategies Related to Distributive and Procedural Fairness**

| Conflict Strategies | Distribution | | | |
| | Unfair Procedure | | Fair Procedure | |
	Fair	Unfair	Fair	Unfair
Avoiding				
Willingness	1.4 (0.59)	1.4 (0.78)	1.4 (0.95)	1.6 (0.95)
Fairness	1.5 (1.2)	1.5 (0.78)	1.2 (0.42)	1.5 (0.90)
Integrating				
Willingness	6.7 (0.51)	6.8 (0.46)	6.7 (0.64)	6.8 (0.49)
Fairness	6.8 (0.70)	6.6 (0.98)	6.8 (0.83)	6.8 (0.41)
Compromising				
Willingness	3.9 (1.6)	4.4 (1.3)	4.4 (1.4)	4.3 (1.8)
Fairness	3.3 (1.7)	3.6 (1.7)	4.0 (2.0)	2.8 (1.8)
Dominating				
Willingness	1.8 (0.92)	2.3 (1.5)	2.9 (1.8)	3.3 (2.0)
Fairness	1.9 (1.3)	2.7 (1.8)	3.7 (2.1)	4.4 (2.2)
Obliging				
Willingness	4.1 (2.1)	2.3 (1.6)	2.9 (2.1)	2.4 (1.7)
Fairness	4.0 (1.9)	2.3 (1.6)	2.0 (1.2)	1.5 (0.75)

To test the hypothesis that the effects of distribution and procedure on willingness to use the strategies of obliging and dominating are mediated by perceived fairness of these strategies, two separate analyses of covariance (ANCOVA) with distribution and procedure as independent variables in both analyses, willingness to use the strategies of obliging and dominating as dependent variables, and perceived fairness of obliging and dominating as a covariate in respective analysis, were conducted. The ANCOVA with willingness to use the obliging strategy as dependent variable revealed that the covariate was significant, $F_{1,155} = 19.70$, $p < 0.001$, $\eta^2 = 0.113$. Effects of distribution and procedure on willingness to use obliging were no longer significant, suggesting that the main and interaction effects of distribution and procedure were accounted for by perceived fairness of obliging. In the corresponding ANCOVA on willingness to use the dominating strategy, the covariate was significant, $F_{1,155} = 66.33$, $p < 0.001$, $\eta^2 = 0.30$, but the effect of distribution disappeared, suggesting that effect of distribution on willingness to use dominating was accounted for by perceived fairness of dominating.

Discussion

The principal aim of the present study was to investigate the independent and combined effects of distributive and procedural justice on willingness to endorse cooperative and competitive strategies of interpersonal conflict management. The hypotheses were partially supported. More specifically, effects of distribution and procedure were obtained on the most cooperative strategy (i.e., obliging) and the most competitive strategy (i.e., dominating), suggesting that taking the opponent's views and interests into consideration is more fair, and not doing so is less fair, when distribution and/or procedure is fair rather than unfair. Furthermore, participants' willingness to use cooperative or competitive strategies was accounted for by the perceived fairness of the strategies. This suggests that the same strategy is perceived as more or as less fair dependent on whether the allocated outcome or the enacted procedure by the supervisor is fair, and that perceived fairness of the strategies affects the extent to which the co-worker is willing to adopt a specific strategy.

Gouldner (1960) called attention to the significance of the reciprocity norm. According to this norm, we expect others to reciprocate good deeds we do for them and we are hardly surprised if others become upset when we do not reciprocate the good deeds they do for us. Similarly, negative deeds (e.g., unfair treatment of employees) evoke resentment and retaliatory behaviors aiming at restoring equilibrium (e.g., Skarlicki and Folger, 1997). The reciprocity norm may provide a plausible explanation of the distributive and procedural justice effects on willingness to employ the obliging strategy to a larger extent and dominating to a lesser extent when distribution and/or procedure aspects are fair rather than unfair. Further research is warranted to test the reciprocity explanation as well as identifying other potential mediating processes (e.g., identification, see Tyler, 2000) in the relationship between fairness and interpersonal conflict management.

Willingness to use the integrating and avoiding strategies were unaffected by fairness of distribution and procedure. This finding appears to be reasonable in that people use integrating as a win-win strategy and, as such, takes the individual's own point of view into account. Note that an individual employing integrating does not have to make any concessions to gain something else in return. Negotiation research indicates that insofar as an integrative solution is known to the parties in conflict, it should be regarded as fair and be preferred to other solutions (cf. Thompson, 1990; Thompson, Peterson and Brodt, 1996). Distrust and high stakes have been shown to prevent conflicting parties to arrive at integrative solutions and to bias their perceptions of the conflict and make them overlook common interests (Thompson, 1990). The integrating strategy aims at generating solutions by which the parties make trade-offs on issues according to their different interests. Thus, each party concedes the most on issues that are unimportant to self but important to the other party. The avoiding strategy, by contrast, is a passive strategy in that it completely neglects the individual's own needs and demands as well as those of the other party. Thus, regardless of the fairness of the distribution and/or procedure, it is not efficient to use avoiding as this strategy does not result in a resolution of the conflict.

What are the practical implications of studying conflict, justice, and conflict management in organizations? First of all, people have different motives, interests and goals that are frequently incompatible with those of others. Thus, conflicts are common occurrences in organizations (e.g., Sheppard, Lewicki and Minton, 1992). Second, material resources are scarce, while people have unlimited wants and desires (e.g., Deutsch, 2000). Third, as organizations must be productive and cost-efficient, managers as well as co-workers have to learn how to deal with conflicts as conflicts are often costly. Conflicts may result in delayed deliveries, absenteeism, sabotage, etc. Finally, research shows that conflicts do not only have negative consequences; they may also generate positive outcomes like increased creativity and enhanced problem solving ability (for overviews see De Dreu, 1997; and Deutsch and Coleman, 2000). The manner in which conflicts are managed determines the outcome. The focus should thus be on conflict *management* and on the promotion of more cooperative solutions generating more positive outcomes.

The present study showed that a fair procedure mitigated or enhanced the effects of an unfair distribution on willingness to use the cooperative strategy of obliging. An implication for organizational management is that as material and economic resources are limited, it is likely that allocated outcomes (e.g., wages, rewards, etc.) may be conceived as unfair. Senior-level managers can, however, fulfill employees' need for fairness by establishing fair formal structural procedures that meet the multiple criteria of *consistency* (equal treatment across persons and over time); *bias suppression* (refraining from self-interest and preconceptions); *accuracy* (using all correct information available); *correctability* (opportunity for second opinions and modification of decisions); *representativeness* (those affected by decisions are involved in making decisions); and *ethicality* (compatibility with universal moral standards and values) (Leventhal, 1980). Fair procedures are likely to boost employees' perceptions of justice and encourage the employment of more cooperative styles of conflict management. Managers can also pay attention to the more informal, interactional aspects of procedures. To be kind, considerate, respectful and treating subordinates by dignity do not incur any monetary costs, but may yet be quite effective in eliciting cooperative conflict management strategies.

Tyler (2000) discussed three boundary conditions to the positive effects of procedural fairness on conflict resolution. In general, Tyler argues that the societal culture within which the conflict occurs may affect the relationship between procedural fairness and effectiveness of conflict resolution. More specifically, the importance attached to fair treatment may vary with cultural context and people from different cultural backgrounds may base their definition of a fair procedure on different criteria. Group boundaries may also pose a limit to the effectiveness of procedural justice mechanisms. Research shows that people do not think in terms of justice when dealing with people belonging to other ethnic or social groups (e.g., Deutsch, 1985; Hafer and Olson, 2003). For instance, when people are in conflict with someone who is outside of their own social group, they tend to focus more on the favorability of a proposed conflict resolution when deciding whether to accept it. Furthermore, procedural justice is more likely to be effective in determining the course of a conflict when the person identifies herself with the group within which the conflict occurs or the authorities involved in the conflict (Tyler and Degoey, 1995). Thus, fair treatment by an authority may influence the way an employee handles a conflict with her supervisor insofar as she identifies herself with the organization.

Concluding Remarks

Social justice research has during the last decade progressively stressed and investigated the role of fairness in predicting and generating positive outcomes, such as creativity, responsibility, trust, and voluntary cooperation in groups (Tyler and Blader, 2000, 2003). The present chapter contributes to this focus by addressing the impact of distributive and procedural justice on fostering cooperation in the management of interpersonal conflicts in an organizational context.

The presented study is important in two respects. First, it addresses an important but neglected link between organizational justice and conflict management. Present findings suggest that distributive and procedural justice enhance the endorsement of the obliging (cooperative) strategy and lowers the endorsement of the dominating (competitive) strategy. Second, distributive justice studies typically overlook subjects' reactions to the way in which the resources are allocated. If, procedural evaluations are neglected, it is possible that observed distress resulting from injustice might be responses to procedural rather than distributive aspects of the situation (Törnblom and Ahlin, 1998) or to the interaction between procedural and distributive factors (Törnblom and Vermunt, 1999). Thus, addressing the independent and combined effects of distributive and procedural fairness contributes to the recent integrative approach in social justice research.

In conclusion, as fairness predicts a great number of organizational outcomes (e.g., Cohen-Charash and Spector, 2001; Colquitt et al., 2001), advance knowledge of how different conflict management strategies are perceived in terms of fairness under various conditions of organizational justice should be useful in learning more about the process of conflict management in the workplace.

References

Bem, D.J. (1972), "Self-Perception Theory" in *Advances in Experimental Social Psychology*. Berkowitz, L. (ed.) (New York: Academic Press), 2–62.

Bies, R.J. and Moag, J.S. (1986), "Interactional Justice: Communication Criteria of Fairness" in *Research on Negotiation in Organizations*. Lewicki, R.J., Sheppard, B.H. and Bazerman, M.H. (eds) (Greenwich, CT: JAI Press), 43–55.

Brockner, J. and Wiesenfeld, B.M. (1996), "An Integrative Framework for Explaining Reactions to Decisions: The Interactive Effects of Outcomes and Procedures", *Psychological Bulletin*, **120**, 189–208. [PubMed 8831296] [DOI: 10.1037/0033-2909.120.2.189]

Cohen-Charash, Y. and Spector, P.E. (2001), "The Role of Justice in Organizations: A Meta-Analysis", *Organizational Behavior and Human Decision Processes*, **86**, 278–321. [DOI: 10.1006/obhd.2001.2958]

Colquitt, J.A., Conlon, D.E., Wesson, M.J., Porter, C.O.L.H. and Ng, K.Y. (2001), "Justice at the Millennium: A Meta-Analytic Review of 25 years of Organizational Justice Research", *Journal of Applied Psychology*, **86**, 425–445. [PubMed 11419803] [DOI: 10.1037/0021-9010.86.3.425]

Cropanzano, R., Byrne, Z.S., Bobocel, D.R. and Rupp, D.E. (2001), "Moral Virtues, Fairness Heuristics, Social Entities, and other Denizens of Organizational Justice", *Journal of Vocational Behavior*, **58**, 164–209. [DOI: 10.1006/jvbe.2001.1791]

De Dreu, C.K.W. (1997), "Productive Conflict: The Importance of Conflict Management and Conflict Issue" in *Using Conflict in Organizations*. De Dreu, C.K.W. and Van De Vliert, E. (eds) (London: Sage), 9–22.

Deutsch, M. (1985), *Distributive Justice: A Social Psychological Perspective* (New Haven, CT: Yale University Press).

Deutsch, M. (1990), "Sixty Years of Conflict", *International Journal of Conflict Management*, 1, 237–263.

Deutsch, M. (2000), "Justice and Conflict" in *Handbook of Conflict Resolution: Theory and Practice*. Deutsch, M. and Coleman, P. (eds) (San Francisco: Jossey-Bass), 41–64.

Deutsch, M. and Coleman, P.T., eds (2000), *The Handbook of Conflict Resolution: Theory and Practice* (San Francisco: Jossey-Bass).

Folger, R. (1986), "Rethinking Equity Theory: A Referent Cognitions Model" in *Justice in Social Relations*. Bierhoff, H.W., Cohen, R.L. and Greenberg, J. (eds) (New York: Plenum Publishing), 145–162.

Folger, R. (1993), "Reactions to Mistreatment at Work" in *Social Psychology in Organizations: Advances in Theory and Research*. Murnighan, J.K. (ed.) (Englewood Cliffs, NJ: Prentice-Hall), 161–183.

Gouldner, A.W. (1960), "The Norm of Reciprocity: A Preliminary Statement", *American Sociological Review*, 25, 161–178. [DOI: 10.2307/2092623]

Greenberg, J. (1990a), "Employee Theft as a Reaction to Underpayment Inequity: The Hidden Costs of Pay Cuts", *Journal of Applied Psychology*, 75, 561–568. [DOI: 10.1037/0021-9010.75.5.561]

Greenberg, J. (1990b), "Organizational Justice: Yesterday, Today, and Tomorrow", *Journal of Management*, 16, 399–432. [DOI: 10.1177/014920639001600208]

Hafer, C.L. and Olson, J.M. (2003), "An Analysis of Empirical Research on the Scope of Justice", *Personality and Social Psychology Review*, 7, 311–323. [PubMed 14650388] [DOI: 10.1207/S15327957PSPR0704_04]

Hollinger, R.C. and Clark, J.P. (1983), *Theft by Employees* (Lexington, MA: Lexington Books).

Konovsky, M.A. and Folger, R. (1991), "The Effects of Procedures, Social Accounts, and Benefits Level on Victims' Layoff Reactions", *Journal of Applied Social Psychology*, 21, 630–650. [DOI: 10.1111/j.1559-1816.1991.tb00540.x]

Leventhal, G.S. (1980), "What Should Be Done with Equity Theory?". in *Social Exchange: Advances in Theory and Research*. Gergen, K.J., Greenberg, M.S. and Willis, R.H. (eds) (New York: Plenum Publishing), 27–55.

Levine, J.M. and Thompson, L. (1996), "Intragroup Conflict" in *Social Psychology: Handbook of Basic Principles*. Higgins, E.T. and Kruglanski, A.W. (eds) (New York: Guilford), 745–776.

Lind, E.A. and Lissak, R.I. (1985), "Apparent Impropriety and Procedural Fairness Judgments", *Journal of Experimental Social Psychology*, 13, 338–350.

Lind, E.A. and Tyler, T.R. (1988), *The Social Psychology of Procedural Justice* (New York: Plenum Publishing).

Mikula, G. and Wenzel, M. (2000), "Justice and Social Conflict", *International Journal of Psychology*, 35, 126–135. [DOI: 10.1080/002075900399420]

Moorman, R.H. (1991), "Relationship between Organizational Justice and Organizational Citizenship Behaviors: Do Fairness Perceptions Influence Employee Citizenship?" *Journal of Applied Psychology*, **76**, 845–855. [DOI: 10.1037/0021-9010.76.6.845]

Podsakoff, P. and Organ, D. (1986), "Self-reports in Organizational Research: Problems and Prospects", *Journal of Management*, **12**, 531–544. [DOI: 10.1177/014920638601200408]

Pruitt, D. and Kim, S.H. (2004), *Social Conflict: Escalation, Stalemate, and Settlement*, 3rd edn (New York: McGraw-Hill).

Rahim, M.A. and Magner, N.R. (1995), "Confirmatory Factor Analysis of the Styles of Handling Interpersonal Conflict: First-Order Factor Model and its Invariance across Groups", *Journal of Applied Psychology*, **80**, 122–132. [PubMed 7706190] [DOI: 10.1037/0021-9010.80.1.122]

Rahim, M.A., Magner, N.R. and Shapiro, D.L. (2000), "Do Justice Perceptions Influence Styles of Handling Conflict with Supervisors? What Justice Perceptions, Precisely?" *The International Journal of Conflict Management*, **11**, 9–31.

Sheppard, B.H., Lewicki, R.J. and Minton, J.W. (1992), *Organizational Justice: The Search for Fairness in the Workplace* (New York: Lexington Books).

Skarlicki, D.P. and Folger, R. (1997), "Retaliation in the Workplace: The Roles of Distributive, Procedural, and Interactional Justice", *Journal of Applied Psychology*, **82**, 434–443. [DOI: 10.1037/0021-9010.82.3.434]

Thibaut, J. and Walker, L. (1975), *Procedural Justice: A Psychological Analysis* (Hillsdale, NJ: Lawrence Erlbaum).

Thompson, L. (1990), "Negotiation Behavior and Outcomes: Empirical Evidence and Theoretical Issues", *Psychological Bulletin*, **108**, 515–532. [DOI: 10.1037/0033-2909.108.3.515]

Thompson, L., Peterson, E. and Brodt, S. (1996), "Team Negotiation: An Examination of Integrative and Distributive Bargaining", *Journal of Personality and Social Psychology*, **70**, 66–78. [DOI: 10.1037/0022-3514.70.1.66]

Törnblom, K.Y. (1988), "Positive and Negative Allocations: A Typology and a Model for Conflicting Justice Principles" in *Advances in Group Processes*, Vol. 5. Lawler, E. and Markovsky, B. (eds) (Greenwich, CT: JAI Press), 141–168.

Törnblom, K.Y. (1992), "The Social Psychology of Distributive Justice" in *Distributive Justice from an Interdisciplinary Perspective*. Scherer, K.R. (ed.) (Cambridge: Cambridge University Press), 177–284.

Törnblom, K.Y. and Ahlin, E. (1998), "Mode of Accomplishing Positive and Negative Outcomes: Its Effects on Fairness Evaluations", *Social Justice Research*, **11**, 423–442. [DOI: 10.1023/A%3A1022123324011]

Törnblom, K.Y. and Vermunt, R. (1999), "An Integrative Perspective on Social Justice: Distributive and Procedural Fairness Evaluations of Positive and Negative Outcome Allocations", *Social Justice Research*, **12**, 39–64. [DOI: 10.1023/ · A%3A1023226307252]

Tyler, T.R. (2000), "Social Justice: Outcome and Procedure", *International Journal of Psychology*, **35**, 117–125. [DOI: 10.1080/002075900399411]

Tyler, T.R. and Bies, R. (1990), "Beyond Formal Procedures: The Interpersonal Context of Procedural Justice" in *Applied Social Psychology and Organizational Settings*. Carroll, J. (ed.) (Hillsdale, NJ: Erlbaum), 77–98.

Tyler, T.R. and Blader, S.L. (2000), *Cooperation in Groups: Procedural Justice, Social Identity, and Behavioral Engagement* (Philadelphia: Psychology Press).

Tyler, T.R. and Blader, S.L. (2003), "The Group Engagement Model: Procedural Justice, Social Identity, and Cooperative Behavior", *Personality and Social Psychology Review*, **7**, 349–361. [PubMed 14633471] [DOI: 10.1207/S15327957PSPR0704_07]

Tyler, T.R. and Degoey, P. (1995), "Collective Restraint in Social Dilemmas: Procedural Justice and Social Identification Effects on Support for Authorities", *Journal of Personality and Social Psychology*, **69**, 482–497. [DOI: 10.1037/0022-3514.69.3.482]

Tyler, T.R. and Lind, E.A. (1992), "A Relational Model of Authority in Groups" in *Advances in Experimental Social Psychology*, Vol. 25. Zanna, M. (ed.) (San Diego: Academic Press), 115–191.

Chapter 8

The Talk of Negotiators: Shaping the Fairness of the Process and Outcome[1]

Karen A. Hegtvedt
Emory University, USA

Labor and management come to some agreement over a wage-benefit package after several lengthy, vicious rounds of bargaining. A mixed-age group of children divide up a bag of candy in a way that benefits the younger children. Those youngsters, however, still think that the division is unfair because the older children had teased them mercilessly about having any candy at all. A couple discusses how to spend their income tax return. Each expresses concern with what the other wants. They end up deciding to splurge on a weekend at the beach, which the wife had wanted, and to wait to build the deck, which the husband wanted, until next year. Both think the decision to go to the beach is fair.

These examples focus on the negotiation of benefits. Because of general beliefs in the value of giving people the opportunity to voice their interests and to compromise with others (i.e., procedural justice), people usually perceive negotiated outcomes as fair (i.e., distributive justice) (Hegtvedt and Cook, 1987). Yet, as these examples illustrate, what is perceived as fair may depend upon the nature of what is said during the negotiations.[2] Labor and management may have come to an agreement, but the viciousness of the negotiations dampened the perceived justice of the outcome. The couple, in contrast, considered the interests of each party when making their decision. This other-focus may have ensured that both parties perceived the discussion and the outcome as fair.

---

1   Paper presented at the IXth International Social Justice Conference, Skövde, Sweden. Address correspondence to the author at Department of Sociology, Emory University, Atlanta, GA 30322 (khegtv@emory.edu). This research was supported by an Emory University grant (URC2-50537). I would like to thank Stephanie Funk and Tim Brezina for their assistance in collecting data, Kim Lupo and Stuart Hysom for their help preparing the data, and Cathryn Johnson, anonymous reviewers, and the editors of this volume for their comments on draft versions.

2   What is said during negotiations may constitute a form of interactional justice (see Bies and Moag, 1986) insofar as communications may convey information about treatment generally or respect, truthfulness, neutrality, justification, and the like more specifically. Only one empirical study (Leung, Tong and Ho, 2004) links negotiation to fair interpersonal treatment, showing that fair treatment produces smaller egocentric biases in negotiation.

Although there is much literature on negotiation (see Lawler and Ford, 1995; Bazerman et al., 2000) and a great deal on perceptions of justice (see Hegtvedt and Markovsky, 1995), few empirical studies focus on the intersection of the two. A couple of conceptual analyses of these links (Hegtvedt and Cook, 1987; Cohen, 1991), moreover, are independent of the two key empirical investigations combining justice and bargaining. Tjösvold (1977) examines how appeals to justice made by a high status negotiator lead to more agreements, and Thompson and Loewenstein (1992) show that disputes drag on when what negotiators label as fair divisions are basically egocentric. My colleagues and I have examined how situational factors (group pay level, the nature of justice conflict in negotiating dyads) affect bargaining communications (Hegtvedt, Brezina and Funk, 1995) and how similar factors impact perceptions of procedural and distributive justice, as well as emotional reactions to injustice (Hegtvedt and Killian, 1999).[3] These integrations of the bargaining and justice literatures, however, fall short of examining the impact of communications— how negotiators actually talk to each other—on the perceived fairness of the negotiations and of the negotiated outcome.

On the theoretical level, this study extends the links between bargaining and justice, and on the empirical level, the Hegtvedt, Brezina and Funk (1995) analysis. Using the Hegtvedt et al. data, which come from an experiment involving two actors, ostensibly members of a three-person group, who must decide how to distribute a group reward, I address two unanswered questions: how do bargaining communications affect perceptions of procedural and distributive justice? To what extent do such communications mediate the effects of situational factors on justice perceptions? Responses to these questions not only fill a gap in knowledge about the intersection of bargaining and justice but also contribute to the growing concern with the role of justice in social conflict (Deutsch, 2000; Mikula and Wenzel, 2000).

In addition, this analysis contributes to the study of procedural justice in two novel ways. First, little work in procedural justice focusses on bargaining situations per se. Although early work examined the importance of procedural justice in negotiations epitomized by legal mediation (see Lind and Tyler, 1988), its role in direct negotiations has hardly been tapped (see Molm, Takahashi, and Peterson [2003] as an exception). And, second, the analysis parcels out the effects of communications and procedural justice on distributive justice perceptions to explore differences between the two theoretical precursors. In some ways, bargaining communications capture elements underlying the group value model of procedural justice, e.g., indicators of the value of an individual to a group (Lind and Tyler, 1988), the extent to which negotiators respect each other, and the status (or "standing") of each bargainer (Tyler and Lind, 1992). Yet, given the critical direct link between what is said in negotiations and the actual outcome, communications may contribute to an understanding of perceptions of distributive justice beyond that embodied in the relationship between perceptions of the fairness of the negotiations and that of the outcome.

---

3   This analysis uses the same data as those previous reports, which did not focus on negotiation communications as a predictor of justice evaluations. The theoretical argument here draws upon, but does not repeat in full, the ideas presented in the other sources. Previous data analysis is not replicated here except as necessary.

To set up the analysis, I first discuss the nature of conflict in bargaining situations. I then turn to the types of communications that negotiators may use, reviewing prior results from these data. These sections along with assumptions about behavior in situations involving conflict over a reward distribution provide the basis for predicting the impact of bargaining talk on perceptions of procedural and distributive justice. Experimental data provide a means to test the hypotheses.

Conflict in Bargaining Situations

Negotiation involves "two or more people (or unitary groups) [who] attempt to resolve competing claims about the allocation or the exchange of valued outcomes" (Carroll and Payne, 1991, p. 3). In a bargaining situation, typically actors pursue self-interested goals, which include coming to some agreement rather than facing no agreement (Chertkoff and Esser, 1976). When negotiating over the distribution of rewards or resources, individuals may suggest divisions that they believe are fair.

People's beliefs about fairness are shaped by a number of factors, including individual motivations, position in the group, attributions of responsibility, availability of rewards, situational goals, the degree to which evaluations are public, etc. (see Törnblom, 1992; Hegtvedt and Markovsky, 1995). As a consequence, people may disagree about what is fair and personal perceptions may deviate from an ideal of justice that is impartial, consensual, and promotes collective welfare (Rawls, 1971; Deutsch, 1985; Hegtvedt and Johnson, 2000). Moreover, conflict between parties over what is just in a bargaining situation may take different forms.

Three potential forms of justice conflict exist. Insofar as individuals are egocentric in their perceptions of justice (Messick and Sentis, 1979), they may define as fair distributions that promote their own material interests. Thus, egocentric justice conflict or, more simply, self-interest conflict involves negotiators whose preferred distributions reflect their material self-interests. Another form of conflict mixes the self-interest of one actor with a partner's claim that represents an existing moral or normative principle (Kaplowitz, 1977). Such cases comparing individual interests to the interests of others constitute self-interest/justice conflict. Finally, a third form involves conflict over different normative standards of justice (see Hegtvedt and Cook, 1987). For this type of justice principle conflict, individuals' claims materially benefit others and thus seem consistent with the ideal of justice. When individuals sacrifice some of their own material outcomes to enhance others' outcomes, they promote collective welfare. Self-interested justice conflict is likely to be the most intense and difficult to resolve because each claim reifies individual material self-interests. In contrast, justice principle conflict is likely to be the least intense and more readily resolved because both actors emphasize a moral concern with the benefits for others, even at a material cost to themselves.[4]

Given conflict over what constitutes a fair distribution, individuals may engage in negotiations to come to resolve their differences. The nature of communications

---

4   In two frameworks that address justice conflict, Lamm (1986) focusses primarily on self-interested justice conflict and Törnblom (1988) includes the possibility of mixed and justice principle conflict. Neither perspective, however, details the resolution of conflict.

involved in conflict resolution, in turn, may affect fairness evaluations at the conclusion of bargaining.

Resolving Conflict and Bargaining Communications

Within the bargaining situation, individuals convey their intentions in two ways: through their actions and through their communications. Many bargaining studies (see Hamner and Yukl, 1977; Lawler and Ford, 1995) examine the size of offers and concessions, the frequency and rate of concessions, and the terminating of concessions. Alternatively, the focus here is on what and how individuals communicate with each other as a way to reveal aspects of their negotiation goals. Indeed, when bargainers are able to communicate, they typically produce better outcome solutions (see McClintock, Stech and Keil, 1983; Chatman, Putnam and Sondak, 1991).

Generally, communications may be characterized as aggressive or conciliatory (Wall, 1985). Aggressive communications tend to focus on the value of one's own claims and the denigration of the opponent's claims by labeling them in a derogatory or pejorative way. Such comments may entail blunt, even hostile, behavior with the intent of decreasing an opponent's outcomes and putting that person on the defensive (Wall, 1985). In contrast, conciliatory communications define common problems and recognize an opponent's viewpoint. Conciliatory comments tend to demonstrate flexibility, to elicit positive responses, to express a desire to work together, and to enhance empathy in general (Chatman, Putnam and Sondak, 1991). In effect, aggressive ways of talking may be more self-focused and conciliatory approaches are more bi-laterally focused (Walcott et al., 1977).

Intuitively, it may seem that appeals to fairness may communicate a conciliatory approach because of the moral connotation such appeals evoke. Under certain conditions, such as when high status negotiators use fairness arguments to indicate concern for the collectivity (Tjösvold, 1977), this potential moral meaning of justice appeals emerges. Yet, more generally in bargaining situations appeals to fairness may fail to communicate a conciliatory approach or moral correctness. Instead, they may be used in a self-serving or strategic way to promote the "rightness" of one's own claims. Research shows that negotiators' fairness judgments tend to reflect egocentrism (see Bazerman et al., 2000). Several theorists also argue that when individuals use justice rhetoric to justify their own self-interested ends the problem of division may grow intractable (Zartman, 1988; Mikula and Wenzel, 2000). Likewise, Bacharach and Lawler (1981) suggest that to the extent that negotiators' appeals to justice correspond to their power position, they may be unsuccessful in arousing empathy in a partner. These theorists, in effect, draw attention to the nature of justice conflict inherent in the negotiating dyad.

Results from Hegtvedt, Brezina and Funk (1995) show that the nature of justice conflict does affect bargaining communications. The "talk" in dyads imbued with self-interest conflict is more likely to involve aggressive comments than that in dyads characterized by justice principle conflict. Likewise, results pertaining to use of fairness arguments parallels those for aggressive comments: dyads characterized by conflict stemming from egocentric claims invoke more fairness appeals than dyads competing over other-oriented claims. Arguments that pertain to joint or partner's well-being appear to decrease the necessity of justice rhetoric to justify one's intended distribution. These results, however, leave unanswered the key questions for this analysis: to what extent does the nature of bargaining communication influence perceptions of justice? And, do such communications mediate the effects of situational factors on justice perceptions?

Communications and Justice Perceptions in a Bargaining Context

The bargaining situation brings together concerns for two different types of justice: procedural and distributive. Procedural justice refers to evaluations of the fairness of the process by which a distribution is determined (Lind and Tyler, 1988). Elements of the process may also call attention to the fairness of interaction between actors (see Tyler and Lind, 1992). In contrast, distributive justice pertains to assessments of the fairness of the outcome or outcome distribution itself (Adams, 1965). Bargaining researchers argue that people typically perceive negotiated outcomes to be fair (Hegtvedt and Cook, 1987) but few test that conclusion in view of other situational factors. Also, although a great deal of research demonstrates that procedural justice is positively related to distributive justice (see Lind and Tyler, 1988), little work looks at the links between the fairness of the negotiation process and of the negotiated outcome.

The nature of the bargaining context may affect the relationship between procedural and distributive justice. Hegtvedt and Killian (1999) examine the effect of situational factors—group pay level, subject's performance, differences between initial pay divisions, and own outcome levels—on perceptions of procedural and distributive justice. Results indicate that greater differences between initial pay divisions decrease the likelihood that individuals will perceive the negotiation process as fair. Findings also show that own outcome level is positively related to perceptions of the fairness of the outcome to self but negatively related to perceptions of the fairness of the outcome to others, regardless of the inclusion of the perceived fairness of negotiations as an additional predictor of evaluations of distributive justice.

Together, the findings from the previous analysis of these data suggest two conclusions about how the bargaining context affects justice perceptions. First, the more conflict in the situation, the less likely individuals are to judge a process as fair. Molm, Takahashi and Peterson (2003) would agree. Their study contrasted negotiated exchange, which appears more procedurally fair with its emphasis on explicit offers and counter-offers, to reciprocal exchange, which captures a form of unilateral gift-giving with no explicit expectation of return. Molm et al. find, however, that reciprocal exchange, not negotiated exchange, was judged as more fair. They argue that reciprocal exchange may engender trust among exchange partners whereas negotiated exchange highlights the conflict between them. Conflict may also threaten an individual's perceived standing or value to the group (Tyler and Lind, 1992) by raising concerns about treatment (see Tyler et al., 1997), which may suppress the perceived fairness of the process. Second, the continuing impact of own outcome level on distributive justice perceptions suggests that individuals' perceptions reflect egocentric concerns. Emphasis on egocentric concerns is not surprising given other research demonstrating that in impersonal situations, individuals tend to express egocentric allocation preferences and justice evaluations (see Hegtvedt and Markovsky, 1995; Bazerman et al., 2000). In effect, characteristics of the bargaining context affect individuals' motivations and perceptions of their treatment, which in turn color how fair they perceive a process and outcome to be.

The impersonal, one-time bargaining situation studied here may stimulate egocentric evaluations of both the process and the outcome (i.e., fairness perceptions generally). Yet, the actual negotiation communications, in conjunction with the nature of the justice conflict, may provide additional information pertinent to shaping justice assessments. To make sense out of a situation, including individuals in it, people are likely to invoke schemas to facilitate their interpretation (Fiske and Taylor, 1991). These "...abstract cognitive structures that represent organized knowledge about a given concept or type of stimulus ... shape how people view and use information" (Howard, 1995, p. 93). Individuals may bring with them to the situation schemas about bargaining and about the fairness of negotiated outcomes. The bargaining schema may include presumptions about goals, reciprocity, and the need to work out some sort of agreement (Chertkoff and Esser, 1976). The justice schema consists of beliefs about how people should treat each other (e.g., civilly, with respect) and what a negotiated outcome should look like (e.g., a compromise between the interests of the negotiating parties or a division that clearly considers the interests of others). The actual starting points of the negotiations (i.e., how distant the proposals are) and the tenor of the "talk" of the negotiations (e.g., conciliatory or aggressive), however, may combine with a priori schema to shape individuals' interpretations of the situation.

In the bargaining situation, what individuals perceive about the discrepancy in their initial pay divisions and what they sense about the negotiation proceedings are likely to affect their justice perceptions. What was said during bargaining may be more salient than the actual differences in pay distributions, given that communications are proximal in both time and consequence. Moreover, communications are two-way, what one individual says may encourage or discourage responses of a particular type in a partner. The dyadic communications, in effect, set the tone for the bargaining session. So, when individuals are asked about how fair they perceive the pay distribution to be, they may reflect on what actually occurred and on what they expected based on their justice schema.

Given that a pure sense of justice involves some degree of impartiality and emphasis on collective well-being, conciliatory communications are more likely to convey such themes. To the extent that conciliatory "talk" takes into consideration other individuals' concerns and evaluations, it is more likely to enhance perceptions of justice. Conversely, use of aggressive "talk" may signal lack of engagement in the welfare of the group and schematic inconsistency, which may attenuate the perceived justice of both the process and outcome. Thus:

Hypothesis 1: Use of conciliatory comments is positively related to perceptions of fairness.

Hypothesis 2: Use of aggressive comments is negatively related to perceptions of fairness.

Although fairness arguments seem to raise the spirit of justice that suggests collective benefit and impartiality, previous research on allocation and bargaining indicates that justice evaluations are often egocentric (e.g., Bazerman et al., 2000; Handgraaf et al., 2003, 2004). To the extent that fairness appeals appear to represent a strategic means to achieve materially self-interested goals, they too fail to evince what is expected based on a justice scheme. Rather than demonstrating some concern about others' interests, egocentric justice claims may be interpreted as simply self-serving. Such an interpretation may give rise to intractable problems in the negotiation and attenuate perceptions of the fairness of the process and outcome. Thus:

> Hypothesis 3: Use of fairness comments is negatively related to perceptions of fairness.

In addition, to the extent that communications are more salient than the initial pay discrepancies, it may be the case that the impact of situational factors decreases once communications are taken into account. Previous analysis (Hegtvedt and Killian, 1999) demonstrates that situational factors—initial differences, own outcome levels—do influence perceptions of justice. That analysis, however, fails to consider how what is said during negotiations may affect fairness evaluations. Indeed, comments during negotiation may alter initial perceptions. To the extent that dyads use more conciliatory comments, the fact that initial divisions were discrepant may weaken in importance. Conversely, an aggressive tone to the negotiations may simply ingrain initial differences, perhaps even exaggerate them. Thus:

> Hypothesis 4: Bargaining communications are likely to mediate between situational factors and perceptions of fairness.

Insofar as negotiation communications are inherent in the process itself of coming to an agreement, they may provide an immediate indicator of how group members are treating each other, which is a key conceptual underpinning of procedural justice (Lind and Tyler, 1988).[5] Yet whether negotiators consider themselves to be group members, concerned about their value to each other, may be questionable. As Molm, Takahashi and Peterson (2003) demonstrated, the tenets of the group value model of procedural justice may be problematic with regard to negotiated exchanges— at least when communications are disallowed as in their experimental situation. Communications, however, may be central to conveying the willingness or reticence of individuals to compromise to resolve their conflict. They are also the inherent means to determine the final outcome. Given the paucity of information about the relevance of the group value model of procedural justice in bargaining situations and the importance of communications in such contexts, the analysis will also explore whether communications directly as hypothesized affect perceptions of distributive justice or whether they work indirectly through perceptions of procedural justice.

---

5   Tyler and Lind (1992) include treatment such as that implied in interactional justice in their conceptualization of procedural justice, along with emphasis on the procedures focusing on the decision per se. Given that bargaining leads to some decision about a pay distribution, I employ the more general term.

Methods

Overview

Data to test the above hypotheses on the effects of bargaining communications on perceptions of justice come from a computerized experiment (see Hegtvedt, Brezina and Funk, 1995; Hegtvedt and Killian, 1999). The situation involved two subjects, ostensibly members of a three-person task group, who first worked on individual tasks that established the basis for the group reward. Each subject suggested a distribution of the reward, and, when differences between distribution preferences emerged, the two negotiated a mutually agreeable distribution, after which they answered a series of questions. Although not the focus of this analysis, below I detail situational factors manipulated in the experiment: group reward level (high/low) and, nested within dyads, individual performance level (high/low) and a justice standard (equity/equality), which set up the justice conflict. Sex is included as a control factor.

Participants

The experiment involved 226 undergraduates (113 same sex dyads) at a South-eastern university who were recruited from introductory sociology and psychology courses. Of these, 20 dyads failed to suggest initial allocations which differed, thus obviating the necessity of bargaining. Thirteen dyads were eliminated for other reasons: extremely incomplete data by one group member (four dyads); existing friendship between dyad members (four dyads); failure of one or both group members to identify correctly in manipulation checks their group reward or individual performance level (five dyads).

All participants were randomly assigned to the conditions. The final analysis involves 160 participants (80 males and 80 females), resulting in 10 dyads of each sex in each of the four conditions combining group reward level with the nested factors. Each subject was paid $6.50 at the end of the 45 minute experiment.

Procedures

Subjects arrived separately to the social psychology laboratory. Experimental assistants directed them to individual rooms, where they were seated at personal computers. The computers were linked to a third machine that controlled all phases of the experiment. Once both participants were ready, the assistant started the program and then remained available to respond to questions and problems.

All information was provided via computer screens. Subjects first learned that they would be participating in a three-person work group like that found in many organizational settings. Although they would work independently on tasks, their combined performances would determine how well the group as a whole did. Because of the focus on dyadic bargaining, a procedure was created to lead subjects to believe that two of the three group members would work on the task at one point in time and the performance of a third group member would occur at a different time, but would be added into their group's performance estimate. Thus, after the

Table 8.1   Subjects' Message Library

Comments on *Own* Division

1.1   My division is more fair than yours.

1.2   Because we worked the same amount of time on the task, my division is the best and only way to go.

1.3   Even though this was a productivity situation, it was also a group effort so we should be paid about equally.

1.4   I understand why you might want more of a proportional division, but we did work the same amount of time on the task.

1.5   This is a team situation, so we all deserve to be paid equally.

1.6   Because we performed at different levels on the task, my division is the best and only way to go.

1.7   Even though this was a cooperative effort, it was also a productivity situation, so we should be paid according to our performance.

1.8   I understand why you might want more of an equal division, but we did perform at different levels on the task.

1.9   This is a productivity situation, so we all deserve to be paid according to how we performed.

Comments on *Partner's* Division

2.1   Your pay division is unfair.

2.2   Your pay division is selfish.

2.3   Your pay division is generous.

2.4   I think that you should give up more of your share.

2.5   I think your proposed pay division may have merit.

Comments on *Negotiation Proceedings*

3.1   I refuse to make another change until you offer a change.

3.2   I really want us to come up with a division we can agree on.

3.3   I think both of our pay proposals might be fair.

3.4   I like the changes you made but think we should go further.

Note: Only message about negotiation proceedings used in the analysis was 3.3.

introduction to the study, the computer ostensibly randomly determined whether subjects would work simultaneously with another group member or work as the third group member whose performance would later be combined with two others. The selection procedure always resulted in the two participants working simultaneously.

The next two phases of the study involved a practice task session and the actual task session. The task involved solving five-letter anagrams. Subjects were told that their performance scores would be based on their speed and accuracy at solving the anagrams, as well as the difficulty of the given anagram. The intention of the complex scoring method was to prohibit subjects from tracking the number of anagrams they solved, which could cast doubt upon the information we provided about their performance level. During the 15 minute task session, subjects tried to solve 45 anagrams.

At the end of the task session, participants learned of their own performance levels and those of the other two group members. Accompanying this information was the group performance score, resulting from the sum of the individual scores, and the corresponding group reward level. The next information provided indicated what individuals in the past thought was a fair way to allocate the group reward. The intention of this information was to set up either equality or equity as a standard of fairness.

After receiving this information, subjects distributed the pay for their group. Each group member then learned how his or her partner allocated the group reward. By design, dyad members should have offered different pay divisions. A negotiation session allowed them to work out these differences. Individuals could send various messages from a pre-set list (see Table 8.1). Individuals each sent an initial message. Then the computer randomly picked one participant to initiate the bargaining. In a turn-taking fashion, participants could offer distributions or send messages. They continued in this fashion, revising their pay divisions through offers and counter-offers and communicating with each other until an agreement was reached or the allotted time ended. All groups came to an agreement in the allotted time.

Upon completion of the negotiations, subjects responded to a questionnaire appearing on their screens. The questionnaire included items to assess the manipulations and perceptions of the fairness of the outcome and process as well as other measures. At the end of the questionnaire, an explanation of the study appeared on the screen. Lab assistants then debriefed subjects further, assessed their suspicions, and paid them.

Independent Variables

Manipulations
Although not of central theoretical interest to the analysis here, originally three variables were manipulated: level of group reward, individual task performance level, and justice standard. After completing the task, the screen indicated subjects' own performance level, those of their partner, and that of the group. The group performance level translated into the group reward level at 1¢ per performance point. Along with the monetary amount, information indicated whether the group's pay was in the low ($12.00) or high ($24.00) range.[6]

Individual task performances ostensibly stemmed from the complex scoring success on the anagram task. To minimize suspicion about the performance scores, tougher anagrams were given to the subjects randomly assigned to lower performance. Subjects were informed that they were either the low performer (scoring 267 or 536 points in the low and high reward conditions, respectively) or the high performer (scoring 532 or 1,065 points in the low and high reward conditions, respectively). The third group member (who the subjects believed had worked on the task at a different time) was always the middle performer, scoring either 401 or 799 points depending on the group reward level.

Each dyad member received different information about the justice standard for the distribution in order to create the potential for conflict. To operationalize an

---

6   Pre-test information suggested that college students would expect $5.50–$6.50 for participation in a one hour experimental session. Thus, the low reward amount was insufficient to cover the pay expectations of three group members whereas the high reward amount was sufficient.

equity standard, subjects were told that individuals in the past divided the money proportionately because each member performed at a different level, and paying them according to how well they did on the task is the fairest type of division. Similarly, to set up the equality standard, subjects learned that individuals in the past had divided the group reward equally because each member worked the same amount of time on the task, and that equal payment is the fairest type of division. Subjects also filled out a form to remind them of their group pay level, performance level, and way people in the past divided the reward. Despite these efforts to create justice standards, a number of initial pay divisions failed to correspond to the manipulations. Subjects, however, often disagreed on their distributions so negotiations ensued.

Assessing Justice Conflict

To indicate justice conflict, subjects' initial distributions were categorized as reflecting the pursuit of material self-advantage or other-advantage. The combination of two measures allows classification of dyads in terms of the respective orientations of negotiators. One measure estimates the distance of each performer's initial reward allocation from a perfectly equal distribution and the other calculates the distance from an exactly equitable distribution.

These distance scores rely upon the actual initial allocations of subjects to the low, medium, and high performers in their group, and compare them to a distribution involving equal amounts to each performer and to equitable amounts, based on performance levels. The distance from a purely equal or equitable distribution is given by the square root of the sums of squared deviations of the actual distribution amounts (x_i) from the theoretical amounts, standardized by the square root of the sums of squared deviation between the theoretical equal (E_i) and equitable or proportional amounts (P_i). In addition, the measures are standardized to create readily interpretable and intuitively understandable integer scores, ranging theoretically from 0 to 100. Equation 1 provides the basis for the equality score (S_e) and Equation 2 for the equity or proportionality score (S_p):

$$S_e = 100 - \left[\sqrt{\Sigma(E_i - x_i)^2} \Big/ \sqrt{\Sigma(E_i - P_i)^2} \right] \; 100 \tag{1}$$

$$S_p = 100 - \left[\sqrt{\Sigma(P_i - x_i)^2} \Big/ \sqrt{\Sigma(E_i - P_i)^2} \right] \; 100 \tag{2}$$

These equations create measures meaningful and comparable across levels of group reward and individual performance level. A high score value represents a close match between the subject's distribution and the referent distribution; a 100 means that the subject's actual allocation was identical to the one derived from the strict application of a given rule. A low value represents a weak preference for a particular type of distribution. A 0 clearly indicates little preference for the referent distribution but does not necessarily imply a clear preference for the alternative distribution (e.g., a score of 0 on the equity measure means that the actual allocation and the strictly equitable one are equally distant from an equal allocation). If a distribution is not strictly equitable, but begins to approach equality, then the two scores are likely to sum to 100. Negative score values arise when the distance between strictly equitable and equal distributions is less than that between the actual distribution and its referent, such as when individuals take all of the rewards for themselves or give all of them to others.

The nature of justice conflict stems from a combination of the equality and equity scores for the low and high performer in each group. The following logical statements set up the sorting. To indicate self-interest, the low performer's equality score had to be greater than that of the high performer, and the high performer's equity score had to be greater than that of the low performer. To indicate other-advantage, akin to justice, the low performer's equity score had to be greater than that of the high performer while the high performer's equality score was greater than that of the low performer. Fifteen dyads failed to conform to these specifications. Two dyads were re-categorized as indicating self-advantage whereas the other 13 dyads (10 male and three female) seemed to represent a mix in which in which the high performer's allocation reflected self-advantage while the low performer's indicated generosity or justice toward others.

In sum, by coupling the closeness of initial divisions to equal and equitable ones with performance level, three types of dyads emerged: 1) both parties are oriented toward self-advantage and thus are involved in self-interest conflict; 2) both parties are oriented toward other-advantaged proposals, creating justice principle conflict; and 3) one actor opts for self-advantage and the other for other-advantage to create a mix, which represents self interest/justice conflict. Theoretically, conflict should be the greatest in self-advantage dyads and the least in dyads characterized by justice principle conflict.[7] Two dummy variables capture the empirical impact of justice conflict: MIXJUST compares dyads in which dyad members conflict over justice principles (0) with those described as using a mix (1); SELFJUST compares dyads characterized by self-interest conflict (1) with those depicted by justice principle conflict (0).

Control Factors

As in previous analyses, two control factors are included. First, to the extent that individuals are egocentric in their assessments of fairness, the final amount of pay that a group member receives may be important. OWNOUTC indicates the subject's proportion of the final pay division. Regardless of group reward level, the subject could receive no money from the final pay division (proportion equals 0) or all of the money (proportion equals 1.00). In reality, subjects usually receive some money. The actual range is from 0.17 to 0.75 (representing $2.04 and $9 in the low group reward condition and $3.08 and $18 in the high group reward condition). The second factor is subject's sex (constant within a dyad).

Bargaining Communications

The pre-set message library was designed to allow participants to "talk" with their partner in ways suggested in the bargaining literature. The messages were derived

---

7   Hegtvedt et al. (1995) argue that reward scarcity exacerbates conflict in dyads characterized by self-interest conflict. Interactive effects of type of conflict and group reward here were non-significant.

from descriptions of types of conciliatory and aggressive communications, noted above, offered by Walcott et al. (1977); Wall (1985), and Chatman, Putnam and Sondak (1991). Table 8.1 shows the messages at the subjects' disposal, divided into three sets of comments about: 1) own pay division; 2) partner's pay division; and 3) the negotiation proceedings (only the fairness comment was used by subjects).

The measures of dyadic communication during bargaining are divided into several types of arguments: fairness; conciliatory; and aggressive. The measure of fairness arguments comes from the compilation of the use of three messages, items 1.1, 2.1, 3.3: "My own division is more fair than yours", "Your pay division is unfair", and "I think both of our pay proposals might be fair." The total usage of these three comments to the overall number of messages sent in the dyad during the negotiation phase constitutes the measure FAIRNESS.

Other items operationalize concepts derived from the bargaining literature pertaining to conciliatory and aggressive communications about own and partner's pay divisions. Many of these items constitute ways to justify equal or equitable distributions. Regarding comments about one's own division of the pay, items 1.4, 1.5, 1.8, and 1.9 are intended to sound conciliatory. For example, 1.4 states "I understand why you might want more of a proportional division, but we did work the same amount of time on the task", which is intended to demonstrate empathy with the partner's point of view. The sum of these comments, standardized by the total number of messages constitutes a measure of conciliatory comments about one's own pay division (NICEOWN). Messages 1.2, 1.3, 1.6, and 1.7 are more aggressive communications, asserting one's own preferences without regard for the partner. For example, 1.6 states, "Because we performed at different levels on the task, my division is the best and only way to go." By summing and standardizing these items, an indicator of aggressive communications (AGGOWN) emerges. In a similar fashion, proportion measures capture conciliatory messages (2.3 and 2.5) about partner's division (NICEPRTNR) and aggressive communications (2.2 and 2.4) about the same (AGGPRTNR). Message 2.2 ("Your pay division is selfish") is an attempt to capture denigration of the partner's claims. All measures of communication are at the dyadic level, constituting a contextual factor hypothesized to influence perceptions of justice.

Dependent Variables

Questionnaire items provide measures of perceptions of justice. To assess perceptions of the fairness of the negotiation process (FAIRPRCS), subjects responded to the question, "How unfair or fair do you think was the process of coming to some agreement about the final overall pay division?" Responses were on a 1 to 9 point scale, where one indicated very unfair and nine indicated very fair. Individuals answered three questions about the fairness of the final pay division, each beginning with "How unfair or fair do you think the final pay division was ..." The three endings to the question were: to yourself (FAIRSELF), to the co-worker with whom you negotiated, and to the co-worker who worked on the task earlier. Subjects responded in terms of the fairness scale specified above. The latter two items (Pearson's correlation = 0.38) were combined additively and standardized to

Table 8.2 **Descriptions of Situational Factors, Communications*, and Perceptions of Fairness**

Variable	Description
GROUPPAY	Amount of money paid to the group, either $12 (coded 0) or $24 (coded 1).
SPERF	Level of subject's task performance, low (coded 0) or high (coded 1)
SEX	Represents sex of the dyad, male (coded 0) or female (coded 1).
MIXJUST	Dummy variable comparing dyads using just rules (coded 0) to those using a combination of self-interested and just rules (coded 1).
SELFJUST	Dummy variable comparing dyads using just rules (coded 0) to those using self-interested and just rules (coded 1).
OWNOUTC	Proportion of final pay distribution earned by the subject (Actual range 0.17–0.75).
NICEOWN	Proportion of conciliatory messages about own pay proposal to all messages during negotiations, range 0–1.
NICEPRTNR	Proportion of conciliatory messages about partner's pay proposal to all messages during negotiations, range 0–1.
AGGOWN	Proportion of aggressive messages about own pay proposal to all messages during negotiations, range 0–1.
AGGPRTNR	Proportion of aggressive messages about partner's pay proposal to all messages during negotiations, range 0–1.
FAIRNESS	Proportion of fairness comments to all messages during negotiations, range 0–1.
FAIRPRCS	Perceived fairness of the negotiation process; varies from *very unfair* (coded 1) to *very fair* (coded 9).
FAIRSELF	Perceived fairness of the final pay division to the self (subject); varies from *very unfair* (coded 1) to *very fair* (coded 9).
FAIROT	Perceived fairness of the final pay division to other group members (combined additively and standardized); varies from *very unfair* (coded 1) to *very fair* (coded 9).

* All measures of communications are at the dyadic level.

create a theoretically meaningful measure of the perceived fairness of the final pay division to others (FAIROT).

Analyses

Table 8.2 lists the variables used in the ordinary least squares regression analyses. Initial analysis reveals how situational factors (group pay level, performance level, sex, own outcome, and the dummy variables comparing dyads characterized by different orientations) alone and how dyadic communications alone influence perceptions of justice. Subsequent analysis shows the combined effects of situational factors and communications on justice perceptions, controlling for other sources of variation. A final equation assesses the effects of communication on perceptions of the fairness of the outcome to self and other, controlling for perceptions of procedural justice.

Table 8.3   Standardized Regression Coefficients (Standard Error) for Effects of Situational Factors and Communications on Perceptions of Justice

Independent Variables	Fairness Perceptions										
	FAIRPRCs			FAIRSELF				FAIROT			
GROUPPAY	0.13	–	0.21*	0.06	–	0.09	0.02	0.00	–	0.02	-0.05
SPERF	-0.02	–	-0.02	-0.17	–	-0.14	-0.13	0.32***	–	0.32**	0.33**
SEX	0.06	–	0.08	0.09	–	0.09	0.07	0.12	–	0.12	0.10
MIXJUST	-0.18*	–	0.16	0.06	–	0.08	0.03	0.09	–	0.07	0.02
SELFJUST	-0.18*	–	-0.15	-0.20*	–	-0.10	-0.05	-0.05	–	-0.06	-0.01
OWNOUTC	0.08	–	0.08	0.38***	–	0.36***	0.34**	-0.45***	–	-0.44***	-46***
NICEOWN	–	0.17	-0.04	–	-0.12	-0.11	-0.09	–	-0.07	-0.08	0.07
NICEPRTNR	–	-0.11	-0.16*	–	0.06	0.02	0.08	–	-0.03	-0.05	0.01
AGGOWN	–	0.08	-0.08	–	0.05	0.05	0.08	–	-0.03	-0.02	0.01
AGGPRTNR	–	-0.14*	-0.16*	–	-0.20**	-0.21**	-0.16*	–	-0.06	-0.03	0.01
FAIRNESS	–	0.10	-0.07	–	0.05	-0.07	-0.05	–	0.05	0.04	0.06
FAIRPRCS	–	–	–	–	–	–	0.35***	–	–	–	0.31***
Constant	5.34	7.31	5.17	4.25	7.36	4.22	2.55	9.29	7.12	9.29	8.02
R^2	0.09	0.06	0.15	0.12	0.08	0.18	0.28	0.13	0.01	0.14	0.22
Adjusted R^2	0.06	0.03	0.08	0.08	0.05	0.12	0.22	0.10	-0.02	0.08	0.16
N	159	159	159	157	157	157	157	156	156	156	156

Significance levels are for one-tail tests if in predicted direction; otherwise they are for two-tail tests.
• $p < 0.05$ **$p < 0.01$ ***$p < 0.001$

Results

Manipulation Check

To determine whether subjects perceived $12 to be an insufficient amount to meet group members' pay expectations and $24 to be sufficient, they answered the following: "Thinking about the pay your group received, how sufficient do you think the funds were to pay all group members?" (1 = not at all sufficient, 9 = very sufficient). Results indicate a significant effect for group pay level ($B = 1.87$[SD = 0.31, beta = 0.44], t = 5.95 [d.f. = 150], $p < 0.001$), controlling for subject's sex and measures of justice conflict. High group reward subjects perceived the amount to be more sufficient than low group reward subjects (calculated predicted values of the means are 6.22 and 4.75, respectively).

Separate Effects of Situational Factors and Communications on Justice Perceptions

Examination of the effects of situational factors on justice perceptions generally replicates results reported in Hegtvedt and Killian (1999). Subtle differences stem from the use here of a measure of the nature of justice conflict, not simply differences between dyad members' initial pay distributions. As hypothesized in Hegtvedt and Killian (1999), conflict affects perceptions of the fairness of the process of negotiation (Table 8.3). Dyads oriented toward self-advantage assess the process as less fair than do dyads oriented toward justice. Interestingly, however, dyads with one member who is oriented to self-interest and another oriented toward justice principles evaluate the negotiations as more fair than dyads in which both pursue other-advantage.

With regard to perceptions of outcome fairness, the size of one's own outcome is positively related to fairness to self but negatively related to fairness to others. The nature of justice conflict in the dyad also affects assessments of the fairness of one's own outcome. Participants in dyads involving self-interest conflict evaluate their outcomes as less fair than those characterized by justice principle conflict. The nature of conflict, however, fails to affect perceptions of fairness to others. The only additional effect is for level of subject's performance. High performers assess the outcomes to others as more fair than do low performers.

Hypothesis 1 suggests that conciliatory communications are likely to be positively related to perceptions of justice. Results (Table 8.3), however, fail to confirm this hypothesis in terms of any type of perceived justice. Neither "nice" communications about one's own division or one's partner's division affects fairness assessments. In contrast, findings provide some support for Hypothesis 2 focusing on negative, aggressive communications. Although aggressive communications about one's own pay division fail to affect perceptions of fairness, such messages about one's partner's proposals do. To the extent that dyadic communications about one's partner's pay division is characterized by denigrating arguments, individuals are less likely to perceive the bargaining process as fair and are less likely to assess their own outcome as fair. Use of fairness arguments, like conciliatory ones, exerts no effects on any type of perceived justice, thus disconfirming Hypothesis 3. Interestingly, no type of communication exerts any effect on perceptions of fairness to others.

Assessing Mediation: The Combined Effects of Situational Factors and Communications on Perceptions of Justice

Table 8.3 also presents results controlling for situational factors in order to assess the extent to which communications attenuate the effects of such factors and thus imply that they mediate between features of the situation and assessments of justice. With regard to perceptions of the fairness of the process of negotiation, the once significant comparisons between dyads (Table 8.3) involving different types of conflict become non-significant, signaling the mediating effects of communications as predicted by Hypothesis 4. Group reward level, however, emerges as significant. Those in high pay groups evaluate the process as more fair than those in low pay groups. The effect of aggressive communications about the partner's division remains significant in the predicted direction. In addition, an effect for positive communications about the partner's division emerges. The direction of the effect is opposite to that expected, however. "Nice" comments about one's partner's division decrease the perceived fairness of the process.

With regard to perceptions of the fairness of the outcome to self, the addition of the communications factors reduces the previously significant effects of the comparisons between dyad types to non-significance. Thus, it appears that that communications mediate the effects of conflict on perceptions of justice, as indicated by Hypothesis 4. Communications, however, do not mediate the effects of own outcome. No evidence emerges with regard to the mediating effects of communications on evaluations of the fairness of the outcome to others.

To explore the effects of communications independent of their meaning for perceptions of procedural justice, I include the measure of fairness of the process in analysis of the effects of situational factors and communications on perceptions of distributive justice. Inclusion of procedural justice perceptions to predict perceived outcome fairness hardly alters the findings (Table 8.3). Not surprisingly, perceptions of procedural fairness are positively related to fairness to self and fairness to others. And, inclusion of procedural assessments nearly doubles the R^2's for both forms of outcome fairness. Despite the addition of process evaluations, negative communications about partner's division continue to be negatively related to perceptions of fairness to self. This finding suggests that communications exert an effect independent of what they might contribute to process evaluations on perceptions of distributive justice.

Discussion

This study attempts to fill a void in the literature regarding the implications of the negotiation process for perceptions of fairness. In particular, emphasis focused on the nature of "talk" during negotiations as an important element influencing subsequent evaluations of the fairness of the process itself and the fairness of the outcomes for self and other. The data allowed assessment of the effects of both conciliatory and aggressive comments about one's own and a partner's pay proposals as well as the use of statements about the fairness of those proposals. Although, as discussed further below, the pre-set message library limits the extent of comments, the results highlight the differential impact of various types of communications for various types of fairness assessments. In doing so, this study is a first step in a more detailed understanding of the impact of bargaining communications on perceived procedural and distributive justice.

The data provide a consistent, albeit limited, response to the main queries of this paper: how do bargaining communications affect justice perceptions? And, to what extent do communications mediate the effects of situational factors on justice perceptions? Aggressive communications about one's partner's pay proposals certainly decrease the perceived fairness of the process of negotiation and of the outcome to oneself, confirming Hypothesis 2. This effect remains regardless of controls for situational factors and, in the case of fairness to self, regardless of the inclusion of evaluations of procedural justice. Thus, communications—a certain type—do mediate the effects of situational factors on certain types of fairness evaluations.

In contrast to the consistent effects of aggressive communications about a partner's proposal, aggressive communications about one's own division failed to affect justice perceptions. It may be that in bargaining situations people expect others to take strong stances about their own interests. However, when negotiators denigrate their partner's ideas they signal a lack of empathy and perhaps less willingness to come to some agreement. A partner may feel insulted as well and act defensively in response. The aggressive comments and reactions in a dyad may exacerbate the conflict underlying the negotiation process. To some extent this pattern may be akin to the types of arguments used by political candidates; putting forth one's own agenda is expected, but opponents as well as the public often react negatively to mud-slinging or revelations of less than stellar personal lives, i.e., "negative campaigning."

That conciliatory messages failed to have the effect predicted by Hypothesis 1 is surprising. The rationale for the hypothesis indicated that such communications convey empathy and empathy denotes concern for the welfare of all parties, a characteristic at the heart of a true justice schema. Several issues, however, surround these findings. First, at the empirical level, the items may not have captured as conciliatory a tone as intended. Although developed to represent recognition of a partner's viewpoint, the phrasing of some items with a clause beginning with "but" may have been interpreted as counter-arguments, thus decreasing empathy. Second, combining empirical and theoretical levels, the impersonal character of electronic messages between strangers, coupled with general beliefs about the competitiveness of negotiations, may have inhibited the development of empathy. In face-to-face situations or even ones in which a person's verbal tone could be assessed, the conciliatory messages might have greater impact. These two issues suggest that future research should vary strategies for measuring and conveying conciliatory communications.

And third, at the theoretical level, the meaning of a conciliatory strategy might be reassessed. In the one instance in which conciliatory comments are significant, the effect on perceptions of justice is in the opposite direction from that predicted. Use of conciliatory comments about partner's division decreased perceived fairness of the negotiation process, suggesting that subjects may have worried about being "suckered." They might have wondered whether their partner said nice things about their division as a strategic attempt to getting them to make more concessions. Although beyond the scope of these analyses, this finding raises concerns with the nature of the combination of messages used. If a person generally employs aggressive communications, a switch to more conciliatory ones may be greeted with skepticism.

Likewise, the nature of fairness communications may have been difficult to interpret. Although earlier analyses (Hegtvedt, Brezina and Funk, 1995) showed that subjects used fairness communications more frequently in materially self-interested dyads compared to dyads offering other-advantaged initial divisions in which conflict is over justice principles, recipients of those communications may have seen them either as strategic actions or as attempts of good-will to facilitate an agreement. The possibility of mixed interpretations in the actual bargaining situation rather than the proposed strategic usage may account for the lack of support for Hypothesis 3.

Although communications do not have as great an impact on perceptions of justice as expected, it is interesting to note that they only impact two types of justice: procedural and distributive regarding one's own outcomes. Communications fail to influence perceptions of outcome justice for others in the situation. To the extent that negotiations themselves draw attention to an individual's own actions and own outcomes, their concern for fairness to others may be minimal, especially in such an impersonal situation. Additionally, of studies investigating what people believe is fair for other group members, most show that concerns about injustice for oneself are more pronounced than concerns about others' injustice. For example, Messick and Sentis (1979), demonstrate that actors believe that lower amounts are fairer to others than to themselves. Such an egocentric bias underlies the results here for the influence of own outcome level on assessments of fairness for self and other. In addition, Lind, Kray and Thompson (1998) show that one's own mild experiences of injustice have a greater impact on impressions of the situation than experiences of severe injustice by another person. But when own injustice experiences create empathy, individuals may be more likely to respond to the severe injustice of another group member (Kray and Lind, 2002). Thus, stimulation of perceptions of another actor's injustice depends upon situational circumstances that solidify a group. Insofar as such conditions do not typically characterize negotiations, the failure of communications to impact evaluations of justice for the partner is understandable.

In bargaining, perhaps only when one's own deserving is at issue does concern with fairness to others grow salient—from an egocentric viewpoint, however. The unexpected effect of subject's performance level on perceptions of fairness to others partially supports this idea. The effect shows that high performers were more likely to see the outcomes as fair to their partners. And, although non-significant, the effect of performance level on fairness to self is in the opposite direction. Assuming egocentrism, together these results suggest that smaller amounts to lower performers are perceived as fair from the perspective of the high performer. And, when assessing fairness to others, it does not matter what was said during the negotiations.

In contrast, what was said during the negotiations matters for the other two types of justice beyond the effect of situational factors (except own outcome level). That the effects of the nature of conflict in the situation grow non-significant with the inclusion of communications implies that the messages may mediate the effects of situational factors as suggested in Hypothesis 4. Such a finding indicates that despite or in view of the context of negotiation, the way bargainers approach the negotiation may have a profound impact on whether the resulting division of outcomes are perceived as fair. For example, husbands and wives may want to avoid using insults and attacks even in their pursuit of self-interested ends with regard to spending income tax returns, deciding of vacation locales, etc.

Avoiding the use of such negative remarks does more than ensure procedural justice. Although communications may constitute one way in which people assess their treatment in a group—their status, the extent to which they are trusted and treated without bias (Tyler and Lind, 1992)—they also appear to create independent meanings about the situation. What is said stimulates an interpretative process (Chatman, Putnam and Sondak, 1991), which appears to go beyond the bounds of the antecedents of procedural justice.

These findings, coupled with those regarding fairness to others, raise issues regarding the role of procedural justice in bargaining situations and, perhaps, in other contexts as well. In terms of the bargaining situation, the typical authority/subordinate relationships characteristic of the organizations in which much procedural justice research is done is absent. In addition, bargaining partners may focus more on the conflict of negotiations (Molm, Takahashi and Peterson, 2003) and thus fail to see themselves as members of the same group. As a consequence, one of the assumptions of the group-value model of procedural justice is not met in the bargaining context (Lind and Tyler, 1988). Future research should delve into the elements underlying what individuals perceive to constitute procedural justice in negotiations or more generally in situations like the one examined here involving equal status actors outside of institutional frameworks. In addition, given the independent impact of communications in this study, another way to augment the typical procedural justice research paradigm may be to investigate the actual dynamics between authorities and subordinates, not simply how they interpret characteristics of the relationship. In other words, procedural justice researchers might also investigate the "talk" between workers and their superiors in order to understand when concerns with group value emerge or fail to do so.

In ongoing situations, not simply one-time negotiation sessions, it may also be possible to explore an alternative to the argument here. While some types of communications may impact perceptions of justice as shown here, it may also be the case that the perceived fairness of the process or of the outcome may affect the nature of communications used in groups. If people perceive themselves to be unfairly treated or compensated, they may be more likely to use negative communications, which may get the authority's attention or exacerbate the injustice of the situation. Whether either scenario is true awaits empirical study. Some findings, however, suggest that perceived justice impacts the style that subordinates use to manage conflict with their supervisors (Rahim, Magner and Shapiro, 2000). Higher levels of all types of justice relate positively to the use of more cooperative conflict management styles.

This study investigates a narrow range of communications in a highly controlled situation. As noted above, the study's methods disallow the richness of communication in many ways: vocal tone, facial gestures, body language. Indeed, face-to-face communication may enhance rapport (Drolet and Morris, 1999), which may in turn affect the impact of communications and the relevance of elements of procedural justice. Study of these processes in face-to-face dyads of a variety of types is an avenue for future research. Also, by controlling on the gender of dyad members, the analysis omits consideration of nuances created in mixed gender dyads. For example, Carli (1990) shows that language akin to the conciliatory comments used here (i.e., tentative language) may increase the influence of women interacting with males whereas aggressive comments used by females in mixed gender dyads may have the reverse effect. Thus, it is important to explore how gender composition of the negotiating dyad affects the impact of communications on perceptions of fairness. The analyses presented here focus solely on the effects of types of communication in the absence of the pattern of those communications as well as of offers and counter-offers, and the size and reciprocity of concession making.

Indeed, the meaning of communications may be linked with the actual behavior of moving toward an agreement. Research on frame analysis in bargaining (Putnam and Holmer, 1991) suggests that negotiators use new information in the situation to revalue their own position and strategy. Such an approach assumes the active, ongoing interpretation of negotiators in the situation, which may help to explain the effect of communications beyond that embodied in procedural justice evaluations. Thus, in order to gain a more precise understanding of how negotiation communications affect perceptions of fairness future research should include analyses that can link communication with concession behavior. Such a study may involve the explicit manipulation of communications, coupled with concession behavior, in order to examine their joint impact, controlling for other factors.

The negotiation of the distribution of benefits occurs in many situations, involving partners who vary in terms of their power positions, affective relations, time perspective, and so forth. In addition, justice is a pervasive value in society. In joining these two aspects of social interaction, this research examines one way in which bargaining communications may create perceptions of justice. By focusing on the nature of the conflict between negotiators, however, the study raises concerns with a fundamental issue of all social groups: the conflict between the fairness that can bind group members and the self-interest that often propels the behavior of most individuals (see van Dijk, De Cremer and Handgraaf, 2004). This study is a small step in understanding that "what is said" ultimately affects the outcome of a conflict.

References

Adams, J.S. (1965), "Inequity in Social Exchange", *Advances in Experimental Social Psychology*, **2**, 267–299.

Bacharach, S.B. and Lawler, E.J. (1981), *Bargaining: Power, Tactics, and Outcomes* (San Francisco: Jossey-Bass).

Bazerman, M.H., Curhan, J.R., Moore, D.A. and Valley, K.L. (2000), "Negotiation", *Annual Review of Psychology*, **51**, 279–314. [PubMed 10751973] [DOI: 10.1146/annurev.psych.51.1.279]

Bies, R.J. and Moag, J.S. (1986), "Interactional Justice: Communication Criteria of Fairness" in *Research on Negotiation in Organizations*, Vol. 1. Lewicki, R.J., Sheppard, B.H. and Bazerman, M.H. (eds) (Greenwich, CT: JAI Press), 43–55.

Carli, L.L. (1990), "Gender, Language, and Influence", *Journal of Personality and Social Psychology*, **59**, 941–951. [DOI: 10.1037/0022-3514.59.5.941]

Carroll, J.S. and Payne, J.W. (1991), "An Information Processing Approach to Two-Party Negotiations", *Research on Negotiation in Organizations*, **3**, 3–34.

Chatman, J.A., Putnam, L.L. and Sondak, H. (1991), "Integrating Communication and Negotiation Research", *Research on Negotiation in Organizations*, **3**, 139–164.

Chertkoff, J.M. and Esser, J.K. (1976), "A Review of Experiments in Explicit Bargaining", *Journal of Experimental Social Psychology*, **12**, 464–486. [DOI: 10.1016/0022-1031%2876%2990078-0]

Cohen, R.L. (1991), "Justice and Negotiation", *Research on Negotiation in Organizations*, **3**, 259–282.

Deutsch, M. (1985), *Distributive Justice: A Social Psychological Perspective* (New Haven: Yale University Press).

Deutsch, M. (2000), "Justice and Conflict" in *The Handbook of Conflict Resolution: Theory and Practice*. Deutsch, M. and Coleman, P.T. (eds) (San Francisco: Jossey-Bass), 141–164.

Drolet, A.L. and Morris, M.W. (1999), "Rapport in Conflict Resolution: Accounting for how Nonverbal Exchange Fosters Coordination on Mutually Beneficial Settlements to Mixed Motive Conflicts", *Journal of Experimental Social Psychology*, **36**, 26–50. [DOI: 10.1006/jesp.1999.1395]

Fiske, S.T. and Taylor, S.E. (1991), *Social Cognition* (New York: McGraw-Hill).

Hamner, W.C. and Yukl, G.A. (1977), "The Effectiveness of Different Offer Strategies in Bargaining", in *Negotiations: Social Psychological Perspectives*. Druckman, D. (ed.) (Beverly Hills, CA: Sage), 137–160.

Handgraaf, M.J.J., van Dijk, E., Wilke, H.A.M. and Vermunt, R.C. (2003), "The Salience of a Recipient's Alternatives: Inter- and Intrapersonal Comparison in Ultimate Games", *Organizational Behavior and Human Decision Processes*, **90**, 165–177. [DOI: 10.1016/S0749-5978%2802%2900512-5]

Handgraaf, M.J.J., van Dijk, E., Wilke, H.A.M. and Vermunt, R.C. (2004), "Evaluability of Outcomes in Ultimatum Bargaining", *Organizational Behavior and Human Decision Processes*, **95**, 97–106. [DOI: 10.1016/j.obhdp.2004.06.005]

Hegtvedt, K.A. and Cook, K.S. (1987), "The Role of Justice in Conflict Situations", *Advances in Group Processes*, **4**, 108–136.

Hegtvedt, K.A. and Johnson, C. (2000), "Justice beyond the Individual: A Future with Legitimation", *Social Psychology Quarterly*, **63**, 298–311. [DOI: 10.2307/2695841]

Hegtvedt, K.A. and Killian, C. (1999), "Fairness and Emotions: Reactions to the Process and Outcomes of Negotiation", *Social Forces*, **78**, 269–303. [DOI: 10.2307/3005797]

Hegtvedt, K.A. and Markovsky, B. (1995), "Justice and Injustice" in *Sociological Perspectives on Social Psychology*. Cook, K., Fine, G. and House, J. (eds) (Boston: Allyn & Bacon), 257–280.

Hegtvedt, K.A., Brezina, T. and Funk, S. (1995), "When Cries of "It's not Fair" are not Fair: Factors Affecting the Negotiated Resolution of Justice Conflict", Paper presented at the Meetings of the American Sociological Association, Washington, D.C.

Howard, J.A. (1995), "Social Cognition" in *Sociological Perspectives on Social Psychology*. Cook, K., Fine, G. and House, J. (eds) (Boston: Allyn & Bacon), 90–117.

Kaplowitz, S.A. (1977), "The Influence of Moral Considerations and the Perceived Consequences of Action", *Journal of Conflict Resolution*, **21**, 475–500.

Kray, L. and Lind, E.A. (2002), "The Injustices of Others: Social Reports and the Integration of Others' Experiences in Organizational Justice Judgments", *Organizational and Human Decision Processes*, **89**, 906–924. [DOI: 10.1016/S0749-5978%2802%2900035-3]

Lamm, H. (1986), "Justice Consideration in Interpersonal Conflict" in *Justice in Social Relations*. Bierhoff, H., Cohen, R.L. and Greenberg, J. (eds) (New York: Plenum Publishing), 43–63.

Lawler, E.J. and Ford, R. (1995), "Bargaining" in *Sociological Perspectives on Social Psychology*. Cook, K., Fine, G. and House, J. (eds) (Boston: Allyn & Bacon), 236–256.

Leung, K., Tong, K. and Ho, S.S. (2004), "Effects of Interactional Justice on Egocentric Bias in Resource Allocation Decisions", *Journal of Applied Psychology*, **89**, 405–415. [PubMed 15161401] [DOI: 10.1037/0021-9010.89.3.405]

Lind, E.A. and Tyler, T.R. (1988), *The Social Psychology of Procedural Justice* (New York: Plenum Publishing).

Lind, E.A., Kray, L. and Thompson, L. (1998), "The Social Construction of Injustice: Fairness Judgments in Response to Own and Others' Unfair Treatment by Authorities", *Organizational Behavior and Human Decision Processes*, **75**, 1–22. [PubMed 9719655] [DOI: 10.1006/obhd.1998.2785]

McClintock, C.G., Stech, F.J. and Keil, L.J. (1983), "The Influence of Communication upon Bargaining" in *Basic Group Processes*. Paulus, P.B. (ed.) (New York: Springer-Verlag), 205–233.

Messick, D.M. and Sentis, K.P. (1979), "Fairness and Preference", *Journal of Experimental Social Psychology*, **15**, 416–434. [DOI: 10.1016/0022-1031%2879%2990047-7]

Mikula, G. and Wenzel, M. (2000), "Justice and Social Conflict", *International Journal of Psychology*, **35**, 126–135. [DOI: 10.1080/002075900399420]

Molm, L.D., Takahashi, N. and Peterson, G. (2003), "In the Eye of the Beholder: Procedural Justice in Social Exchange", *American Sociological Review*, **68**, 128–152. [DOI: 10.2307/3088905]

Putnam, L.L. and Holmer, M. (1991), "A Framing, Reframing, and Issue Development" in *Communication and Negotiation*. Putnam, L.L. and Roloff, M.E. (eds) (Newbury Park, CA: Sage), 128–155.

Rahim, M.A., Magner, N.R. and Shapiro, D.L. (2000), "Do Justice Perceptions Influence Styles of Handling Conflict with Supervisor? What Justice Perceptions, Precisely?" *International Journal of Conflict Management*, **11**, 9–31.

Rawls, J. (1971), *A Theory of Justice* (Boston: Harvard University Press).

Thompson, L. and Loewenstein, G. (1992), "Egocentric Interpretations of Fairness and Interpersonal Conflict", *Organizational Behavior and Human Decision Processes*, **51**, 176–197. [DOI: 10.1016/0749-5978%2892%2990010-5]

Tjösvold, D. (1977), "Commitment to Justice in Conflict between Unequal Status Persons", *Journal of Applied Social Psychology*, **7**, 149–162. [DOI: 10.1111/j.1559-1816.1977.tb01336.x]

Törnblom, K.Y. (1988), "Positive and Negative Allocations: A Typology and Model of Conflicting Justice Principles", *Advances in Group Processes*, **5**, 141–168.

Törnblom, K.Y. (1992), "The Social Psychology of Distributive Justice" in *Justice: Interdisciplinary Perspectives*. Scherer, K. (ed.) (Cambridge: Cambridge University Press), 177–236.

Tyler, T.R. and Lind, E.A. (1992), "A Relational Model of Authority in Groups", *Advances in Experimental Social Psychology*, **25**, 115–191.

Tyler, T.R., Boeckmann, R.J., Smith, H.J. and Huo, Y.J. (1997), *Social Justice in a Diverse Society* (Boulder, CO: Westview Press).

Van Dijk, E., De Cremer, D. and Handgraaf, M.J.J. (2004), "Social Value Orientations and the Strategic Use Fairness in Ultimatum Bargaining", *Journal of Experimental Social Psychology*, **40**, 697–707. [DOI: 10.1016/j.jesp.2004.03.002]

Walcott, C., Hopmann, P.T. and King, T.D. (1977), "The Role of Debate in Negotiation" in *Negotiations: Social Psychological Perspectives*. Druckman, D. (ed.) (Beverly Hills, CA: Sage), 193–212.

Wall, J.A. (1985), *Negotiation: Theory and Practice* (Glenview, IL: Scott, Foresman).

Zartman, I.W. (1988), "Common Elements in the Analyses of the Negotiation Process", *Negotiation Journal*, **4**, 31–43. [DOI: 10.1007/BF01000902]

Chapter 9

Social Injustice in Indian Country: Historical Antecedents of Current Issues

Laurence Armand French
University of New Hampshire, USA

Nancy Picthall-French

Introduction

American Indians have suffered injustices within the United States from the beginning of white contact in the sixteenth century up to the present. Although the days of overt genocide are over a more subtle form of exploitation continues today as is evident in the current controversies surrounding the mismanagement of the Individual Indian Trust Fund and the deliberate exploitation of gaming tribes by lobbyist and politicians. Clearly, any analysis of Native Americans' (American Indians and Native Alaskans/Eskimos) justice in the United States needs to focus on the uniqueness of this relationship of a conquering colonial power over the subjugated indigenous population and how it differs from other minority groups in the United States and even Canada's aboriginals (First Nations and Inuit). American Indians, because of their federal protection status within Indian Country (federally-recognized tribal reservations), obviates any comparison with other racial minorities including, Blacks, Hispanics/Latinos and Asians. These other minority groups of color have historically benefited from class mobility, albeit limited and mostly within their own ethnic/cultural communities, hence adhering to the socio-economic benefits of the larger societal value system. This is not to say that problems relevant to procedural (due process) and distributive (goods/wealth) injustices are not present—but, when they exist, they appear to be more a factor of economic class than culture, religion or race (Park, 1964). In this chapter, we first would like to show how the situation of American Indians differs from that in Canada, which factors are important to explain the injustices done to them, and what the main differences are between the Native American culture and the society at large. To get an accurate picture of the contemporary treatment of American Indians it is necessary to describe the genesis of United States Indian Policy as it has developed from the earliest period on. The next part of the chapter will describe contemporary social justice issues. The chapter will conclude with suggestions for a better understanding and treatment policy of Native Americans.

The Position of the American Indians

Native Americans in US and Canada

While political structure of both the United States and Canada are, for the most part, products of the British system, Canada has managed to treat its indigenous peoples better than the Americans. Historically, Canada had periods where it treated its aboriginal peoples poorly but things have improved greatly since passage of the Constitutional Act of 1982. Since 1876, Canada has done a far better job in allowing its Aboriginals to practice their traditional cultural way hence demonstrating the ability to tolerate and embrace the aboriginal communitarian cultural ways while adhering to Protestant capitalism within the larger societal order. Canada's adherence to a fundamental justice model gives it an advantage in addressing multicultural needs, including those of its First Nations and Inuit. On the other hand, America's *due process* procedural justice model has proven to be incompatible with the communitarian distributive justice model associated with Indian tribes eventually leading to the imposition of the Euro-American justice model in Indian country at the expense of aboriginal traditional custom inherent in the *Harmony Ethos*. Essentially, the Canadian system is more in line with the Rawlsian and Kymlicka models of multiculturalism where there is a mix of Euro-Canadian and traditional customs such as restorative justice (Kymlicka, 1995; Rawls, 1999). By the same token, the failure of the United States to recognize aboriginal cultural ways makes Walzer's historical antecedents of value progression argument a weak one when looking at multicultural justice in America (Walzer, 1983). The progressive integration of the US due process model with that of aboriginal customs and mores did not evolve due to the harsh repression of tribal traditionalism and the forced imposition of a white-dominated justice system. Actually, United States treatment of American Indians is more in concert with the old apartheid system in South Africa challenging Nozick's contention that fair forms of distributive justice will evolve in systems where procedural justice is purported to be equal for all parties involved and with only free will determining differential outcomes (Nozick, 1977). Iris Marion Young's feminist concept relevant to the failure of distributive justice in white, male-dominated societies provides the best model for explaining the dilemma of Native American injustices in the United States (Young, 1990). Her thesis of a paternalistic double standard of justice equally applies to the US Government's treatment of Native Americans and its regulation of Indian country. Here, American Indians have long been viewed as immature humans not capable of responsible adult behaviors hence requiring the benevolent supervision of the White-dominated society in making all major decisions regarding their lives.

Factors Affecting the Position of American Indians

Clearly, America's strong conservatism and sense of white supremacy plays a critical role here (Stephanson, 1995). The superiority of white, Anglo-Saxon Protestants (WASP) was established early in the United States under the doctrine of *Manifest Destiny* which justified WASP Divine Providence and the inherent superiority of white over other race and ethnic groups. These two factors, in turn, tended to support an unwavering doctrine of individualistic free will and capitalism and a strong aversion to communal life-styles like those inherent in aboriginal cultures. Indeed, America's aversion to communism predated Marx and Engels's (1967) 1848 work, *The Communist Manifesto*, by 70 years beginning with the establishment of the new Republic. American Indians were the first to experience the punitive wrath of America's intolerance for any system other than their model of Protestant capitalism (Weber, 1930). These differences played themselves out within the contravening justice models used by American Indians versus their Euro-American counterparts. The history of US/Indian relations is based on the United States attempting to destroy the communitarian Harmony Ethos and its focus on balance and restorative justice and replace it with the Christian capitalistic *due process* procedural justice model. Added to this problem is the fact that American Indians have rarely had real access to the due process provisions imposed upon them since they rarely have held equal status before the white courts.

The American Indian Harmony Ethos

The *Harmony Ethos* provided the foundation of restorative, communitarian justice for North American Indians prior to European influence. Most notable of this system was the shared ownership of land and material wealth. Individuals had few possessions that they owned outright. Mother Earth (land) was not owned but leased from her by those occupying it at any given time. Property boundaries were determined at the clan or tribal level with large tracks of forest and grazing lands open to all. Moreover, infractions of mores and folkways were dealt with at the clan and not at the individual level. The restoration of group balance and not individual culpability drove the aboriginal systems of justice. Many elements of this aboriginal world view survived to the present. Common tenets of this ethos transcend the hundreds of American Indian and Native Alaskan groups residing in North America (northern Mexico, the United States except it Pacific islands, and Canada) despite variations in their *creation myths*—the justifying epistemological methodology for subscribing to the Harmony Ethos. The Harmony Ethos stress the importance of individual independence and the avoidance of overt aggressiveness. Third persons or objects were often used to convey dissatisfaction in intra-tribal interactions. Other characteristics of the Harmony Ethos include: a resentment of authority; a hesitancy to command others; a reluctance to refuse requests made by others in their group; an obligatory hospitality and sharing with kinfolk; an impassivity regarding greetings and exchanges; the refusal, or unwillingness, to contradict others; and the absence of gestures in public speaking. These attributes differ considerably from those spelled out in the Protestant Ethic which stresses competition, personal aggressiveness, and individual accountability. The Harmony Ethos calls for group cooperation and not individual competition. Balance and in-group cooperation are the norms of the aboriginal Harmony Ethos. Even during wars the purpose was to balance the kill from pervious battles. Blood vengeance, even for serious offenses like murder, usually had a de jure statute of limitations of one calendar year (Reid, 1970). The ideal of the Harmony Ethos was restorative justice and fair compensation to the clan offended. Punishment per se is not the desired outcome as it is within America's *due process* model. Moreover, community (clan, family) participation in the judicial process evened the playing field avoiding the blatant injustices long associated with the US model of selective justice as is evident in the current reevaluation of the US death sentence and its obvious prejudice against minorities and the poor which until recently included the mentally retarded and youth (French, 1977, 2005).

Given these contravening judicial ideals the fact is that aboriginals of North America have long suffered from both physical and cultural genocide at the hands of the European colonists. This situation was especially true in the United States where federal policy originally sanctioned ethnic cleansing in the form of genocide and forced removal. These policies decimated the Native American population from tens of millions to less than a million by the time of President Grant's *Peace Policy* of 1870. This was the beginning of a more subtle form of discrimination under the pretense of *distributive justice*. And with the pretense of distributive justice came the justification for the abolition of treaty making with Native American tribes. The idea here was that by dividing up tribal lands into individual allotments American Indians would no longer require treaty protection given that this process would assimilate them into the larger US society. The problem with distributive and procedural justice in the United States at that time was that American Indians were still disenfranchised and did not have the weight of a non-Indian before state or federal courts, federal or state. US citizenship for American Indians did not come until 1924 and even then many states refused to provide state citizenship with New Mexico being the last doing so in 1982.

American Indians continue to be exploited by those mandated to protect their interests. This is evident with the current Individual Indian Money Trust investigation and the bilking of gaming tribes by Republican lobbyist Jack Abramoff. A brief of the history of US/Indian relationships is required to best understand the nature of Indian exploitation. The practice of *federal paternalism* stemming from President Grant's (1870) Peace Policy served to obviate critical elements of decision and process control. Clearly, there was no fairness in the model of procedural justice imposed upon Indian country by the US Congress and the US Department of the Interior via the Bureau of Indian Affairs (BIA). The *interactive justice* process was one-sided with Indian tribes having little or no real power or authority to accept, reject, or otherwise influence decisions about their fate while they often fared poorly under the US model of procedural justice. The Intercourse Acts gave whites superior standing before the US Courts with Indians having little recourse to the due process model of justice. Public Law 280 in the 1950s illustrates a current example of discriminatory interactive justice. Certain tribes were forced to accept state intervention in Indian country with out their consent and in violation of previous federal treaties. Under these and similar circumstances anti-Indian sentiments played a major role with the adjudication of American Indians by non-Indian police, prosecutors, judges and correctional officers, a phenomenon that continues to the present (Sweeney and McFarlin, 1993; Morris, 2000; Beugre and Baron, 2001; French, 2003).

The Genesis of US Indian Policy

The introduction of Western judicial and martial justice came with the Europeans and their struggle over control of North America. Indian/European alliances changed the circumstances of dealing with traditional enemies. No longer was the enemy body count related to accommodating a balance for their own dead, now the tribes were indoctrinated with the European concept of annihilation. This introduction to the European concept of martial justice set the stage for the long and brutal history of Indian/white wars that began during the Colonial Era and extended to the early 1970s. During the early days of the United States, non-hostile administrative rules were developed as well outlining the nature of trade with Indian groups. The Trade and Intercourse Acts (1790; 1793; 1796; 1799; 1802; 1822; 1834) began shortly after the establishment of the War Department in 1789. From then on the military played a critical role in policing Indian country.

Rules governing criminal justice emerged over the years as well. Initially, federal and state criminal jurisdiction pertained only to Indian/white interactions either in or out of Indian country. Intra-tribal offenses were pretty much left to traditional Indian justice. Again there was a wide variance between types of justice with the Five Civilized Tribes (Cherokee, Choctaw, Chickasaw, Creek and Seminole) adopting the Euro-American style of justice in the early nineteenth century and carrying this form of government with them to Indian territory (Oklahoma) following removal while other tribes continued to maintain their aboriginal forms of justice. Of these eastern tribes the Cherokee were the largest with over 60 permanent villages covering a vast area in western North Carolina, northern Georgia, southern Virginia, eastern Tennessee and parts of Alabama.

The Cherokee were encouraged to abandon their pre-Columbian traditional ways and adopted those of the Euro-Americans in an effort to keep their homeland. In doing so, they had to disenfranchise women who had an equal vote with adult males and acquire black slaves, a concept alien to aboriginal folkways. The transition to US procedural law required the establishment of criminal justice system based on the due process model along with the establishment of police forces, courts and jails. This required shifting justice issues from the seven traditional clans to a formal control mechanism with set procedures and record keeping. Historically, Cherokee folklore vested these responsibilities in the clan structure and its system of blood vengeance. Moreover, no negative sanction lasted more than a year within the aboriginal system regardless of the seriousness of the offense. Balance was maintained at beginning of the new year with all offenses forgiven. Essentially, traditional Cherokee folkways provided the clans only a year to avenge any wrong before the statute of limitations ran out. Despite these changes the seven Civilized Tribes were forcefully removed, with considerable cost of lives, by the US Army under President Andrew Jackson's directive, west of the Mississippi to Indian Territory (now the state of Oklahoma). Cohen noted that the historical precedent for criminal justice within Indian country rested with the Trade and Intercourse Acts.[1]

---

1   The exercise of federal jurisdiction over non-Indian offenders against Indians in Indian country was first put on a statutory basis by the original Trade and Intercourse Act, the Act of July 22, 1790.... These provisions were reenacted with minor modifications in the later temporary Trade and Intercourse Acts of 1793, 1796, and 1799, and were embodied in the first permanent Trade and Intercourse Act of 1802 as sections 2 to 10, inclusive. The general rule established by these statutes was confirmed in the Act of March 3, 1817 (Federal Enclaves

The basis of Indian jurisprudence emerged out of the US Supreme Court decisions forged under Chief Justice John Marshall. Three cases, known as the *Marshall trilogy*, determined early on what the relationship between American Indians and the US would be as well as what authority each branches of government would have in these matters. In 1823, in *Johnson v McIntosh*, the Court determined that with the establishment of the United States Indian tribes could no longer transfer their land to other parties without the consent and approval of the federal government. This establishment of federal supervision over tribes' was based on the court's determination that tribe sovereignty was diminished with the establishment of the United States. Then in 1831 in *Cherokee Nation v Georgia*, the US Supreme Court determined that tribes, specifically the Cherokee Nation, were not foreign states but merely *domestic dependent nations* existing within the confines of the greater United States. This ruling established the federal trust relationship with tribes. Consequently the Court ruled that tribes could not sue states in federal court. A year later, in 1832, in *Worchester v Georgia*, the US Supreme Court ruled that states could not interfere with tribal jurisdictions given that tribes (Indian country) constituted distinct communities, occupying their own territory with clearly defined boundaries. The results of Marshall's trilogy gave the US Congress total and exclusive authority over Indian country even if this meant abrogating previous treaties. Essentially the US Supreme Court empowered Congress to regulate the tribes. This power subsequently included challenging the sovereign powers of the tribe when dealing with criminal offenses within Indian country.

In these early years of the republic, the War Department provided the enforcement arm in Indian country while the Indian Agent (later upgraded to the position of Commissioner of Indian Affairs in 1832) determined which issues required adjudication. The regulation of non-Indians within Indian country was first articulated by Congress in 1817 with the Federal Enclaves Act, also known as the General Crimes Act. The purpose of the Federal Enclaves Act was to extend the entire body of federal law into Indian country. The justification for this action was that the federal government held exclusive jurisdiction in Indian country, especially for crimes committed against Indians by non-Indians. The Federal Enclaves Act was subsequent modified by the Assimilative Crimes Act of 1825, the Major Crimes Act of 1885, and Public Law 280 in 1953.

The Assimilative Crimes Act (1825) stipulated that offenses in Indian country, while still under federal jurisdiction, would use state or territorial statutes and sentences as a guide for federal adjudication. Hence, the local state or territorial laws where the reservation was located would be used by the federal government for those crimes not specifically defined under the federal criminal code. While the intent was for tribal justice to operate within Indian country for crimes by Indians

---

or General Crimes Act).... The Trade and Intercourse Act of June 30, 1834, reenacted the rule developed in the earlier statutes. This rule was subsequently incorporated in the Revised Statutes as section 2,145 and in Title 25 of the United States Code as section 217. The exceptions contained in Title 25 of the United States Code, section 218, relating to offenses by Indians against Indians and to offenders punished by tribal law have no application to offenses committed by non-Indians against Indians (Cohen, 1942, pp. 364–365).

against Indians, the white Indian Superintendent held virtually absolute authority in dealing with issues in Indian country. Most significantly, he had the US Army at his disposal as an enforcement agent for his dictates. Initially, the Indian Superintendent was responsible 1) for providing the provisions to the tribe that were guaranteed by treaty; 2) for keeping the Indians within the confines of Indian country as it was defined by treaty; and 3) for enforcing methods for the civilizing (Christianizing) the Indian.

Crow Dog and the End of Aboriginal Restorative Justice

The Crow Dog Sioux case which extended the Federal Enclaves (General Crimes) Act in 1885 to include the "Major Crimes". An element of Congress was attempting to further apply state jurisdictions within Indian country at the time of the killing of Spotted Tail in 1881 on the Brule reservation at Rosebud. Although considered to be a puppet of the US Government, Spotted Tail was a warrior and war chief who was seriously injured fighting the US Army at Bluewater, Nebraska in the Sioux War of 1855. This resulted in his incarceration at Fort Leavenworth, Kansas. But by 1865 he emerged as the head chief of the Brulé, and along with Red Cloud and the Oglala Sioux, participated in the treaties, held at Fort Laramie in the late 1860s, that determined the Great Sioux Reservation. His status with the USA was elevated considerably when he kept the Brulé out of the 1876 Sioux War which resulted in the defeat of Lieutenant Colonel George A. Custer and the Seventh Calvary at the Little Big Horn River. By the early 1880s, extralegal retribution by both the US Army and the Indian Superintendents in the Dakotas was fierce and severe resulting in the questionable execution of Crazy Horse in 1877 and the exile of Sitting Bull—two of the leaders of the Little Big Horn River group that defeated Custer.

Crow Dog, on the other hand, was a more traditional Sioux leader given that historically the Sioux never had a strong head chief until this position was made necessary when dealing with the US Government relevant to treaty negotiations creating leaders such as Red Cloud and Spotted Tail. Crow Dog was once the chief of the Orphan band of the Brulé Sioux and remained a leader of the survivors of Big Raven's band following the massacre of Big Raven and all his warriors in the 1844 conflict with the Shoshone. Crow Dog was closely associated with Crazy Horse and even accompanied him when he surrendered in 1877. Crow Dog is credited with preventing bloodshed when soldiers attempted to kill Crazy Horse at the time he surrendered. Crow Dog also went to Canada and met with Sitting Bull while he and his band were in exile. Thus, in the early 1800s, while Spotted Tail was seen as an ally of the US, Crow Dog was seen as the leader of Sioux traditionalism and antagonistic to the US Government. Just prior to the altercation that took Spotted Tail's life, Crow Dog served as the chief of the Indian police at the Rosebud Agency in 1879 and 1880.

Clearly, both Spotted Tail and Crow Dog were vying for positions of power within the new Rosebud Agency established in 1878. These leaders reflected the two camps existing at that time—the progressives (accommodation with the US) lead by Spotted Tail and the traditionalists led by Crow Dog. The hostility between Spotted Tail and Crow Dog has been attributed to ideological differences, bitterness and jealously. Some felt that Crow Dog was bitter at Spotted Tail for dismissing him as chief of police while others saw this as a personal problem involving a woman, Light-in-the-Lodge. Here, Spotted Tail is accused of taking Light-in-the-Lodge away from her disabled, elderly husband and making her his second wife. Crow Dog then took it upon himself to represent the wronged husband. At any rate, on August 5, 1881, the 47-year-old Crow Dog shot the 58-year-old Spotted Tail as they approached each other on a road near the Agency. Crow Dog shot and killed Spotted Tail during this altercation. Given that this was an Indian v Indian crime and was exempt at that time from federal jurisdiction under the Federal Enclave/General Crimes Act, the matter was resolved between the clans involved utilizing the traditional peacemakers. The resolution, according to Brulé traditions was for Crow Dog's clan to compensate Spotted Tail's clan with a payment of $600, eight horses, and one blanket. This determination was quickly met and harmony was then restored to the tribe according to their customary law.

The US Supreme Court decision regarding Crow Dog was unpopular with a number of factions including the US Army, the Indian Agency and Spotted Tails supporters (not family and clan which agreed to the dictates of tribal justice). Accordingly, Agent Lelar sent Chief Hollow Horn Bear to arrest Crow Dog and his alleged co-conspirator, Black Crow, after Eagle Hawk, the chief of the agency police failed to do. Once he was arrested Crow Dog was brought to Fort Niobrara, Nebraska. Within 20 days of the killing, the US Attorney General and the Secretary of the Department of Interior jointly concluded that the Federal Enclaves Act, as modified by the Assimilative Crimes Act and incorporated into the various Sioux treaties, allowed the territorial death statute to apply to Crow Dog. Interestingly, Crow Dog was only one of a number of parallel murder cases the BIA was attempting to get the Courts to qualify as falling under state or territorial law, a clear forerunner to Public Law 280. At this time, the BIA Commissioner, Henry Price, stated that the BIA wanted to impose any available criminal jurisdiction, federal, state, or territorial, over the tribes. The US attorneys joined the BIA in this early Public Law 280 effort but the Nevada Supreme Court rejected this argument stating that states had no jurisdiction over Indians because of the exclusive federal authority in Indian affairs set by the Marshall court.

Crow Dog's trial itself reflected the political emotions surrounding it and the assertion that he represented the "bad Indians" such as Crazy Horse and Sitting Bull and needed to be punished in order to send a message to other renegades. It was clear from the outset that the trial and all-white jury would find Crow Dog guilty despite his claim of self-defense. In the jury selection, the defense attorney, A.J. Plowman, questioned the jurors about their prejudices against Indian witnesses. The general consensus was that the testimony of a white would greatly outweigh that of an Indian. One juror stated that the testimony of one white man would outweigh that of a hundred Indians. Nonetheless, the jury was quickly approved and seated. In the end, the jury convicted Crow Dog of capital murder and sentenced him to hang. The US Supreme Court, on December 17, 1883 upheld Crow Dog's petition and released him in *Ex Parte Crow Dog*. In its decision, the Court upheld the Marshal's Court contention of tribal sovereignty in *Worcester v Georgia*. It posed a serious challenge to the BIA policy of cultural genocide and instead upheld the equality of tribal traditions and sovereignty (Harring, 1994).

The Major Crimes Act emerged as a conservative reaction to the US Supreme Court decision in *Ex Parte Crow Dog* but also had the support from an unlikely source, the Indian Rights Association (IRA), a group of eastern liberal reformers who also shared the tenet of civilizing and Christianizing American Indians. The Major Crimes Act (1885) extended original and exclusive federal jurisdiction in Indian country to include murder, manslaughter, rape, assault with intent to kill, arson, burglary, and larceny. Crow Dog's prosecution violated the Enclaves Act which precluded federal prosecution of Indian defendants who had been punished by his/her tribe. Now tribal justice was exempt from adjudicating these crimes. (The Index Crimes listed under the Major Crimes Act has been expanded to now include 13 crimes.) This also set the stage for state (or territorial) statutes to become the standard for the adjudication of all other crimes committed by anyone, including Indians off the reservation as well as non-Indian offenders in Indian country. The Major Crimes Act initially gave federal exclusive jurisdiction only in Indian country, but was later extended to any federal lands not covered by the Uniform Code of Military Justice (UCMJ).

J. Edgar Hoover is credited with this expansion in order to curtail lawlessness in the US during the turbulent years following the First World War and during the Great Depression. Hoover then used federal major crime statistics to gather data for what he coined the "Index Crimes" with these data published yearly in his *FBI Uniform Crime Report*. These index crimes are also the reason that the FBI has such a presence in Indian country. In 1886, the US Supreme Court upheld the constitutionality of the Major Crimes Act in *US v Kagama*, a case involving murder among Indians on the reservation. The Court now argued that due to the federal trust relationship with Indian tribes, Congress has the duty and authority to regulate tribal matters. Later, in *Lone Wolf v Hitchcock* (1903), the US Supreme Court went a step further stating that Congress could, by statute, abrogate the provisions of an Indian treaty. These Congressional powers were deemed so powerful that complaints against these actions had to be brought to the same body that dictated them—the US Congress. This ruling specifically had significance on not only Allotment but on Public Law 280 as well.

At the time of the Crow Dog incident, the Interior Department and its enforcement/administrative arm, the BIA, were attempting to consolidate their power and authority in Indian country at the expense of traditional rites and customs. This led to the establishment of the *Courts of Indian Offenses* in 1883, also known as BIA courts. The Secretary of the Interior, Henry M. Teller initiated the Congressional action that provided the Courts of Indian Offenses. These courts were the first attempts to legislate morality in Indian country given that his intent was to use these BIA courts to eliminate the heathenish practices that he felt plagued American Indians impeding their Christianization and civilization. These were, in fact, Courts of Cultural Genocide (Courts of Indian Offenses, 1883). Prior to the establishment of the BIA Courts of Indian Offenses, the BIA agent held martial law status serving as prosecutor and judge with the authority to summarily charge, prosecute and sentence Indians under his control. Revisions in 1892 established District Courts within Indian country and provided for the appointment of Indian judges in the BIA Court of Indian Offenses. The Commissioner of Indian Affairs or BIA Agent appointed both the tribal police and judges using the patronage system. While the district judges were now Indians they kept their job as long as they held allegiance to the white BIA agents. Not only did the BIA determine the judges and police, who served as prosecutors, any judgment had to be approved by the white BIA official. These courts were effective in carrying out their mandate of cultural genocide punishing the practice of Indian customs and religious rituals such as the sun dance, use of medicine men, and joint clan ownership of property. On the other hand, certain tribal customs were sanctioned by the BIA Courts including banishment and restitution. The BIA Courts of Indian Offenses set the stage for Allotment and the attempt to dissolve Indian country.

Grant's main architect for the peace plan was his choice to head the BIA, Commissioner of Indian Affairs, Ely Parker. Parker was of mixed Indian (Seneca) and white blood and served as a brigadier general in the Union Army. A trusted protege of President Grant and strong supporter of this new dimension of ethnic cleansing, he supported these efforts to not only uproot tribes but force them to abandon their traditional ways in lieu of the Western-Christian perspective. Removal continued to be the primary vehicle for getting unwanted Indians off lands desired by white settlers and the railroads. Congress aided the Executive Branch in this process by refusing to ratify any more Indian treaties. In 1854, the US Senate, in executive session, read each unratified *US/Indian* treaty three times, as required by law, and then denied ratification for all. The tribes involved were not notified of this clandestine move and had little recourse after-the-fact (Deloria, 1974; French, 1994).

After most of the remaining tribes were removed to *Indian Territory* (Oklahoma) efforts were under way to take this land away from them, including the *Five Civilized Tribes* (Cherokee, Choctaw, Chickasaw, Seminole and Creek). They were termed such due to their adoption of the Euro-American legal and economic model during the early years of the Republic, and they brought their US-styled laws, courts, police and corrections with them to Indian Territory (Oklahoma) during Removal. Given that they had already accommodated the western-model of justice, they were generally exempt from the dictates of the Courts of Indian Offenses and other federally-imposed judicial authority except for that which dealt with non-Indian offenders within Indian country. However, the civilized tribes fell out of favor with the federal government for their support of the Confederacy during the Civil War and suffered severe sanctions during Reconstruction. This set in motion plans to include them in the allotment plan—the foundation for cultural genocide at this time—which was already being imposed on other tribes (Curtis Act, 1898; Meriam, 1928).

Allotment represented the imposition of the Western Protestant Ethic model of economic competition and individual responsibility that was diametrically opposite of the aboriginal communal, collective responsibility model. Moreover, the aboriginal traditional Indian cultural model reflected *social communism*. The 160-acre family allotments were comparable to the land alloted to *homesteaders* who staked claims on federal public lands opened to settlers. This plan would free up so-called *surplus lands* held in common by the tribe through treaties. In the past some of this land was used to relocate other removed tribes but the plan now was to make this land available to non-Indian homesteaders. Initially, the alloted Indian land was to be held in trust by the US Government in order to prevent the land from being taxed or being taken illegally by non-Indians. Nonetheless, many Indians lost their allotment when challenged in court. Lastly, the Allotment Act was intended to have universal application within Indian country and was imposed without any requirement of consent of the tribes or Indians affected. The program was quite effective in that the total amount of treaty-granted, Indian-held land fell from 138 million acres in 1887 to 48 million acres in 1934, with much of this being desert or poor agricultural land. Besides, many Indian landowners eventually lost their allotments to the states for failure to pay property taxes (French, 1987; Canby, 1988).

All told, Allotment was a great success for proponents of manifest destiny and another dire failure for American Indians. Allotment abrogated treaty protection for Indians in Indian Territory forcefully imposing the dominant societal politico/economic system on them without the same protections offered their non-Indian counterparts. It also freed up the territory for white settlement and eventual statehood. It was during this time and under these circumstances that the current federal fraud was initiated cheating the Indians of tens of billions of dollars via the treaty-bound trust relationship with the US Departments of Interior and Treasury. In summary, the General Allotment Act (Dawes Act) of 1887 took back 90 million acres from Indian tribes and gave it to white homesteaders. The remaining 54 million acres of Indian lands were determined by allotments ranging from 30 to 40 acres with those lands not individually allotted held in trust by the US Government. Today the allotted trust lands belong to some 300,000 American Indians. Herein lies the current problem. These lands were then unilaterally leased out to non-Indian enterprises (grazing, timber, oil and gas activities) with the money going to the US Treasury supposedly held in trust for distribution to individual Indians under a program know as the Individual Indian Money (IIM) trust. The mismanagement of these monies was first noticed in 1928 by the General Accounting Office, the independent investigative arm of Congress. This was part of the reform movement leading to the Meriam Report. The mismanagement continued and was not addressed until 1994 with passage of the Indian Trust Reform Act.

There is also suspicion that this effort to defraud Native Americans paved the way for both Termination and Relocation during the Eisenhower Administration during the 1950s. These federal policies were renewed efforts to again attempt to destroy the American Indian traditional communal life-style. Interestingly President Eisenhower appointed Dillon Myer, a former head of the Japanese-American Relocation Centers, to the position of Commissioner of the BIA during his administration. His dictatorial style set the stage for a combined Executive and Congressional endeavor to reverse the progress gained under the Wheeler-Howard and Johnson-O'Malley acts. The first act in this series was House Concurrent Resolution 108. On August 1, 1953, the Eighty-third Congress enacted a fundamental change in Indian policy which again reinforced the concepts of cultural genocide and ethnic cleansing by attempting to abolish federal obligations to Indian groups. By passing an "act of Congress", they attempted to deny American Indians any special recognition and thereby relegate them as common members of the states where their reservation existed (Emmons, 1954; Canby, 1988).

Two weeks later Public Law 280 went into effect. It extended state criminal jurisdiction over offenses committed by or against Indians in Indian country taking this authority from the tribal courts. A major problem with this legislation was that it exacerbated the often-hostile relationship that existed between non-Indians and Indians in states where reservations exit. This provided the non-Indians their chance to further exploit their American Indian neighbors now that they no longer had federal protection. Less than a year later, in June 1954, the Menominee Indians of Wisconsin were added to the list by Congress. They soon became the example of how devastating the policy of Termination was in Indian country. Termination and Public Law 280 were unilateral policy decisions made by the US Congress and forced upon Indian tribes. No tribe has ever accepted the terms of Public Law 280. Despite this fact, it continues in those so-designated States (Fixio, 1992).

If anything, the combination of Termination and Relocation contributed to a new social problem—that of *psychocultural marginality*—whereby American Indians were caught between two worlds without being allowed to fully belong to either. This represented the ultimate form of cultural genocide. With their culture and language again being attacked by the combined effects of Termination and Relocation, a new generation of American Indians living off reservations and in urban Indian ghettos were socialized in a world of both psychological and cultural ambiguity—the foundation of marginality (Stonequist, 1937; French, 1997). With this process came increased social, health and legal problems. Costo and Henry noted this process in their book, *Indian Treaties: Two Centuries of Dishonor*:

> Religious groups and white-controlled humanitarian organizations generally embodied the worst of the growing paternalism toward the Natives. Finally, the federal government, jockeying precariously between policies of assimilation and the growing recognition that the tribes simply would not disappear together with their unique cultures, originated what has become know as the "Relocation Program". Indians were induced to go to the cities for training in the arts of the technological world. There they were dumped into housing that in most cases was ghetto-based, into jobs that were dead end, and training that failed to lead to professions and occupations. The litany of that period provides the crassest example of government ignorance of the Indian situation. The "Indian problem" did not go away. It worsened. The policies of the Eisenhower administration, which espoused the termination of federal-Indian relationships, was shown to be a failure, a gross injustice added to a history of injustice (Costo and Henry, 1977, p. 41).

Termination ended with the failed Menominee experience but did nothing to reverse the damage done by either Relocation or Public Law 280. Wisconsin exemplified state hostility toward Indians within their boundaries. Indeed, the state went too far in its interpretation of the combined authority of Termination and Public Law 280. Wisconsin felt that the law made all state statutes applicable to the dissolved reservation including specified exemptions such as hunting and fishing rights. In 1964, the US Supreme Court held that the Termination Act did not abrogate Indian treaty rights since these rights were reserved by Public Law 280 which was passed by the same Congress. Continued poverty and exploitation eventually led to the Menominee Restoration Act in December 1973 which repealed the Termination Act of June 17, 1954 restoring tribal status and federal supervision (Menominee Restoration Act, 1973).

Contemporary Social Justice Issues: The IIM Trust and the Exploitation of Gaming Tribes

The IIM Trust controversy and the exploitation of gaming tribes are two contemporary issues that strain the special trust the federal government imposes on American Indians relevant to monetary resources.

The Individual Indian Trust Fund Debacle

The Individual Indian Trust Fund mismanagement suit was filed with the aid of the Native American Rights Fund (NARF) on June 10, 1996 when Babbitt was Secretary of the Interior. In the original suit, the Assistant Interior Secretary (BIA Director) was Ada Deer while Robert Rubin was the Secretary of the Treasury. The suit was filed by Elouise Cobell, a Blackfoot Indian and Montana banker, who, along with the NARF lawyers, accuse the US Government of violating their trust responsibility for the collection of monies from the leasing of Indian lands to non-Indian businesses for grazing, logging, mining and oil drilling. The plaintiffs note tens of billions dollar shortfall due either to theft, corrupt deals or shoddy bookkeeping practices. This certainly challenges any concept of fair distributive justice for American Indians even today.

In describing the suit, John Echohawk, Executive Director of the Native American Rights Fund noted that:

> The Bureau of Indian Affairs has spent more than 100 years mismanaging, diverting and losing money that belongs to Indians. They have no idea how much has been collected from the companies that use our land and are unable to provide even a basic, regular statement to Indian account holders. Everyday the system remains broken, hundreds of thousands of Indians are losing more and more money. (Echohawk, 2001)

The catch-22 is that the Department of Interior approves all leases of resources in Indian country. Moreover, the law requires Indians to use the federal government as their bank so these transactions occur without Indian input or accountability.

The court-appointed federal monitor reported to the court that the current Secretary of the Interior, Gale Norton, presented compulsory reports that were untruthful leading to a contempt charge leveled against her. This placed her in the same status as her predecessor, Bruce Babbitt. Moreover, the Native American Rights Fund (NARF) notified Judge Lambert that 16 Federal Reserve Banks, including the New York Federal Reserve Bank, have been on an Anderson/Enron-like binge destroying Indian trust account documents clearly in violation of the federal judge's order. The federal judge has now held Secretary Norton in contempt of Court—a distinction that has not been assigned a high-ranking member of the US administration since the 1800s.

During the 10 years of the suit, other tribes have looked at their trust funds for evidence of corruption and deals between US Corporations and the US Government. The Navajo, the largest Indian tribe in the United States with the largest reservation discovered secret deals between the US Department of the Interior and Peabody Coal greatly restricting fair market royalties for coal taken from their land. The Navajo suit is for 600 million dollars. These issues have led to considerable distrust of the federal government in Indian country. Many tribal members see these blatant abuses as contributing to many of the social and health problems long plaguing Indian country. They feel that inadequately funded programs are due to a severe shortfall of resources guaranteed under the IIM trust fund. Indeed, the National Congress of American Indians (NCAI), the most senior and respected voice in Indian country, has voiced its distrust of the US Federal Government in general and the Bush Administration in particular:

> The trust is a shambles and in need of top-to-bottom reconstruction. We hope, and expect, that the Court will not delay justice for another six months or a year while the Secretary (Norton) rearranges the chairs at her Department—stripping the Native American employees of the BIA, in the meantime, of their trust responsibilities, as if this mess is their fault. (Martin, 2001, p. 3) (see Appendix A)

The Exploitation of Tribal Gaming

The Indian gaming controversy emerged as a result of cutbacks to trial funding by the Reagan administration. While appropriations and expenditures for Indian affairs is stipulated under the Snyder Act of 1921, no particular funding formula has ever been derived, allowing the federal government to determine the appropriate amount for "general and incidental expenses in connection with the administration of Indian affairs". President Reagan wanted the tribes to generate their own money with gaming but this proposal quickly led to state challenges. The first federal Indian gaming court case involved a Public Law 280 state, Florida. In 1979, the Seminole Tribe began operating a high-stakes bingo operation on reservation land near a major metropolitan area in southern Florida. Threatened with criminal prosecution under Public Law 280 regulation by the county sheriff, the Seminole took the case to the federal court with the fifth US Circuit Court ruling in the tribe's favor (*Seminole Tribe of Florida v. Butterworth*, 1981). Moreover, the court stipulated that Indian gaming issues were civil/regulatory, and not criminal/prohibitory, cases as stipulated under Public Law 280. Given that Florida allowed bingo gaming, the court argued, Indian gaming on a federal Indian reservation did not constitute conduct prohibited as being against the public policy of the state of Florida.

It took a US Supreme Court decision, *California v Cabzon Band of Mission Indians* in 1987, to move Congress to establish a federal regulatory ruling regarding gaming within Indian country. *Cabzon* was yet another Public Law 280 case, where a state had attempted to enforce laws restricting the operation of bingo games in Indian country. With both the Supreme Court and the executive branch supporting Indian gaming, Congress set forth to authorized and regulate Indian gaming among federally recognized tribes. Congress forged a law that provided a statutory foundation for Indian gaming while at the same time promoting the self-determination economic considerations indicated by President Reagan. These federal standards were incorporated into the *Indian Gaming Regulatory Act of 1988* (IGRA Public Law 100–497).

The IGRA distinguishes between three types of gaming in Indian country, with Class I activities reserved for traditional Indian games of chance, those that have survived from aboriginal times. Under the IGRA, Public Law 280 or federal authority under the Assimilative Crimes Act (ACA) can no longer attempt to regulate these traditional customs. Class II gaming pertains to bingo, pull-tabs, and similar games. This was the initial form of Indian gaming that was protected by the federal courts. Class III, on the other hand, represents casino-type gaming including slot machines, casino games, sports and racing betting. Class III gaming required a state-tribe compact before it could be federally sanctioned. This factor alone upset the distributive justice intent of Indian gaming itself. Now tribes were pitted against each other as well as against big business and political interests. Here, conservative, Mormon-dominated states like Utah and Hawaii were successful in outlawing all types of gaming. Utah's influence affected the largest US reservation—the 25 million-square-mile Navajo Nation.

Many tribal leaders saw the IGRA's rules pertaining to Class III gaming as another means toward Public Law 280 constraints previously overruled in Federal court. They argued that Public Law 280 (state) authority was being expanded to non-PL 280 states through the tribal-state compact. In 1989, the Red Lake Band of Chippewa Indians and the Mescalero Apaches in New Mexico filed suit against the constitutionality of the Indian Gaming Regulatory Act, on the grounds that the tribe-state compact undermined both tribal sovereignty and federal responsibility to Indian tribes. In 1992, seven more tribes joined the class-action suit. Litigation over the IGRA continues today with the greatest obstacle coming from the western states—the region that appears to harbor the greatest prejudice against American Indians. One of the strongest anti-Indian voices, in addition to the Mormons, is the Western Governors' Association.

Clearly the inequity in the gaming opportunity among federally-recognized tribes challenged their long-held tradition of fair distributive justice. It also set the scene for continued exploitation. Congress looked at tribal exploitation as a cash cow for political influence given that they regulated Indian Country. In 2000, under the George W. Bush administration, the Republican dominated Congress exempted tribes from limits toward political contributions. They are not restricted to the $101,400 cap therefore making them fair game for influence peddling by members of Congress and lobbyists. Essentially, Congress changed the rules so that they could blackmail tribes to get them to think they were making favorable rulings for the tribes which they regulated to begin with. In order to make it easier to bilk the tribes Congress also exempted them from registering as political action committees. It appears Congress set it up so that their wards, the 212 federally recognized Indian tribes, are the only group that could be solicited without any record keeping whatsoever.

Clouding the issue of tribal solicitations is the continued exploitation of Indian tribes relevant to federal influence for their gaming interests. Two associates of Congressman Tom DeLay (Republican from Sugarland, Texas), Jack Abramoff and Mike Scanlon, are the center of a federal scandal involving the fleecing of over 60 million dollars from Indian tribes under the pretense of representing their gaming interests. DeLay, Abramoff and Scanlon are also linked to George W. Bush's PAC, "Texans for Political Justice" (TPJ). US Senator Ben Nighthorse Campbell, the only Native American currently in the Senate and Chairman of the US Senate Committee on Indian Affairs, held hearings on Indian Tribal lobbying matters on November

17, 2004. This hearing led to the eventual downfall of Jack Abramoff. During the hearing Senator Nighthorse Campbell noted the contempt that Abramoff held for his tribal clients calling them "monkeys", *troglodytes*, "morons", to mention a few. The hearings also addressed the deliberate exploitation of the Tiguas tribe of Texas. Abramoff and Scanlon took the tribes money with the promise of supporting their gaming enterprise while, at the same time, persuaded the state of Texas to force the closure of the Tribe's casino in El Paso. More despicable, Abramoff took out term-life insurances on tribal leaders with his private Jewish academy being the beneficiary. Abramoff is recorded as saying: "I wish those moronic Tiguas were smarter in their political contributions. I'd love to get our mitts on that moolah! Oh well, stupid people get wiped out".

More on this matter was disclosed in the May 2 2005 issue of *Newsweek*, stating that Mr Abramoff created a charity, the Capital Athletic Foundation, as a front to launder the monies he obtained from Tribal clients. But instead of going to projects for inner-city youth, the money was funneled instead to Israel to fight the Palestinian. Apparently the Indian monies were used to purchase camouflage suits, sniper scopes, night-vision binoculars and other military equipment to aid West Bank Jewish settlers mobilize against the Palestinians. And the West Bank security payments are not the only misuse of the Indian Tribal monies by Abramoff. Ostensibly, about $4 million was used for a now-defunct Orthodox Jewish school in suburban Maryland that two of Abramoff's sons attended. The investigation into the DeLay, Abramoff and Scanlon now estimates that some $80 million was taken from Tribal coffers in the guise of favorable treatment by the Bush Administration.

On January 3, 2006, Jack A. Abramoff pled guilty to three federal felonies associated with his defrauding Indian tribes. Part of the plea-bargain is his cooperation in the larger influence peddling in Congress and the Administration. Many in Washington are worried given that Abramoff was a top figure in Tom DeLay's "K Street Project" designed to solidify Republican dominance in Washington, DC. Also implicated in Abramoff's Indian scam is J. Steven Guiles, former Deputy Secretary of Interior—the agency responsible for protecting Indian County. Guiles was a top lobbyists for the oil and mining industries prior to his appointment to the Bush administration. His collusion with Abramoff in the Indian gaming scandal is currently unfolding and will likely extend to Secretary Norton as well.

Some Concluding Remarks

The ongoing corruption and exploitation in Indian Country by those mandated to protect them clearly makes a mockery of both US procedural due process justice and the special mandate of distributive justice afforded Indian tribes via treaty obligation. Ostensibly, the only avenue for Native Americans to access the due process model of procedural justice is to abandon their communitarian traditional form of distributive justice. Even then, allowing the ongoing process of cultural genocide to take its course is no guarantee that Native Americans will be accepted as first class citizens. The example of the *Civilized Tribes* is a clear example of this double standard of social justice in America. Social injustices are clearly measured by the quality of life and care in Indian country. Recent assessments by the US Commission on Civil Rights indicate that the health status of tribal members continues to be the worse in the United States. American Indians today have the shortest life expectancy and have higher maternal and infant mortality rates. Moreover, American Indians are the group most likely to die from tuberculosis, diabetes, alcoholism and the flu. Suicide rates among American Indian youth are the highest in the Nation while those with other health problems have the poorest survival rates of any group (Healy, 2004).

To decrease or stop the deprived economic and cultural position of Native Americans, the US policy towards them should be changed dramatically. To achieve this a cultural switch in the dominant social system is necessary. One way to do this is to look over the border to Canada and how they have improved the position of the American Indians and Inuit. Moreover, accepting the diversity of cultures is a necessary precondition for the improvement of Native Americans in the US. Specifically the differences in conceptions of justice—procedural justice—between the Native Americans and the dominant society should be recognized and accepted: the Protestant Ethic is different from the Harmony Ethos. Only then a beginning can be made of the economic and cultural improvement of American Indians.

Appendix A: Cobell v Norton

Declarative Judgment of Indian Suit Against the US Government

A comprehensive text describes *Eloise Pepion Cobell et al. v Bruce Babbitt, Secretary of the Interior, Lawrence Summers, Secretary of the Treasury, and Kevin Gover, Assistant Secretary of the Interior* (US District Court, District of Columbia, Civil No. 96-1285 (RLC)). In the text the Plaintiffs, representing federally-recognized Indian tribes whose monies are administered by the BIA and US Department of the Interior claim that the Defendants, the BIA and US Department of the Interior, have mismanaged the federal program known as the Individual Indian Money (IIM). In the Introduction to the Memorandum Opinion it was noted:

> It would be difficult to find a more historically mismanaged federal program than the Individual Indian Money (IIM) trust. The United States, the trustee of the IIM trust, cannot say how much money is or should be in the trust. As the trustee admitted on the eve of the trial, it cannot render an accurate accounting to the beneficiaries, contrary to a specific statutory mandate and the century-old obligation to do so. More specifically, as Secretary Babbitt testified, an accounting cannot be rendered for most of the 300,000-plus beneficiaries, who are now plaintiffs in this lawsuit. Generations of IIM trust beneficiaries have been born and raised with the assurance that their trustee, the United States, was acting properly with their money. Just as many generations have been denied any such proof, however. "If courts were permitted to indulge their sympathies, a case better calculated to excite them could scarcely be imagined." *Cherokee Nation v Georgia*, 30 US (5 Pet.) 1, 15 (1831) (Marshall, C.J.)

The Court ordered the following action:

Declaratory Judgment

Pursuant to the Declaratory Judgment Act, 28 USC. Section 2201, and the Administrative Procedure Act, 5 USC. Sections 702 & 76, the court HEREBY DECLARES that:

1. The Indian Trust Fund Management Reform Act, 25 USC. Section 162a et seq. & 4011 et seq., requires defendants to provide plaintiffs an accurate accounting of all money in the IIM trust held in trust for the benefit of plaintiffs, without regard to when the funds were deposited.
2. The Indian Trust Fund Management Reform Act, 25 USC. Section 162a et seq. & 4011 et seq., requires defendants to retrieve and retain all information concerning the IIM trust that is necessary to render an accurate accounting of all money in the IIM trust held in trust for the benefit of plaintiffs.
3. To the extent that prospective relief is warranted in this case and to the extent that the issues are in controversy, it has been shown that defendant Bruce Babbitt, Secretary of the Interior, and defendant Kevin Gover, Assistant Secretary of the Interior, owe plaintiffs, pursuant to the statutes and regulations governing the management of the IIM trust, the statutory trust duty to:
    a. establish written policies and procedures for collecting from outside sources missing information necessary to render an accurate accounting of the IIM trust;
    b. establish written policies and procedures for the retention of IIM-related trust documents necessary to render an accurate accounting of the IIM trust;
    c. establish written policies and procedures for computer and business systems architecture necessary to render an accurate accounting of the IIM trust; and
    d. establish written policies and procedures for the staffing of trust management functions necessary to render an accurate accounting of the IIM trust.
4. To the extent that prospective relief is warranted in this case and to the extent that the issues are in controversy, it has been shown that defendant Lawrence Summers, Secretary of the Treasury, owes plaintiffs, pursuant to the statutes and regulations governing the management of the IIM trust, the statutory trust duty to retain IIM trust documents that are necessary to render an accurate accounting of all money in the IIM trust held in trust for the benefit of plaintiffs.
5. Defendants are currently in breach of the statutory trust duties declared in subparagraphs II (2)–(4).
6. Defendants have no written plans to bring themselves into compliance with the duties declared in subparagraphs II (2)–(4).
7. Defendants must promptly come into compliance by establishing written policies and procedures not inconsistent with the court's Memorandum Opinion that rectify the breaches of trust declared in subparagraphs II (2)–(4).

8. To allow defendants the opportunity to promptly come into compliance through the establishment of the appropriate written policies and procedures, the court HEREBY REMANDS the required actions to defendants for further proceedings not inconsistent with the court's Memorandum Opinion issued this date.

Continuing Jurisdiction and Further Proceedings

To ensure that defendants are diligently taking steps to rectify the continuing breaches of trust declared today and to ensure that defendants take the other actions represented to the court upon which the court bases its decision today, the court will retain continuing jurisdiction over this matter for a period of five years, subject to any motion for an enlargement of time that may be made. Accordingly, the court ORDERS that:

1. Beginning March 1 2000, defendants shall file with the court and serve upon plaintiffs quarterly status reports setting forth and explaining the steps that defendants have taken to rectify the breaches of trust declared today and to bring themselves into compliance with their statutory trust duties embodied in the Indian Trust Fund Management Reform Act of 1994 and other applicable statutes and regulations governing the IIM trust.
2. Each quarterly report shall be limited, to the extent practical, to actions taken since the issuance of the preceding quarterly report. Defendants' first quarterly report, due March 1 2000, shall encompass actions taken since June 10, 1999.
3. Defendants Secretary of the Interior and Assistant Secretary of the Interior— Indian Affairs shall file with the court and serve upon plaintiffs the revised or amended High Level Implementation Plan (HLIP). The revised or amended HLIP shall be filed and served upon completion but no later than March 1 2000.
4. Defendants shall provide any additional information requested by the court to explain or supplement defendants' submissions. Plaintiffs may petition the court to order defendants to provide further information as needed if such information cannot be obtained through informal requests directly to defendants.
5. The court DENIES plaintiffs' request for prospective relief that have not already been granted by this order. The court based much of its decision today—especially the denial of more extensive prospective relief—on defendants' plans (in both substance and timing) to bring themselves into compliance with their trust duties declared today and provided for explicitly by statue. These plans have been represented to the court primarily through the High Level Implementation Plan, but also through the representations made by government witnesses and government counsel. Given the court's reliance on these representations, the court ORDERS defendants, as part of their quarterly status reports, to explain any changes made to the HLIP. Should plaintiffs believe that they are entitled to further prospective relief

based upon information contained in these reports or otherwise learned, they may so move at the appropriate juncture. Such a motion will then trigger this court's power of judicial review.

Certification of Order for Interlocutory Appeal

For the reasons stated in the court's accompanying Memorandum Opinion, and pursuant to 28 USC Section 1292(a)(4), the court HEREBY FINDS that it is of the opinion that this order involves controlling questions of law as to which there is substantial grounds for difference of opinion. An immediate appeal of the court's order may materially advance the ultimate termination of the litigation. Accordingly, the court HEREBY CERTIFIES this order for interlocutory appeal pursuant to 28 USC Section 1292(b). Further proceedings in this case shall not be stayed during the pendency of any interlocutory appeal that may be taken.

SO ORDERED. Royce C. Lamberth, United States District Judge.

Not only did the defendants not comply, they were charged by the plaintiffs with engaging in an Oliver North procedure—the deliberate destruction of records. Judge Lamberth subsequently held the defendants in contempt of court in February 2000 for admitting to the improper destruction of thousands of records and for not filing the required quarterly reports. The American Indian plaintiffs are requesting appointment of a "Special Master" to enforce Judge Lamberth's Court Order. And this action comes from one of the most Indian-friendly administrations in US history! Clearly, contravening US policy and procedures toward American Indians continues unabated into the twenty-first century.

References

Assimilative Crimes Act (1825), 18 U.S.C.A., 13.
Beugre, C.D. and Baron, R.A. (2001), "Perceptions of Systemic Justice: The Effects of Distributive, Procedural, and Interactive Justice", *Journal of Applied Social Psychology*, **32**, 324–339. [DOI: 10.1111/j.1559-1816.2001.tb00199.x]
California v Cabzon Band of Mission Indians, 480 US 202 (1987).
Canby, W.C., Jr (1988), *American Indian Law* (St Paul, MN: West Publishing Company).
Cherokee Nation v Georgia. 30 US (5 Pet.) 1, 15 (1831)
Cobell et al. v Babbitt et al. (civil No. 96-1285), 1996.
Cohen, F. (1942), "Crimes in Indian Country by Non-Indians against Indian (Chapter 18: Criminal Jurisdiction)", *Handbook of Federal Indian Law* (Washington, DC: US Government Printing Office), 364–365.
Costo, R. and Henry, J. (1977), "The New War against the Indians", *Indian Treaties: Two Centuries of Dishonor*, Costo, R. and Henry, J. (San Francisco, CA: Indian Historian Press), 42.

Courts of Indian Offenses, *Annual Report of the Secretary of the Interior* Washington, DC: House Executive Document, No. 1, 48th Congress, 1st Session, serial 2190, November 1, 1883, x-xiii.

Curtis Act, US Statutes at Large, 30: 497−98, 502, 504−05, June 28, 1898.

Deloria, V., Jr (1974), *Behind the Trail of Broken Treaties* (New York: Dell).

Echohawk, J. (2001), "Cobell v. Norton", *NARF Legal Review*, **26**, 5.

Emmons, G.L. (1954), "Relocation of Indians in Urban Areas", *Annual Report of the Secretary of the Interior* (Washington, DC: US Government Printing Office), 243.

Ex Parte Crow Dog, 109 US Reports, 557, 571−72, December 17, 1883.

Federal Enclaves Act (1817), 18 U.S.C.A., 1152.

Fixio, D.L. (1992), *Termination and Relocation: Federal Indian Policy, 1945-1960* (Albuquerque, NM: University of New Mexico Press).

French, L.A. (1977), "The Selective Process of Criminal Justice", *International Journal of Criminology and Penology*, **5**, 63−78.

French, L.A. (1987), "The Accommodative Antithesis", *Psychocultural Change and the American Indian: An Ethnohistorical Analysis* (New York: Garland), 123−159.

French, L.A. (1994), "Reservations and Federal Paternalism", *The Winds of Injustice* (New York: Garland), 45−74.

French, L.A. (1997), *Counseling American Indians* (Lanham, MD: University Press of America).

French, L.A. (2003), *Native American Justice* (Chicago, IL: Burnham, Inc./Lexington Books).

French, L.A. (2005), "Mental Retardation and the Death Penalty: The Clinical and Legal Legacy", *Federal Probation*, June, 16−20.

General Allotment Act (Dawes Act), US Statutes at Large, 24, 388-91, February 8, 1887.

Harring, S.L. (1994), *Crow Dog's Case* (New York: Cambridge University Press).

Healy, B. (2004), "The Shame of a Nation", *US News and World Report* (October 4th), 26.

House Concurrent Resolution 108, 83rd Congress, 1st Session, 67 US Statutes at Large, B132, August 1, 1953.

Indian Citizenship Act, US Statutes at Large, 43:253, June 24, 1924.

Indian Gaming Regulatory Act, US Statutes at Large, 102: 2467−69, 2472, 2476, October 17, 1988.

IRA: Indian Reorganization Act, US Statutes at Large, 48:984−88, June 18, 1934.

Indian Removal Act, US Statutes at Large, 4:411−12, May 28, 1830.

Johnson v McIntosh, 21 US (8 Wheat.) 534, 1832.

Kymlicka, W. (1995), *Liberalism, Community and Culture* (Oxford: Clarendon).

Lamberth, R.C. (1999). "History surrounding IIM Trust Establishment", *Memorandum Opinion: Findings of Fact and Conclusions of Law,* US District Court for District of Columbia (*Cobell v Babbit, Sumners, & Gover,* Civil No. 96-1285, 9−10).

Lone Wolf v Hitchcock, 187 US Reports, 553, 564-8, January 5, 1903.

Major Crimes Act, US Statutes at Large, 23: 385, March 3, 1885.

Martin, J. (2001), "Interior Trust Management Plan Criticized: NCAI Says BIA to Be Stripped of Trust Responsibilities", *Cherokee One Feather*, **36**(46) (November 21st), 1, 17.

Marx, K. and Engels, F. (1967), *The Communist Manifesto*. Randall, F. ed. (New York: Washington Square Press).

Menominee Restoration Act, US Statutes at Large, 87: 700ff, December 22 1973.

Meriam, L. (1928), *The Problem of Indian Administration* (Baltimore, MD: Johns Hopkins Press), 346.

Morris, M.W. (2000), "Justice for All? Progress in Research on Cultural Variation in the Psychology of Distributive and Procedural Justice", *Applied Psychology*, **49**, 100–132. [DOI: 10.1111/1464-0597.00007]

Nozick, R. (1977), *Anarchy, State, and Utopia* (New York: Basic Books).

Park, R.E. (1964), *Race and Culture* (New York: Free Press).

Public Law 280, US Statutes at Large, **67**, 588–590, August 15, 1953.

Rawls, J. (1999), *A Theory of Justice*, revised edn (Boston, MA: Harvard University Press).

Reid, J. (1970), *A Law of Blood* (New York: New York University Press).

Seminole Tribe of Florida v. Butterworth, 658 F.2d 310 (5th Cir. 1981).

Snyder Act, US Statutes at Large, 42: 208–209, November 2 1921.

Stephanson, A. (1995), *Manifest Destiny* (New York: Hill and Wang).

Stonequist, E. (1937), *The Marginal Man* (New York: Russell and Russell).

Sweeney, P.D. and McFarlin, D.B. (1993), "Workers' Evaluations of the 'Ends' and the 'Means': An Examination of Four Models of Distributive and Procedural Justice", *Organizational Behavior and Human Decision Processes*, **55**, 23–40. [DOI: 10.1006/obhd.1993.1022]

Termination of Menominee Indians, US Statutes at Large, 68, 250–52, June 17 1954.

Title 25 (2002), Indians. *United States Code* (St. Paul, MN: West Publishing Company).

Trade and Intercourse Act, US Statutes at Large, 4, 729–35, June 30, 1834.

US v Kagama, 118 US 375, 382–85, May 10, 1886.

Walzer, M. (1983), *Spheres of Justice* (New York: Basic Books).

Weber, M. (1930), *The Protestant Ethic and the Spirit of Capitalism*. Parsons, R. trans. (London: Allen & Unwin).

Worcester v. Georgia, 31 US (6 Pet.) 515, 1832.

Young, I.M. (1990), *Justice and the Politics of Difference* (Princeton, NJ: Princeton University Press).

PART IV
Distributive and Procedural Justice Research: Epistemology, Method and Application

Chapter 10

Subjective Impartiality: Justice Judgements between Morality and Self-Interest[1]

Holger Lengfeld

University of Hagen, Germany

Introduction

The research reported in this chapter explores employees' justice judgments of their salary, either they are *moral* judgments, or predominantly reflect material *self-interests* in higher wages. Until now, this question has been widely neglected in organizational research. In this research tradition, standardized questionnaires using the term "justice" as a stimulus are common practice. Consequently, justice judgments are part of moral judgments *by definition*. Therefore, the analytical concept is based on the respondents' understanding of the term "justice" and not on a construct postulated by the researcher (Walster and Walster, 1975). Philosophical theories of justice, however, do not consider these judgments as moral *per se*. Instead, the philosophical perspective repeatedly points to two criteria in order to clarify whether a judgment should be viewed as a moral one. The first criterion is judging a person's impartiality in relation to other persons who are involved in the distribution. The second criterion is whether the judging person refers to moral rules for distribution (cp. Barry, 1995; Liebig, 2001; Soltan, 1987: 25 et seq.; Singer, 1997; Swift, 1999).

To further clarify the close connection between justice and *impartiality*, let us consider John Rawls' "Theory of Justice" (Rawls, 1971). Rawls argues that everyday ideas of a just distributive order are affected by people's social structural positions within a given society. Particularly, age, sex, educational background, social class position, occupational status and income are important social structural features. Furthermore, Rawls assumes that individuals act according to their self-interests, and that nobody wants to be worse off in the future. But usually, the available amount of goods cannot satisfy all individual interests. Therefore, Rawls introduces the concept of the "original position". The "original position" is a thought experiment in which people, regardless of

---

1   The data used in this chapter originates from the project "Veränderungsprozesse und Gerechtigkeit in Organisationen" (VGIO), funded by the Deutsche Forschungsgemeinschaft (DFG) from 1996–2000 at the Humboldt Universität zu Berlin (Berlin) and the University of Heidelberg. I am grateful to Stefan Liebig, Mike Steffen Schäfer and the editors for helpful comments.

their social structural position, decide on the principles that should be used to distribute goods in a way that is considered just. Since the "original position" ensures impartial judgment, it is considered a central precondition to create social justice. If people are unaware of their position in society, they cannot help but judge in a morally *fair* way. This occurs, even if they know that the society is unequally structured in general.

But what are the implications of this philosophical conception when we are analyzing employees' judgments concerning the fairness of their wages? Let us suppose that a semi-skilled female employee considers her wage unjust, i.e. too low. In this case, can we assume that she makes a moral judgment free of self-interest? Of course not, because when she judges her wage, she is certainly not in the "original position" as envisaged by Rawls. We can assume that she was well aware of her social structural position. Therefore, we have to conclude that her judgment might have been caused by her material self-interest. We can also expect that she is *dissatisfied* with her pay, if it barely covers the cost of living. Consequently, this dissatisfaction influences her justice judgment.

Considering this, do we have to conclude that any judgment about one's own pay is ultimately nothing more than a judgment about personal satisfaction? Or can we assume that at the same time, the employee articulates a moral claim about the behavior of his or her organization, a moral claim requesting distributive justice? To answer these questions, the empirical construct of distributive justice has to be validated. Usually, standardized employee surveys such as those reported by Cohen-Charash and Spector (2001), Colquitt et al. (2001), Folger and Konovsky (1989) or Freedman and Goodman (1967) measure distributive justice using ordinal or metrically scaled items. This chapter aims to contribute to the validation of this measurement with regard to the philosophical critique on the empirical definition of justice. Toward this end, I will proceed in three steps. First, I will compare and discuss the concepts of "satisfaction" and "justice", which I assume reflect different attitudes towards people's wage. Second, I attempt to demonstrate that satisfaction judgments predominantly reflect motives of self-interest, while judgments on justice are predominantly grounded in moral attitudes. For that purpose, I identify two social institutions, the firm and the works council, that have to face both moral and self-interest judgments in various ways. In the third step, I will verify my previous hypotheses empirically, using a standardized employee survey carried out in 21 firms of Germany's metal industry.

Satisfaction and Justice as Different Attitudes towards Individual Wages

The motivational structure behind people's justice judgments can be examined in different ways. In this chapter, I will employ an empirical construct validation (cp. Cronbach and Mehl, 1955). Therefore, the general question is whether the semantic meaning of a term used in a standardized survey, i.e., its operational definition, has the same content as its nominal definition. Otherwise, the operational and the nominal definition of a given term will vary and, consequently, their meanings will refer to different phenomena. In the following analysis, I will scrutinize the terms "justice" and "satisfaction". Since it has already been proposed that these two constructs measure different things, it seems reasonable to use discriminant validation (for previous theoretical and experimental attempts see Austin et al., 1980; Blau, 1964; Messick and Sentis, 1979, 1983). First, the theoretical relations between the two constructs will be examined. Then, I will empirically verify whether both constructs measure the same or different things.

Why does it make sense to compare the employees' justice judgments towards their pay with their pay satisfaction? The latter concept primarily expresses an employee's interest in an appropriate wage. This becomes evident when we look closely at some of the basic assumptions of work satisfaction research. Particularly in the field of the psychology of work, a large number of surveys have dealt with the causes and effects of work satisfaction. Thirty years ago, Locke (1976) concluded that about 4,000 relevant psychological studies had been conducted. Thus, research interest in this field has been substantial. Two main reasons can be identified. First, work satisfaction is considered to be one of the main determinants of employees' work performance. Numerous surveys focus on the effects of work satisfaction on work performance, work motivation, frequency of absence or illness (e.g., Brown and Peterson, 1993; Faragher et al., 2005; Iaffaldano and Muchinsky, 1985). Second, work satisfaction has attracted a lot of interest because it is relatively easy to measure empirically in standardized surveys, either by using a one-item measurement (e.g., Hackman and Oldham, 1975) or multiple item-based scales (e.g., DeMeuse, 1985; Ironson et al., 1989; Smith et al., 1969; Spector, 1997).

In the face of the considerable amount of research described above, it is not surprising that various concepts of work satisfaction have been suggested (Locke, 1976). Two basic conceptions can be distinguished, a psychological conception focussing on needs and an attitude-based conception. The psychological variant, which focuses on needs, defines work satisfaction as a condition of mental well-being resulting from the fulfilment or non-fulfilment of individual needs (e.g., Wolf, 1970). The attitude-based variant conceptualizes work satisfaction as an attitude towards the individual's work situation. Such attitudes can refer to four different aspects of the work situation: rewards, colleagues, the nature of the work that is being done, and organizational context (Locke, 1976).

It should be emphasized that there are fundamental differences between the concept of work satisfaction as described above, and the concept of justice. Judgments concerning justice relate to *normative* dimensions of interaction. Since employees evaluate certain distributive rules as socially binding, they expect others to conform to these rules. The nature of this relation has been emphasized especially by status-value theory (Berger et al., 1972). According to this theory, income distributions are judged as fair or unfair only if the evaluating person applies a normative frame of reference. This frame of reference expresses normative standards which the evaluating person considers socially binding. According to Messick and Sentis (1983: 68), most empirical theories emphasize equality as the basic principle of justice. Equality of outcome, equality of outcome per unit input, or equality above a minimum level are variations of this basic distributive principle. Here, the difference between the concept of justice and satisfaction becomes clear. Although both evaluations are based upon social comparisons, satisfaction does not relate to underlying, socially binding principles. Rather, it predominantly relates to individual experiences of past outcomes regarding payment, chances for promotion, tenure, or challenging tasks (Messick and Sentis, 1983; Prentice and Crosby, 1987).

As a result, can we conclude that justice judgments exclusively represent normative motives of evaluation; whereas, satisfaction judgements solely embody motives of self-interest? Keeping the philosophical critique on empirical justice research in mind, one might argue that both categories empirically contain elements of the other. Let us assume that an employee considers her own wage unjustly low. What rationales can be identified? On the one hand, she can compare her wage to the wage of co-workers performing similar tasks. In terms of equity theory (e.g., Adams, 1965; Walster and Walster, 1975), her judgement can be definitely classified as a justice evaluation. On the other hand, and apart from any normative criteria involved, the employee's judgement could also refer to self-interested motives. She might argue that her actual wage does not supply her material wants, e.g., a desired vacation trip or a new compact car. Consequently, these utilitarian criteria might be incorporated into her justice judgment.

Empirically, the reverse situation seems to be more important, i.e. the situation in which moral judgments are part of the individual's general set of evaluation criteria. In this case, the reason for pay dissatisfaction is rooted in the fact that one's own wage is seen as unjustly low, although this does not refer to a conception of the individual's self interests. This conception is supported by the results of several empirical surveys. For instance, Folger and Konovsky (1989) looked at the employee's justice judgments towards rising wages. Using multiple regression analysis, they showed that distributive justice judgments have a significant positive impact on pay satisfaction, whereas perceptions of procedural justice only influence organizational commitment and trust in superiors. McFarlin and Sweeney (1992) achieved a similar result via an employee survey in a US bank. As an indicator for fair wages, the authors asked to what extent current wages compensate for varying workloads. They were able to show that payment justice enhances overall work satisfaction (McFarlin and Sweeney, 1992). Similar effects were reported from other surveys (Dittrich and Carrell, 1976; Klein, 1973; Randall and Mueller, 1995).

Let us now return to our initial question whether justice judgments differ from satisfaction judgments. Philosophical theory states that "real life" justice judgements do not meet the criterion of impartiality, a basic requirement for social justice (Barry, 1995; Singer, 1997: 95 et seq.; Swift, 1999). In this respect, "real life" justice judgements are more or less guided by motives of self-interest, which is comparable to satisfaction judgements. In contrast to philosophy, social psychology shows that justice and satisfaction judgments are different evaluation categories. Therefore, it can be expected that this difference is reflected in an employee's survey response concerning his pay. Although we will observe a positive correlation between both issues, justice and satisfaction judgements are not assumed to converge with one another.

Determinants of Evaluations towards Pay

Subsequently, we can now examine to what extent the two judgment categories differ from one another. To answer whether they display the two latent constructs of morality and self-interest, we need some more substantial arguments. Among other things, these arguments have to reveal whether these constructs have different effects on attitudes and behavior. In order to answer this question, it is useful to look for social institutions that employees hold responsible for establishing and securing justice and satisfaction concerning their wages. Both organizational sociology and industrial relations research demonstrate that employees hold different expectations towards the firm as an economic institution and towards the works council (or the labor union, respectively) as a representative of their interests (Lengfeld and Liebig, 2002; Metcalf et al., 2000; Voos, 1997). The firm is expected to offer the highest wages possible. In contrast, employees expect the works council to (1) surpervise adherence to social rights in the firm and (2) to enforce distributive justice regarding pay.

Moral Claims towards the Works Council

Within organizational sociology, it has proven useful to differentiate between "collective" and "corporative" actors (Coleman, 1974, 1990; Olson, 1996). *Collective actors* are characterized by a high consensus of interests among their members. By assuming that the unification of individual interests improves the chances for their realization, these actors are brought into being. They are supported through active participation and passive membership, as individual and collective goals coincide with each other. Since the members of collective actors have equal rights, binding decisions are legitimate only if they are carried out using a bottom-up approach.

The German works council is a typical example of a collective actor. It is brought to life either by the initiative of several employees or by labor unions represented in the respective firm. Its members are elected (Schnabel, 2000). Employees expect the works council to enforce *moral* standards vis-à-vis the firm's management, which affect and even define the relation between employees and management (Lengfeld and Liebig, 2002). This expectation results from the position the works council takes within industrial relations. The works council embodies the theory of democratic co-determination, according to which the citizens' social and political rights should be applicable both in states and in firms alike (Marshall, 1973). To ensure this, the establishment of works councils in German firms was legally established in 1920. However, it took decades of intensive political fighting between capital and labor until works councils were accepted *de facto*. Workers' requests encountered substantial resistance from employers and their associations (Müller-Jentsch, 1995b). They claimed that any statutory, institutionalized co-determination is alien to the capitalist system, since it infringes upon the elementary norm of free capital expenditure. Moreover, it was said to decrease efficiency because it reduced capital gains. Since they were the bearers of economic risk, firms believed they were entitled to these gains, (Furubotn, 1988; Jensen and Meckling, 1979). It took decades until both sides eventually learned to reconcile their differences with institutionalized works councils (Müller-Jentsch, 1995a, 1995b).

Why do German employees regard the works council as an entity that is capable of enforcing distributive justice? The answer is that the distribution of goods and burdens is part and parcel to the works council's duties (Lengfeld, 2003). The central assignments of the works council are co-determination for regulations concerning overtime and the selection of personnel to be laid-off, the compilation of social compensation plans and surveillance of collective wage agreements. The works council has an all-encompassing right to co-determination concerning payment schemes. According to German jurisdiction, the works council has to ensure the just distribution of the fixed salary to all employees, as determined by the employer (cp. Däubler, 1990: 561). This includes the right to co-determine regulations concerning the distributive order of extra-pay.

Following these considerations we can draw two conclusions. First, we can assume that the statutory role of the works council, ensuring the just distribution of fixed wages, will be reflected in the employee's attitudes towards justice. More specifically, the works council is expected to assert the employees' moral demands for a socially just distribution of wages. If the employees view their wages as unjust, we can assume that the works council will be held responsible. This judgment will be reflected in the employees' attitudes towards the works council. In effect, if workers consider themselves unjustly underpaid, then they will voice dissatisfaction with the performance of the works council.

Second, I assume that the employees will not expect the works council to push for increasing wages, as it is statutorily forbidden to initiate collective actions (organizing strikes, refusal to work or wage bargaining). Consequences of the limited influence of the works council regarding wage increases and the relationship between satisfaction and justice may be as follows. Let us assume that pay satisfaction is a valid indicator to measure judgments on wages that are rooted in self-interest. Since the works council is not responsible for maximizing wages, workers dissatisfied with their wages will not hold the works council primarily responsible for it. In a nutshell, pay dissatisfaction does not (or to a much lesser degree) affect the employees' evaluation of the works council's activities.

Expectations of Benefit Maximization towards the Firm

Now let us turn our attention to the firm as a "corporate actor". A corporate actor is established to satisfy particular objectives of its founder. Since the founder cannot achieve his goals alone, he depends on the cooperation of other members, primarily individual employees. They, of course, have goals of their own which might differ from the goals of the corporate actor. This results in a fundamental conflict of interests between the firm and the employees. Regarding this conflict, organizational theory has produced several proposals (e.g., Coleman, 1990; McGregor, 1960; Roethlisberger and Dickson, 1939; Simon, 1962; Taylor, 1911). All of them are based on an assumption expressed quite early on by Chester Barnard (1938): Employees will only be prepared to perform the necessary tasks and to give up the freedom of action if the firm provides financial and non-material incentives. Employees will only give up the freedom of their action, if they consider these incentives to be appropriate for the satisfaction of their personal interests, (see also Coleman, 1990, for details). Therefore, we can assume that employees see the firm primarily as a means to maximize their wages.

In contrast to the works council, employees will not significantly view the firm as a means to ensure fair wages. As a series of empirical analyses have proven, employees do have normative demands towards firms (Cohen-Charash and Spector,

2001; Colquitt et al., 2001; Cropanzano, 1993; Greenberg, 1990a, 1990b; Folger and Cropanzano, 1998). Nonetheless, it is unlikely that normative requests and self-interested expectations are posed to the firm to quite the *same degree*, since individual employees and firms are entangled in a basic conflict over the distribution of any cooperatively attained gains. Although this conflict can be institutionally regulated, it will never entirely disappear. The opponents will and cannot expect the other side to behave impartially. This is why employees do not expect the firm to neglect its interests in favor of becoming an impartial actor that realizes the employees' ideas concerning social justice.

Indeed, organizational research demonstrates that identification with the firm is a useful indicator for judgments towards the firm. The more the employees are satisfied, the more they identify with the firm's goals (e.g., Kohn and Schooler, 1973, 1982; Lincoln and Kalleberg, 1990). Accordingly, we can make the following assumption, which is also underlined by research on work satisfaction. If employees believe that their organizational membership satisfies their interests in high wages, satisfaction with their wage should lead to identification with the firm. In short, the more satisfied employees are with their wages, the more positively they will evaluate their firm. Since the firm is not expected to accept the employees' moral demands for a socially just distribution of pay, however, perceptions of just pay will not significantly affect identification with the firm.

Hypotheses

At the beginning of this chapter I asked whether justice judgments of individual wages are primarily moral judgments, or whether they predominantly express an employee's interest in maximizing his wage. To assess this question, two constructs were identified and differentiated: fairness of wages and pay satisfaction. It was further argued that both constructs are empirically distinct and that they stand in a positive relationship to each other. Thus, a first hypothesis may be stated as follows:

> Hypothesis 1: The more employees evaluate their wages as just the more satisfied they are with it.

Although it is important to test the relationship between justice evaluations and satisfaction, it is not a necessary precondition to clarify the correlation between them. Thus, I have focused on the question whether satisfaction and justice evaluations entail different consequences within the firm. The answer to this question was based on the following arguments. First, employees expect the works council to enforce their moral requests regarding fair wages. Second, they view the firm as a means to maximize their interests in higher wages. Furthermore, it was argued that neither the works council is primarily expected to maximize salaries nor that the firm is primarily regarded as a means for just distributions. Using judgments of justice and satisfaction to evaluate the performance of the works council and identification with the firm, Hypotheses 2 and 3 can be put forward:

Hypothesis 2a: The more employees judge their wages as unjust, the more they will evaluate the works council's activities negatively.

Hypothesis 2b: Justice evaluations of wage will have a smaller impact on identification with the firm than wage satisfaction.

Hypothesis 3a: The more employees are dissatisfied with their wages, the less they will identify with the firm.

Hypothesis 3b: Wage satisfaction will have a smaller impact on the evaluation of the performance of the works council than justice evaluations of wage.

Method

Participants

The data used in this chapter originates from a standardized employee survey "Veränderungsprozesse und Gerechtigkeit in Organisationen—VGIO" ("Organizational Change and Social Justice"), which was conducted in 21 firms of the German metal industry. The firms were situated in two regions in the western part of Germany that introduced semi-autonomous group work two years prior to the survey. The firms were selected through a screening process in January 1999. In this process, short questionnaires were administered to 4,010 firms consisting of questions about the type of group work carried out, along with relevant information about the respective firms. Out of 250 firms with more than 100 employees, 21 firms were willing to participate in the employee survey. From these firms 685 workers, 72 supervisors, 37 works council members and 42 CEOs were questioned. The empirical instrument was a standardized questionnaire. The main part was identical for all surveyed groups, except for a few specific questions that varied for workers, supervisors, works councils and CEOs.

A commercial survey institute carried out on-site questioning, as well as data input and data scrubbing. All workers received the questionnaire at work and filled it out at home. After a four day deadline, the worker's questionnaires were collected anonymously at the workplace. All supervisors of the respective working units were questioned. Managers and works council members were chosen systematically. Generally, only employees who participated in the conception and implementation of the group work were questioned. Completed questionnaires were sent through firm-internal mail. The return rate was 73.3 per cent in total (70.3 per cent from workers, 88.8 per cent from supervisors, 92.5 per cent from works council members and 95.5 per cent from CEOs).

Procedure

In order to test the first hypothesis regarding the discrimination between justice and satisfaction, it is useful to look at the frequencies of both variables, since possible differences between the two constructs might be revealed already on the descriptive level. In a second step, the average value of satisfaction judgments and justice judgments will be compared. Respondents were asked whether they feel unjustly underpaid, justly paid or unjustly overpaid (see details below). For analysis, the justice scale was broken into a two part-scale ("underpaid" and "overpaid") and arranged according to scale points. I did this for two reasons. First, due to the midpoint "justly paid", including the entire rating scale in the regression analysis produces ambiguous results. Second, it is plausible that the effects of unjust underpayment on pay satisfaction are quite different from feelings of being overpaid. Unjust overpayment might evoke pay satisfaction, whereas unjust underpayment might result in a higher rate of pay dissatisfaction. Subsequently, the average values are presented graphically in Figures 10.1–10.3. By using a linear regression equation, the gradient angle (β) of both part-scales will be shown. Thereby the judgments of all interviewed groups make up the data pool (N=686).

To verify the second and third hypotheses, I will proceed in two steps. First, I carry out a principle components analysis to identify the two indicators, "identification with firm" and "evaluation of works council," that will be used to show the consequences of justice and satisfaction judgments. Second, I calculate two regression equations with robust standard errors (Huber-Regression in consideration of firm clusters; cp. Huber, 1967) where these indicators subsequently become independent variables. Several control variables are included in this model. Among them are the effects of satisfaction judgments and justice judgments on the two consequences, "identification with firm" and "evaluation of works council". Due to the fact that not all employee groups were questioned regarding firm identification in the VGIO survey, only the workers' answers are presented in the regression model (N=356).

Variables

Justice Judgments and Satisfaction Judgments
In the VGIO survey, the employees were asked to judge their wages in terms of justice. Three different judgments were possible. First, it is possible that one's wage is perceived as unjustly low. Secondly, it can be considered unjustly high. Or thirdly, employees might regard their wage as just. To display all three possibilities empirically, employees were given a scale ranging from -5 to +5. Using this scale, they were asked to judge whether their wages are just (zero-point of the scale) or, in case of a perceived injustice, unjustly low (-1 to -5) or unjustly high (+1 to +5). To acquire "pure" justice judgments concerning individual wages, employees were explicitly asked only about their wage in the firm. Therefore, this inquiry did not pertain to their general income that would also include social security payments, income tax etc. Furthermore, the particular name of the respective firm was used in this question. In order to examine the different effects of the three judgments within the scope of the regression equation, the scale was divided into a two part-scale (underpaid, overpaid) and two dummy variables ("underpaid", "just paid"; reference category is "overpaid").

Pay satisfaction was assessed using an 11-point scale reaching from 0 (very dissatisfied) to 10 (very satisfied). Here, too, the firm's name and the term "payment" were used in the phrasing of the questions.

Table 10.1   Identification with the Firm and Evaluation of the Works Council (Factor Analysis)

			h^2
I am satisfied with work at [name of firm]	**0.851**	0.189	0.759
I am proud to belong to [name of firm]	**0.891**	0.171	0.822
I would recommend [name of firm] to my friends	**0.845**	0.154	0.738
The works council at [name of firm] represents my interests	0.150	**0.911**	0.851
The works council at [name of firm] represents the interests of all workers	0.164	**0.902**	0.841
The works council at [name of firm] provides information to the workforce very well	0.210	**0.782**	0.655
Eigenvalue	1.442	3.224	

Notes   n = 356, principle-components factor analysis with subsequent varimax rotation

Consequences of Justice Judgments and Satisfaction Judgments
Identification with the firm was measured with three items. Respondents were asked on a 4-point scale ("yes indeed" to "not at all") to specify whether they were satisfied with the tasks carried out in the firm, whether they were proud to work for their firm, and whether they would recommend the firm to good friends. The evaluation of the works council was also measured on a 4-point scale ("yes indeed" to "not at all") with three items. These pertained to whether the respondent regarded the works council as competent to assert and enforce his individual interests as well as the general interests of all employees, and whether the respondent felt well informed by the works council. Two indicators,"identification with the firm" and "evaluation of the works council," were deduced from principle components factor analysis (see Table 10.1).

Control Variables
Apart from regular demographic characteristics such as age, sex and educational degree, other control variables were included such as the respondent's relative income, the duration of his employment with the firm, as well as the identification with the goals of the trade unions (see details below).

Income   We can assume a positive relation exists between the employee's income and his identification with the firm. Respondents were asked to state their average monthly net income (after reductions). On this basis, each employee's individual deviation from the set average income was calculated. Compared to the absolute income, this indicator has the advantage of identifying the position of each employee within the firm's income hierarchy.

Duration of employment   We can assume that the longer an employee works for a given firm, the higher his identification with the firm and the more positive his evaluation of the works council will be. To verify this, we asked for the starting year of the respondent's employment. This value was recoded into the duration of employment (in years). Subsequently, a quotient was calculated from the duration

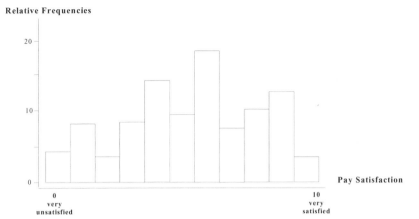

Figure 10.1   Pay Satisfaction (Relative Frequencies, n = 688)

of employment and the duration of professional life. For blue collar workers in Germany, an average age by firm entry of 16 years was assumed. This indicator provides information as to the proportionate association with the firm in relation to the previous career.

Identification with trade unions   We can assume that identification with trade unions has a positive effect on the evaluation of the works council; whereas, identification with the firm will have a negative effect. To control for these effects, an 11-point scale was used, from 0 (not at all) to 10 (very much).

Results

Let us start with a closer look at the separation of justice judgments and satisfaction judgments. Whereas standardized surveys report a rather high satisfaction rate (e.g., Lincoln and Kalleberg, 1990), Figure 10.1 shows a broad coverage of all cells with a slight asymmetry to the right. The mean of 5.38 underlines this tendency. Figure 10.2 shows the justice judgments. Here, the asymmetry leans to the left, i.e., judgments that employees are "unjustly underpaid" are represented more often. The mean is about -0.79. Some 30 per cent of the respondents state that they consider themselves to be justly paid or even overpaid. Comparing these findings with those of satisfaction judgments, we note two observations. First, both attitudes differ in terms of their distribution. Second, we find a considerably high occurrence of statements relating to unjust overpayment.

These results can be further underlined if we look at the relation between satisfaction and justice judgments (Figure 10.3). Consistent with Hypothesis 1, judgments of being unjustly underpaid negatively affect pay satisfaction; whereas, perceived overpayment leads to rising satisfaction. These findings can be ascribed to the fact that overpayment is necessarily in the respondent's material self-interest and, therefore, leads to a higher degree of pay satisfaction. β-coefficients, however, tell us that satisfaction and justice judgments do not converge. Surprisingly, the

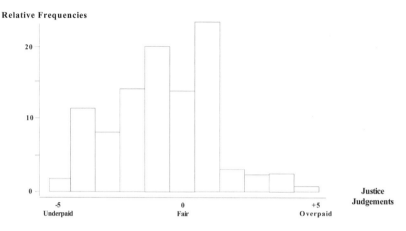

Figure 10.2   Justice Judgments of Pay (Relative Frequencies, n = 688)

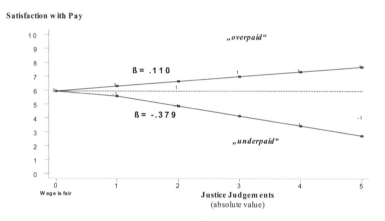

Figure 10.3   Justice and Satisfaction Judgments (Regression Lines)

Notes: n = 686; Comparison of means of pay satisfaction by justice judgments (part scales). Beta-coefficients with robust standard errors (Huber-regression, clustered by firm affiliation).

overpayment regression line is only gently inclined. Although it cannot be directly tested by the data, one can suppose that perceptions of unjust overpayment might evoke moral doubts. Although being overpaid conforms to the interest of payment maximization, a "bad conscience", in turn, might lessen this joy.

The second and third hypotheses postulate that justice judgments and satisfaction judgments mirror different attitude dimensions concerning morality and material self-interests. Accordingly, pay dissatisfaction was expected to influence firm identification negatively (Hypothesis 3a). Perceptions of injustice were assumed to evoke negative judgments towards the works council (Hypothesis 2a). Effects of justice judgments on firm identification and satisfaction with works council's evaluation are expected to exert a smaller influence than the other factors (Hypotheses 2b and 3b). The

Table 10.2 Determinants of Firm Identification and Works Council's Evaluation (Regression Analysis)

	Identification with Firm	Evaluation of Works Council
Socio-demographic characteristics		
Age	0.007 (1.72)	-0.001 (-0.27)
Sex (women = 1)	-0.398 (-2.16)	-0.339 (-2.03)
Education (highest degree)	-0.086 (-1.96)	-0.005 (-0.13)
Relative Income	-0.000 (-2.06)	-0.000 (-0.29)
Duration of Employment	-0.270 (-1.67)	-0.472 (-1.83)
Attitudes		
Identification with Unions	-0.034 (-1.42)	**0.099*** (4.74)**
Pay Satisfaction	**0.091*** (4.21)**	0.012 (0.53)
Being unjust underpaid	-0.293 (-1.96)	**-0.363** (-3.49)**
Being fair paid	0.002 (0.01)	-0.261 (-1.54)
Intercept	0.452 (0.96)	0.409 (1.06)
R^2	**0.138**	**0.125**

Notes: n = 356; Listed are beta-coefficients with robust standard errors (Huber-regression, clustered by firm affiliation); $^*p_t < 0.05$; $^{**}p_t < 0.01$; $^{***}p_t < 0.001$

respective results are shown in Table 10.2 (β-coefficients are reported; t-values in brackets). Let us first look at the regression model in the left column. It is striking that neither socio-demographic nor organizational-structural variables significantly affect firm identification. In contrast, employees increasingly identify themselves with their firm if they are satisfied with their wages (β = 0.091 on the 0.001-level of significance). This result supports Hypothesis 3a, which postulates a positive effect of pay satisfaction in firm identification. Moreover, it is noteworthy that not even one of the dummy variables concerning just payment has a significant effect on firm identification. The effects do not reach the 0.05-level of significance. This last finding is consistent with Hypothesis 2b, which expects only a weak effect of justice evaluation on firm identification.

The opposite has to be said for attitudes towards the works council. While individual and organizational-structural variables show no significant effect, identification with trade unions is positively linked to judgments towards the works council. This is plausible because German metal workers are highly unionized and works councils are traditionally recruited from "IG Metall", one of the world's largest trade unions. The most important finding is that workers, who regard themselves as unjustly underpaid, evaluate the works council's activities negatively. This finding supports Hypothesis 2a, which postulates a negative impact of injustice on the evaluation of the works council. On the other hand, and in line with Hypothesis 3b, whoever is dissatisfied with his wage does not hold the works council responsible.

In sum, these findings seem to validate the second and third hypotheses. Perceived injustice of wages has a significant negative effect on the evaluation of the works council, but this does not influence the employee's identification with the firm. Conversely, pay dissatisfaction leads to a low firm identification, but not to a negative evaluation of the works council.

Conclusions: Subjective Impartiality

Do justice judgments, as approached by ordinary survey research, really express moral demands, or do they more or less mirror the employee's material self-interest of maximizing their wage? This question was discussed in this chapter because of some scepticism raised by philosophical theory concerning the validity of the empirical definition of justice. This theory contends that "real life" justice judgements do not meet the criterion of impartiality, one of the basic requirements of social justice. In this respect, "real life" justice judgements are more or less guided by motives of self-interest, which is comparable to satisfaction judgements. To answer the aforementioned question, a discriminant validation was carried out. Two indicators were distinguished – pay satisfaction as an indicator of the individual's self-interest, and justice of pay as an indicator for moral demands. Based on data taken from a standardized employee survey conducted within the German metal industry, it could be shown that both constructs differ from one another. Perceived unjust underpayment leads to dissatisfaction, whereas unjust overpayment, to a much lesser extent, strengthens satisfaction. The relative weakness of both relations, especially in the case of overpayment, might justify the conclusion that the operational definitions of justice and satisfaction measure different things.

Furthermore, using insights from organizational sociology and industrial relations research, I have identified two social institutions which are held responsible for asserting employees' material self-interests and moral demands. It was empirically shown that employees demand the works council to ensure social justice within firms. If the works council cannot fulfil this duty, this results in negative evaluations for the works council's activities. Moreover, it was postulated that employees evaluate their association with the firm according to the benefits they get from it. Accordingly, pay dissatisfaction decreases identification with the firm.

What consequences arise from these findings in the broader context of the philosophical critique of empirical research outlined above? The philosophical perspective stated that justice judgments should be made from an impartial standpoint and with reference to moral principles. Obviously, people are, to a large extent, unable to judge impartially according to philosophical theorists because their judgements are more or less guided by motives of self-interest (cf. Rawls, 1971). When judging in terms of justice, they cannot discern the social relations and restrictions in which they are embedded. To weigh moral principles and distributions of scarce goods, in the philosophical sense, requires a high degree of cultural capital (e.g., formal education, linguistic competence, access to art and culture; see Bourdieu, 1979) which workers, for the most part, do not possess. Although empirically observed justice judgements are, nevertheless, inherently moral, people fail to meet the rigorous criteria of impartiality stated by philosophical theories of justice.

Contrary to the philosophical point of view, I would like to point out that "real life" justice judgments still are moral judgments. However, these judgements differ from the philosophical ones insofar as they express the people's call for asserting moral norms in the social world. These are norms that the people expect are agreed upon by everyone involved in the distribution. In other words, it is not the ability to judge in an impartial way that constitutes justice judgments in "real life", *but the subjective claim to do so*. To clearly indicate the contradiction between the ability and the subjective claim to act impartially, I would like to suggest the term "subjective impartiality". This term expresses that people struggling for just distributions expect that they as well as others abandon self-interests. In that case, in a distributional conflict, they assume from each other that their judgments should apply to the same socially binding norms.

Unfortunately, in the majority of cases, people are wrong in believing that others will hold the same normative standards of judgment. Remember our example stated above: the female worker demanding justice of pay is sure about two things. First, from her point of view, she believes to claim high moral standards. Second, she is strongly convinced that every person in her position would arrive at the very same moral conclusion. Nonetheless, others will be very likely to refuse the female workers' claims for justice. In social reality, people obviously develop competing claims of justice, and they are often incapable of mutually recognizing these claims. One might call this the "egocentric bias" of justice evaluations, i.e., a "tendency for subjects to judge more money to be fair for them than for another in the same situation" (Messick and Sentis, 1983: 71).

References

Adams, J.S. (1965), "Inequity in Social Exchange" in *Advances in Experimental Social Psychology*, Vol. 2. Berkowitz, L. (ed.) (New York: Academic Press), 267–299.

Austin, W., McGinn, N.C. and Susmich, C. (1980), "Internal Standards Revisited: Effects of Social Comparisons and Experiments on Judgments of Fairness and Satisfaction", *Journal of Experimental Social Psychology*, **16**, 426–441. [DOI: 10.1016/0022-1031%2880%2990049-9]

Barnard, C. (1938), *The Functions of the Executive* (Cambridge MA: Harvard University Press).

Barry, B. (1995), *Justice as Impartiality* (Oxford: Clarendon Press).

Berger, J.M., Zelditch, M., Anderson, B. and Cohen, B.P. (1972), "Structural Aspects of Distributive Justice: A Status-Value Formulation" in *Sociological Theories in Progress*, Vol. 2. Berger, J.M., Zelditch, M. and Anderson, B. (eds) (New York: Houghton Mifflin), 119–146.

Blau, P.M. (1964), *Exchange and Power in Social Life* (New York: Wiley).

Bourdieu, P. (1979), *La Distinction. Critique sociale du jugement* (Paris: Éditions de Minuit).

Brown, S.P. and Peterson, R.A. (1993), "Antecedents and Consequences of Salesman Job Satisfaction: Meta-Analysis and Assessment of Causal Effects", *Marketing Research*, **30**, 63–77. [DOI: 10.2307/3172514]

Cohen-Charash, Y. and Spector, P.E. (2001), "The Role of Justice in Organizations: A Meta-Analysis", *Organizational Behavior and Human Decision Processes*, **86**, 278–321. [DOI: 10.1006/obhd.2001.2958]

Coleman, J.S. (1974), *Power and the Structure of Society* (New York: Norton).

Coleman, J.S. (1990), *Foundations of Social Theory* (Cambridge MA: Belknap Press of Harvard University Press).

Colquitt, J.A., Conlon, D.E., Wesson, M.J., Porter, C. and Ng, K.Y. (2001), "Justice at the Millennium: A Meta-Analytic Review of 25 years of Organizational Justice Research", *Journal of Applied Psychology*, **86**, 425–445. [PubMed 11419803] [DOI: 10.1037/0021-9010.86.3.425]

Cronbach, L.J. and Meehl, P.E. (1955), "Construct Validity in Psychological Tests", *Psychological Bulletin*, **52**, 281–302. [PubMed 13245896] [DOI: 10.1037/h0040957]

Cropanzano, R. (1993), *Justice in the Workplace: Approaching Fairness in Human Resource Management* (Hillsdale: Lawrence Erlbaum).

Däubler, W. (1990), *Das Arbeitsrecht 1: Leitfaden für Arbeitnehmer* (Reinbek bei Hamburg: Rowohlt).

DeMeuse, K.P. (1985), "A Compendium of Frequently Used Measures in Industrial/Organizational Psychology", *The Industrial-Organizational Psychologist*, **23**, 53–59.

Dittrich, J.E. and Carell, M.R. (1976), "Dimensions of Organizational Fairness as Predictors of Job Satisfaction, Absence and Turnover", *Proceedings of the Academy of Management, 1976*, 79–83.

Faragher, E.B., Cass, M. and Cooper, C.L. (2005), "The Relationship between Job Satisfaction and Health: A Meta-Analysis", *Occupational and Environmental Medicine*, **62**, 105–112. [PubMed 15657192] [DOI: 10.1136/oem.2002.006734]

Folger, R. and Cropanzano, R. (1998), *Organizational Justice and Human Resource Management* (Thousand Oaks: Sage).

Folger, R. and Konovsky, M.A. (1989), "Effects of Procedural and Distributive Justice on Reactions to Pay Raise Decisions", *Academy of Management Journal*, **32**, 115–130. [DOI: 10.2307/256422]

Freedman, A. and Goodman, P. (1967), "Wage Inequity, Self-Qualification, and Productivity", *Organizational Behavior and Human Performance*, **2**, 406–417. [DOI: 10.1016/0030-5073%2867%2990005-0]

Furubotn, E. (1988), "Codetermination and the Modern Theory of the Firm: A Property-Rights Analysis", *Journal of Business*, **61**, 165–181. [DOI: 10.1086/296426]

Greenberg, J. (1990a), "Employee Theft as a Reaction to Underpayment Inequity: The Hidden Cost of Pay Cuts", *Journal of Applied Psychology*, **75**, 561–568. [DOI: 10.1037/0021-9010.75.5.561]

Greenberg, J. (1990b), "Organizational Justice: Yesterday, Today, and Tomorrow", *Journal of Management*, **16**, 399–432. [DOI: 10.1177/014920639001600208]

Hackman, J.R. and Oldham, G.R. (1975), "Development of the Job Diagnostic Survey", *Journal of Applied Psychology*, **60**, 159–170. [DOI: 10.1037/h0076546]

Huber, P.J. (1967), "The Behavior of Maximum Likelihood Estimates under Non-Standard Conditions" in *Proceedings of the Fifth Annual Berkeley Symposium on Mathematical Statistics and Probability*, Vol. I. LeCam, L.M. and Neyman, J. (eds) (Berkeley CA: University of California Press), 221–233.

Iaffaldano, M.T. and Muchinsky, P.M. (1985), "Job Satisfaction and Job Performance: A Meta-Analysis", *Psychological Bulletin*, **97**, 251–273. [DOI: 10.1037/0033-2909.97.2.251]

Ironson, G.H., Smith, P.C., Brannick, M.T., Gibson, W.M. and Paul, K.B. (1989), "Construction of a Job in General Scale: A Comparison of Global, Composite and

Specific Measures", *Journal of Applied Psychology*, **74**, 1–8. [DOI: 10.1037/0021-9010.74.2.193]

Jensen, M.C. and Meckling, H. (1979), "Rights and Production Functions: An Application to Labor-Managed Firms and Codetermination", *Journal of Business*, **52**, 469–506. [DOI: 10.1086/296060]

Klein, S.M. (1973), "Pay Factors as Predictors of Satisfaction: A Comparison of Reinforcement, Equity, and Expectancy", *Academy of Management Journal*, **16**, 598–610. [DOI: 10.2307/254693]

Kohn, M.L. and Schooler, C. (1973), "Occupational Experience and Psychological Functioning", *American Sociological Review*, **38**, 97–118. [DOI: 10.2307/2094334]

Kohn, M.L. and Schooler, C. (1982), "Job Conditions and Personality", *American Sociological Review*, **87**, 1257–1286. [DOI: 10.1086/227593]

Lengfeld, H. (2003), *Mitbestimmung und Gerechtigkeit: Zur moralischen Grundstruktur betrieblicher Verhandlungen* (München, Mering: Hampp).

Lengfeld, H. and Liebig, S. (2002), "Collective Bargaining, Co-Determination, and Justice Ideologies in the Firm", *Social Justice Research*, **15**, 246–270. [DOI: 10.1023/A%3A1021062529317]

Liebig, S. (2001), "Lessons from Philosophy? Interdisciplinary Justice Research and Two Classes of Justice Judgments", *Social Justice Research*, **14**, 265–287. [DOI: 10.1023/A%3A1014367907348]

Lincoln, J.R. and Kalleberg, A.L. (1990), *Culture, Control and Commitment: A Study of Work Organization and Work Attitudes in the United States and Japan* (Cambridge: Cambridge University Press).

Locke, E.A. (1976), "The Nature Causes of Job Satisfaction" in *Handbook of Industrial and Organizational Psychology*. Dunnette, M.D. (ed.) (Chicago: Rand McNally), 1297–1349.

Marshall, T.H. (1973), *Class, Citizenship, and Social Development* (Westport CT: Greenwood Press).

McFarlin, D.B. and Sweeney, P.D. (1992), "Distributive and Procedural Justice as Predictors of Satisfaction with Personal and Organizational Outcomes", *Academy of Management Journal*, **35**, 626–637. [DOI: 10.2307/256489]

McGregor, D. (1960), *The Human Side of Enterprise* (New York: McGraw-Hill).

Messick, D.M. and Sentis, K. (1979), "Fairness and Preference", *Journal of Experimental Social Psychology*, **15**, 418–434. [DOI: 10.1016/0022-1031%2879%2990047-7]

Messick, D.M. and Sentis, K. (1983), "Fairness, Preference, and Fairness Biases" in *Equity Theory: Psychological and Sociological Perspectives*. Messnick, D.M. and Cook, K.S. (eds) (New York: Praeger), 61–94.

Metcalf, D., Hansen, K. and Charlwood, A. (2000). *Unions and the Sword of Justice: Unions and Pay Systems, Pay Inequality, Pay Discrimination, and Low Pay*. CEP-Discussion Paper (London: London School of Economics and Political Science).

Müller-Jentsch, W. (1995a), "Germany: From Collective Voice to Co-Management" in *Works Councils: Consultation, Representation, and Cooperation in Industrial Relations*. Rogers, J. and Streeck, W. (eds) (Chicago, London: The University of Chicago Press), 53–78.

Müller-Jentsch, W. (1995b), "Industrial Democracy: From Representative Codetermination to Direct Participation", *International Journal of Political Economy*, **25**, 50–60.

Olson, M. (1996), *The Logic of Collective Action* (Cambridge MA: Harvard University Press).

Prentice, D.A. and Crosby, F. (1987), "The Importance of Context for Assessing Deservingness" in *Social Comparison, Social Justice, and Relative Deprivation*. Masters, J.C. and Smith, W.P. (eds) (Hillsdale NJ): Lawrence Erlbaum), 165–182.

Randall, C.S. and Mueller, C.W. (1995), "Extensions of Justice Theory: Justice Evaluations and Employees' Reactions in a Natural Setting", *Social Psychology Quarterly*, **58**, 178–194. [DOI: 10.2307/2787041]

Rawls, J. (1971), *A Theory of Justice* (Cambridge MA: Belknap Press of Harvard University Press).

Roethlisberger, F.J. and Dickson, W.J. (1939), *Management and the Worker* (Cambridge MA: Harvard University Press).

Schnabel, C. (2000), "Nonunion Representation in Germany" in *Nonunion Employee Representation: History, Contemporary Practice, and Policy*. Kaufman, B.E. and Taras, D.G. (eds) (Armonk, London: M. E. Sharpe), 365–385.

Simon, H.A. (1962), *Administrative Behaviour: A Study of Decision-Making Process in Administrative Organization* (New York, London: Macmillan).

Singer, M. (1997), *Ethics and Justice in Organisations* (Aldershot: Avebury).

Smith, P.C., Kendall, L.M. and Hulin, C.L. (1969), *Measurement of Satisfaction in Work and Retirement* (Chicago: Rand McNally).

Soltan, K.E. (1987), *The Causal Theory of Justice* (Berkeley: University of California Press).

Spector, P.E. (1997), *Job Satisfaction: Application, Assessment, Cause, and Consequences* (Thousand Oaks: Sage).

Swift, A. (1999), "Public Opinion and Political Philosophy: The Relation between Social-Scientific and Philosophical Analyses of Distributive Justice", *Ethical Theory and Moral Practice*, **2**, 337–363. [DOI: 10.1023/A%3A1009903718660]

Taylor, F.W. (1911), *The Principles of Scientific Management* (New York, London: Harper & Brothers).

Voos, P. (1997), "Economic and Social Justice through Collective Bargaining: The USA in the Coming Century", *Industrial Relations Journal*, **28**, 292–298. [DOI: 10.1111/1468-2338.00065]

Walster, E. and Walster, G.W. (1975), "Equity and Social Justice", *Journal of Social Issues*, **31**, 21–43.

Wolf, M.G. (1970), "Need Gratification Theory: A Theoretical Reformulation of Job Satisfaction/Dissatisfaction and Job Motivation", *Journal of Applied Psychology*, **54**, 87–94.

Chapter 11

Studying Justice: Measurement, Estimation, and Analysis of the Actual Reward and the Just Reward[1]

Guillermina Jasso
New York University

1 Introduction

In the study of distributive justice, there are two fundamental actors and three fundamental quantities. The *observer* reflects on the situation of a *rewardee*. The observer perceives the rewardee's *actual reward*, forms or retrieves an idea of the *just reward* for the rewardee, and assesses the fairness or unfairness of the actual reward, producing the *justice evaluation*. These three quantities form the crucial nexus. Though much comes before (reward-relevant characteristics, for example) and much will follow (a strategy to alter the actual reward, for example), this trio occupies a central place, illuminating the essence of distributive justice processes and generating their long reach.[2]

The observer and rewardee may be the same person—in which case the situation is called *reflexive*—or they may be different persons—in which case the situation is called *nonreflexive*. Situations and research designs pertaining to *justice for self* thus involve reflexive quantities, those pertaining to *justice for others* involve nonreflexive quantities, and those pertaining to *justice for all* involve both reflexive and nonreflexive terms.

The reward may be any personal quantitative characteristic salient for individuals and societies, including *goods* (things of which more is preferred to less) and *bads* (things of which less is preferred to more). The quintessential good in the study of justice is money, in all its many forms, and the quintessential bad is time in prison. The one confers the illusion of perfection, as Weber (1904–1905/1958) understood, and the other destroys freedom—and perfection and freedom are among the fundamental engines of

---

1   I am grateful to Wil Arts, Gabrielle Ferrales, John Hagan, Samuel Kotz, Jui-Chung Allen Li, Stefan Liebig, Eva Meyersson Milgrom, Kjell Törnblom, Riël Vermunt, Murray Webster, Bernd Wegener, and Christopher Winship for many valuable discussions.

2   Sometimes there is a third actor—the allocator. In general, the allocator need not be a human person; it may be society or a deity. If human, the allocator need not be alive, as in the case of bequests and inheritance.

behavior (Jasso 2003a). Among children, an important good is the grades they receive in school, the natural counterpart to the income for which their parents work.

The actual reward is sometimes called the *perceived-actual reward*, because the observer's information about the rewardee's actual reward may be imperfect. Even in the reflexive case, if the reward under consideration is ordinal—such as beauty, intelligence, or athletic skill—so that measurement is by relative rank, the observer may misperceive his or her own relative rank.

Given that it is the perceived-actual reward which is compared to the just reward, leading to the assessment of justice or injustice, the perceived-actual reward plays an important part, in the spirit of the Thomas Theorem, formulated by W. I. Thomas, which highlights the actor's definition of the situation.

Accordingly, in order to understand the justice evaluation—that is, to understand the observer's assessments of justice and injustice—it is crucial to understand the observer's ideas of the rewardee's actual reward and just reward, termed, respectively, the *observer-specific/rewardee-specific perceived-actual reward* and the *observer-specific/rewardee-specific just reward*. Hereafter, the phrases "actual reward" and "just reward" are shorthand for the longer expressions, and denoted A and C, respectively; the justice evaluation is denoted J.

The three fundamental quantities—A, C, and J—may each be arrayed in an observer-by-rewardee matrix, as depicted in Table 11.1. If observers and rewardees are the same, the matrix is square, and the principal diagonal contains the reflexive terms.

It is obvious that the justice evaluation is the outcome of a process in which the observer compares the actual reward to the just reward—a process captured in the *justice evaluation function*:[3]

$$J = \theta \ln \left(\frac{A}{C} \right) \tag{1}$$

where θ denotes the signature constant, to be described below. The actual reward and the just reward, too, are understood as the outcomes of two processes, called the *actual reward function* and *just reward function*, respectively, and written:

$$A = A(X, Y; \varepsilon) \tag{2}$$

and:

$$C = C(X, Q; \varepsilon), \tag{3}$$

where X, Y, and Q denote vectors of rewardee and situational characteristics—X affecting both the actual and the just reward—and ε and ε denote stochastic errors.

The actual reward function (ARF), just reward function (JRF), and justice evaluation function (JEF) depicted in Equations 1, 2, and 3 are three of the four

---

3   Here we present the logarithmic-ratio specification of the justice evaluation function. For development of the general justice evaluation function and discussion of other potential specific forms of the justice evaluation functions, see Jasso (1990, 1996, 1999).

Table 11.1   Observer-by-Rewardee Matrices of the Actual Reward, the Just Reward, and the Justice Evaluation

1. Actual Reward Matrix

$$A = \begin{bmatrix} a_{11}\, a_{12}\, a_{13}\, \cdots\, a_{1R} \\ a_{21}\, a_{22}\, a_{23}\, \cdots\, a_{2R} \\ a_{31}\, a_{32}\, a_{33}\, \cdots\, a_{3R} \\ \cdots\ \cdots\ \cdots\ \cdots\ \cdots \\ a_{N1}\, a_{N2}\, a_{N3}\, \cdots\, a_{NR} \end{bmatrix}$$

If there are no perception errors, the actual reward matrix collapses to a vector:

$$a_x = [\, a_{.1}\, a_{.2}\, a_{.3}\, \cdots\, a_{.R}\,]$$

2. Just Reward Matrix

$$C = \begin{bmatrix} c_{11}\, c_{12}\, c_{13}\, \cdots\, c_{1R} \\ c_{21}\, c_{22}\, c_{23}\, \cdots\, c_{2R} \\ c_{31}\, c_{32}\, c_{33}\, \cdots\, c_{3R} \\ \cdots\ \cdots\ \cdots\ \cdots\ \cdots \\ c_{N1}\, c_{N2}\, c_{N3}\, \cdots\, c_{NR} \end{bmatrix}$$

C. Justice Evaluation Matrix

$$J = \begin{bmatrix} j_{11}\, j_{12}\, j_{13}\, \cdots\, j_{1R} \\ j_{21}\, j_{22}\, j_{23}\, \cdots\, j_{2R} \\ j_{31}\, j_{32}\, j_{33}\, \cdots\, j_{3R} \\ \cdots\ \cdots\ \cdots\ \cdots\ \cdots \\ j_{N1}\, j_{N2}\, j_{N3}\, \cdots\, j_{NR} \end{bmatrix}$$

Notes: Observers are indexed by o = 1,…,N; rewardees are indexed by r = 1,…,R. Thus, c_{or}, a_{or}, j_{or} represent the observer-specific/rewardee-specific just reward, actual reward, and justice evaluation, respectively.

fundamental functions in justice analysis (the fourth fundamental function being the justice consequences function, whose principal independent variable is *J*).

Estimation of the actual reward function and the just reward function yields the micro and macro effects known, in the *A* case, as the *effects of the reward-relevant characteristics* and the *reward inequality*, and in the *C* case as the *principles of microjustice and macrojustice*.

Note that the *A* and *C* functions can be jointly estimated, leading to assessment of the correlation among the unobservables in the two equations.

This chapter develops several research designs for measuring and estimating the trio of fundamental justice quantities and the associated fundamental justice functions. Section 2 presents designs for measuring the actual reward and the just reward, both for self and others, including fictitious others. The protocols for measuring the actual reward and the just reward for fictitious others rely on the *factorial survey method* pioneered by Peter H. Rossi (1951, 1979). All the procedures for measuring the just reward discussed in Section 2 ask respondents directly what they think is the just reward, and thus have come to be called *direct methods* for approximating the just reward.

Section 3 begins by observing that the just reward obtained via the direct designs introduced in Section 2 may yield distorted measures of the just reward. Respondents may be reluctant to disclose their inner ideas of fairness or may feel the pressures of socialization and social desirability. This possibility, formalized by Jasso and Wegener (1997), led to the distinction between the *true just reward* and the *disclosed just reward* and to new efforts to devise techniques for estimating the true just reward.

Two keys make it possible to estimate the true just reward—*the justice evaluation function* and the factorial survey method. Section 3 summarizes the justice evaluation function.

With these two keys in place, we examine in Section 4 three *indirect methods* for estimating the true just reward, one pertaining to self, proposed by Evans (1989), and two pertaining to fictitious others and utilizing factorial survey methods, the first proposed by Jasso and Rossi (1977) and Jasso (1990) and the other proposed by Jasso and Webster (1999). As will be seen, the justice evaluation function and the factorial survey method are partners in a marriage of true minds. Indeed, in the case of one of the indirect methods, the progeny—estimates of the true just reward—depend equally on both parents, and cannot be obtained from one without the other. This indirect method is illustrated in Section 5.

2 Direct Measures of the Actual Reward and the Just Reward

We may conceptualize the actual reward and the just reward as corresponding to a person or to a particular characteristic. Because a person is a bundle of characteristics, we may think of the one-characteristic case as unidimensional and the person case as multidimensional. In the unidimensional case, the focal characteristic may be sex, age, schooling, occupation, and so on. For example, *Leviticus* (27:3–4) prescribes the value of a male (age 20–60) at fifty shekels and of a female (also 20–60) at thirty shekels; in this case, the dimension of interest is sex, and age is held constant for both sexes. The most widely studied characteristic in the unidimensional case is occupation. In the multidimensional case, characteristics typically include age, sex, education, occupation, and experience.

2.1 Unidimensional Case—Occupation

Four large survey projects have measured the actual reward and/or the just reward for particular occupations.

2.1.1 International Social Science Programme
The International Social Science Programme (ISSP) has asked respondents, via the Inequality Modules fielded in 1987, 1992, and 1999, to provide both the actual reward and the just reward for sets of 9–11 occupations. Table 11.2 reports the occupational titles in each of the four surveys.[4]

---

4   For further information on the ISSP program of surveys, documentation, and public-use data, see www.issp.org.

Table 11.2   Occupations Studied in ISSP, ISJP, NIS and GSOEP

Occupation	ISSP			ISJP	NIS	GSOEP
	1987	1992	1999	1991–2006	NIS-2003-1	2005
unskilled worker in a factory	✓	✓	✓	✓	✓	✓
bricklayer	✓	✓			✓	
farm laborer	✓	✓			✓	
city bus driver	✓	✓				
doctor in general practice	✓	✓	✓		✓	
bank clerk	✓	✓			✓	
owner of a small shop	✓	✓			✓	
chairman of a large natl corp	✓	✓	✓	✓	✓	✓
skilled worker in a factory	✓	✓	✓		✓	
secretary	✓	✓			✓	
member of the cab in fed govt	✓	✓	✓			
secondary school teacher					✓	
engineer					✓	
college professor					✓	
shop assistant			✓			
owner-manager of large factory			✓			
judge in high court			✓			
lawyer			✓			

Note: The wordings differ somewhat for the GSOEP occupations; see text.

The wording of the two questionnaire items is as follows:

Actual Reward Questionnaire Item: "We would like to know what you think people in these jobs actually earn. Please write in how much you think they usually earn, each year, before taxes. Many people are not exactly sure about this but your best guess will be close enough. This may be difficult, but it is very important. So please try. Please write in how much they actually earn each year."

Just Reward Questionnaire Item: "Next, what do you think people in these jobs ought to be paid—how much do you think they should earn each year before taxes, regardless of what they actually get? Please write in how much they should earn each year."

2.1.2 International Social Justice Project

The International Social Justice Project (ISJP) has asked respondents in its fieldings of 1991, 1996, 2000, and 2006 to provide the actual reward and the just reward for two of the occupations studied in the ISSP. The two occupations are "unskilled worker in a factory" and "chairman of a large national corporation" (Table 11.2).[5]

The wording of the two items is as follows:

---

5   For further information on the ISJP program of surveys, documentation, and public-use data, see www.butler.edu/isjp/.

Actual Reward Questionnaire Item: "We would like your estimate of the income which people in some occupations actually earn per (YEAR/MONTH) on average. (Your best guess will be fine.)"

Just Reward Questionnaire Item: "You have told me what you think people with these occupations actually earn. Now tell me what you think would be a *just and fair* average (YEARLY/MONTHLY) income for people in these occupations."

2.1.3 New Immigrant Survey

The US New Immigrant Survey (NIS), in the first round of surveying the 2003 immigrant cohort (NIS-2003-1), asked respondents to provide the actual reward for seven occupations, both in the United States and in their country of last residence. The seven occupations consisted of the two studied in both the ISSP and the ISJP—unskilled worker in a factory and chairman of a large national corporation—plus five other occupations randomly selected from among 10 occupations, 7 of which were studied in the ISSP (Table 11.2).[6]

The wording of the two items is as follows:

Actual Reward Questionnaire Item—United States: "We would now like to know what you think people in various jobs actually earn in the United States. Please state how much you think workers usually earn, each year, before taxes. Many people are not exactly sure about this, but your best guess will be close enough. This may be difficult, but it is very important, so please try. Please estimate in US dollars how much each worker actually earns per year before taxes."

Actual Reward Questionnaire Item—Country of Last Residence: "We are also interested in what you think workers in these jobs earned in your country of last residence just before you came to the United States. Please make your estimates in the currency of that country. How much do you think each worker earned per year in your country of last residence before taxes?"

2.1.4 German Socio-Economic Panel

The German Socio-Economic Panel (GSOEP) asked respondents in its fielding of 2005 to provide the actual reward and the just reward for versions of the two occupations studied in the ISSP and the ISJP. The two occupations are "unskilled worker" and "manager on the board of directors of a large company" (Table 11.2).[7]

The wording of the two items is as follows:

Actual Reward Questionnaire Item: "How high on average is the monthly net income of an [_____]?"

Just Reward Questionnaire Items: The actual reward item is followed by two items. First, the respondent is asked, "Would you say that this income has a just relation to the job

---

6   For further information on the NIS, documentation, and public-use data, see http://nis.princeton.edu.

7   For further information on the GSOEP, documentation, and public-use data, see http://www.diw.de/english/sop/index.html.

demands?" If the response is, "No, the respondent is asked the further question, "How high would a just monthly income of [_____] be, from your point of view?"

2.2 Multidimensional Case—Self and Other

A person is a combination of many characteristics. It is a person who receives an actual reward, and it is a person about whom many judgments of just rewards are made. When the rewardee is self—i.e., in the reflexive case—the multidimensionality is implicit. Similarly, when the rewardee is a named other, the multidimensionality, too, may be implicit. Yet there is substantial interest in assessing ideas of the worth of characteristics and in moving from the particular to the abstract. To estimate the effects of rewardee sex, age, schooling, experience, etc., on observers' ideas of the just reward, a sharp instrument is the factorial survey, in which fictitious persons are generated by randomly combining many levels of many characteristics. In all these situations, the actual and just rewards can be directly measured.

2.2.1 Actual and Just Reward for Self

Actual Reward for Self   In the domain of earnings, the actual reward for self is measured in virtually all surveys and censuses. These include, besides the four data sets in Table 11.2, national censuses, the major cross-sectional data bases (such as the General Social Surveys), and the major longitudinal data bases (such as the National Longitudinal Studies of Labor Market Experience, the Panel Study of Income Dynamics, and the Health and Retirement Survey).

For example, actual earnings was measured in the ISJP-1991 via the question: "What is the income *you yourself* received from a job or business (BEFORE/AFTER) taxes) (during 1990/in last 12 months/per month)?" In the New Immigrant Survey, a large set of questions tap wages, salaries, overtime pay, and so on, for each job a respondent has.

Surveys on students also routinely ask for information about the student's grades. For example, the Israeli Junior High School Study (IJHSS), fielded in 1986, asked students to report their grades in five subjects (Dar and Resh, 1993, 1996). The questionnaire item asked: "What was the grade you received in [subject] in the last semester?"

Once the actual rewards for self are measured, it is straightforward to estimate the actual reward function for a population—for example, wage attainment and grade attainment functions. These are among the most intensely studied relations in all social science.

Just Reward for Self   The just reward for self is a more specialized quantity, and it is not routinely measured. The IJHSS and the ISJP innovated with inclusion of direct measures of the just reward. The questionnaire item in the IJHSS states: "What is the grade you think you deserved to get in [subject]?" The questionnaire item in the ISJP states: "What income do you feel you *deserved* from your (job/business)?" The GSOEP (2005) asks two questions, "Is the income that you earn at your current job just, from your point of view?" and if the answer is negative, follows with, "How high would your net income have to be in order to be just?"

As with the actual rewards, once the just rewards for self are obtained, it is straightforward to estimate the just reward function for a population. Examples include Jasso and Wegener (1999) and Jasso and Resh (2002).

Two Remarks   First, consider a population of individuals reflecting on their own and others' rewards. Measurement of the actual and just rewards for self generates the entries for the principal diagonal of the A and C matrices in Table 11.1. Second, note that whenever both the actual and just rewards for self are obtained in the same survey (as they were in both the IJHSS and the ISJP), it becomes possible to estimate jointly the actual reward equation and the just reward equation, thus obtaining a window into the correlation between the unobservables in the two equations.

2.2.2 Actual and Just Reward for Fictitious Others
The factorial survey method pioneered by Peter H. Rossi and developed with associates (Rossi et al. 1974, Rossi 1979, Rossi and Anderson 1982, Rossi and Berk 1985, Jasso 2006b) provides a systematic way to generate fictitious individuals whose actual and just rewards can be directly measured. Briefly, the investigator 1) chooses a set of reward-relevant characteristics (such as age, sex, schooling, experience); 2) chooses a set of levels for each characteristic (e.g., two sexes, 10 levels of age, 12 levels of schooling, etc.); 3) randomly combines all levels of all characteristics to obtain the population of fully crossed characteristics; and 4) deletes impossible combinations (such as a 25-year-old with 30 years of work experience). This adjusted population of fictitious individuals, which can be very large, is then the sampling frame from which random samples are drawn for presentation to respondents. The size of the random samples is roughly in the 30–60 range, enabling assessment of respondent-specific equations of the effects of rewardee characteristics on the actual reward and the just reward. Each description of a fictitious person is called a *vignette*; thus, each respondent judges a *deck* of vignettes.[8]

Direct Measure of the Actual Reward for Fictitious Other   If the research objective is to obtain respondent perceptions of the actual reward, then the task assigned to the respondent is to provide an estimate of the actual reward for each vignette. For an example of this design, we turn to the ongoing research on executive compensation carried out by Jasso and Meyersson Milgrom (unpublished). In this research, fictitious chief executive officers (CEOs) were generated by randomly combining the levels of such characteristics as age, sex, industry sector, and firm capitalization. Table 11.3 presents the characteristics and their levels. Table 11.4 provides a facsimile of the instructions to respondents. Table 11.5 depicts a sample vignette with space for the respondent to write in the perceived actual reward.

The obtained data make it possible to estimate for each respondent his or her own actual reward function, and hence to assess interrespondent variability in perceptions of actual returns to reward-relevant characteristics. This type of equation is an example of the positive-beliefs equation described and analyzed in Jasso (2006b).

---

8   A brief introduction to Rossi's factorial survey method is provided in Jasso (2003b).

Table 11.3   Characteristics of Fictitious CEOs, Salary Perceptions Study

---

1. Age
11 levels, in increments of five years, from 20 to 70 years.

2. Sex
  1. Male
  2. Female

3. Years of Schooling Completed
15 levels, in increments of one year, from completion of sixth grade to a doctoral degree.

4. Years as CEO
16 levels, in increments of one year, from 0 to 15 years.

5. Firm Headquarters
  1. United States
  2. Europe
  3. Asia

6. Industry of This Firm
  1. Manufacturing
  2. Finance and insurance
  3. Information
  4. Wholesale trade

7. Size of Firm—Capitalization
27 levels, from $50 million to $600 billion.
[50m, 75m, 100m, 125m, 150m, 175m, 200m, 250m, 500m, 600m, 700m, 800m, 900m, 1b, 5b, 10b, 15b, 20b, 25b, 50b, 75b, 100b, 200b, 300b, 400b, 500b, 600b]

Note: The population of fictitious CEOs (called "vignettes") consists of all the logically possible combinations of characteristics. Logically impossible combinations are deleted. These are defined as meeting one of the following conditions: (i) age minus schooling less than 5; and (ii) age minus years as CEO less than 16. Random samples are drawn from the adjusted population for presentation to respondents.

Direct Measure of the Just Reward for Fictitious Other   If the research objective is to obtain respondent perceptions of the just reward, the task involves providing direct estimates of the just reward. For an example of this design, we consider the ongoing research on prison sentences carried out by Hagan, Ferrales, and Jasso (unpublished). In this research, judicial case scenarios consisting of fictitious prison guards accused of torturing fictitious prisoners were generated by randomly combining the levels of pertinent case characteristics, including characteristics of both prison guards and prisoners. Respondents are then asked to provide their idea of the just prison sentence for the accused prison guards.

Data obtained in this design enable estimation of each respondent's just reward equation, and hence assessment of interrespondent variability in the principles of microjustice. In this case, the equation is of the normative-judgments type described and analyzed in Jasso (2006b).

Two Remarks   First, these protocols for direct measurement of the actual and just rewards in factorial survey studies yield estimates for nonreflexive *A* and *C* matrices. The observers and rewardees are two different sets of persons—the one a set of real persons, the other a set of fictitious persons—and the matrices need not be square.

Table 11.4   Facsimile of Instructions in CEO Salary Perceptions Study

---

Survey of Perceptions of Ceo Salaries

To the Respondent:

Chief executive officers (CEOs) and their firms differ in a lot of ways. We have made up descriptions of different kinds of CEOs and firms. The firms' market value is expressed in US dollars (note that a billion corresponds to what in Europe is called a milliard). All the CEOs are newly hired at the firms. Some have been a CEO before at other firms. We would like to know what you think is that CEO's total compensation for the first year. This total compensation amount includes salary, signing bonus (if any), value of restricted stock, savings and thrift plans, and other benefits, but excludes stock options. The total compensation amount is expressed in US dollars.

     When you read each description of a CEO, please write the dollar amount which best represents what you think is that CEO's total compensation for the first year.

     You may change any of the amounts.

     Your responses are completely confidential.

     Thank you very much for your participation.

Respondent ID _____

Table 11.5   Facsimile of CEO Vignette in Salary Perceptions Study

---

The CEO is 30 years old,
a man who completed 10 years of school.
He was a CEO elsewhere for 2 years.
The firm, headquartered in the United States,
is in the information sector.
The firm has a market value of $ 300 billion.

ACTUAL TOTAL COMPENSATION_____

Importantly, every cell is susceptible of being populated (if every respondent provides an estimate for every vignette). Second, if the research design calls for all respondents to provide both actual rewards and just rewards, then the actual reward equation and the just reward equation can be estimated jointly and, as in the case of justice for self described above, the correlation between the unobservables can be explored.

3. Interlude: Direct and Indirect Measures of the Just Reward

Our purpose is to approximate the actual reward and the just reward and to estimate the actual reward function and the just reward function. It would seem that we have achieved our purpose. This chapter could come to a close right here, or at least the expository part before providing an illustration. We have laid out methods for every case of interest—the actual reward and the just reward for both self and other. We could pack up and go home.

There is a nagging thought, however, one that never fails to surface in reviewers' comments and in colloquia, and it affects the just reward. How do we know that the estimates provided by respondents represent their true ideas of justice? The survey research enterprise has long been cognizant of response effects and social desirability bias. Suppose that there is a discrepancy between what respondents say and what they really think. Suppose that there are two just rewards rather than one—the *true just reward* and the *disclosed just reward*.

Such were the concerns that led Jasso and Wegener (1997) to propose the existence of two just rewards and to posit a *disclosure function* which converts the true just reward into the disclosed just reward. It was already thought that both the just reward and the justice evaluation exhibit variation across different *contexts*. These contexts are formalized by the mnemonic *brots*—where each letter stands for a context which may differentially shape the operation of the sense of justice: *b* for the benefit or burden under consideration, *r* for the type or identity of the rewardee, *o* for the observer, *t* for the time period, and *s* for the society.

Now, Jasso and Wegener (1997) argued that the discrepancy between the true just reward and the disclosed just reward may differ systematically not only by the five *brots* dimensions but by more specific elements within the *brots* dimension, such as observer age and gender. And they suggested that research was needed to document this discrepancy and its correlates. Such work would yield a protocol for calibration as well as a clear sense of the kinds of respondents or situations not susceptible of disclosure mechanisms and thus on whom direct methods can be safely used versus the kinds of respondents and situations for which indirect methods are superior.

But first, it was necessary to examine the possibilities for indirect measurement of the just reward. How could it be done? Perhaps projective techniques? Perhaps designs utilizing advances in brain imaging? How could one get inside a person's head and capture the true just reward?

Help would come from an unexpected quarter—the justice evaluation function. Indeed, two indirect procedures for estimating the just reward had already been proposed, one for self by Evans (1989) and one for fictitious others by Jasso (1990), the latter using data collected by the method developed in Jasso and Rossi (1977).

To understand these and a third indirect method, we begin with an overview of the justice evaluation function.

Justice Evaluation Function As discussed above, the observer compares the rewardee's actual reward to the observer's idea of the just reward for the rewardee, producing the experienced justice evaluation, denoted J^*:

$$J^* = \ln\left(\frac{A}{C}\right). \tag{4}$$

If this mathematical relation faithfully represents the justice evaluation process, then it could be used to construct an indirect measure of the just reward. For the fundamental comparison at the heart of a justice evaluation is between the actual reward and the *true* just reward, and thus if we know the actual reward and the justice evaluation, we can solve for the just reward!

But we were not out of the woods yet. Two challenges remained. First, it was important to think hard about the correct form of the justice evaluation function, continuing the work reported in Jasso (1990). Second, the formula in Equation 4 represents the experienced justice evaluation function, and work by Jasso (1980) and Jasso and Wegener (1997) indicated that the justice evaluation, too, was susceptible of distortion in the empirical context, and could be thought of as two justice evaluations, the *experienced justice evaluation* and the *expressed justice evaluation*.

The Form of the Justice Evaluation Function   The log-ratio form in Equations 1 and 4 possesses several useful and appealing properties. The first three noticed were: 1) exact mapping from combinations of A and C to J; 2) integration of rival conceptions of J as a ratio (Homans, 1974, 1976) and as a difference (Berger et al., 1972); and 3) deficiency aversion, viz., deficiency is felt more keenly than comparable excess (and loss aversion, viz., losses are felt more keenly than gains). These properties were quickly discussed (e.g., Wagner and Berger, 1985) and remain the most often cited (Whitmeyer, 2004). In the course of further scrutiny of the JEF, two new properties emerged: 4) additivity, such that the effect of A on J is independent of the level of C, and conversely; and 5) scale invariance (Jasso, 1990). Six years later two other desirable properties were noticed: 6) symmetry, such that interchanging A and C changes only the sign of J; and 7) the fact that the log-ratio form of the JEF is the limiting form of the difference between two power functions,

$$\lim_{k \to 0} \frac{A^k - C^k}{k} = \ln \left(\frac{A}{C} \right) \tag{5}$$

which both strengthens integration of the ratio and difference views and also integrates power-function and logarithmic approaches (Jasso, 1996). More recently, an eighth (almost magical) property has come to light, linking the JEF and the Golden Number, $(\sqrt{5} - 1)/2$ (Jasso, 2006c).

The logarithmic-ratio form is the only functional form which satisfies both scale invariance and additivity (Jasso, 1990).

The JEF connects the two great literatures in the study of justice, the literature on ideas of justice and the literature on reactions to injustice. As well, it generates several useful links, via the justice index (the arithmetic mean of J): 1) a link between justice and two measures of inequality, Atkinson's (1970, 1975) measure defined as one minus the ratio of the geometric mean to the arithmetic mean and Theil's MLD; 2) a link with ideology, via decomposition of the justice index into the amount of overall injustice due to reality and the amount due to ideology; and 3) a link with poverty and inequality, via another decomposition of the justice index into the amount of overall injustice due to poverty and the amount due to inequality (Jasso, 1999).

Of course, scientific questions are never completely closed. To that end, it is useful to examine alternative functional forms, to consider which features of the log-ratio form are too important to give up (say, loss aversion and scale invariance?), and to empirically try alternate forms. Work with alternative forms is reported in Jasso (1990, 1996, 2006b), the last article reporting an empirical analysis using the power-difference form in Equation 5.

Note that the indirect method for measuring the just reward to be presented below can be used with any additive functional form, as illustrated by the analysis in Jasso (2006b).

Experienced and Expressed Justice Evaluations   The experienced justice evaluation J^* is the quantity that generates behavioral consequences. However, individuals differ in their style of expression, some given to hyperbole, others to understatement, and thus the experienced justice evaluation is transformed into the expressed justice evaluation J (Jasso, 1980; Jasso and Wegener, 1997). Meanwhile, justice evaluations arise about both goods and bads. Accordingly, justice analysis introduces a quantity called the *signature constant* and denoted θ; by its sign the signature constant indicates whether the observer regards the reward as a good or as a bad, and by its absolute value the signature constant indicates expressiveness. Thus, the justice evaluation function becomes, as shown in (1) and repeated here:

$$J = \theta \ln\left(\frac{A}{C}\right). \tag{6}$$

The True Just Reward   Immediately, a new expression for the true just reward is generated:

$$C = A \exp(-J/\theta). \tag{7}$$

This new expression points the way to systematic construction of indirect methods for estimating the true just reward. Look at Equation 7. The true just reward is a function of three quantities: the actual reward, the expressed justice evaluation, and the signature constant. Accordingly, the true just reward can be estimated from a design in which 1) the investigator provides the actual reward, 2) the respondent provides the expressed justice evaluation, and 3) the signature constant is estimated.

A New Approach   The road is becoming clear. To transform the theoretical (mathematical) justice evaluation function into an empirical (statistical) justice evaluation function, we may write, for every judgment made by every respondent:

$$\text{expressed justice evaluation} = \theta \ln(\text{actual reward}) - \theta \ln(\text{just reward}) + \varepsilon. \tag{8}$$

The just reward is unobserved, of course. If a respondent makes several judgments, these can be aggregated according to the usual regression setup, producing the estimable form:

$$\text{expressed justice evaluation} = \alpha + \theta \ln(\text{actual reward}) + \varepsilon. \tag{9}$$

The exact interpretation of Equation 9 and, in particular, the properties of θ depend on the research design. *A priori*, we can distinguish two possible research designs. In the first research design, the respondent judges the fairness or unfairness of several actual rewards for a single rewardee. This case, now called the *multiple-rewards-per-rewardee* design, generates a constant just reward, the constant is absorbed into the equation intercept, and estimation of θ is straightforward. This design was developed by Evans (1989) for estimating the just reward for self and by Jasso and Webster (1999) for estimating the just reward for fictitious others.

In the second research design, the respondent judges the fairness or unfairness of one actual reward for each of several rewardees. This case, now called the *one-reward-per-rewardee* design, generates as many just rewards as there are rewardees. Equation 9 is straightforwardly estimated, but because there are many unobserved just rewards—one for each actual reward—it is urgent to guard against correlation between the actual rewards and the unobserved just rewards. Any such correlation would bias the estimate of the signature constant, as discussed below.

Properties of θ The signature constant θ does a lot of work. It enables estimation of both the experienced justice evaluation and the true just reward. Thus, the utmost care must be taken in estimation of θ. Jasso (1990) pointed out that if the actual rewards are uncorrelated with the unobserved just rewards, then the estimate of θ is unbiased and consistent and, under the assumption that the errors are independently distributed with mean zero and constant variance, is best linear unbiased (BLUE). However, if the actual rewards are correlated with the unobserved just rewards, then the estimate of theta obtained from Equation 9 is biased. Thus, the challenge in the one-reward-per-rewardee design is to satisfy orthogonality. And, indeed, it is this danger of failure to satisfy orthogonality that led Jasso and Webster (1999, pp. 370–372) to develop the multiple-rewards-per-rewardee design.

Orthogonality and the Factorial Survey Method The solution to the problem of estimating theta in the one-reward-per-rewardee design lay in the researchers' backyard. Jasso had begun her justice work with a vignette study, under the tutelage of Peter H. Rossi, who pioneered the factorial survey method. Look again at Equations 8 and 9. In the factorial survey designs presented in Section 2, fictitious individuals are generated by randomly combining all the levels of a set of potentially reward-relevant characteristics. If the design is modified to include an actual reward randomly attached to each fictitious individual, then the orthogonality condition is exactly met—there is zero correlation between the actual reward and the reward-relevant characteristics and, hence, the unobserved just reward. It follows that the estimate of θ is unbiased and consistent and indeed, as already noted, may be BLUE.

Further methodological issues remain to be discussed, including properties of the estimated just rewards and such additional features as emphasizing in the instructions to respondents that the actual rewards are random, so that respondents will not infer a correlation between actual reward and just reward. Section 4 covers these matters.

But for now we can celebrate a wedding. In the one-reward-per-rewardee research design, the marriage of the justice evaluation function and the factorial survey method enables unbiased and consistent estimation of the signature constant θ, and the signature constant θ in turn enables estimation of the experienced justice evaluation and the true just reward.

4 Two Indirect Methods for Estimating the Just Reward: The One-Reward-per-Rewardee Method and the Multiple-Rewards-per-Rewardee Method

This section describes two indirect methods for estimating the just reward for fictitious others, an early love child and a late love child, as it were, of the marriage of the justice evaluation function and the factorial survey method, and describes as well an indirect method for estimating the just reward for self, a middle child not requiring the factorial survey method. The data collection protocol for the early love child follows exactly and in every particular the design formulated by Jasso and Rossi (1977), an application to the study of justice of the factorial survey method pioneered by Rossi. The data collection protocol for the late love child, developed by Jasso and Webster (1999), is a modification of the initial protocol. The data analysis protocols for both methods developed over the years, as experience with the factorial survey method and the justice evaluation function revealed new possibilities. The indirect method for estimating the just reward for self, developed by Evans (1989) and first implemented in the 1987 round of the International Social Science Survey/ Australia (Kelley and Evans, 1987), is discussed together with the Jasso and Webster (1999) design, as they are both multiple-rewards-per-rewardee methods.

As in all factorial survey studies, the data collection protocol in the two designs for fictitious others has three elements, a respondent sample—omitted from consideration here—a vignette sample, and a rating task. General topic-independent procedures for both data collection and data analysis in factorial surveys are described in Jasso (2006b). In the data analysis summaries below, we focus on estimation of the true just reward.

4.1 The One-Reward-per-Rewardee Method

In the one-reward-per-rewardee method, each respondent is given descriptions of a set of rewardees and asked to judge the fairness of the (one) actual reward attached to each rewardee. This is the original design developed by Jasso and Rossi (1977).

4.1.1 Data Collection Protocol
Vignette Sample   The design calls for generating the population of all possible combinations of all levels of a set of variables including 1) potentially reward-relevant characteristics and 2) the actual reward. This population is then adjusted by deleting any impossible combinations (such as a physician who only completed the eighth grade). Random samples are then drawn from the adjusted population. Note that the zero correlation between the actual reward and each of the reward-relevant characteristics is unimpaired by deletion of the impossible combinations. Thus, the data satisfy the orthogonality condition discussed above.

Table 11.6   Facsimile of Instructions in Study of the Justice of Earnings, Using the One-Reward-per-Rewardee Design

---

Survey of Judgments on the Justice of Earnings

To the Respondent:

People and their jobs differ in a lot of ways. We have made up descriptions of different kinds of people and jobs. All the persons described work full-time; and all have worked continuously and full-time since finishing school. Each person is randomly assigned a hypothetical earnings amount. We would like to know what you think about whether each person is fairly or unfairly paid, and, if you think that a person is unfairly paid, whether you think the person is paid too much or too little.

We would like you to use numbers to represent your judgments. Let zero represent the point of perfect justice. Let negative numbers represent degrees of underreward, and positive numbers represent degrees of overreward. The greater the degree of underpayment, the larger the absolute value of the negative number you choose (for example, if two persons receive ratings of -68 and -23, the person receiving the -68 is viewed as more underpaid than the person receiving the -23). Similarly, the greater the degree of overpayment, the larger the positive number (for example, a person receiving a rating of +200 is viewed as more overpaid than a person receiving a rating of +75). In other words, mild degrees of underreward and of overreward are represented by numbers relatively close to zero; larger degrees of underreward and of overreward are represented by numbers farther away from zero.

The justice evaluation scale may be visualized as follows:

```
----+----+----+----+----+----+----+----+----+----+----+----+----+---
                               0
```
Underreward   Overreward

When you read each description of a person, please write the number that best matches your judgment about the fairness or unfairness of that person's earnings. There is no limit to the range of numbers that you may use. For example, some respondents like to map their personal scale to the numbers from -100 to +100; others prefer to use smaller regions, and still others, larger regions. Of course, you may choose any real number (for example, decimals and fractions as well as whole numbers) to represent a judgment.

You may rate the descriptions in any order.

You may change any of your ratings.

Your responses are completely confidential.

Thank you very much for your participation.

Rating Task   The rating task reinforces the orthogonality condition by explicitly describing the actual reward as "hypothetical" and "randomly attached" to the fictitious individual. Table 11.6 presents a facsimile of the instructions to respondents in the one-reward-per-rewardee method.

Table 11.7 provides an example of the vignettes in this design.

4.1.2 Data Analysis Protocol

Recall the basic justice evaluation regression equations in Equations 8 and 9. According to justice theory, the respondent forms or retrieves a true just reward

Table 11.7   Facsimile of Vignette in Study of the Justice of Earnings, Using the One-Reward-per-Rewardee Design

A man 35 years old,
who completed 12 years of school,
graduating from high school.
He is a warehouse supervisor.
His yearly salary is $37,500.

YOUR RATING_____

using the information in the reward-relevant characteristics, next compares the actual reward to the true just reward, producing an experienced justice evaluation which is transformed by the signature constant theta into the numerical rating *J*. Thus, the "silent partner" in the ratings is the set of unobserved true just rewards.

The justice evaluation regression equation in Equation 8 may be re-written to express the estimated true just reward as a function of the actual reward *A*, the estimated signature constant theta, and the expressed justice evaluation *J*:

$$\textit{estimated true just reward} = \textit{actual reward} \times \exp\left(-\frac{\textit{expressed justice valuation}}{\textit{estimated } \theta}\right) \quad (10)$$

or, more compactly:

$$\hat{C} = A \exp(-J/\hat{\theta}). \quad (11)$$

Estimation of Equation 9, separately for each respondent, yields each respondent's estimated theta. As already noted, this estimate is unbiased and consistent and may be BLUE.

The estimated true just rewards, being nonlinear transformations of estimated θ, lose the property of unbiasedness but by Slutsky's theorem retain the property of consistency. This is one of the reasons why premium is placed on having each respondent judge a large number of vignettes.

The estimated true just rewards are ready to be displayed in the just reward matrix (as in Table 11.1, panel 2) and used in analyses of the just reward function and the just reward distribution to obtain the estimates of the principles of microjustice and the principles of macrojustice.

Section 5 provides an illustration of the one-reward-per-rewardee indirect method for estimating the just reward.

4.2 The Multiple-Rewards-per-Rewardee Method

Evans (1989) developed a procedure for measuring just earnings for self, in which each respondent was given five hypothetical earnings amounts for self and asked to judge the fairness or unfairness of each. This procedure was first applied in the 1987 round of the International Social Science Survey/Australia (Kelley and Evans, 1987). Jasso and Webster (1999) developed a procedure for measuring the just reward for others, in which each respondent was given seven hypothetical earnings amounts

**Table 11.8   Facsimile of Instructions in Study of the Justice of Earnings,
                Using the Multiple-Rewards-per-Rewardee Design**

Survey of Judgments on the Justice of Earnings

To the Respondent:

People and their jobs differ in a lot of ways. We have made up descriptions of different kinds of
people and jobs. All the persons described work full-time; and all have worked continuously
and full-time since finishing school. Each person is randomly assigned several hypothetical
earnings amounts. We would like to know what you think about whether, at each earnings
amount, each person is fairly or unfairly paid, and, if you think that a person is unfairly paid,
whether you think the person is paid too much or too little.

   We would like you to use numbers to represent your judgments. Let zero represent the
point of perfect justice. Let negative numbers represent degrees of underreward, and positive
numbers represent degrees of overreward. The greater the degree of underpayment, the larger
the absolute value of the negative number you choose (for example, if two earnings amounts
receive ratings of -68 and -23, the earnings amount receiving the -68 is viewed as greater
underpayment than the earnings amount receiving the -23). Similarly, the greater the degree
of overpayment, the larger the positive number (for example, an earnings amount receiving a
rating of +200 is viewed as greater overpayment than an earnings amount receiving a rating
of +75). In other words, mild degrees of underreward and of overreward are represented
by numbers relatively close to zero; larger degrees of underreward and of overreward are
represented by numbers farther away from zero.

   The justice evaluation scale may be visualized as follows:

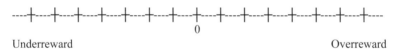

Underreward   Overreward

When you read each description of a person and an earnings amount, please write the number
that best matches your judgment about the fairness or unfairness of that earnings for that person.
There is no limit to the range of numbers that you may use. For example, some respondents
like to map their personal scale to the numbers from -100 to +100; others prefer to use smaller
regions, and still others, larger regions. Of course, you may choose any real number (for
example, decimals and fractions as well as whole numbers) to represent a judgment.

   You may change any of your ratings.

   Your responses are completely confidential.

   Thank you very much for your participation.

---

for each of ten fictitious rewardees and asked to judge the fairness or unfairness of
each.

   Both the Evans (1989) for-self procedure and the Jasso and Webster (1999) for-
others procedure share the same basic data analysis protocol. Data collection in the
for-self procedure is straightforward; the investigator presents a set of hypothetical
actual rewards, and asks the respondent to judge the justice of each. Here we
describe the data collection protocol for the for-others procedure, which utilizes
factorial survey methods. This method was designed to overcome the danger that
respondents, despite the labeling of the actual reward as random, might inject a

Table 11.9   Facsimile of Vignette in Study of the Justice of Earnings, Using the Multiple-Rewards-per-Rewardee Design

A man 43 years old,
who completed 16 years of school,
graduating from college with a B.A. Degree.
He is a grade school teacher.

ANNUAL EARNINGS	YOUR RATING
$ 12,500	_____
15,000	_____
20,000	_____
25,000	_____
30,000	_____
55,000	_____
70,000	_____

correlation between the actual rewards and the reward-relevant characteristics, thus damaging the good properties of the estimated theta.

4.2.1 Data Collection Protocol in the For-Others Application of the Multiple-Rewards-per-Rewardee Method

Vignette Sample   In the for-others application of the multiple-rewards-per-rewardee method, the design begins with the population of all possible combinations of all levels of a set of potentially reward-relevant characteristics. This population is next adjusted by deleting any impossible combinations (such as a physician who only completed the eighth grade). Random samples are then drawn from the adjusted population. Finally, a set of rewards randomly drawn from a larger set of rewards is attached to each fictitious individual. In this design, not only is there zero correlation between the actual rewards and the reward-relevant characteristics, but the presence of several hypothetical actual rewards underscores their random nature and averts the possibility of the respondent seeing a link between reward and reward-relevant characteristic. This design a fortiori satisfies the orthogonality condition.

Rating Task   The rating task requests that the respondent judge the fairness or unfairness of each of the actual rewards attached to each rewardee. Table 11.8 presents a facsimile of the instructions to respondent in the multiple-rewards-per-rewardee method.

Table 11.9 provides an example of the vignettes in this design.

4.2.2 Data Analysis Protocol

As before, recall the basic justice evaluation regression equations in Equations 8 and 9. When the respondent judges the fairness of several potential actual rewards for a particular rewardee (self or fictitious other), the just reward (in the respondent's mind) is constant and can be retrieved via estimation (separately for each respondent-rewardee combination) of the regression Equation 9. It will be useful to have

Table 11.10   Facsimile of Instructions in Study of the Justice of Earnings, Using the One-Reward-per-Rewardee Design, Spring 1996

Survey of Judgments on the Justice of Earnings

To the Respondent:

People and their jobs differ in a lot of ways. We have made up descriptions of different kinds of people and jobs. All the persons described work full-time; and all have worked continuously and full-time since finishing school. Each person is randomly assigned a hypothetical earnings amount. We would like to know what you think about whether each person is fairly or unfairly paid, and, if you think that a person is unfairly paid, whether you think the person is paid too much or too little.

We would like you to use numbers to represent your judgments. Let zero represent the point of perfect justice. Let negative numbers represent degrees of underreward, and positive numbers represent degrees of overreward. The greater the degree of underpayment, the larger the absolute value of the negative number you choose (for example, if two persons receive ratings of -68 and -23, the person receiving the -68 is viewed as more underpaid than the person receiving the -23). Similarly, the greater the degree of overpayment, the larger the positive number (for example, a person receiving a rating of +200 is viewed as more overpaid than a person receiving a rating of +75). In other words, mild degrees of underreward and of overreward are represented by numbers relatively close to zero; larger degrees of underreward and of overreward are represented by numbers farther away from zero.

The justice evaluation scale may be visualized as follows:

0

Underreward   Overreward

When you read each description of a person, please write the number that best matches your judgment about the fairness or unfairness of that person's earnings. There is no limit to the range of numbers that you may use. For example, some respondents like to map their personal scale to the numbers from -100 to +100; others prefer to use smaller regions, and still others, larger regions. Of course, you may choose any real number (for example, decimals and fractions as well as whole numbers) to represent a judgment.

You may rate the descriptions in any order.

You may change any of your ratings.

Your responses are completely confidential.

Thank you very much for your participation.

---

distinctive notation for the multiple-rewards-per-rewardee method, and thus we re-write Equations 8 and 9 for this case:

$$J = \theta \ln A - \theta \ln C + \varepsilon$$
$$= \theta \ln A + \upsilon + \varepsilon \tag{12}$$

Under the assumption that the errors are independently distributed with zero mean and constant variance across the multiple ratings within the respondent-rewardee combination, the slope θ in the second equation in Equation 12 provides an unbiased and consistent estimate of the signature constant, and the intercept υ provides an unbiased and consistent estimate of the negative of the product of the signature constant θ and the log of the just reward. Thus, the estimate of the respondent-specific/rewardee-specific true just reward is obtained by the following formula:

$$\hat{C} = \exp(-\hat{\upsilon}/\hat{\theta}) \tag{13}$$

Because the estimated just rewards are nonlinear transformations of the slope and intercept in Equation 12, they lose the unbiasedness property; however, by Slutsky's theorem they retain consistency.[9]

For illustrations of the for-others application of the multiple-rewards-per-rewardee method, see Jasso and Webster (1999) and Jasso (2006a). The latter analysis shows how this design enables test of two new kinds of impartiality, framing-impartiality and expressiveness-impartiality.

5 Illustration: Measurement and Estimation in a Factorial Survey of the Justice of Earnings Using the One-Reward-per-Rewardee Method

To illustrate, we use the data for one respondent from a larger study described in Jasso (unpublished). Like the other respondents, this respondent judged the justice of the earnings of 20 fictitious workers, providing for each one an expressed justice evaluation. Each worker was described in terms of earnings-relevant characteristics. The descriptions were generated according to the standard Rossi factorial survey protocol, in which all the levels of all characteristics are fully crossed, with impossible combinations (such as a physician with an eighth-grade education) deleted. A hypothetical earnings amount was randomly attached to each description. Tables 11.10 and 11.11 present the instructions for the rating task and an example of a vignette, respectively. Note that the rating task uses the number matching technique pioneered by Stevens (1975) in which each respondent is given maximal freedom to map the subjective justice continuum onto numbers. Note also that the real-number continuum is activated by explicitly mentioning decimals and fractions in the instructions.

Table 11.12 presents, in the two leftmost columns of panel A, the raw data for one respondent, namely, the actual earnings randomly attached to the fictitious worker and the respondent's expressed justice evaluation. Estimation of Equation 9, that is, regression of the expressed justice evaluation on the natural log of actual earnings, yields an estimate of the signature constant θ of 5.77 (panel B).[10]

---

9   This design enables a new possibility for the signature constant, namely, that not only does it differ across respondents but also that, within respondent, it differs across rewardee. The procedure described in the text and Equation 13 pertain to the case in which θ is rewardee-specific. If statistical tests indicate that θ does not differ across rewardees, then the procedure for estimating the true just reward differs from the procedure in the text.

10   The raw data in Table 11.12 can be used by the interested reader to generate everything else in Table 11.12—the estimates of the justice evaluation function, the experienced justice

Table 11.11 Facsimile of Vignette in Study of the Justice of Earnings, Using the One-Reward-per-Rewardee Design, Spring 1996

A woman 35 years old,
who completed 12 years of school,
graduating from high school.
She is a warehouse supervisor.
Her yearly salary is $25,000.

YOUR RATING_____

Table 11.12 Measurement/Estimation in Empirical Justice Analysis: Data and Estimates of the Expressed Justice Evaluation Equation, the Experienced Justice Evaluation, and the True Just Reward

A. Raw Data and Estimates of the Experienced Justice Evaluation and the True Just Reward for 20 Fictitious Workers

Worker	Raw Data		Estimates	
	Actual Earnings (1999 $)	Expressed Justice Evaluation	Experienced Justice Evaluation	True Just Earnings (1999$)
1	25,000	2.5	0.433	16,211
2	5,000	-10	-1.73	28,281
3	30,000	2.5	0.433	19,453
4	7,500	-9	-1.56	35,673
5	15,000	-1	-0.173	17,838
6	35,000	1	0.173	29,432
7	35,000	2.5	0.433	22,695
8	25,000	0	0	25,000
9	5,000	-8.5	-1.47	21,808
10	55,000	7.5	1.30	14,996
11	7,500	-2.5	-0.433	11,566
12	10,000	-3	-0.520	16,817
13	45,000	3	0.520	26,758
14	15,000	0	0	15,000
15	55,000	4	0.693	27,501
16	10,000	-4	-0.693	19,999
17	100,000	10	1.73	17,679
18	55,000	5	.866	23,126
19	70,000	7.5	1.30	19,085
20	25,000	-0.5	-.0866	27,263

B. Estimated Expressed Justice Evaluation Equation

intercept = -57.4   signature constant = 5.77 $R^2 = 0.912$

Note: Data for one respondent, drawn from a larger study reported in Jasso (unpublished). Workers #1–#5 and #16–#20 are women, the rest men.

evaluations, and the true just rewards—as well as all the estimates in Table 11.13 except those of the principles of microjustice.

As evident in Equations 4 and 6, the experienced justice evaluation for a particular worker, denoted j_r^*, is estimated by dividing the expressed justice evaluation, denoted j_r, by the expressiveness coefficient:

$$\hat{j}_r^* = \frac{j_r}{|\hat{\theta}|}. \tag{14}$$

The estimated experienced justice evaluations, corresponding to each of the fictitious workers, are reported in the third column of panel A. For example, this respondent's expressed justice evaluation for Worker # 1 was +2.5 (Table 11.12). The estimated signature constant was 5.77. The estimated experienced justice evaluation is thus:

$$\hat{j}_1^* = \frac{j_1}{|\hat{\theta}|} = \frac{2.5}{5.77} \approx 0.433. \tag{15}$$

It is useful that the justice evaluation function, in combination with the factorial survey justice design, makes it possible to estimate the experienced justice evaluation from a single datum obtained from the respondent—the expressed justice evaluation. But what is truly remarkable is that this same marriage of the justice evaluation function and the factorial survey justice design also makes it possible to estimate the true just reward. Recall the expressed justice evaluation function in Equation 6; there are four quantities, the expressed justice evaluation, the actual reward, the true just reward, and the signature constant. The factorial survey justice design provides the actual reward, the expressed justice evaluation is obtained from the respondent, and the signature constant is estimated via statistical estimation of the equation (as shown above). Thus, there remains only one unknown—the true just reward.

Using Equation 11 we obtain estimates of the true just reward in the eyes of each respondent for each fictitious worker. Continuing with the illustration referring to one respondent, Table 11.12 reports, in the rightmost column of panel A, the estimated true just reward amounts. The estimated true just reward for Worker # 1 is \$16,211, obtained by applying Equation 11:[11]

$$25{,}000 \times \exp(-2.5/5.77) \approx 16{,}211. \tag{16}$$

Now that the just rewards have been estimated, we can confirm that, indeed,

$$\hat{j}_1^* = \ln\left(\frac{a_1}{\hat{c}_1}\right) = \ln\left(\frac{25{,}000}{16{,}211}\right) \approx 0.433$$

$$j_1 = \hat{\theta} \ln\left(\frac{a_1}{\hat{c}_1}\right) = 5.77 \times 0.433 \approx 2.5. \tag{17}$$

---

11 The just reward amounts in Table 11.12 are calculated using a less rounded version of the signature constant than 5.77. Thus, arithmetic computation using the rounded version shown in Equation 17 yields an estimate of the true just reward slightly different from the one shown.

Of course, the estimated justice evaluation equation provides further information. First, the sign of the signature constant, known as the framing coefficient, indicates whether the respondent regards the reward as a good or a bad; in this case, the sign is positive, indicating that the respondent regards earnings as a good.

Second, the intercept in the justice evaluation equation provides the product of $-\theta$ and the expected value of the logged just earnings amounts, and we can confirm that this quantity indeed equals approximately -57.4.

Third, the equation R^2 indicates whether the actual inequality, put experimentally into the actual rewards, is regarded by the respondent as larger or smaller than the just inequality. If a respondent's justice evaluation function has an R^2 larger than 0.5, the respondent considers the actual inequality to be higher than the just inequality, and if a respondent's justice evaluation function has an R^2 smaller than 0.5, the respondent considers the actual inequality to be lower than the just inequality.[12] In this case, the value of R^2 is 0.912, which exceeds 0.5, and thus this respondent considers the actual inequality to be larger than the just inequality.

Now that the experienced justice evaluations and the true just rewards have been estimated, it becomes possible to estimate the many quantities and relations for which the just reward and the justice evaluation function are the basic ingredients—the quantities and relations collected under the rubric of nonfundamental quantities and relations in Jasso and Wegener (1997, p. 416), as augmented by the more recent work in Jasso and Webster (1999) and Jasso (1999)—and thus to strike out in a number of new research directions. First, the just reward function can be estimated, giving rise to the estimated principles of microjustice. Second, the principles of macrojustice can be estimated by calculating measures of location and inequality in the distribution of the just rewards. Third, just gender earnings gaps can be calculated. Fourth, each respondent can be characterized by the proportions of rewardees that he/she regards as underrewarded, justly rewarded, and overrewarded. Fifth, the experienced justice evaluations can be used to calculate the justice indexes, and thence decomposition into the amount of injustice due to poverty and the amount due to inequality.

For example, to estimate the respondent-specific just reward functions, we regress, separately for each respondent, the natural logarithm of the just reward on the rewardee characteristics. The obtained estimates, or transformations thereof, constitute estimates of the respondent-specific principles of microjustice. To illustrate, in a just earnings function, the coefficient of schooling provides an estimate of the just return to investment in an additional year of schooling. The exponential of the coefficient of the binary sex variable, measures the gender multiplier; women are coded "1" and thus the multiplier is applied to the earnings of females, so that subtracting one yields the tax (if negative) or bonus (if positive) on women's earnings, relative to the earnings of comparable men, in percentage points. The gender multiplier has a natural interpretation as the ratio of female to male earnings; a gender multiplier of 0.8 would indicate the view that the just earnings for a woman is 80 per cent of the just earnings of a comparable man.

---

12 This interpretation is derived by analyzing the variance decomposition; fuller details are provided in Jasso (unpublished).

Table 11.13   Measurement/Estimation in Empirical Justice Analysis: Estimates of Additional Justice Quantities—the Principles of Microjustice and Macrojustice, the Just Gender Wage Gap, and the Justice Indexes

A. Quantities Pertaining to the First Central Question: What Do Individuals and Societies Think Is Just, and Why?	
1. Principles of Microjustice	
just base wage	$10,207
just rate of return to schooling	0.0562
just gender multiplier	1.05
R^2 of just earnings function	0.476
2. Principles of Macrojustice	
just Gini's inequality	0.160
just Atkinson's inequality	0.0363
just Plato's ratio	3.08
just relative minimum	0.530
just relative maximum	1.64
3. Just Gender Wage Gaps	
mean-based female/male ratio	1.06
median-based female/male ratio	0.886
B. Quantities Pertaining to the Third Central Question: What Is the Magnitude of the Perceived Injustice Associated with Given Departures from Perfect Justice?	
1. Qualitative Justice Evaluation	
percent workers unjustly underpaid	40
percent workers justly paid	10
percent workers unjustly overpaid	50
2. Justice Indexes	
JI1	0.0606
mean component of JI1	0.368
inequality component of JI1	-0.307
JI2	0.728

Note: Data are from one respondent, drawn from a larger study reported in Jasso (unpublished).

All of the foregoing estimation and analysis is carried out for each respondent separately. A further set of analyses compares the respondents. The distributions of each respondent-specific estimate—for example, the distributions of the principles of microjustice and macrojustice—are inspected to establish the extent of disagreement on each principle. A variety of statistical tests are carried out to assess respondent differences on expressiveness, inequality in the just reward distribution, and so on. Multilevel methods provide for the joint estimation of many of these quantities and equations, as discussed in Jasso (2006b).

Here we continue with our illustration focusing on a single respondent. Table 11.13 presents all the quantities estimated for this one respondent. For clarity, the quantities are grouped into two sets, those pertaining to the first central question in the study of justice and those pertaining to the third central question. As shown, the estimates of the just earnings function indicate that this respondent considers the just base wage for a male to be approximately $ 10,207 (panel A.1). This respondent views the just rate of return to schooling as 5.6 percent for each additional year of schooling.

Table 11.13 also reports, in panel A.2, estimates of the principles of macrojustice guiding this respondent's ideas of just earnings. Three measures of inequality are provided, together with the just relative minimum—the just minimum income is slightly more than half the mean—and the relative maximum—a low 1.6. Not surprisingly, Plato's ratio (the ratio of the maximum to the minimum) is slightly over 3, smaller than most estimates of the actual value of Plato's ratio and smaller even than the 5 which for Plato signaled extreme inequality. As is well-known, different measures of inequality capture different features of a distribution, and thus a set of five indicators provides a fuller picture of the respondent, and will in particular be useful when this respondent is compared to the others in the study.

As well, Table 11.13 provides three different ways of assessing the respondent's views on gender and justice. The just gender multiplier, estimated from the just earnings function, and the mean-based gender gap both indicate that, in the eyes of this respondent, women should earn more than otherwise comparable men. However, the median-based gender gap indicates the opposite. As with inequality, the set of three measures provide a fuller picture of the respondent than a single measure would provide; and this will be especially useful when this respondent is compared with the other respondents.

This respondent also judged half the fictitious workers to be overpaid, 40 per cent to be underpaid, and only 10 per cent to be justly paid (Table 11.13, panel B.1). Moreover, the justice index JI1 estimated for this respondent is positive, indicating that the center of gravity of his/her justice evaluations lies in the overreward region of the justice evaluation scale (Table 11.13, panel B.2). The decomposition of JI1 further indicates that this respondent thinks that both the mean earnings and the earnings inequality are too high.

Exploring further the results of the decomposition of JI1, we calculate the mean of the actual earnings amounts, obtaining $31,500, and the mean of the just earnings amounts, obtaining $21,809. This respondent indeed judges that the actual mean earnings is larger than the just mean earnings; we can confirm that the mean component of JI1, shown in Table 11.13, panel B, is:

$$JI1_{Mean} = \ln\left(\frac{31,500}{21,809}\right) \approx 0.368 \tag{18}$$

Similarly, exploring the inequality component of JI1, which is based on one of Atkinson's (1970, 1975) measures of inequality (the measure defined as one minus the ratio of the geometric mean to the arithmetic mean), we find that the Atkinson-inequality of actual earnings is 0.291 and of just earnings is 0.0363. This respondent thus finds actual inequality much larger than just inequality; we can confirm that the inequality component of JI1, shown in Table 11.13, panel B, is:

$$JI1_{\text{Ineq}} = \ln\left(\frac{1 - 0.291}{1 - 0.0363}\right) \approx -0.307 \tag{19}$$

Of course, the estimates presented in Tables 11.12 and 11.13 become substantially more meaningful when they are compared across respondents. Moreover, groups and collectivities can then be characterized by the degree to which their members are similar to each other or exhibit agreement with respect to the justice quantities and relations. For example, it turns out that this respondent, whose justice life we have highlighted in our illustration, is similar to the overwhelming majority in judging that the actual inequality in the vignettes is too high. However, the hypothesis that the respondents can be described by the same just earnings function is soundly rejected, as is the hypothesis that the respondent-specific just earnings distributions are drawn from the same underlying distribution (Jasso, unpublished).

6 Concluding Note

This chapter described procedures for measuring and estimating the fundamental quantities in justice analysis. We examined a variety of methods for measuring the actual reward and the just reward, for both self and other, including direct and indirect methods for measuring the just reward, and we provided an illustration of one of the two indirect methods, the one-reward-per-rewardee method.

The justice evaluation function makes it possible to estimate the true just reward in the multiple-rewards-per-rewardee method, and the combination of the justice evaluation function and Rossi's factorial survey method makes it possible to estimate the true just reward in the one-reward-per-rewardee method. This is a marriage of true minds, and its progeny include not only the true just reward measures but also measures of the experienced justice evaluation, as well as all the quantities and relations which depend on good measures of the experienced justice evaluation and the true just reward—among them the just reward function, the principles of microjustice and macrojustice, the justice indexes, and the components of injustice due to poverty and to inequality.

The tasks ahead include systematic contrasts of all the methods collected here, in order to establish calibration factors by respondent and situational characteristics.

References

Atkinson, A.B. (1970), "On the Measurement of Inequality", *Journal of Economic Theory*, **2**, 244–263.

Atkinson, A.B. (1975), *The Economics of Inequality* (London: Oxford).

Berger, J., Zelditch, M., Jr., Anderson, B. and Cohen, B.P. (1972), "Structural Aspects of Distributive Justice: A Status-Value Formulation" in *Sociological Theories in Progress, Volume 2*. Berger, J., Zelditch, M. and Anderson, B. (eds) (Boston: Houghton Mifflin), 119–246

Dar, Y. and Resh, N. (1993), "Exploring the Multi-dimensional Structure of Deprivation Among Israeli Adolescents", *Megamot*, **35**, 38–61.

Dar, Y. and Resh, N. (1996), "Exploring the Persistence of Academic Achievement Gap: Social Differentials in Family Resource Returns in Israel" in *Research in Sociology of Education and Socialization, Vol. 11*. Pallas, A. (ed.) (Greenwich CT: JAI Press), 233–261.

Evans, M.D.R. (1989), "Distributive Justice: Some New Measures", Presented at the meeting of the International Sociological Association's Research Committee 28 on Social Stratification and Mobility, Stanford, California, August.

Hagan, J., Ferrales, G. and Jasso, G. (Unpublished), "How Law Rules: Terror, Torture, and the Normative Judgments of Iraqi Judges", Paper presented at the annual meeting of the American Sociological Association, Montreal, Canada, August 2006.

Homans, G.C. (1974), *Social Behavior: Its Elementary Forms*. Rev. ed. (New York: Harcourt, Brace, Jovanovich).

Homans, G.C. (1976), "Commentary" in *Advances in Experimental Social Psychology, vol. 9*, Berkowitz, L. and Walster, E. (eds) (New York: Academic Press), 231–244.

Jasso, G. (1978), "On the Justice of Earnings: A New Specification of the Justice Evaluation Function", *American Journal of Sociology*, **83**, 1398–1419.

Jasso, G. (1980), "A New Theory of Distributive Justice", *American Sociological Review*, **45**, 3–32.

Jasso, G. (1990), "Methods for the Theoretical and Empirical Analysis of Comparison Processes", *Sociological Methodology*, **20**, 369–419.

Jasso, G. (1996), "Exploring the Reciprocal Relations between Theoretical and Empirical Work: The Case of the Justice Evaluation Function (Paper in Honor of Robert K. Merton)", *Sociological Methods and Research*, **24**, 253–303.

Jasso, G. (1999), "How Much Injustice Is There in the World? Two New Justice Indexes", *American Sociological Review*, **64**, 133–168.

Jasso, G. (2003a), "Basic Research" in *The Sage Encyclopedia of Social Science Research Methods, Volume 1*. Lewis-Beck, M., Bryman, A. and Futing Liao, T. (eds) (Thousand Oaks CA: Sage Publications), 52–53.

Jasso, G. (2003b), "Factorial Survey Method (Rossi's Method)" in *The Sage Encyclopedia of Social Science Research Methods, Volume 1*. Lewis-Beck, M., Bryman, A. and Futing Liao, T. (eds) (Thousand Oaks CA: Sage Publications), 374–376.

Jasso, G. (2006a), "Emotion in Justice Processes" in *Handbook of the Sociology of Emotions*. Stets, J.E. and Turner, J.H. (eds) (New York: Springer), 321–346.

Jasso, G. (2006b), "Factorial Survey Methods for Studying Beliefs and Judgments", *Sociological Methods and Research*, **34**, 334–423.

Jasso, G. (2006c), "Homans and the Study of Justice", in *George C. Homans: History, Theory, and Method*. Treviño, A.J. (ed.) (Boulder CO: Paradigm Press), 203–227.

Jasso, G. (unpublished), "A General Justice Research Design".

Jasso, G., and Meyersson Milgrom, E.M. (Unpublished), "Perceptions of CEO Compensation", Paper presented at Stanford Workshop on Executive Compensation and Factorial Survey Methods, June 2005.

Jasso, G. and Resh, N. (2002), "Exploring the Sense of Justice about Grades", *European Sociological Review*, **18**, 333–351.

Jasso, G. and Rossi, P.H. (1977), "Distributive Justice and Earned Income", *American Sociological Review*, **42**, 639–651.

Jasso, G. and Webster, M. (1999), "Assessing the Gender Gap in Just Earnings and Its Underlying Mechanisms", *Social Psychology Quarterly*, **62**, 367–380.

Jasso, G. and Wegener, B. (1997), "Methods for Empirical Justice Analysis: Part I. Framework, Models, and Quantities", *Social Justice Research*, **10**, 393–430.

Jasso, G. and Wegener, B. (1999), "Gender and Country Differences in the Sense of Justice: Justice Evaluation, Gender Earnings Gap, and Earnings Functions in Thirteen Countries", *International Journal of Comparative Sociology*, **40**, 94–116.

Kelley, J. and Evans, M.D.R. (1987), "IsssA: International Social Science Survey/ Australia: Ideology of Inequality 1987–88: Questionnaire", International Survey Centre and Research School of Social Sciences, Australia National University.

Rossi, P.H. (1951), *The Application of Latent Structure Analysis to the Study of Social Stratification*. Unpublished Ph.D. dissertation, Columbia University.

Rossi, P.H. (1979), "Vignette Analysis: Uncovering the Normative Structure of Complex Judgments" in *Qualitative and Quantitative Social Research: Papers in Honor of Paul F. Lazarsfeld*. Merton, R.K., Coleman, J.S. and Rossi, P.H. (eds) (New York: Free Press), 176–186.

Rossi, P.H. and Anderson, A.B. (1982), "The Factorial Survey Approach: An Introduction" in *Measuring Social Judgments: the Factorial Survey Approach*. Rossi, P.H. and Nock, S.L. (eds) (Beverly Hills: Sage), 15–67.

Rossi, P.H. and Berk, R.A. (1985), "Varieties of Normative Consensus", *American Sociological Review*, **50**, 333–347.

Rossi, P.H., Sampson, W.A., Bose, C.E., Jasso, G. and Passel, J. (1974), "Measuring Household Social Standing", *Social Science Research*, **3**, 169–190.

Stevens, S.S. (1975), *Psychophysics: An Introduction to Its Perceptual, Neural, and Social Prospects*. Stevens, G. (ed.) (New York: Wiley).

Wagner, D. and Berger, J. (1985), "Do Sociological Theories Grow?", *American Journal of Sociology*, **90**, 697–728.

Weber, M. (1958), *The Protestant Ethic and the Spirit of Capitalism*. Translated by Talcott Parsons. (New York: Scribner's). First published 1904-1905.

Whitmeyer, J.M. (2004), "Past and Future Applications of Jasso's Justice Theory", *Sociological Theory*, **13**, 432–444.

Chapter 12

Justice Conflicts and the Justice of Conflict Resolution

Leo Montada
University of Trier, Germany

The present chapter is an essay relating some lines of justice research to the analysis and understanding of social conflicts with the purpose of forming a culture of conflict resolution by mediation. The impact of the justice motive in social conflicts is discussed in this chapter. Social conflicts result from perceived injustice and subjective justice is required for their settlement. Conflicts are unavoidable because the justice motive is universal but the views of what is just and what is unjust are not at all universally shared. For the settlement of conflicts the opponents' views of justice have to become convergent. Conflict mediation is emphasized as an effective procedure to create social peace. The main strategies in mediation to settle conflicts and their psychological background are outlined. The justice of free and informed contracts is highlighted.

1. The Concern for Justice as an Anthropological Universal

Claims for justice and protests against injustice are ubiquitous in social life. Political movements, revolutions, and wars are initiated under the banner of justice. Justice is a prominent issue in all fields of politics. The courts are swamped with law suits, and many of their judgments arouse protest or bitterness by those who consider them as unjust. Perceived injustices are at the core of everyday conflicts in private life. Close relationships are put at risk by experienced injustice. Victims of misfortune have to cope with the perceived injustice of their fate and, moreover, with being derogated and blamed by observers who try to preserve their belief in a just world by insinuating the misfortune was self-inflicted. Humans are averse to injustice. They have a justice motive (Lerner, 1980; Ross and Miller, 2002). The concern for justice seems to be an anthropological universal.

2. Divergent Views about Justice

Beliefs about what is just and what is unjust are not at all universally shared. Consequently, conflicts about justice are universal. Everybody is speaking of justice in the singular as if for every case one single view of justice would be the valid one and had to be acknowledged and shared by everybody (Rüthers, 1991). However, looking at all the various and diverging sources of normative standards which may shape and implement the sense of justice the use of the singular means misjudging reality, if it does not serve as a strategic means to put through specific claims for justice.

It is worthwhile to become aware of the long list of sources for the development and socialization of justice beliefs: human rights, constitutions of states, legal codes, religions, justice principles, moral norms, conventional norms, social roles and practiced interaction scripts, game rules, bylaws of organizations, contracts, implicit contracts, promises, etc.

Many of the innumerable norms and normative maxims contained within these sources are highly diverging and contradict each other, e.g., the legal codes of different states are diverging, each single law can be criticized on the basis of some justice principle, quite a few of legal codes worldwide violate human rights or the rules of some religion. Moreover, the laws and normative maxims in these sources are open to interpretation, e.g. human rights, principles of justice as well as large parts of legal codes—which is, by the way, one of the reasons why the outcome of a law suit may be difficult to predict. Nevertheless, all these sources may have impact on the cultural and individual shaping of justice beliefs. Within pluralistic societies many diverging sources are available and have influence on the formation of normative beliefs and expectations of subpopulations and individuals. Diverging normative views, expectations and conflicts within the society are the consequence.

3. Social Conflicts Result from Perceived Injustice

All social conflicts may be interpreted as justice conflicts. Conflicts result from violated normative expectations how other people, agencies, authorities, companies, etc. have to behave, from violated or disregarded claims whatever their normative basis may be: human rights, a legal code, the oughts of a religion, a formal or an implicit contract, or good manners.

The contents of claims for justice have large spectrum of contents, much larger than the spectrum of justice principles studied in empirical research, so far.

Nevertheless, justice research has significantly enriched the body of knowledge about justice beliefs and their function for the emergence of conflicts, for their settlement and their prevention (cf. Tyler et al., 1997; Montada and Kals, 2007; Mikula and Wenzel, 2000; Montada, 2003).

Perceived Injustices, not Incompatibilities Instigate Social Conflicts

Incompatible goals, plans, and opinions may bear the risk of conflicts, but only if normative expectations are violated. Diverging views may be appreciated as creative and worthy of consideration or else as disrespectful or insulting. Diverging goals may be considered as legitimate or as an offence. Diverging religious beliefs may be tolerated as matter of personal freedom or condemned as a betrayal or a threat to the community.

Fair competition is not a social conflict. If all actors in competitive markets and sports are considered to behave legitimately, e.g. pursuing their legitimate self-interest, frustrations and losses are possible but they do not evoke resentment. There are winners and losers but not victimizers and victims. The losers may have performed poorly, they may have been unfortunate, but they have nothing to reproach the winners for, unless they believe that the competition has not been carried out fairly. Being treated unjustly is quite another experience than having lost a game.

However, competition as such is not always considered to be legitimate by everybody. Instead, solidarity and mutual support, not competition, are normatively expected in some social contexts, e.g. within close partnership, friendship or within the family, and in all situations, when a common goal of a social group, when solidarity and loyalty are at stake.

4. Understanding Social Conflicts

People expect that others meet normative standards, entitlements and claims they believe to be just ones. Social conflicts result from perceived violations of subjectively just normative standards or the disregard of entitlements and claims derived from these standards (cf. Mikula and Wenzel, 2000). In conflicts people may claim justice for themselves or for others for whom they feel sympathy, responsibility, or with whom they declare their loyalty.

People react with *resentment* when they view the perpetrating actors as responsible and when they do not see any convincing justification for the norm violation. Conflicts will become manifest, when "the victims" reproach "the perpetrators" for their behavior and "the perpetrators" do neither change nor excuse or justify their behavior convincingly. "The perpetrators" may also calm down the victim's resentment by serious apologies. If "the victims" claims for refraining from their blamed behavior or for redressing it are ignored or refused, the conflict is manifest.

Such claims will be ignored or refused when the addressees are convinced that their behavior is justified, e.g. as legitimate self interest, by legal, moral, or social norms, or as a just retaliation of an antecedent behavior of the claimant.

Typically, the conflict parties justify their own behavior and reproach the behavior of the adversaries. That is the reason why the terms victims and perpetrators are written with quotation marks.

Resentment is the Key Symptom of Conflicts

Perceived injustice instigates resentment, reproaches, wishes for retaliation, or claims for compensation or punishment. A look at aggression research reveals that it is not mere frustration that is instigating aggressive tendencies, but only arbitrary, "illegitimate" frustration (Pastore, 1952; Moore, 1978). Relative deprivation instigates aggression if it is considered unjust (Crosby, 1976). Aggression theories which emphasize anger as emotional antecedent of aggression share this basic assumption (Berkowitz, 1993; De Rivera, 2003). Aggression may have other motives, e.g., selfishness, envy, or striving for power, but, no doubt, resentment is one of the motives of aggression.

5. The Settlement of Conflicts

This conception of social conflicts has implications for the settlement of conflicts. What does it mean to settle a conflict? Peace and the healing of social relationships presuppose a settlement of conflicts. A conflict may be brought to an end without its resolution, i.e., the quarrels, disputes, or fights are not continued, but that the relationship between the adversaries remains poisoned, the conflict continues to be a mortgage for future exchanges, or the exchanges are broken off. Which options exist for settling a conflict?

5.1 Settling Conflicts by Trial?

One of the standard ways of conflict resolution in the western world is to bring the case to trial. If litigants accept the authority of courts, the decisions of judges will terminate the conflict. This does not necessarily mean that the conflict is settled. Conflicts are settled only if all parties, especially the losers, are convinced that the judgment is just. Judges can try to convince the losers that the judgment is just. To that end they have to give voice to all parties, make sure that they have understood their views and positions, and take time and effort to justify their views of the law, the case, and their judgment with convincing arguments. If that is done in a respectful way, judges have a good chance that the losers get the impression of being treated in a fair manner. This impression triggers the fair process effect (cf. Lind and Tyler, 1988; Tyler et al., 1997) meaning that even unfavorable judgments are accepted without resentment, when the procedure is considered fair. A conflict is settled, when the views of the parties are brought more into line, when feelings of injustice get resolved or are prevented. However, judges have to obey the law. And the law may not adequately fit the essential features and contents of an actual conflict. The laws may be criticized as unjust with some good reason.

5.2 Settling Conflicts by Mediation

In conflict resolutions by mediation the laws of a legal code is not given particular weight in relation to the opponents' subjective sense of justice—as long as compulsory laws are not violated. The parties have the opportunity to advocate their personal views of the conflict and their personal normative beliefs. The parties have the freedom to negotiate a "social contract" for their future exchanges on the basis of their personal sense of justice.

Social conflicts may be settled by mediation in two different ways: 1) by getting more convergence of the opponents' normative views, or 2) by lessening the subjective weight or importance attributed to the conflicting views and positions. Strategies for both ways will be outlined.

5.2.1 Making Normative Views Converge
According to the model of social conflicts, perceived injustice is resulting from the following views: the adversary is blameworthy because he or she has violated a valid normative expectation without remorse and apologies and without having an

acceptable justification; and he or she is responsible for this behavior. All components of this view can be used as starting points for a settlement.

5.2.1.1 Qualifying attributions of responsibility   Attributions of responsibility can be qualified or recognized as an error (cf. Semin and Manstead, 1983; Hamilton and Hagiwara, 1992; Montada, 2001). If a person did not have volitional control over his or her behavior because of lacking competences, fatigue, external forces, effects of drugs, etc., he or she is not responsible. If the consequences of an action have not been foreseeable, nobody is responsible, either. Less responsibility will be attributed when malevolent intentions are no longer presumed, when, instead, the behavior is qualified as careless, as well intended but badly performed, or when co-responsibility of others is assumed. Responsibility can also be denied by asserting that the "victim" has consented to participate in a risky activity having a bad end (e.g., losses at the stock markets).

5.2.1.2 Qualifying Blameworthiness by Justifications   The blameworthiness of an actor can be qualified by convincing justifications: offering good reasons for the resented behavior, e.g., making reference to legitimate self interest, to professional or social obligations, claiming the right to defend one's freedom or one's reputation (Montada, 2001). Quite often, own behavior is justified as retaliation for a misdeed of the adversary. Justifications may be convincing and will be accepted. In that case they calm down resentment (Montada and Kirchhoff, 2000; Bernhardt, 2001). They may also be resentfully rejected. For instance, reproaches of having behaved selfishly may not be calmed down by the argument that selfishness is legitimate.

5.2.1.3 Apologies   Sincere apologies are another way to settle a conflict. As Goffman (1971) has emphasized, by remorse and apologies the perpetrator expresses that he or she fully shares the victim's view of the case. He or she is considering the violated norm as a valid ought, concedes to have offended the norm, to be responsible and blameworthy, because the offence was not justified. Moreover, the perpetrator concedes that it is up to the victim to accept or to reject the apology. It is empirically proven that sincere apologies reconcile victims as well as judges and observers and that they reduce the desire for retribution (Ohbuchi, Agarie and Kameda, 1989; Montada and Kirchhoff, 2000, Vidmar, 2000). A perpetrator's attempt at reparation has similar effects and implies all the components of a sincere apology (Darley and Shultz, 1990). The courts, too, reduce the penalties, when in perpetrator-victim reconciliation an agreement is reached (Rössner, 1998).

In escalated conflicts sincere apologies of one side may not be expected, as the adversaries may justify their own offenses as retaliation of anteceding offenses done by the other party. Who should be the first one to concede unjustified offenses? Would that not mean a loss of face? One strategy to make use of the pacifying potential of apologies might be to induce all parties to concede offenses mutually and simultaneously. This might preferably be done without any specifications in order to avoid new disputes about details of the concrete cases.

5.2.1.4 Normative Discourses   In conflicts, the opponents are convinced to be in the right with their own views and claims and the adversaries being wrong. It is the nature of normative beliefs that their validity is taken for granted and, consequently, that they have to be respected by everybody. Conflicts about diverging normative beliefs cannot be settled by simple compromises. One possible solution might be that the opponents consent to appeal to an authority for a decision. The approach in mediation is to reflect the conflicting beliefs and positions in normative discourses.

In philosophy, ethical discourses aim at gaining knowledge of universal ethical truths (Ackerman, 1980; Habermas, 1981) but, as Habermas (1981) has argued, the justification of the validity of a moral maxim or principle is to be distinguished from the justification of decisions in concrete cases where competing principles are considered relevant with good reason. This argument entails the insight that moral maxims may have diverging consequences when they are applied.

The aim of conflict mediation is settling an actual conflict by an agreement that allows productive and peaceful future exchanges between the opponents.

The function of discourses in mediations is not the search for universal ethical truths. They serve to further the insight that good reasons can be put forward, not only for one's own normative views and claims but, equally, for the opponent's views and claims.

Mediators try to generate a culture of communication similar to the one which was designed for ideal ethical discourses: A rhetoric of persuasions and manipulations is banned, mutual understanding and unbiased free deliberation are actively supported. One major goal of normative discourses in mediation is imparting insight into normative dilemmas underlying the conflict, a second goal is to further the mutual understanding of diverging views of relevant facts.

5.2.1.4.1 Imparting insight into existing normative dilemmas   Settling conflicts is made easier when the opponents acknowledge that divergent norms or principles of justice may be advocated with good reasons, i.e., that a normative dilemma exists and, consequently, that neither party is solely right or wrong. If the opponents recognize that their conflict reflects a normative dilemma, they no longer view the position of the other side as completely illegitimate and their own position as the only legitimate one. Thus, every claim that a single principle of distributive justice had exclusive validity should be questioned in conflict mediation (Montada and Kals, 2007). Two examples are given:

- Should the inheritance of parents be divided equally among their children or equitably according to their merits (e.g., their provided care for the parents, their contributions to the social status of the family) or according to their neediness (e.g., their income or the number of grandchildren), should persons who have been very close to the parents receive a share?
- Which employees should be dismissed first, when business is running low? Several justice principles may be considered: seniority, acquired merits by previous performances or loyalty, current performance level, neediness (e.g., number of dependent children), gender, age, nationality, etc.? Moreover, should employers have the right to decide at their own discretion or should a works committee have a say?

A second category of justice dilemmas underlying social conflicts shall be mentioned. It is a matter of fact that attempts to remove one injustice frequently cause other injustices. Some examples are given (cf. Montada, 2003):

- Is it just that young women are privileged by affirmative action programs in competition with young men in the labor market as a compensation for the unquestionable historical discrimination of women in the labor market? Or else, are only those young women to be privileged who have individually suffered discrimination, and are they to be privileged only when they compete with young men who have been unjustly privileged before? In other words: May we apply the justice principle of compensation for suffered disadvantages and undeserved advantages at the level of social categories (women and men) or only at the level of individuals and perhaps social groups (cf. Griffith, Parker and Törnblom, 1993)
- Is the raising of taxes for caused pollution a just measure? Pollution causes risks and costs for others who do not have profit or fun by the polluting activities (e.g., industrial productions, air conditioning, car-driving). Raising taxes for pollution prevents or reduces the unjust externalization of costs, and the tax revenues may be used to compensate for suffered impairments by pollution, to reduce risks, etc. However, raising of taxes may also cause new injustices because rich people can pay the taxes and, nevertheless, continue their polluting activities, whereas poorer ones may have to give up or restrict them (cf. Montada and Kals, 2000).
- When the "benefit of doubt" (which doubtless is a significant progress in the history of criminal law) is applied to a defendant, the victims' claims for punishment and retribution may be violated, assuming that the victims have no doubts that the defendant is the perpetrator.
- Legal punishment for a crime may be deserved, but it also bears the risk of unjust public discrimination of those who are close to the perpetrator, for instance his or her children, who are not at all responsible for the punished deed.

Similar unjust side effects of measures to prevent or to reduce injustices are quite common, from social welfare policies to the containment of terrorism. They all should remind us that using justice in the singular is a mistake.

In normative discourses conflicting claims for justice are advocated When good arguments are put forward, the opponents may qualify their views and claims. They recognize that none of the conflicting claims is solely valid. This is not a *normative relativism* meaning "No norm or normative maxim is really valid!" In contrast, it is the insight in a normative dilemma, meaning "No normative maxim has exclusive validity. Many maxims may be applied with good reason in a specific case." Applying, for instance, one single principle of distributive justice would violate all other principles that might be also taken into consideration. When the opponents come to realize, that a dilemma is underlying their conflict, the conflict will be defused which might, in turn, be a good precondition for future cooperation.

It is the wisdom of institutions to consider various principles of justice in their regulations and decisions   The social market economy, for instance, is an attempt to harmonize the right of all citizens to free economic activities with the maxims of the social welfare state. Rawls' well-known "maximin-principle" is also a suggestion for the freedom to economic activity—that produces common wealth—with the entitlement of every citizen to participate in the common prosperity (Rawls, 1971). This holds equally to the basic maxims of the French Revolution: equality, freedom and fraternity: applying only one of the three maxims excluding the other two would result in quite diverging constitutions of the state.

In many institutional orders for the allocation of scarce resources several principles of distributive justice are considered. This is evidenced by comparative research on the allocation of university positions, subsidized lodgings, transplants in medicine, legal regulations for the lay off of employees, etc. (Elster, 1992). Making reference to these facts as well as to observations that various norms of justice are used in different spheres of justice (Walzer, 1983) may help to qualify rigid insisting on one single maxim. Another strategy may be to remind the opponents that they themselves are used to apply different principles of justice in different situations and context. In order to transcend the actual conflict between the opponents, mediators may offer further normative standards which are or could be applied in similar cases. Becoming aware that their conflicting claims are not the only ones that can be advocated contributes to a different perspective.

The general strategy in discourses is to impart insight into the normative dilemmas entailed in justice conflicts. Settling conflicts is made easier when the opponents have gained insight that divergent principles of justice may be advocated with good reason. When the parties recognize that a justice dilemma exists, they no longer view the position of the opponents as completely illegitimate and their own position as the single legitimate one.

5.2.1.4.2 Disputes about facts   Not only principles of justice may be the object of disputes, but also relevant facts. The opponents may apply the same principle but have diverging views of the facts. Siblings may have consent that the inheritance should be distributed according to their merits or their neediness but may have serious dissent about their individual merits and neediness, respectively. The diverging views have to be communicated and mutually understood.

5.2.2 Uncovering the Real Conflict behind the Topics of the Disputes

The topics of the disputes are not always the true causes of the conflict. To uncover the true causes, the question has to be answered why the topics of the conflict are that important for the opponents. For instance, in many conflicts about the validity of personal opinions, beliefs or appraisals it is essential to know which personal concerns are affected by drawing these views into doubt or by disputing them. Is this interpreted as a sign of disrespect, as an attack on one's social status or social identity, as termination of a close relationship, as a shameful public defeat, as a sign of distancing from a social community? Dealing merely with the topics of the disputes may not be helpful for a settlement of the true conflict.

5.2.3 Qualifying the Subjective Importance of the Conflict

Heavy conflicts frequently produce a mental constriction   The opponents are beside themselves insofar as they are no longer aware of the whole spectrum of their important concerns and their self-concept. The blameworthiness of the opponents, winning or retaliation became the dominant mental topics.

In conflicts both the blameworthiness of the adversaries and the impairments caused by them are frequently exaggerated. An injury caused by a biker in a pedestrian precinct will be dramatized compared to a similar injury resulting from an own failure. Therefore, reducing the subjective importance attributed to the conflict may open the mind to think about constructive solutions. Transcending the conflict is the general advice for qualifying the importance of conflicts. Several strategies may be used in mediation. Some of them will be outlined below.

5.2.3.1 Reminding the Opponents of the Whole Spectrum of their Concerns   This strategy might be illustrated by an example. A couple, both spouses in the fifties, has a serious conflict about the question whether they should take the mother of the husband into their family because she needs care. The husband feels himself under the obligation to do this. His wife rejects this idea strictly and confronts her husband with the question: do you take care for her or for me? The husband's response: do you really wish me to violate my moral responsibility. Both feel betrayed by the partner. The strategy in mediation is to transcend the actual conflict.

This can be done by making the opponents aware of the whole spectrum of their important concerns and their self concepts. In this specific case, this procedure will reveal a lot of shared concerns: both partners love each other; they share moral concerns; they are concerned about the view of their children who love their grandmother; they want to set a good example for their children; they also share economic concerns and fear that the income and property of the mother would get used up for private nursing; when they would organize the needed care for the mother within the family, the mother's nursing insurance would pay a certain amount monthly sufficient to hire professional help at times, the mothers income and property would be saved. Having all these concerns in mind, the couple is ready to generate options how the needed care can be organized within or outside their home and to check which ones fit best to their concerns.

5.2.3.2 Exploring Opportunities for Positive Exchanges   In conflicts, the exchanges are negative: criticisms, blame, hindrances, harm, exclusion, slandering, mistrust, hostility, etc. The exchange of mutual retaliations is costly for all, a looser—looser outcome for the sake of retributive justice. Refraining from retaliations is not costly but avoids anger and harm of the opponents. One of the important changes of perspective in mediation is that from negative exchanges to the opportunities of positive exchanges, positive with respect to important concerns of the parties.

The opponents have to become aware which positive exchanges are feasible ones—from material goods, information, and practical support to friendliness, consideration, sympathy, and emotional support. It is easy to create win—win outcomes when the opportunities of positive exchange are used. Neighbors may exchange services like care for kids, pets or plants, manifold supports and favors, and they can save money by sharing equipment and tools, etc. Although what is offered may be easily accomplished and inexpensive, it may be very valuable for the recipient. That is why both parties may win (subjectively) much more than they invest.

One common recommendation for negotiations and mediations is "to enlarge the cake" to be distributed. However, not every conflict is about distributions, and it is not always possible to increase the cake. However, it is always possible to look at additional concerns of the parties than merely the ones at stake in the actual conflict. In so doing, the number of options for positive exchanges will certainly grow.

5.2.3.3 Including Unsettled Previous Conflicts in an Overall Solution   In long lasting social relationships, an actual conflict may be preceded by a series of conflicts that are not settled at the time being. *Let a neighborhood conflict illustrate this situation.* Neighbor A has intervened when B wanted to put up a basket for his sons to play basketball at the side of a dead end street. B's reaction was to refuse A's request to build a carport on the borderline of his property. As a counter move, A has rejected B's request to fell a tree throwing shadow on his kitchen garden. B's answer was to mow his lawn extensively on afternoons, when B sat with guests on his terrace, etc. Supposing that most of these mutual impairments have been retaliations, one may assume that complying with the neighbor's requests would not have been costly for everyone. Therefore, a win—win agreement is possible when both comply with each other's requests which, in turn, would be a starting point for mutually productive exchanges.

5.2.3.4 Considering the Concerns of Affected Third Parties   Many conflicts affect and impair third parties who are not directly involved. Conflicts between parents have effects on their children, the grandparents and others. Conflicts at the workplace may have impact on colleagues, on the whole organization, on the families, etc. The same is true for resolutions of conflicts: though not directly involved, third parties are affected. This fact may be used to transcend the conflict by stipulating the opponents to take the concerns of others into consideration, at least of those they feel close to. Reflecting the concerns of others constitutes a change of perspective and may qualify the subjective perception and importance of the conflicting positions.

5.2.3.5 Making Internal Conflicts Aware   Not seldom do opponents in a social conflict hold vigorously a claim repressing own doubts and internal conflicts regarding this position, e.g., a young couple had given a lot of thoughts to the problems how to make compatible their professional careers and their desire to have children. It now happened that the young wife got a very attractive offer for an academic position. This position would, however, need her full commitment requiring her to postpone the desire to have a child. Her spouse strongly pleaded to reject this offer. Thereby, he caused heavy reactance on the part of his wife. The result was a serious conflict between the spouses. She was emphasizing all positive aspects of an academic career, reproached her husband for hindering her career, and claimed that it is her free personal decision whether and when she wants a child. The social conflict suppressed their internal conflicts. Making these visible again may calm down the social conflict and facilitate a discourse about the complex issues of personal freedom in close relationships and about the shared responsibilities of both parents for their children.

All these strategies to transcend the conflict open new perspectives that may allow the opponents to qualify the views and claims they hold in the conflict and encourage them to explore new options for social exchanges.

5.2.4 Does Justice become Irrelevant when New Perspectives on the Conflict Become Salient?

Transcending the conflict and opening the mind to think about win-win solutions does not mean that justice concerns become irrelevant, as might be deduced from the recommendation given in the Harvard Model of Negotiation (Fisher and Ury, 1981): think of your interests instead of persisting on your positions. With "positions" is meant: normative claims in the conflict. What is meant with interests is open to interpretation. If the authors only think of self-interest, the whole spectrum of personal concerns with impact on social conflicts would be blinded out, e.g., concerns for others, concerns for a community or social group, concerns for values of all kinds. Moreover, one may argue, that everybody is entitled to pursue his or her concerns. Insofar, the concern for justice in the broad sense introduced above (concern for normatively justified positions) is a "meta-concern" which cannot be put aside in settling conflicts.

It is surprising that concerns for justice are not a central issue in the literature about conflict mediation (cf. Montada and Kals, 2007). Even warnings to bring up justice issues can be found (cf. Pruitt and Carnevale, 1993. Normative standards cannot be excluded when social exchanges are appraised. Normative standards are crucial in social conflicts, and they are crucial for the resolution of conflicts and for agreements about exchanges in the future.

5.2.5 Settling Conflicts by an Agreement

Conflicts are social exchanges. They result from perceived violations or threats of normative expectations and subjective entitlements. Conflicts may be costly for one or for all parties. They may be a mortgage for future exchanges or even end in lasting hostility destroying social relationships.

Productive and sustainable conflict resolutions presuppose that a new basis and/ or new contents for exchanges will be found or created.

In the agreement might be specified whether and how impairments in the past will be regulated, what shall be exchanged in the future, and which rules shall be observed in the exchanges. These questions have to be answered with reference to justice. Exchange relationships are only peaceful and productive if they are considered just.

5.2.5.1 The Justice of Contracts   *The contract is a prototypical form for regulating social exchanges*   Contracts are regarded as just when the partners are equally informed and equally free to consent (Nozick, 1974). In conflict mediation the ultimate criterion for the appraisal of a solution as just is the agreement of the parties according to the famous principle in Roman law: "Consenti not fit iniuria." A contract

the parties have agreed upon freely and informed cannot be unjust. However, justice is violated if relevant information was withheld, if pressure was exerted, or if a party was not free to refuse the contract on account of a predicament, e.g., neediness.

Because contracts are of eminent importance in social life, many legal norms have been established which specify the obligations of the contracting parties. Above all, specific legal rules have been established to protect the supposedly less powerful or less informed parties.

5.2.5.2 The Justice of Contracts with Regard to Third Parties A contract is just between the contracting parties if they have equal freedom to consent or not to consent and if they share all available relevant information. These two preconditions for justice within the internal exchange between the contracting parties—equal freedom and information—is not sufficient to guarantee that a contract would be just also for the exchange with third parties.

Assessing the justice of contracts would be incomplete without having a look at their impact on third parties. Adverse effects on third parties raise new justice problems. Contracts may be fair with respect to the exchanges between the contracting parties but may be seriously unfair with respect to third parties or the larger community. For instance, cartel contracts may be fair for the contracting parties, but they are made at the expense of others.

Some examples may illustrate the statement. Exclusive contracts of sale put other suppliers at a disadvantage. Labor contracts between employers' organizations and unions may be viewed as a fair distribution of profits, but they may also be impairments for others or the public if they result in layoffs or prevent an expansion of the workforce. In close relationships, too, adverse effects on third parties are not unusual. Parents may enjoy the loyal support of their partner in cases of conflict with their adolescent children who, in turn, consider this loyalty to be a coalition at their cost. In case of divorce the financially dependent partner is not allowed to renounce continuous material support by the divorced partner to avoid the risk of becoming dependent on public welfare.

Therefore, it is prudent to expand the view from the contracting parties to the impact of an agreement on third parties and the public. Contract at the cost of third parties are externally unjust and a cause for new conflicts.

References

Ackermann, B. (1980), *Justice in the Liberal State* (New York: Yale University Press).

Berkowitz, L. (1993), *Aggression: Its Causes, Consequences, and Control* (New York: Mac Graw Hill).

Bernhardt, K. (2001), "Ein kognitives Trainingsprogramm zur Steuerung von Empörung". Universitätsbibliothek Trier, http://ub-dok.uni-trier.de/diss/diss11/2001.

Crosby, F. (1976), "A Model of Egoistical Relative Deprivation", *Psychological Review*, **83**, 85–113. [DOI: 10.1037/0033-295X.83.2.85]

Darley, J. and Shultz, T. (1990), "Moral Rules: Their Content and Acquisition", *Annual Review of Psychology*, **41**, 525–556. [DOI: 10.1146/annurev. ps.41.020190.002521]

De Rivera, J. (2003), "Aggression, Violence, Evil, and Peace" in *Handbook of Psychology*. Weiner, J. (ed.), Vol. 5 (Hoboken NJ: Wiley), 569–598.

Elster, J. (1992), *Local Justice* (New York: Russel Sage Foundation).

Fisher, R. and Ury, W. (1981), *Getting to Yes: Negotiating Agreement without Giving In* (Boston: Houghton Mifflin).

Goffman, E. (1971), *Relations in Public: Microstudies of the Public Order* (Harmondsworth: Penguin).

Griffith, W.J., Parker, M.J. and Törnblom, K.Y. (1993), "Putting the Group Back into Intergroup Justice Studies", *Social Justice Research*, **6**, 331–342. [DOI: 10.1007/ BF01050335]

Habermas, J. (1981), *Theorie des kommunikativen Handelns (Bd. 1 und 2)* (Frankfurt/ M.: Suhrkamp).

Hamilton, V.L. and Hagiwara, S. (1992), "Roles, Responsibility, and Accounts across Cultures", *International Journal of Psychology*, **27**, 157–179.

Lerner, M.J. (1980), *The Belief in a Just World: A Fundamental Delusion* (New York: Plenum Publishing).

Lind, E.A. and Tyler, T.R. (1988), *The Social Psychology of Procedural Justice* (New York: Plenum Publishing).

Mikula, G. and Wenzel, M. (2000), "Justice and Social Conflicts", *International Journal of Psychology*, **35**, 126–135. [DOI: 10.1080/002075900399420]

Montada, L. (2001), "Denial of Responsibility" in *Responsibility: The Many Faces of a Social Phenomenon*. Auhagen, A.E. and Bierhoff, H.W. (eds) (London: Routledge), 79–92.

Montada, L. (2003), "Justice, Equity, and Fairness in Human Relations" in *Handbook of Psychology*. Weiner, J. (ed.), Vol. 5 (Hoboken NJ: Wiley), 537–568.

Montada, L. and Kals, E. (2000), "Political Implications of Psychological Research on Ecological Justice and Pro-Environmental Behaviors", *International Journal of Psychology*, **35**, 168–176. [DOI: 10.1080/002075900399466]

Montada, L. and Kals, E. (2007), *Mediation: Ein Lehrbuch auf Psychologischer Grundlage* (Weinheim: Beltz PVU).

Montada, L. and Kirchhoff, S. (2000), "Bitte Um Verzeihung, Rechtfertigungen und Ausreden: ihre Wirkungen auf soziale Beziehungen", *Berichte aus der Arbeitsgruppe "Verantwortung, Gerechtigkeit, Moral" Nr. 130* (Trier: Universität Trier, Fachbereich I—Psychologie).

Moore, B. (1978), *Injustice: The Social Bases of Obedience and Revolt* (London: Macmillan).

Nozick, R. (1974), *Anarchy, State and Utopia* (New York: Basic Books).

Ohbuchi, K., Agarie, N. and Kameda, M. (1989), "Apology as Aggression Control: Its Role in Mediation Appraisal of and Response to Harm", *Journal of Personality and Social Psychology*, **56**, 219–227. [PubMed 2926625] [DOI: 10.1037/0022-3514.56.2.219]

Pastore, N. (1952), "The Role of Arbitrariness in the Frustration-Aggression Hypothesis", *Journal of Abnormal and Social Psychology*, **47**, 728–731. [DOI: 10.1037/h0060884]

Pruitt, D.G. and Carnevale, P.J. (1993), *Negotiation in Social Conflict* (Buckingham: Open University Press).

Rawls, J. (1971), *A Theory of Justice* (Cambridge: Harvard University Press).

Ross, M. and Miller, D.T. (eds) (2002), *The Justice Motive in Everyday Life* (New York: Cambridge University Press).

Rössner, D. (1998), "Mediation und Strafrecht" in *Mediation für die Praxi*. Strempel, D. (ed.) (Berlin: Haufe), 42–54.

Rüthers, B. (1991), *Das Ungerechte an der Gerechtigkeit: Defizite eines Begriffs* (Zürich: Edition Interfrom).

Semin, G.R. and Manstead, A.S.R. (1983), *The Accountability of Conduct: A Social Psychological Analysis* (New York: Academic Press).

Tyler, T.R., Boeckmann, R.J., Smith, H.J. and Huo, Y.J. (1997), *Social Justice in a Diverse Society* (Boulder: Westview Press).

Vidmar, N. (2000), "Retribution and Revenge" in *Handbook of Justice Research in Law*. Sanders, J. and Hamilton, V.L. (eds) (New York: Kluwer), 31–69.

Walzer, M. (1983), *Spheres of Justice: A Defense of Pluralism and Equality* (New York: Basic Books).

Index